INFLATION IN THE UNITED STATES
1940-1948

INFLATION IN THE UNITED STATES

1940-1948

By Lester V. Chandler, 1905—

GORDON S. RENTSCHLER PROFESSOR OF ECONOMICS

PRINCETON UNIVERSITY

HARPER & BROTHERS PUBLISHERS

NEW YORK

Contents

29,128

Contents

Charts

Preface

The purpose of this book is to describe the process of inflation in the United States during and following World War II and to analyze the principal public and private policies which were responsible for it. No attempt is made to describe in detail the movements of individual prices, to analyze all the broad social effects of the inflation, or to deal with every factor that was relevant to the inflationary process. To do this would have required a much longer book and would probably have obscured the basic policies and actions that generated the huge inflationary forces. Attention is therefore concentrated on the major policies and actions that were responsible for breaking the deflationary deadlock and for producing the rise of prices between 1940 and 1948.

The role of fiscal and monetary policies is emphasized. The great rise of federal spendings coupled with a much smaller increase of tax collections produced huge federal deficits, which directly increased the total demand for output, added greatly to private disposable money incomes, generated inflationary forces during the war, and enabled the private sectors of the economy to enter the postwar period with huge accumulations of savings. And wartime federal borrowing and monetary policies were such that these private savings were accumulated largely in the form of money and other highly liquid assets. The very easy monetary policy was continued in the postwar period, though with some modifications after mid-1947. These fiscal-monetary policies appear to have been the dynamic inflationary factor during the defense and war periods. But to explain the course and extent of the inflation it is necessary to consider other factors as well. Attention is therefore given to the behavior of real output, direct controls over prices, wages, and the production and use of goods and services, private controversies over the distribution of income, the wartime accumulation of a backlog of demand for output, and foreign conditions that affected the demand for our exports and that forced a continuation of large government spendings. The analysis is not solely in terms of monetary or even of monetary-fiscal policy.

This was indeed the best-measured inflation that we have ever had. For no other inflationary period have we had access to so many statistical series. It has been difficult, however, to relate some of these series to each other and some of them are far from precise. This is especially true of the measurements of real output. The reader is warned that some of the measurements presented here are highly approximate and should be looked upon only as indicators of general magnitude. For the purposes of this study it was not worthwhile to attempt more precise estimates.

Though it is hoped that this book will be of some interest to professional economists it is written in such a way as to be understandable by anyone with a general knowledge of economic processes. The first three chapters are addressed primarily to those who are not professional economists and who are not familiar with the course of the inflation. They outline the inflationary process and explain the most important concepts on which the later analysis is based.

This study was made while I was Professor of Economics at Amherst College and it was made possible by a grant to the College by the Merrill Foundation for the Advancement of Financial Knowledge. I wish to record here my gratitude to the Merrill Foundation for its generous assistance and to Amherst College for its many kindnesses. Neither the Foundation nor the College is responsible for any of the views expressed or for any of the errors made in this book; for these I assume sole responsibility. I also wish to express my appreciation to Andrew L. Kelemen and Richard G. Bateson for their excellent research assistance and to Mary Alice Fitzpatrick for her invaluable aid in preparing the manuscript for publication

LESTER V. CHANDLER

January, 1951

INFLATION IN THE UNITED STATES
1940-1948

I

Introduction

WITH every one of its major wars the United States has experienced a major inflation. Wholesale prices rose more than 40 percent during the War of 1812, about 120 percent during the Civil War, and about 170 percent during and immediately following World War I. World War II was no exception to this general pattern of price behavior. Between the outbreak of war in September 1939 and August 1948, when the inflationary trend was at least temporarily stopped and reversed, wholesale prices in this country rose 115 percent and prices of cost-of-living items rose 76 percent. The dollar lost 53 percent of its purchasing power over commodities in wholesale markets and 43 percent of its purchasing power over cost-of-living items.

The purpose of this book is to describe the course of the inflation, to analyze its causes, and to suggest reasons why the rise of prices was not even greater, as it might well have been. The major emphasis will be placed on the government's fiscal-monetary policy, for there can be no doubt that the dominant dynamic force was the government's spending-taxing-borrowing policy and the passive and easy monetary policy which was used to assure the Treasury of an adequate supply of money at continuously low interest rates. During the entire defense period, the war period, and the first few months of the postwar period the Government was engaged in a huge deficit-spending program whose magnitude was adapted to defense and war needs rather than to stabilization of

1

economic activity and price levels. Monetary policy was passively adapted to the needs of the Treasury. But the degree, duration, and timing of the price increases cannot be adequately explained by fiscal-monetary policies alone. To tell the complete story it is necessary to give attention to other governmental policies, such as direct controls over prices, wages, and the production and use of goods and services, and to describe the responses of the private sectors as they were evidenced in private investment, consumption, and savings.

Before launching into a description of the policies producing the inflation it will be useful to describe the economic conditions prevailing at the outbreak of the war and to trace out the course followed by the rising price levels.

ECONOMIC CONDITIONS IN 1939

When the war began in September 1939, the situation was far from inflationary in America and in the world generally. For nearly ten years the world's principal economic disease had been not the fever of inflation but the chill of deflation. Depressed demand, shrunken production, mass unemployment, lowered living standards, and falling prices were worldwide phenomena. This "poverty in the midst of plenty," the failure of economic systems to utilize fully their productive capacity because the money demand for output was too low, contributed strongly to the political upheavals of the period. Some countries moved sharply toward fascism or socialism; others, like the United States, cast the incumbent political party out of office and elected parties with programs of the New Deal type. At the depth of the depression in the United States in 1933 there were at least 13,000,000 unemployed, national output had fallen more than 50 percent in terms of money and at least 25 percent in physical terms, wholesale prices were down 33 percent, and the cost of living was 25 percent below 1929 levels. The recovery from 1933 to 1939 was far from complete. As war broke out abroad we still had more than

9,000,000 unemployed; national output, despite the growth of population and the continued improvements in technology during the preceding decade, was still 13 percent below 1929 in terms of money and only about 5 percent above 1929 in real terms; wholesale prices had been relatively stable for many months at a level about 30 percent above the low point of 1933 but still 17 percent below 1929 levels; and the cost of living was still 18 percent below its level of a decade earlier, though it had risen about 9 percent above the low point of 1933. In short, our economy was still running in low gear with a vast amount of unutilized productive capacity because of an inadequate money demand for its potential output. How much output had been lost through lack of employment became clear only during the war and postwar period.

Our long and bitter experience with deflation and unemployment during the decade of the thirties must be kept in mind if we are to understand the course of the subsequent inflation and our national policies related to it. In the first place, the large amounts of unused productive capacity served to delay price rises as spendings for output rose. With their plants at least partially idle, with raw materials easily available, and with a great unemployed labor reserve awaiting hire, business firms enjoying an increased money demand for their products responded at first with relatively large expansions of their output and relatively small increases of their prices. But later, as productive capacity was approached and as bottlenecks appeared in plants, materials, and labor, further increases in the rate of spendings were reflected to an increasing extent in rising price levels and to a decreasing extent in enhanced real output. The availability of unused productive resources goes far toward explaining why price inflation did not become significant until 1941. The favorite prescription, "the best preventive and cure of inflation is increased production," could be an effective protection against inflation in 1940; it was not, however, so effective in the postwar period when we were already pressing the limits of our existing productive capacity.

In the second place, the long deflation and the controversies surrounding it created a profound impression on the minds of government officials and of the population in general. The evils of deflation were obvious, current, and vividly felt; the evils of inflation were only dimly remembered after the passage of nearly two decades and seemed to belong to a different era. To some it seemed almost impossible that deflation could give way to an undesirable degree of inflation, and many, exaggerating the "secular stagnation theory," doubted that inflation or even full employment could continue more than briefly after the termination of fighting. To them the most likely postwar prospects were for a resumption of deflation, not serious and prolonged price increases. This deflation-depression psychology exerted several types of influence on the course of the inflation. For one thing, it helped prevent a flight from money to goods that would have aggravated the rise of prices. Inflations have usually been intensified by a rising velocity of money, especially after they have been in process for some time and people have come to fear a further depreciation of their money. In extreme cases people have literally fled from money; immediately upon receiving money they would run, bicycle, or motor to the nearest market to purchase anything that might be a better store of value. That throughout the inflation in this country the velocity of money failed to rise above depression levels, people continuing to hold more money in relation to their spendings than was customary before 1929, is at least partially attributable to a widespread and persistent belief that prices would not rise much further and would turn down again "before long."

The expectation and fear of deflation was also one of the factors deterring public officials from following more aggressive anti-inflationary policies. In 1941 and even into 1942 it was felt that restrictive financial policies should be delayed until our productive resources were more fully utilized. Throughout the period of active war the desirability of allowing businesses and individuals to accumulate large reserves of money and other liquid assets to act as a cushion against postwar depression was one of the reasons frequently advanced for refusing to increase taxes. And after the end of the war the avoidance of deflation and depression was one of the most persuasive arguments employed for removing direct controls over commodities, wages, and prices; for lowering taxes; for continuing high government spendings; and for continuing very liberal monetary policies.

It would be interesting to know how much different the course of the inflation would have been if the war had started while the United States was in a period of relatively full production and employment.

THE COURSE OF THE INFLATION

Chart 1 shows the behavior of spendings for output, wholesale prices, and the cost of living from 1939 through 1948. At least two important facts stand out. The first is the extent of the price increases from 1939 to the peak in August 1948. Wholesale prices rose 120 percent and the cost of living 76 percent. Equally interesting is the timing of the increases. To analyze this the longer period should be divided into at least three parts: (1) from 1939 to May 1942, (2) from May 1942 until the end of 1945, and (3) from the end of 1945 until August 1948.

The general indexes indicate that less than a quarter of the total inflation between 1939 and August 1948 occurred in the first period from 1939 to May 1942, wholesale prices rising 27 percent and the cost of living 15 percent despite the fact that the rate of spendings for output rose by 70 percent. And most of this price increase occurred in the latter part of the period, in 1941 and early 1942. At first the increased rate of spendings was reflected largely in enhanced output; later, as unutilized capacity decreased and "bottlenecks" began to appear, further increases of spendings were reflected to a greater extent in price increases though the rate of output also expanded further.

It is interesting to note what a small part of the total rise of prices occurred during the three and a half-year period extending from about May 1942 to the end of 1945. The cost-of-living index rose only 16 points, representing about one-fifth of its total

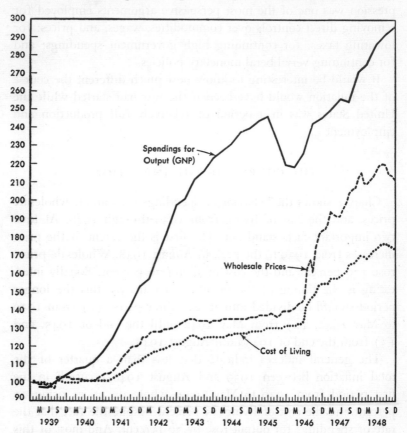

Chart 1.   Indexes of Spendings for Output, Wholesale Prices, and the Cost of Living in the United States, 1939-1948 (1939 = 100). (Note: Spendings for Output figures are quarterly; others are monthly.)

increase from 1939 to August 1948, while the wholesale-price index rose 12 points, which represented only about a tenth of the total rise during the longer period. This limited rise of prices appears the more remarkable when one remembers that it was during this period of about three and a half years that we were most actively engaged in war, the withdrawal of men from industry for military service was at its height, the war was taking at least 40 percent of our output, and both governmental and private spendings were continuing to rise. The explanation is, of course, the imposition of price ceilings by the OPA, buttressed by subsidies, wage controls, rationing, and other direct controls over the supply and use of goods and services. Direct limitations on price increases began in 1941 as "selective controls" over certain scarce and strategic commodities, the number of commodities covered was gradually increased after Pearl Harbor, and in the spring of 1942 most prices were frozen by the General Maximum Price Regulation. In general, legal price increases after that time were allowed only when necessary to relieve hardship on sellers, to enhance the supply of specific commodities, or to permit farm prices to rise to the minimum level at which the price control law enacted by Congress would allow ceilings to be imposed. It is true, of course, that the price indexes understate somewhat the extent of price increases during this period. They do not fully reflect the rise of prices in black markets, the dropping of low-price lines of goods, and quality deterioration. But even full allowance for these factors, if this could be computed, would add only a few points to the price indexes by the end of 1945.

The greater part of the inflation occurred between the end of 1945 and August 1948. During this period occurred more than two-thirds of the total rise of wholesale prices and 60 percent of the increase in the cost of living. Prices rose only slowly until June 1946. But after price control was first crippled by restrictive legislation and then removed the upward spiral of prices and wages accelerated. During 1946 alone wholesale prices rose more than they had during the entire period 1939-1945, and the cost of living advanced two-thirds as much as it had during the preceding six years.

One of the principal tasks of this study will be to explain why the major part of the inflation occurred after the fighting war

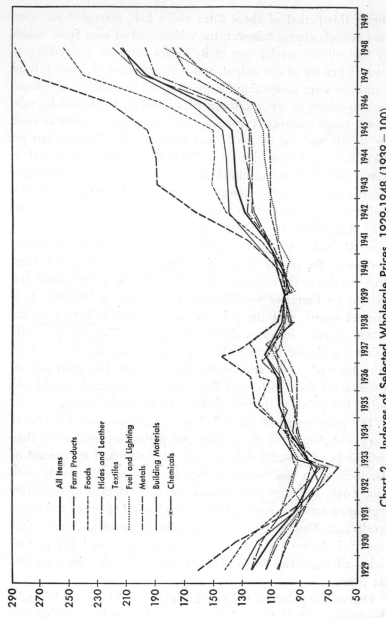

Chart 2. Indexes of Selected Wholesale Prices, 1929-1948 (1939 = 100).

Legend:
All Items
Farm Products
Foods
Hides and Leather
Textiles
Fuel and Lighting
Metals
Building Materials
Chemicals

had been over for several months, government spendings had been markedly reduced from their wartime peak, and a large amount of productive capacity formerly devoted to war purposes had been freed for the use of the civilian economy.

THE DISPERSION OF PRICES

The preceding section dealt with the behavior of the general indexes of average prices of wholesale and cost-of-living items. No less important are the differences in the behavior of the individual prices that are averaged in the more comprehensive price indexes. Price inflation would be of little consequence if all the prices in the economic system, including not only the prices of the various goods and services produced but also the prices of labor, rentals, interest, bonds, stocks, real estate, etc., changed at the same speed and in the same proportion. People would receive and spend more money, but their real purchasing power would be unaltered, for the "prices" received by them would change in exact proportion to the "prices" paid by them. But this is far from an accurate description of actual price relationships during the inflation. Some prices responded quickly and rose greatly while others responded tardily and moved more narrowly. This is shown in a general way in Charts 2 and 3 and in somewhat more detail in Table 1.

There were, of course, many reasons for the varied behavior of individual prices under inflationary conditions. A full explanation would require a complete analysis of the economic system, but only a few of the major factors can be noted here. (1) Differences in the behavior of money demand for various products. As total spending power was enhanced the increase was distributed unequally among the various types of spenders—governmental units, business firms, and individuals with widely varying tastes and spending habits. This shift in the balance of spending power would alone have produced some variations in the behavior of the demand schedules for different products. Moreover, even when

TABLE 1.   The Dispersion of Wholesale Prices, 1939-1948[1]

Commodity	Percentage Increase from the 1939 Average to	
	December 1945	August 1948
Average of all commodities	39	120
Average of all manufactured products	28	105
Average of all raw materials	70	159
Average of all semimanufactured products	27	107
Oils and fats	111	273
Meats	40	255
Livestock and poultry	80	246
Lumber	69	243
Cotton goods	87	206
Grains	104	174
Dairy products	64	166
Hides and skins	39	151
Petroleum and products	18	134
Fruits and vegetables	108	127
Leather	19	113
Nonferrous metals	10	113
Cereal products	28	106
Paper and pulp	33	105
Drugs and pharmaceuticals	44	96
Plumbing and heating equipment	20	94
Paint and paint materials	30	91
Woolen and worsted goods	45	90
Shoes	24	85
Clothing	31	81
Brick and tile	28	74
Furniture	25	74
Hosiery and underwear	20	71
Iron and steel	5	70
Fertilizer materials	21	69
House furnishings	18	64
Chemicals	15	49
Cement	10	46
Rayon	5	44
Automobile tires and tubes	11	13
Gas	−8	3
Electricity	−13	−16

[1] Computed from data in the *Survey of Current Business*.

an individual enjoys an increased spending power he does not distribute the increase pro rata over the things that he was previously purchasing; instead, he may actually reduce his demand for some things (such as foods that he considers of "low quality"), maintain relatively unchanged his demand for certain other things,

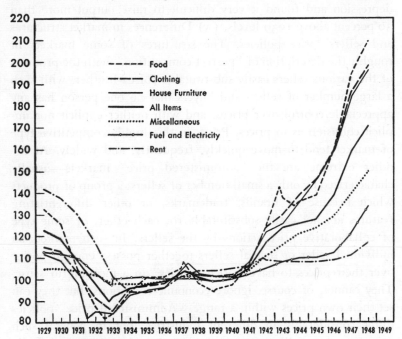

Chart 3.   Indexes of the Cost of Living and Its Components, 1929-1948 (average 1935-1939 = 100).

and increase greatly his demands for still others. (2) Differences in the difficulty and cost of expanding the supplies of various commodities. Starting from a given situation, the supply of some commodities can be expanded quickly, greatly, and with only slowly increasing costs per unit, whereas the output of other commodities can be expanded only slowly and to a small extent without encountering rapidly rising costs per unit. For example, when the war broke out the iron and steel industries and many machinery manufacturers were operating far below capacity levels and there was a large unemployed labor reserve to which they had access; they could increase their output markedly before encountering large increases in their unit costs. Farmers, however, had maintained their production at relatively high levels throughout the depression and found it very difficult to raise output more than 30 percent above 1939 levels. (3) Differences in market structures and sellers' price policies. The structures of some markets fit roughly the description of "perfect competition," with the products of the various sellers easily substitutable for each other, with such a large number of sellers and buyers that no one person has any appreciable control over prices, and with neither explicit nor implicit collusion as to prices. Prices in this highly competitive type of market tend to move quickly, frequently, and widely. At the other extreme are the "administered price" markets—usually characterized by only a small number of sellers; a group of products which because of brands, trademarks, or other differentiating features are not easily substitutable for each other; or some type of collaborative price actions by the sellers. In such markets an individual seller or several sellers together possess enough power over their prices to have "price policies" in a meaningful sense. They cannot, of course, ignore economic conditions, but they can set their own prices within a range. "Administered price" policies differ considerably in different industries, but in general such prices are changed less frequently than those in more atomistically competitive markets, and they often vary less widely. For example, it was clear in 1948 that neither steel nor automobile manufacturers were charging all that they could get for their products; there was a flourishing "grey market" in steel above the manufacturers' prices, and many new cars were selling through used-car lots at prices several hundred dollars above the manufacturers' suggested retail lists. Monopolistic power is probably objectionable on other grounds, but it does not seem to have been a major contributing factor to the inflation. (4) Differences in contracts and customs relating to the freedom to change prices. Some prices are free to move immediately and without limit in response to changes in economic conditions. Others, however, are bound for a time by term contracts or market customs. Rentals, interest rates, teachers' salaries, power rates, and many other prices are typically fixed by contract for terms of varying length and can be changed only after a delay. In some markets custom is also against frequent price changes. (5) Government regulation. Many prices can be advanced only with the approval of some regulatory agency, which is sometimes given only reluctantly and after a delay. Among these are, outstandingly, rates charged by public utilities: railroads, buses, trucks, telephones, gas, water, electricity, and so on. In 1948 rents were still held down by direct controls.

It is largely because of the widely varied behavior of individual prices—using the term "price" in a broad sense to include rates and money values of all individual goods and services—that inflation alters so greatly the relative economic positions of different people. Some find that their purchasing power is reduced as the prices of the things they buy rise more than the amount of money that they can command on income and capital account. Pensioners, schoolteachers, annuitants, bondholders, government employees, and many others can attest to this fact. On the other hand, some are helped rather than injured by the rise of prices, for the decreased purchasing power of each dollar is more than compensated by the increase in the number of dollars that they command.

THE BEHAVIOR OF REAL OUTPUT

To deal only with price inflation from 1939 to 1948 could easily lead to a serious misunderstanding of economic events during the period as a whole. The accompanying rise of real output must also be borne in mind. With the rise of money spendings for output, which to producers appeared as an increased money demand for their products, the response was not only to raise prices but also to increase real production by putting into use unemployed workers and other productive facilities. The number of unemployed people was reduced to a minimum and plants again worked full time. In 1948 national output in *real* terms, after full allowance for increases in price levels, was at least 50 percent above the 1939 level, and the increase was probably even more than this. We were producing far more goods and services—both in the aggregate and per capita—than at any time before the war, and had demonstrated clearly how wasteful underemployment had been during the decade of the thirties. But this does not mean that a price inflation of the magnitude that we experienced was necessary to achieve full employment and production. It was clear that full employment could not be achieved with 1939 levels of spendings and prices unless cost levels could be reduced without an offsetting decline of spendings for output—a difficult achievement in our economy. Some rise of spendings and prices was desirable. It hardly follows, however, that the attainment and maintenance of high employment and production required such a great inflation of spendings and prices as did in fact occur. This applies particularly to the spiral after the end of the war, as spendings, prices, wages, other costs, and profits raced each other up the mountain.

‖‖‖

II

Spendings and Inflation

WHY did prices rise so much during the 1939-1948 period? Stated in the most elementary terms, the behavior of price levels can be explained by comparing the flow of money spendings into the market with the flow of goods and services into the market. Price levels fall when the flow of money spendings decreases *relative to* the flow of goods and services to be purchased. And price levels rise when the flow of spendings increases *relative to* the flow of goods and services. The inflation following 1939 was not due to any reduction in the volume of goods and services available for purchase. The inflation occurred as the volume of spendings rose so much more than the supply of goods and services could be augmented. The dynamic factor was the rise of spendings.

The above statements, though valid, are far from being an adequate explanation of either the "basic causes" or the process of the inflation. To give them meaning it is necessary to explain the behavior of spendings and output in terms of the motivations and actions of government, business firms, and individuals. Such questions as the following need to be answered. Who was responsible for the rising rate of spendings, and what motivated the increases? Why did spendings rise so much after having remained at low levels for a long period? Were some types of spendings more dynamic than others in the sense that increases in them induced increases in other types of spendings? What were the roles of government, business, farmers, labor, consumers, and

15

banks in the inflation? Attempts to answer these questions will be made in later sections. First, however, it will be useful to outline quantitatively the behavior of spendings and output during the period.

SPENDINGS FOR OUTPUT: GROSS NATIONAL PRODUCT (OR EXPENDITURES)

The great increase of spendings following 1939 extended not only to currently produced goods and services but also to real estate, capital goods produced and carried over from earlier periods, and "second-hand" goods in general. The inflated prices of farm lands, urban dwellings, second-hand automobiles, and many other items carried over from the past attest to this fact. This study, however, will concentrate most of its attention on the current output (production) of goods and services—its amount, the behavior of spendings for it, and its prices. This is done because the rate of real output and the rate of spendings for output appear to be the key factors in the operation of our economy.

In analyzing the behavior of real output and of spendings for output we are fortunate to have the excellent statistical series on "gross national product" (GNP) prepared by the Department of Commerce.[1] Though the series is well known and widely used, a short description of it at this point may be useful.

"Gross national product" is usually defined as the output of goods and services in the United States during a stated period of time, usually a year, *valued at its current market prices*. But it may also be defined as spendings for output during a stated period.[2] Total spendings for output during any period are made

---

[1] For a description of this series and for much valuable statistical material, see *National Income Supplement to the Survey of Current Business*, July, 1947; and the *Survey of Current Business*, July, 1948 and July, 1949. Current statistics appear in many places, including the *Survey of Current Business* and the *Federal Reserve Bulletin*.

[2] This is not strictly accurate. GNP includes not only output sold in the market, but also certain goods and services, such as the rental value of owner-occupied houses and food consumed by farmers out of their own production,

up of four broad classes of spendings: (1) personal consumption expenditures, (2) gross private domestic investment, (3) net foreign investment, and (4) government purchases of goods and services. The effective money demand for ouput during any period is equal to the sum of these four types of spendings.

Personal consumption expenditures, as the name implies, are spendings by consumers in this country for goods and services to be used for consumption purposes. Some are for consumers' nondurable goods, such as food, clothing, gasoline, fuel oil, and beverages; some are for consumers' durable goods, such as pleasure automobiles, furniture, and refrigerators; and others are for various types of consumer services, such as shoe repair, theater admissions, medical services, barber and beauty services, and domestic help. Personal consumption expenditures are the largest single type of spendings for output in our economy.

Gross private domestic investment consists of the spendings of nongovernmental units—individuals and private organizations, mostly business firms—for currently produced goods with which to maintain or increase the stock of capital goods in this country. It includes spendings for new construction—residential, commercial, and industrial; spendings for new producers' durable goods —such as motors, machinery, railroad equipment, farm equipment, electrical generating machinery, store fixtures, and so on; and net changes in business inventories. A net increase in business inventories adds to the flow of spendings as the business firms increasing their inventories during a period buy the goods from other firms or hire labor and other productive factors with which

---

that are used by their producers and are not sold in the market. But since these are a relatively small part of the total and do not vary much relative to GNP, we can without much inaccuracy consider GNP as synonymous with spendings for output. It will be noted that GNP includes only spendings for output at its final stage; it avoids multiple counting by leaving out intermediate interfirm sales, such as the sale of steel to parts manufacturers, the sale of parts to auto manufacturers, and the sale of autos from manufacturer to dealer. The retail price of the automobile includes the value of all its components and is the sum of the "values added" by the various firms contributing to its delivery to the final buyer.

to produce the goods in their own plants. A net decrease of business inventories, however, should be subtracted from other types of spendings to arrive at total spendings for output; it indicates that business firms as a group have not spent for production during the period as much as they have sold to final buyers. It will be noted that these are *gross*, not *net*, spendings for private domestic investment; they include spendings for currently produced capital goods to offset the depreciation of existing capital as well as to make net additions to it. To arrive at *net* private domestic investment during a given period it is necessary to subtract from the gross spendings for private domestic investment the amount of estimated capital depreciation owing to wear and tear and obsolescence during the period. Gross private domestic investment is very important in the fluctuations of spendings, output, and prices; it is one of the most widely fluctuating types of spendings, and it is dynamic in the sense that its fluctuations tend to produce variations in other types of spendings.

Net foreign investment represents the net amounts that foreigners contribute to spendings for our output during a given period by selling capital assets here, or by borrowing from us, or by shipping gold to us. By buying capital claims from them or by taking gold from them we can enable foreigners to buy from us more goods and services than we buy from them, thus enabling them to make a net contribution to spendings for our output. It must be noted, however, that this figure does not always measure the full excess of our exports over our imports; it measures only the net purchases by foreigners permitted by their sales of capital claims to us or by shipping gold to us. To find the full impact of our net exports of goods and services to foreign countries during a period we would have to add to our net foreign investment the amount of net gifts made to foreigners by our people and government. Net gifts to foreigners by our people are included in personal consumption expenditures; net gifts to foreigners by our government are included in government purchases of goods and services. These items have been very important since 1939, for through net gifts to foreigners as well as through net foreign investment we have made it possible for our exports of goods and services to exceed our imports by many billions of dollars.

Government purchases of goods and services include, as the name implies, spendings by federal, state, and local governmental units for the current output of goods and services. Some of these spendings are for the output of goods and services by business firms—construction materials and services, office equipment, automobiles, military materiel, paper, and the countless other items needed by modern governments. Other spendings are directly for the services of workers—for officials, clerks, policemen, firemen, construction workers, military personnel, and many other types of labor. Government purchases represent a contribution to the demand for output and to national money income just as surely as do business or personal spendings. One should not allow his opinions as to the appropriate scope of government activity to obscure this point.

In summary, GNP, or total spendings for output, during any period are made up of the following types of spendings: (1) personal consumption expenditures, (2) gross private domestic investment, (3) net foreign investment, and (4) government purchases of goods and services. And total spendings for output fluctuate with the sum of these types of spendings.

Chart 4 shows how widely GNP has fluctuated since 1929. From 1929 to 1933 total spendings for output fell from an annual rate of $103.8 billion to $55.8 billion, a fall of 46 percent. This reflected declines of 41 percent in personal consumption spendings, 92 percent in gross private domestic investment, 80 percent in net foreign investment, and 6 percent in government purchases. It is small wonder that many employers, struck by the drastic decline in the effective money demand for their products, not only reduced their prices but also released masses of workers to lengthen the lines of the unemployed and either closed their plants or operated them on only a part-time basis.

By 1939, after a recession in 1938, spendings for output had

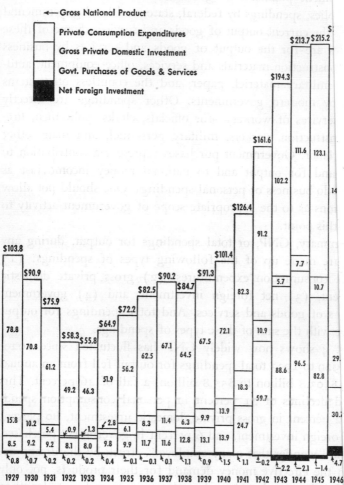

← Gross National Product

☐ Private Consumption Expenditures

☐ Gross Private Domestic Investment

☐ Govt. Purchases of Goods & Services

■ Net Foreign Investment

Year	GNP				
1929	$103.8	78.8	15.8	8.5	0.8
1930	$90.9	70.8	10.2	9.2	0.7
1931	$75.9	61.2	5.4	9.2	0.2
1932	$58.3	49.2	0.9	8.1	0.2
1933	$55.8	46.3	1.3	8.0	0.2
1934	$64.9	51.9	2.8	9.8	0.4
1935	$72.2	56.2	6.1	9.9	−0.1
1936	$82.5	62.5	8.3	11.7	−0.1
1937	$90.2	67.1	11.4	11.6	0.1
1938	$84.7	64.5	6.3	12.8	1.1
1939	$91.3	67.5	9.9	13.1	0.9
1940	$101.4	72.1	13.9	13.9	1.5
1941	$126.4	82.3	18.3	24.7	1.1
1942	$161.6	91.2	10.9	59.7	−0.2
1943	$194.3	102.2	5.7	88.6	−2.2
1944	$213.7	111.6	7.7	96.5	−2.1
1945	$215.2	123.1	10.7	82.8	−1.4
1946		14	29.	30.	4.7

Chart 4. Gross National Product and Its Components, 192
(in billions of dollars).

climbed to an annual rate of $91.3 billions, 63 percent above the low point of 1933 but still 12 percent below 1929 levels. As the war broke out the downward spiral of deflation had been at least temporarily halted and we had enjoyed a considerable measure of recovery in employment and production. Yet, as noted earlier, there were still more than 9,000,000 unemployed and no signs of impending runaway price increases. The major problem was still to achieve a sufficiently high effective demand for output to permit the attainment of a satisfactorily high level of employment and production. Ironically, the war solved this problem, at least for the time, though it compensated by providing a host of new problems. A whole chain of events—the intensification of war preparation abroad, relaxation of our neutrality policy, the introduction of lend-lease, our own preparation for war, our participation in the war, and our contribution to foreign relief and reconstruction in the postwar period—these provided the dynamic force that hoisted spendings for output to an unprecedentedly high level. After rising above $215 billion during the war period, GNP continued upward to reach $262.4 billion in 1948. This rate of spendings was by far the greatest ever attained in this country; it was 153 percent above the levels of prosperous 1929, about 370 percent above the low point in 1933, and 187 percent above the level of 1939. By keeping in mind this great rise of spendings one can avoid a common elementary mistake in analysis. Some observers, relying on the overly-simple rule that an increase in the price of a product decreases the quantity of it that can be sold, argued erroneously that general price increases would decrease sales and bring on unemployment. What they forgot was that the price increases were supported and even actively "caused" by a marked increase in both the ability and willingness to spend by government, business, and individuals.

During the 1939-1948 period as a whole the marked rise of GNP reflected increases in all four types of spendings for output. This is shown in Table 2. Personal consumption rose 165 percent, gross private domestic investment 355 percent, net foreign investment 111 percent, and government purchases 180 percent. It is to be noted, however, that a mere comparison of percentage increases may lead to a misunderstanding of the respective roles of the four types of spendings, for some of these components are much larger than others. For example, personal

TABLE 2.   GNP and Its Components, 1939-1948

| | Amounts in Billions | | 1948 as Percentage of 1939 | Percentage of Increase Due to Rise of This Type of Spendings |
	1939	1948		
GNP	$91.3	$262.4	287.4	100
Personal consumption	67.5	178.8	264.9	65.1
Gross private domestic investment	9.9	45.0	454.5	20.5
Net foreign investment	0.9	1.9	211.1	0.6
Government purchases of goods and services	13.1	36.7	280.2	13.8

TABLE 3.   GNP and Its Components, 1939-1941

| | Amounts in Billions | | Last Quarter of 1941 as Percentage of 1939 | Percentage of Total Rise Due to Rise of This Type of Spendings |
	1939	Last Quarter 1941 (Annual rate)		
GNP	$91.3	$139.6	152.9	100.0
Personal consumption	67.5	85.9	127.3	38.2
Gross private domestic investment	9.9	18.8	189.9	18.4
Net foreign investment	0.9	2.1	233.3	2.5
Government purchases of goods and services	13.1	32.8	250.4	40.9

consumption spendings showed a smaller percentage rise than GNP, but because they were such a large part of total spendings they contributed 65 percent of the total increase of GNP.

The quantitative importance of increases in the different types of spendings varied in different parts of the inflation period. This can be shown by dividing the period into three subperiods: (1)

from 1939 until our entrance into the war in late 1941, (2) from the end of 1941 until the peak of our war spendings in the first quarter of 1945, and (3) from the first quarter of 1945 until 1948.

All four types of spendings contributed heavily to the total rise of spendings up to the end of 1941, as is shown in Table 3. The rise of government spendings reflected the increase of defense activities—construction of strategic plants, purchases of war materials, increasing military personnel, and growing lend-lease aid

TABLE 4. GNP and Its Components, 1941-1945

	Amounts in Billions at Annual Rates		First Quarter of 1945 as Percentage of Last Quarter of 1941	Percent of Total Rise Due to Rise of This Type of Spendings
	Last Quarter of 1941	First Quarter of 1945		
GNP	$139.6	$222.6	159.5	100.0
Personal consumption	85.9	119.0	138.5	39.9
Gross private domestic investment	18.8	7.7	41.0	−13.4
Net foreign investment	2.1	−2.7	—	− 5.8
Government purchases of goods and services	32.8	98.6	300.6	79.3

to our future allies. Net foreign investment rose somewhat as warring countries borrowed here or sold capital assets to us in order to purchase materials with which to carry on the war, though lend-lease aid, which is included in government purchases, supplied a large part of these needs during the latter part of the period. Gross private domestic investment spendings, which had been in the doldrums during the depression and were a key factor in the prolongation of unemployment, rose for the first time in more than a decade to levels above those of 1929, both responding to the general rise of demand and contributing greatly to it. Personal consumption spendings also rose, both as a response to the general rise of incomes and as a contributing factor.

The continued rise of total spendings for output from late 1941 until the peak of our war effort in the first quarter of 1945 reflected widely differing patterns of behavior by the component types of spendings, as is shown in Table 4. Government expenditures rose greatly; to supply the almost insatiable appetite of the allied war machine they increased more than 200 percent to a level about seven and a half times that of 1939. Personal consumption spendings, responding to the rise of money incomes and despite the various measures adopted to curb consumption, rose 38.5 percent to a level 76 percent above that in 1939. Spendings for gross private domestic investment actually declined 59 per-

TABLE 5. GNP and Its Components, 1945-1948

	Amounts in Billions at Annual Rates First Quarter		1948 as Percentage of First Quarter of 1945	Percent of Total Rise Due to Rise of This Type of Spendings
	1945	1948		
GNP	$222.6	$262.4	117.9	100.0
Personal consumption	119.0	178.8	150.3	150.3
Gross private domestic investment	7.7	45.0	584.4	93.7
Net foreign investment	−2.7	1.9	—	11.6
Government purchases of goods and services	98.6	36.7	37.2	−155.6

cent; this was due to no decrease in either the ability or the eagerness to spend for investment purposes but to the fact that only essential capital maintenance and construction could be permitted during the wartime shortages of labor and materials and much of the investment that did occur was done by the government. Net foreign investment was negative during most of the war period; we borrowed, sold assets abroad, or exported gold in order to import goods and services to help meet our war and civilian needs. Our exports far exceeded our imports, but most of our exports did not yield current payments to us, for they were supplied under lend-lease arrangements. As a result we sold capital assets, including gold, and borrowed abroad in order to pay for a part of our imports, especially for those from South American countries. Only a few billion dollars worth of goods and services were acquired in this way, however.

There can be no doubt that the continuously rising government spendings were the key factor in the rising levels of total spendings and prices from 1939 to the first quarter of 1945 when our war effort reached its peak. During this period government spendings rose 653 percent and directly contributed 65 percent of the total increase of spendings for output. Moreover, the rise of government spendings was indirectly responsible for most, if not all, of the rise of private consumption and investment spendings. But the period from the first quarter of 1945 into 1948 presents a far different picture, as shown in Table 5. Government expenditures actually declined by nearly $62 billion, or 63 percent, though they remained far above prewar levels. The postwar rise of total spendings for output was due solely to the rise of nongovernmental spendings. The rise of net foreign investment contributed nearly 12 percent of the rise of total spendings between the first quarter of 1945 and 1948, but most of the increase of GNP was traceable to the rise of domestic private spendings for consumption and investment. Personal consumption expenditures rose by $59.8 billion, an amount equal to 150 percent of the net rise of GNP, while gross private domestic investment rose $37.3 billion, an amount equal to nearly 93 percent of the net rise of GNP. Thus the major part of the inflation occurred while government spendings had fallen far below their wartime peak, and it was supported by the big increase of private and foreign spendings, mostly the former.

Though the preceding sections described statistically the behavior of GNP and its components during the 1939-1948 period they are not well adapted to showing why these various types of spendings for output behaved as they did. They do not answer questions such as these: Why did private spendings for consumption and capital goods come out of their depression doldrums and increase markedly and continuously? What kinds of spendings were dynamic in the sense that their increase supplied the original upward stimulus and induced increases in other types of spendings? Which types of spendings rose merely as a response to rises in other spendings, and through what process did these induced increases of spendings occur? These questions will now be considered. As a first step it will be useful to look at the relationship between GNP and gross national income—the amount of gross money income received by the government, business firms, and individuals during any period.

GROSS NATIONAL PRODUCT AND GROSS NATIONAL INCOME

As noted above, the GNP for any period is the amount of total spendings for output. It is evident, however, that all of these spendings become gross money income for the various members of the community—the government, business firms, and individuals. Spendings for output, and only these spendings, create money income and the total money income received during any period is equal to the amount of spendings for output.

This principle is illustrated in Chart 5, which shows the shares of gross national income received by the various claimants in 1947. Total spendings for output during that year were $235.7 billion. All of these spendings were received by someone as either gross or net income. A part of these receipts for output were paid over to our various governmental units as indirect business taxes. These, which are a part of the government's income, do not include income and excess-profits taxes on business, but they do include several other kinds of taxes, notably property taxes on business and taxes on the production or sale of such things as liquor, beer, tobacco, gasoline, and so on. Another part of the spendings for output accrued to business firms as allowances to cover the current depreciation of their capital because of obsolescence and wear and tear. The remainder of GNP, after deducting indirect business taxes and current capital depreciation, is the *national income*. This is the *net* money income of the factors of production before any taxes except indirect business taxes. All of this accrued to the members of our nation as compensation of employees, corporate net profits (before income and excess-profits

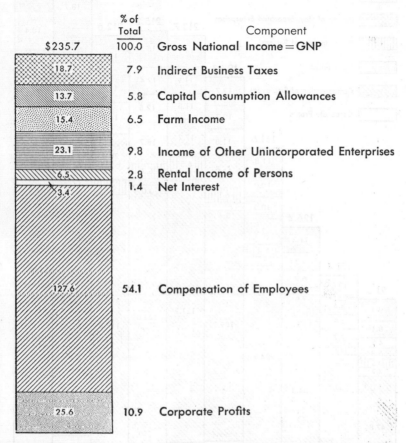

	% of Total	Component
$235.7	100.0	Gross National Income = GNP
18.7	7.9	Indirect Business Taxes
13.7	5.8	Capital Consumption Allowances
15.4	6.5	Farm Income
23.1	9.8	Income of Other Unincorporated Enterprises
6.5	2.8	Rental Income of Persons
3.4	1.4	Net Interest
127.6	54.1	Compensation of Employees
25.6	10.9	Corporate Profits

Chart 5. Gross National Income and Its Distributive Shares, 1947 (in billions of dollars).

taxes), incomes of farm proprietors, incomes of other unincorporated enterprises, rental incomes of persons, and net receipts of interest.

This fact, that spendings for output create an equal amount of

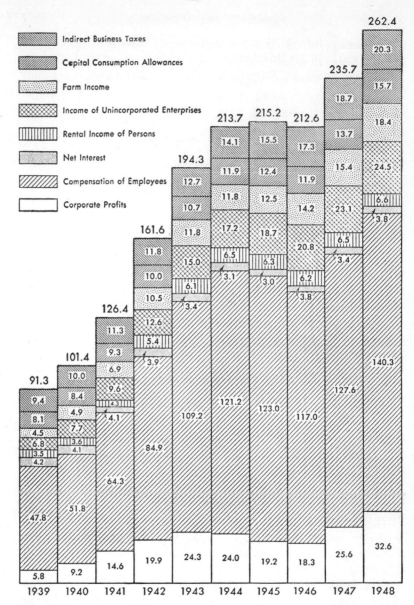

Chart 6. Gross National Income and Its Distributive Shares, 1939-1948 (in billions of dollars).

gross money income for our government, business firms, and persons, helps to explain much about the behavior of our economy. A decrease of total spendings for output, whatever the source of the decrease, reduces the amount of money income received in the community; it reduces total spending power. And a rise of spendings for output creates an equal increase of money income generated and received; it creates additional spending power.

Chart 6, showing the levels of gross national income received during each of the years 1939-1948, illustrates two principal points: (1) For each of these years the total money income received by the members of the nation was equal to total spendings for output. (2) The amount of income generated and received fluctuated exactly with total spendings for output. Thus, the marked decline of GNP from 1929 to 1933 reduced money incomes correspondingly, the major part of the decline being suffered by individuals and business firms. And the great rise of spendings for output between 1939 and 1948 generated an equal increase in money incomes received, and the largest part of the increase accrued to the private sectors of the economy.

GNP AND THE TOTAL DISPOSABLE INCOMES OF PERSONS, CORPORATIONS, AND THE GOVERNMENT

As a measure of changes in the spending power of the various sectors of the economy, the income figures cited above have the disadvantage of showing the distribution of income before any taxes except indirect business taxes and also before certain other transfers of money income among the various sectors of the economy. What is needed for this purpose is a series showing the distribution of money income remaining at the disposal of persons, corporations, and governmental units after all taxes have been paid and after certain other transfers have taken place. This will be called "disposable gross income." Its total for any period is equal to total spendings for output.

Disposable government income for any period is equal to the

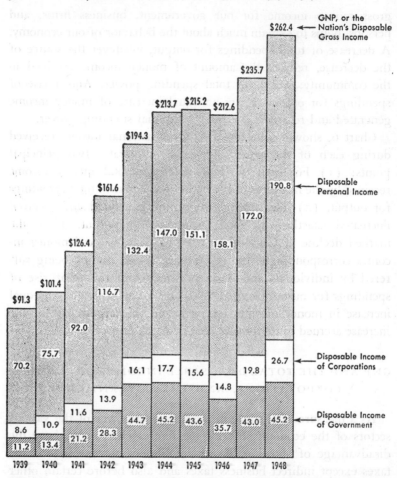

Chart 7. Gross National Product and the Nation's "Disposable Gross Income," 1939-1948 (in billions of dollars).

government's total income or revenue minus certain transfer payments to business firms and persons. The government's income or revenue includes all of its tax collections—indirect business taxes, income and excess-profits taxes, poll taxes, etc.—and certain other types of income, such as fines, fees, and administrative charges. Not all of this remains with governmental units as disposable government income, however; a part of it is paid out as *transfer payments*—payments for which the government receives currently no goods or services—to business firms and individuals. These transfer payments include such things as social security benefits, pensions and other benefits to veterans, interest on the public debt, and net subsidies to business. These transfers, though deducted from government revenue to find "disposable government income," appear as a part of the disposable incomes of corporations and persons.

Disposable corporate gross income is equal to the sum of corporate depreciation and obsolescence allowances and undistributed corporate net profits after payment of all corporate taxes. Or, to describe it another way, is is the amount left at the disposal of corporations out of their depreciation and obsolescence allowances and net profits after they have paid their taxes to the government and have distributed dividends to their stockholders.

Disposable personal income is the amount of income of all kinds, including transfer payments received, remaining at the disposal of persons after they have paid all their taxes.

Chart 7 shows several facts about the "disposable gross income" of the nation.

In the first place, the disposable gross income of the nation (i.e., the sum of the disposable incomes of government, corporations, and persons) for any period is equal to the GNP for the same period. Spendings for output create these incomes and determine their total size. In the second place, the great increase of GNP after 1939 created an equal increase in the disposable gross income of the nation; increased spendings for output created increased spending power. And in the third place, the increase of government tax collections, though very large, was far too small to prevent great increases in the disposable incomes (incomes after taxes) of corporations and persons. Even during the period of preparation for war and during the war period itself, when the government was taking constantly increasing amounts of our national output for its purposes, the amount of taxes collected lagged so far behind that corporations and persons had progressively larger amounts of money income left at their disposal.

It is now possible to cast additional light on some of the questions raised earlier: Why did private spendings in the form of gross private domestic investment and personal consumption rise so much after 1939 in contrast to the preceding decade in which they had persistently remained at such low levels as to produce deflation and unemployment? What started the upward movement and then sustained it? The answer is complex in its details, but not in its general outline. To provide this answer it will be convenient to divide the inflation period into two subperiods: (1) from 1939 to the end of the war, and (2) from the end of the war until the peak of the inflation in 1948.

There can be little doubt that the dynamic factor breaking the depression deadlock was the advent of war. The first impact was felt as other countries increased their purchases here by sending us gold, by borrowing here, and by reselling American securities to us, thereby injecting increased spendings for our output. This was strongly reinforced as our government continuously increased its rate of expenditures for goods and services to supply lend-lease aid to our future allies, to implement its expanding defense program, and to meet the mounting needs of total war. The direct effect of this great increase of foreign and government spending for output was not only to add to the total demand for goods and services but also to increase gross national income, and since tax collections increased far less than government spendings the effect was to increase greatly the disposable money incomes of business firms and individuals.

The continuing rise of foreign and government spendings induced increases in private spendings for investment and consumption purposes. Gross private domestic investment had been at a low level during the depression. But with the rapid rise of foreign and government spendings entrepreneurs again became both willing and able to spend large amounts for capital maintenance and accumulation. They were willing because with the rising level of

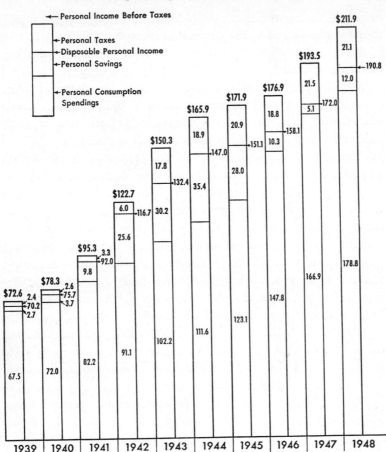

Chart 8.   Personal Income and Its Disposal, 1939-1948, Annual Figures,
(in billions of dollars).

demand for output they could foresee satisfactory profits on large
amounts of new investment, and they were able to spend more
both because of their rising profits and because credit was kept
highly available at low interest rates. During the war period itself
private investment spendings were held in check only by a shortage
of labor and materials and by direct government controls. This rise

of private investment after 1939 added still further to total spendings for output and to the disposable incomes of individuals and business, and it helped to induce increases in personal spendings for consumption.

Why did personal consumption spendings rise so much? Why, after having doggedly remained below $70 billion for several years before 1939, did they rise progressively until they surpassed $123 billion in 1945? What started the rise, and what sustained it? The rate of personal spendings for consumption varies with (1) the amount of personal disposable income, and (2) the propensity of people to consume and to save. There can be no doubt that the amount of disposable income left in people's hands after they have paid their taxes is a major determinant of the amount that they spend for consumption. It would be amazing if people spent no more for consumption when their disposable incomes were $150 billion than when their disposable incomes were only $70 billion. But the propensity to consume and to save is also an important determinant. People do after all have the right to decide what parts of their disposable incomes they will consume and what parts they will save—that is, not spend for consumption. And they may at times alter the proportions devoted to each of the two uses.

Chart 8 shows the behavior of personal income, personal taxes, disposable personal incomes, personal consumption, and personal savings. Several facts stand out. (1) Personal income increased so much more than personal taxes that disposable personal income increased greatly. The increase of personal taxes was not even sufficient to absorb all the increase of income contributed by government spendings, to say nothing of the increase of income contributed by private spendings. From a level of $70 billion in 1939, disposable personal income rose to $151 billion in 1945. (2) With rising disposable incomes, people spent increasing amounts for consumption. Without declining in a single year, personal spendings for consumption rose from $67.5 billion in 1939 to $123 billion in 1945. It is clear from the figures that the rise of disposable personal incomes was the major factor in the rise of consumption spendings. (3) The rise of consumption spendings did not, however, precisely parallel the rise of disposable personal income. This is shown in Table 6.

TABLE 6. The Distribution of Disposable Personal Income Between Consumption and Saving, 1939-1948

	Amounts in Billions			Personal Consumption as Percentage of Personal Disposable Income	Personal Saving as Percentage of Personal Disposable Income
Year	Disposable Personal Income	Personal Consumption	Personal Savings		
1939	$ 70.1	$ 67.5	$ 2.7	96.3	3.7
1940	75.7	72.1	3.7	95.2	4.8
1941	92.0	82.3	9.8	89.5	10.5
1942	116.7	91.2	25.6	78.1	21.9
1943	132.4	102.2	30.2	77.2	22.8
1944	147.0	111.6	35.4	75.9	24.1
1945	151.1	123.1	28.0	81.5	18.5
1946	158.1	147.8	10.3	93.5	6.5
1947	172.0	166.9	5.0	97.0	3.0
1948	190.8	178.8	12.0	93.7	6.3

In 1939 our people as a group elected to spend 96.3 percent of their disposable income for consumption and to save 3.7 percent of it. As their disposable incomes rose they spent larger absolute amounts for consumption, but a smaller percentage. They saved a larger percentage. To some extent this rise in the percentage of disposable incomes used for saving reflected the widespread appeals to save and lend to the government in order to win the war and help fight inflation. To a much greater extent, however, it reflected the limited ability of the economy to provide enhanced supplies of consumption goods and services and the fact that price ceilings prevented, or at least limited, the ability of buyers to bid up the prices of the limited supplies. Much of the abnormally high rate of saving during the war represented "forced saving"; it was done under various types of compulsion.

In short, the rise of personal consumption spendings between

1939 and 1945 was an induced rise—a rise induced by the increase of disposable personal incomes. The great rise of foreign and government spendings contributed the original upward thrust both directly by contributing to personal disposable incomes and indirectly by inducing a rise of private investment spendings which contributed still further to the rise of personal disposable incomes. Responding to these increases of their incomes, people increased their spendings for consumption, thereby greatly aggravating the rise of both spendings for output and money incomes. Though the rise of personal consumption was a major contributor to the rise of total spendings and to the mounting inflationary pressures from 1939 to 1945, it was not an "original cause"; there is no reason to believe that it would have occurred in the absence of the great rise of foreign and government spendings and the induced rise of private investment.

Though there can be little doubt that the great rise of government spendings was the principal dynamic factor in the inflation during the 1939-1945 period, the postwar situation was far different. The further rise of spendings after the end of the war occurred despite a marked decline of government expenditures; the postwar inflation might have been less severe if government spendings had declined more, but the causes of the continued rise of spendings and prices must be sought elsewhere. They are to be found in a combination of conditions: (1) the high and insistent demand for our goods and services by foreign countries, (2) the willingness and ability of our business firms and others to spend large and increasing amounts for gross private domestic investment, and (3) the increased willingness and ability of our people to spend for consumption. The reasons for this combination of conditions will be developed in detail in later chapters, but they can be outlined here.

The willingness of other countries to spend large amounts for our output was traceable to their huge needs for reconstruction, development, and the easing of social tensions, and to the unavailability of the needed goods and services elsewhere in the world. Their ability to spend so much here was due largely to the willingness of our government to make huge grants and loans and also to the ability of other countries to ship gold to us and to sell assets and borrow in our markets.

The willingness of our business firms and others to spend very large and rising amounts for investment was due to a number of things: (1) a deficiency of capital goods traceable in part to the very low rate of investment during the prewar depression and during the war period itself, (2) expectations of a high and rising level of demand for output, and (3) the highly liquid condition of business at the end of the war. The ability to spend such large and rising amounts for investment was due to the huge accumulation of liquid savings by business during the war, to the large current earnings of business during the postwar period, and to the maintenance of very easy credit conditions.

A major factor in the continued rise of spendings after the war was the rise in the proportion of their disposable incomes that people elected to spend for consumption. The decline of this proportion during the war has already been noted. In 1939 people as a group spent 96.3 percent of their disposable incomes for consumption; by 1944 this percentage had declined to 75.9 percent.[3] This marked wartime decline in the percentage of income consumed and the rise in the percentage of income saved did not, however, represent the "free choice" of income receivers. It was accomplished largely through compulsions—fervent pleas to save in order to fight inflation and win the war, and shortages of consumer goods and services accompanied by rationing and price ceilings. As soon, however, as supplies for civilians began to increase and direct controls over goods and prices began to be relaxed, consumer spendings surged upward. Despite the continued rise of disposable personal incomes, the percentage of these incomes spent for consumption rose from 75.9 in 1944 to 81.5 in 1945, 93.5 in 1946, 97.0 in 1947, and 93.7 in 1948. In fact, during each of the postwar years except 1948 the rise of con-

[3] See Table 6 on p. 35 above.

sumption spendings exceeded the rise of disposable personal
incomes. This is shown in Table 7. For each dollar increase in their
disposable incomes people as a whole increased their consumption
spendings by $2.80 in 1945, $3.53 in 1946, and $1.38 in 1947.
This marked increase in the propensity to consume was a major
dynamic factor in the postwar rise of spendings and prices.

TABLE 7.   Increase of Personal Disposable Incomes, Consumption, and Savings,
1939-1948
(Increases or decreases (−) in billions of dollars)[4]

Year	Personal Disposable Incomes	Personal Consumption	Personal Saving	(Col. 4) Increase of Personal Consumption as Percentage of Increase of Personal Disposable Income	(Col. 5) Increase of Personal Saving as Percentage of Increase of Personal Disposable Income
1939	$ 4.7	$ 3.0	$ 1.7	63.8	36.2
1940	5.6	4.6	1.0	82.1	17.9
1941	16.3	10.2	6.1	62.6	37.4
1942	24.7	8.9	15.8	36.0	64.0
1943	15.7	11.0	4.6	70.0	30.0
1944	14.6	9.4	5.2	64.4	35.6
1945	4.1	11.5	− 7.4	280.4	−180.5
1946	7.0	24.7	−17.7	352.9	−252.9
1947	13.9	19.2	− 5.3	138.2	− 38.1
1948	18.8	11.8	7.0	62.8	37.2

Only a few of the many factors that accounted for this marked
increase in the propensity to consume can be noted at this point.
(1) The increased availability of consumer goods and services
and the relaxation of wartime compulsions to "save." As social
pressures for saving were weakened and direct controls over supplies and prices were relaxed at the end of the war people were
again free to bid against each other for goods and services, and they

[4] Computed from data in the Department of Commerce series. The increases
shown were derived by deducting from the amounts during a given year the
amounts during the year before. Column 4 is the marginal propensity to consume, and Column 5 is the marginal propensity to save.

did so with alacrity. (2) The tremendous accumulation of savings during the war, most of them in highly liquid forms. Later sections will show how the government's deficit spending during the war permitted both businesses and individuals to save huge amounts. Personal savings alone aggregated $132.6 billion during the years 1940-1945, and the major part of these was represented at the end of the war by increased holdings of currency, checking and time deposits, government securities, and other highly liquid assets. In terms of money, people were far richer than at the beginning of the war. Because of this, some people felt free in the postwar period to consume beyond their current incomes. Others did not actually spend past savings but many of them felt justified in consuming an abnormally large proportion of their current incomes. (3) The "backlog of demand" for consumer's goods created during the war. The supply of many types of consumer's goods, and especially of durable items, was severely curtailed during the war, and many other things were available only in limited amounts. As a result of this as well as of an unjustified feeling that they had suffered serious economic deprivation during the war period, people in general felt justified in going on a mild spending spree.

The postwar rise of total spendings and prices cannot be blamed upon any one type of spendings; it was a resultant of the behavior of all four principal types and of the policies behind them. These will be discussed in detail in later chapters. First, however, it will be useful to see how the rise of spendings during the inflation period was financed.

SPENDINGS FOR OUTPUT, THE SUPPLY OF MONEY, AND THE VELOCITY OF MONEY

The preceding sections described the behavior of total spendings for output and analyzed briefly the roles played by consumer spendings, gross private domestic investment, net foreign investment, and government purchases. In many respects this is the most useful type of analysis, for it enables us to relate the rate of spendings to the motives and actions of the various kinds of spenders and income receivers. But it is also useful to employ the

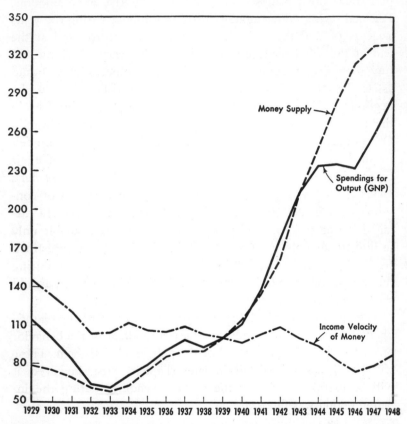

Chart 9.   Indexes of Spendings for Output (GNP), the Money Supply, and the Income Velocity of Money, 1929-1948   (1939 = 100).

"quantity theory" approach to show the relations among spendings, the supply of money, and the velocity of money. It is a truism that the amount of spendings for output during any period is equal to the supply of money multiplied by the "income velocity of money"—the average number of times each dollar of the money supply is spent for output during the period.[5] Thus, increased spendings for output can be financed by an increased supply of money, an increased velocity of money, an increase of both, or an increase of one not fully offset by a decline of the other.

Chart 9 shows that for the 1939-1948 period as a whole the increased spendings for output were financed entirely by an increased money supply. The quantity of money—checking deposits plus coin and currency in circulation—rose from less than $35 billion in 1939 to about $110 billion in 1948, an increase of 214 percent.[6] During the same period spendings for output rose only 187 percent. It has long been established that the rate of spendings need not vary proportionally with the supply of money, but our experience after 1939 has again shown that it is dangerous to ignore the influence of an expanded money supply.

It is interesting to note the types of money whose supply increased, who issued the money, and the process by which the additional money was created and injected into the stream of spendings. Of the $75 billion increase in the total money supply from 1939 to 1948, about 75 percent was in the form of additional checking deposits and 25 percent in the form of additional coin and paper currency—mostly the latter. Practically none of the increased supply of money was issued by the government itself. In line with twentieth-century methods of inflation, the Treasury avoided the direct issuance of paper money to finance its deficits and relied instead on the Federal Reserve and our 14,000 commercial banks to create the additional money that it needed. The new money was created and injected into the stream

[5] The "income velocity of money" used here was computed by dividing GNP by the total of demand deposits adjusted plus currency outside banks.

[6] These figures include coin and currency outside banks plus demand deposits adjusted. Demand deposits adjusted exclude interbank deposits and U. S. Government deposits. A case could be made for including in the money supply some part of time and savings deposits, for some of these are in fact used as means of payment. In general, however, our definition of the money supply can be defended on the ground that payments are made predominantly by the transfer of checking deposit credits and of coin and currency.

of spendings in two principal ways: (1) by gold imports, and (2) by increases in bank loans and bank holdings of securities. Between 1939 and 1948 about $6 billion was added to our money supply as foreigners shipped gold here, exchanged it for checking deposits, and injected the new money into the spending stream by purchasing our goods and services. But most of the new money was created through increased loans and security holdings by the banking system. Up to the end of 1945 the major part of the increase in the money supply was attributable to purchases of government securities by the Federal Reserve and commercial banks. Unable, or at least unwilling, to raise enough money through taxation or borrowing of current savings, the federal government sold large amounts of its securities to the Federal Reserve and commercial banks, who in turn gave it deposit credits. The government then paid over these deposit credits to individuals and business firms in exchange for the various goods and services that it required. Though a major part of the increased money supply resulted from increased bank holdings of government securities, it is important to note that these were supplemented by increased bank loans to private borrowers, especially during the periods from 1939 to Pearl Harbor and after the end of the war. In fact, bank holdings of governments declined somewhat after the end of the war, but this decline was more than offset by the rise of bank credit extended for private purposes. Banks created new deposits for private borrowers, who then injected them into the spending stream through the purchase of goods and services for consumption or investment purposes.

To a student of money, one of the most interesting aspects of this inflation was the behavior of the velocity of money. Inflations in the past have usually been accompanied by an increasing velocity of money as people and business firms received higher money incomes, felt that their future money incomes would be larger, and feared that money would continue to lose its purchasing power. But throughout this inflation the velocity of money remained at or below depression levels. During the prosperity period, 1923-

1929, inclusive, the income velocity of money—the average number of times each dollar was spent for output during a year—averaged about 3.7. This meant that people and business firms as a whole elected to hold at any one time enough money to cover about 27 percent of their annual spendings for output.[7] The income velocity of money fell during the depression period and in 1939 stood at about 2.6, which was 22 percent below the average of the twenties. Chart 9 shows that thereafter the income velocity of money rose gradually until the first quarter of 1942, at which time it was about 10 percent above its level in 1939, then fell steadily until the latter part of 1945 when it was nearly 30 percent below 1939 levels, and then rose somewhat during the next three years. A major part of the increase of spendings after the end of the war was financed by an increase in the velocity of money above the very low wartime level; but in 1948 the income velocity of money was still, despite the continued rise of prices, about 13 percent below 1939 levels and nearly 40 percent below the level of the twenties.

It is difficult to explain fully the continued low velocity of money—the willingness of people and business firms to hold unusually large amounts of money relative to their spendings—despite the continued decline in the purchasing power of money, but some of the operating factors can be pointed out. Let us look first at the period of active war. One of the relevant factors during this period was the large amount of "forced saving" by people who were unable, because of scarcities and price controls, to spend all their money for the kinds of goods and services that they most wanted in the long run. Of course, their abnormally large money savings could have reëntered the spending stream quickly if people had exchanged them for securities or savings accounts at banks, but several factors tended to prevent this. Among these

[7] By the income velocity we mean GNP divided by the money supply; that is, demand deposits adjusted plus coin and currency outside banks. Since GNP also includes government spendings we should perhaps include government deposits in the money supply. If we did this the velocity of money would show an even greater decrease during the war period.

were the facts that many of the savers were not accustomed to having any savings at all and even less accustomed to buying and holding securities, that many did not have convenient access to a savings institution, that many savings institutions did not greatly encourage further deposits, that interest rates paid on savings were very low, and that many wanted to be in a highly liquid condition when the war was over. Business firms were also accumulating very large amounts of money by reducing inventories, by large depreciation allowances, and by large retentions of profits; shortages of goods and services, supplemented by price controls, prevented them from spending these funds for additional inventories or capital improvements. They did return a considerable part of these money accumulations to the spending stream through repayment of loans and purchases of securities, but they also added large amounts to their checking deposit balances to be held idle until the postwar period.

The limited rise of velocity after the end of the war in the face of accelerated inflation is more difficult to explain, but the following conditions were relevant. (1) The large amount of accumulated savings. With abnormally large amounts of savings which they did not want to use immediately for consumption, many people—especially those who did not deal in the stock market and were unfamiliar with securities in general—preferred to hold large money balances. (2) Low interest rates, especially at savings institutions. With interest on savings accounts at very low levels and with many savings institutions unenthusiastic about accepting more funds, people sacrificed only a small income by holding idle money balances. (3) Shortages of many goods, especially durable goods, and the "stickiness" of administered prices. Many people had earmarked a part of their savings for specific things such as automobiles, new houses, or expensive electric appliances which were limited in supply and whose prices were kept by their producers from rising to the level which would have reduced demand to equality with the supply. Unable to get these physical products or to bid up their prices freely, many people elected to hold money until they could get delivery of the things they wanted most. (4) The continued expectation of deflation and of an imminent cessation of the price rise. Large sections of the population postponed purchases to wait for the widely predicted downturn. It is frightening to contemplate what might have happened to price levels in the absence of the widespread fear of an early postwar depression.

This chapter has outlined the behavior of spendings for output after 1939 and analyzed some of the factors responsible for it. The next chapter will deal with the behavior of physical output.

III

||||||||||||||||||||||||||||||||||||||||||||||||||||||||||||||||||||||||||||||||||||||||||||||||||||||||||||||||||||||||||

Real Output During the Inflation

THE inflation was neither caused nor aggravated by any actual decline in the amount of goods and services available for purchase. It occurred despite the fact that real output rose to record-breaking levels. Only by keeping this fact in mind can one understand the behavior of our price levels and the differences in the degree of inflation here and abroad.

As pointed out in an earlier section, our economy was running in low gear when the war broke out in 1939. More than 9 million people who were willing and able to work were unemployed; many others were working only part time; and many factories, mines, and farms were either idle or operating considerably below capacity levels. And, it must be emphasized, our productive capacity was being underutilized only because the effective money demand for output was so low that enterprisers did not find it profitable to offer full employment in order to achieve full production. In such a situation it was only to be expected that a rise of spendings for output, which to enterprisers appeared as an increase in the money demand for their products, would bring about an increase of real output as well as price rises. The early response was a large increase in output and a relatively small increase of prices; but as production approached capacity levels and producers encountered more and more bottlenecks in facilities, labor, or materials, further increases of spendings were reflected

46

to a greater extent in price rises and to a lesser extent in increases of real output.

The increase of output was achieved by an increased employment of labor and other productive facilities. Virtually all the unemployed were absorbed into either civilian employment or the armed forces, several million people who ordinarily would not seek employment took jobs for patriotic reasons, to increase their family incomes, or to replace the income of a member of the family who had gone to war, and the average number of hours worked per week increased by between 15 and 20 percent. Other productive facilities were also utilized more intensively; plants that had been idle were brought into use, many that were not already running 24 hours a day and 7 days a week increased their hours of operation, plants generally operated at a higher tempo, and many new facilities were created, especially in the munitions industries. It was in these ways that the output of our economy was raised to unprecedentedly high levels during the war period despite the fact that more than 11 million men and women were in the armed forces. This rise of output helped to limit the degree of inflation.

With the termination of fighting many people who ordinarily do not seek employment withdrew from the labor force and overtime work largely disappeared. Nevertheless, after a temporary lull, the output of goods and services rose to record peacetime levels. Our productive facilities had come through the war practically unscathed, millions of men returned from the armed forces to civilian employment, and unemployment remained at an almost irreducible minimum. Two important facts about our output in the postwar period should be borne in mind. First, real output was far above any prewar levels; this availability of an unprecedented peacetime output of goods and services helped to limit the extent of inflation here. Second, it proved to be impossible to raise output above wartime levels in a short period of time, so that further increases of spendings for output had to be reflected largely in price inflation. With the economy already operating at near capacity levels there was not the "cushion" of unused productive facilities that existed in 1940 and even in 1941. Our long-run prospect is, we hope, for large increases in output as we improve our technology and add to our capital equipment but this is a slow process and cannot offset great increases of spendings during short periods of time.

A comparison of our economy with the economies of war-torn countries brings out the importance of increased output in limiting the degree of inflation here. While our output was reaching unprecedented levels the output of many other countries remained below, in some cases far below, prewar levels. Exhaustion of soil fertility because of the unavailability of fertilizers, destruction of livestock, lack of farm machinery, damage to factories both by wear and tear and by military action, destruction and deterioration of transportation and communication facilities, malnutrition of workers and their families, loss of income from foreign investments, social discontent and political uncertainties, military occupation—all these factors served to reduce productivity in many countries so that increased spendings there were necessarily reflected in price inflation. This is not to say that our increased output is the sole explanation of our lesser degree of inflation; in some countries monetary and fiscal policies were also much more inflationary. But we should realize that our escape from bombing and from land warfare within our own borders was a real aid in limiting the extent of our inflation.

THE AMOUNT OF THE INCREASE OF OUTPUT

There can be no doubt that during both the war and the postwar periods our output of real goods and services has been far above prewar levels. The rise was too great to permit any questioning of this conclusion. It is extremely difficult, however, to measure the rise of output with any degree of accuracy, especially during the war period. This is largely because of the marked change in the composition of output and the difficulty of establishing equivalents between wartime and peacetime products. The most marked shift was, of course, from civilian to military products. When such a shift occurs, how is one to measure the change in physical output? A tank equals how many farm tractors? A bomber is equivalent to how many civilian transport planes? A marine uniform is the equivalent of how many low-price civilian suits? Thousands of such difficulties arise in equating war and civilian goods. Moreover, civilian goods themselves changed in wartime. In many cases ersatz materials had to be used. Rubber heels were made of reclaimed rather than virgin rubber, children's toys of wood or paper rather than iron or steel, clothing of lower quality materials, shoes of poorer leather, and so on. Also, some producers discontinued their low-profit items and concentrated on those with higher profit margins. It is very difficult to measure changes in real output when such shifts in the composition of output occur.

There are three principal methods of measuring physical output: (1) to deflate the market value of output by an appropriate price index, (2) to construct indexes of the physical amounts of goods and services produced, and (3) to use an index of man-hours worked and adjust this by an estimate of changes in productivity per man-hour. Each of these has its shortcomings for our purpose. The first is inaccurate because we lack a price index that is properly weighted for the purpose of correcting for price changes in the GNP. We shall later offer a rough measure of changes in real output computed by deflating GNP by the cost of living index, but this will probably overestimate somewhat the rise of physical output during the war because the cost of living index probably understates the rise of prices that actually occurred. An index of physical production can accurately reflect the behavior of real output where the product is not altered; it is therefore useful in measuring the output of such things as grain, iron ore, coal, electricity, copper, and so on. It cannot, however, measure output accurately where products are altered significantly. In such cases recourse must be had to an index of man-hours worked with adjustments for estimated changes in productivity per man-hour. Such adjustments are likely to be very approximate, yet by 1944 more than half of the Federal Reserve industrial production index was computed in this way.[1]

The measures of output in Table 8 are offered with the caution that they are at best only approximate indicators. Columns 2 and 3 show the behavior of gross national product in dollars of

TABLE 8.   Gross National Product in Current and 1939 Dollars

Year	Col. 1 GNP in Current Dollars (In billions)	Col. 2 GNP in 1939 Dollars (In billions)	Col. 3 Index of GNP in 1939 Dollars (1939 = 100)	Col. 4 GNP Minus Compensation of Military Personnel in 1939 Dollars (In billions)	Col. 5 Index of GNP Minus Compensation of Military Personnel in 1939 Dollars (1939 = 100)
1939	$ 91.3	$ 91.3	100	$ 90.9	100
1940	101.4	100.6	110	100.1	110
1941	126.4	119.5	131	117.8	130
1942	161.6	137.9	151	132.4	146
1943	194.3	156.3	171	144.7	159
1944	213.7	169.2	185	152.8	168
1945	215.2	166.6	182	149.1	164
1946	212.6	151.7	166	146.1	161
1947	235.7	147.1	161	144.6	159
1948	262.4	152.4	167	150.1	165

1939 purchasing power. The figures in column 2 were arrived at by dividing GNP by the cost of living index converted to a 1939 base. They indicate that real output rose 85 percent from 1939 to 1944 and then declined somewhat though it continued after the war to be more than 60 percent above the level of 1939. These output figures include the services of military personnel. If the latter are omitted the rise during the war was somewhat smaller, as is shown in columns 4 and 5. Nevertheless, output excluding the services of military personnel rose 68 percent between 1939 and 1944 and then declined slightly in the postwar period.

[1] War Production Board, *American Industry in War and Transition*, 1945, Part II, p. 21.

Table 9 presents some physical production indexes. These do not include all types of output, the most notable omissions being consumer services and the services of government employees. They do, however, bring out some interesting facts. (1) The total output of goods rose more than 85 percent between 1939 and the peak of the war effort and then in the postwar period averaged about 65 percent above the 1939 level. (2) Some types of production rose much more than others. For example, non-

TABLE 9.   Physical Production Index, 1939-1948
(1939=100)[2]

Year	Total Pro- duction	Agri- cultural Pro- duction	Total	Minerals	Manu- factures	Con- struction	Trans- portation	Electric and gas Utilities
					Nonagricultural Production			
1939	100	100	100	100	100	100	100	100
1940	112	104	113	110	116	108	110	121
1941	139	108	147	118	154	148	138	126
1942	170	121	180	122	194	164	175	141
1943	190	118	205	125	237	91	208	164
1944	186	123	200	132	231	49	217	172
1945	168	122	178	129	196	55	209	170
1946	153	126	158	126	162	104	189	171
1947	164	122	174	141	178	119	200	196
1948	172	132	180	146	182	141	197	217

agricultural production increased considerably more than agricultural output. This does not, of course, reflect unfavorably on agriculture, for farmers had not reduced their output so much in the preceding depression period and therefore entered the war era with far less unemployed labor, land, and other productive facilities.

These measures of real output, inaccurate as they are, show clearly that real output during the war and even the postwar period was far above the 1939 level.

[2] SOURCE: *Midyear Economic Report of the President,* July, 1949, p. 98. These indices have been converted by the writer to a 1939 base.

HOW THE INCREASE OF REAL OUTPUT
WAS ATTAINED

How was our economy able to attain such a great increase in its real output of goods and services? Many factors contributed, though their importance varied in different parts of the period: (1) an increase in the number of people at work, (2) an increase in the number of hours worked and in some cases in the intensity of work, (3) a more intensive utilization of existing facilities, (4) additions to facilities, and (5) improvements in technology.

TABLE 10.   The United States Labor Force, 1939-1948
(In thousands of persons, 14 years of age and over)[3]

Year	Col. 1 Total Labor Force, Including Armed Forces	Col. 2 Number Unemployed	Col. 3 Number Employed in Armed Forces and Civilian Employment	Col. 4 Number in Armed Forces	Col. 5 Total	Col. 6 Nonagri-cultural	Col. 7 Agricultural
					Number in Civilian Employment		
1939	55,600	9,480	46,120	370	45,750	36,140	9,610
1940	56,030	8,120	47,900	390	47,520	37,980	9,540
1941	57,380	5,560	51,820	1,470	50,350	41,250	9,100
1942	60,230	2,660	57,570	3,820	53,750	44,500	9,250
1943	64,410	1,070	63,340	8,870	54,470	45,390	9,080
1944	65,890	670	65,220	11,260	53,960	45,010	8,950
1945	65,140	1,040	64,100	11,280	52,820	44,240	8,580
1946	60,820	2,270	58,550	3,300	55,250	46,930	8,320
1947	61,608	2,141	59,467	1,440	58,027	49,761	8,266
1948	62,748	2,064	60,685	1,307	59,378	51,405	7,973

Table 10 shows the estimated labor force and its utilization. Column 3 shows the great increase between 1939 and 1944 in the number of people utilized in the armed forces and in civilian employment; this increase amounted to about 19 million persons, or more than 40 percent. Where did this increased manpower come from? Nearly 9 million came from the ranks of the unemployed, as unemployment declined from about 9.5 million in 1939 to less than 700,000, in 1944. The remainder came from an

[3] SOURCE: *Ibid.*, p. 93. The figures for 1939 are from the Department of Labor; for subsequent years they are from the Department of Commerce.

increase in the size of the labor force. Youths terminated or interrupted their education to enter the armed forces or take civilian jobs, elderly people delayed retirement or came out of retirement to work, many women who would not ordinarily seek employment took part-time or full-time jobs, and others sacrificed leisure to help win the war. Both by reducing unemployment and by increasing the total labor force we were able to add nearly 11 million persons to our armed forces and at the same time increase the number engaged in civilian employment by about 6 million, or more than 13 percent, between 1939 and 1944.

TABLE 11. Average Weekly Hours per Worker in Selected Industries, 1939-1948
(Index, 1939=100)[4]

Year	All Manufacturing		Building Construction		Bituminous Coal Mining		Retail Trade	
	Hours	Index	Hours	Index	Hours	Index	Hours	Index
1939	37.7	100	32.6	100	27.1	100	43.0	100
1940	38.1	101	33.1	102	28.1	104	42.9	100
1941	40.6	108	34.8	107	31.1	115	42.5	99
1942	42.9	114	36.4	112	32.9	121	41.6	97
1943	44.9	119	38.4	118	36.6	135	40.5	94
1944	45.2	120	39.6	121	43.4	160	40.3	94
1945	43.4	115	39.0	120	42.3	156	40.3	94
1946	40.4	107	38.1	117	41.6	154	40.5	94
1947	40.3	107	37.8	116	40.7	150	40.2	93
1948	40.0	106	37.3	114	37.7	139	40.0	93

The supply of labor was also augmented by increasing the average number of hours per week, as is shown for a few selected industries in Table 11. For industry as a whole the increase in the average length of the work week from 1939 to 1944 was probably between 15 and 20 percent, though there were wide differences among industries. For example, while the average work week in retail trade was shortened by about 6 percent, increases in other lines were 20 percent in manufacturing as a whole, 21 percent in building construction, 60 percent in bituminous coal mining,

[4] SOURCE: *Statistical Supplement to the Survey of Current Business,* 1947, pp. 60-63; and *Surveys of Current Business.*

47 percent in anthracite mining, and 8 percent in metalliferous mining. Farmers also worked longer hours; this contributed significantly to their ability to set new records in agricultural production despite the decline in the number of persons engaged in farming.

Along with the increase in the number of working people and the longer work week occurred a more intensive utilization of existing facilities. Previously idle plants were brought into operation, many plants operated extra shifts and more days each

TABLE 12.   Value of Manufacturing Plant Built, 1940-1944, and the Estimated Replacement Value of Prewar Manufacturing Plant
(In billions of dollars)[5]

Industry	Replacement Value of 1939 Plant	Additions, 1940-1944	1940-1944 Additions as Percentage of Replacement Value of 1939 Plant
Total	$49.0	$25.6	52
Transportation equipment, except autos	1.1	6.6	600
Chemicals	3.9	5.4	138
Nonferrous metals	1.4	1.7	121
Iron and steel	8.6	4.9	57
Autos and equipment	2.8	0.9	32
Machinery	3.2	0.9	28
Petroleum and coal products	4.0	1.0	25
Food	6.7	1.3	19
Other	17.3	2.9	17

week, and machinery and processes were speeded up. Moreover, large plant additions were made, many of them government financed, in a number of industries producing war or essential civilian products. For example, it has been estimated that additions to manufacturing plant in the years 1940-1944 amounted to $25.6 billion, and that these additions were equal to 52 percent of the replacement value of manufacturing plants in 1939 (see Table 12). The 1940-1944 additions exceeded the replacement value of the prewar plant in the industries producing chemicals,

[5] SOURCE: War Production Board, *American Industry in War and Transition,* 1945, Part II, p. 29.

nonferrous meals, and transportation equipment other than autos; in the iron and steel industries they exceeded 55 percent of the replacement value of prewar plant, and in several others they were 25 percent or more. Many of these additions retained their usefulness for postwar production; some others, such as ship-building facilities and shell-loading plants, were of only limited usefulness for peacetime purposes.

It is impossible to estimate accurately the contribution of improved technology to the rise of output during the war, but many improvements were made. New methods and machines were devised, incentive payment plans increased the output of workers in many cases, the ease of selling reduced real marketing costs, and standardization—especially of military items—contributed to productivity. For example, the standardization of military uniforms and shell casings enabled producers to work day after day without making new patterns or repeatedly adjusting machinery to turn out a variety of products.

All these factors, together with weather conditions that were unusually favorable for farm production, help to explain the great rise of real output between 1939 and the peak of production during the war period. But why did real output in the postwar period fall somewhat below its wartime peak? The decline was especially large if we include in real output the services of people in the armed services (see Table 8 above). It was still significant, however, if we exclude the services of the armed forces. The decline was largely, though not solely, traceable to (1) the decline in the size of the labor force, and (2) a shorter work week. Whereas the total labor force, including the armed forces, rose to nearly 66 million in 1944 it fell several millions after the end of the war as youths returned to school, many women withdrew from the labor force, elderly people retired, and some others no longer elected to work (see Table 10). If, however, we look only at the number engaged in civilian employment we find that it rose after the end of the war, and by 1948 was 30 percent above 1939 and even 10 percent above 1944. This helps to explain why real output exclusive of the services of the armed forces fell less than real output including those services.

With the end of the war, overtime work largely disappeared and average hours worked per week declined below the wartime peak, though they remained somewhat above 1939 levels (see Table 11). There were many reasons for this, including employers' desires to avoid overtime pay rates, workers' fatigue, union fears of losing the basic 40-hour week, union contracts providing a shorter work week without decreased pay, paid vacations, paid holidays, and time lost in labor disputes.

THE UTILIZATION OF GNP

The preceding sections described the behavior of total real output and emphasized its great rise over prewar levels. It will be useful at this point to look at the proportions of output that were devoted to governmental and export purposes and to private consumption and investment purposes.

The latter part of Table 13 shows that between 1939 and the peak of the war effort a continuously rising proportion of output was used for government and export purposes. In 1939 only 15.3 per cent of total output was employed in these ways; in 1943-1944 these purposes absorbed more than 44 percent of total output. The percentage of output available for private consumption and investment declined from 84.7 in 1939 to less than 56 percent in 1943 and 1944. It should be noted, however, that the rise of output was so great that the total volume of goods and services available for private consumption and investment were above 1939 levels throughout the war. It appears that at no time during the war was the amount of real output available for private consumption and investment less than 12 percent above 1939 levels. These overall figures do, however, hide great variations in the availability of the different types of goods and services. In the first place, the volume of real output available for private capital maintenance and accumulation declined markedly,

TABLE 13. Disposition of Gross National Product, 1939-1948
(In billions of dollars)[6]

| Year | In Current Dollars | | | | In 1939 Dollars | | | |
	Col. 1 Total GNP	Col. 2 Government Purchases plus Net Foreign Investment	Col. 3 Gross Private Domestic Investment	Col. 4 Personal Consumption	Col. 5 Gross Private Domestic Investment	Col. 6 Personal Consumption	Col. 7 Sum of Col. 5 and Col. 6	Col. 8 Index of Col. 7 (1939=100)
1939	$ 91.3	$14.0	$ 9.9	$ 67.5	$ 9.9	$ 67.5	$ 77.4	100
1940	101.4	15.4	13.9	72.1	13.8	71.4	85.2	110
1941	126.4	25.8	18.3	82.3	17.3	77.6	94.9	123
1942	161.6	59.5	10.9	91.2	9.3	77.9	87.2	113
1943	194.3	86.4	5.7	102.2	4.6	82.4	87.0	112
1944	213.7	94.4	7.7	111.6	6.1	88.6	94.7	122
1945	215.2	81.4	10.7	123.1	8.3	95.4	103.7	134
1946	212.6	35.4	29.5	147.8	21.1	105.6	126.7	164
1947	235.7	37.7	31.1	166.9	19.4	104.3	123.7	160
1948	262.4	38.6	45.0	178.8	26.2	104.0	130.2	168

PERCENTAGE OF TOTAL

Year	Col. 1	Col. 2	Col. 3	Col. 4
1939	100	15.3	10.8	73.9
1940	100	15.2	13.7	71.1
1941	100	20.4	14.5	65.1
1942	100	36.8	6.7	56.4
1943	100	44.5	2.9	52.6
1944	100	44.2	3.6	52.2
1945	100	37.8	5.0	57.9
1946	100	16.7	13.9	69.5
1947	100	16.0	13.2	70.8
1948	100	14.7	17.1	68.2

[6] The figures for output at 1939 prices were computed by dividing the GNP at current values by the cost-of-living index converted to a 1939 base. They are therefore only rough approximations and should be used only to show general magnitudes.

while consumers' goods and services enjoyed a large increase. And in the second place, the availability of the various types of consumers' goods and services behaved quite differently. In general, nondurable consumers' goods and services were available in unprecedented amounts. Food, tobacco, beverages, clothing, jewelry, amusement services—these and many other things were available for purchase at the height of the war effort in amounts far above prewar levels. It is true that they were often "hard to get" and that long lines often formed when stores offered them for sale, but this was due to the great increase in people's disposable money incomes rather than to any decrease in the volume of such things offered for sale. On the other hand, many types of consumers' durable goods were either unavailable or were available only in reduced quantities. Among these were automobiles, bicycles, electrical equipment, and most other goods made of metal or lumber. At the end of the war there had accumulated large backlogs of consumer demands for these durable goods and for some nondurable goods that during the war had been available in quantities that were very large yet not large enough to satisfy the swollen demands accompanying the rise of personal incomes.

These facts point to one important conclusion: that the wartime inflationary pressures under the prices of goods and services for private purchase were not due to any general decrease in the absolute amount of these things available for purchase. Instead, they were traceable to the fact that the amount of money income left in the hands of the private sectors was allowed to rise so much more than the volume of goods and services available for private purchase. This resulted from a tax policy that was far too mild to subtract from private money incomes an amount large enough to match the amount of real output being taken for government and export purposes.

As the war drew to a close the volume of goods and services available for private purposes began to rise to still higher levels. With the end of the war in Europe the amount of output taken for government purposes began to decline, and the decline accelerated after V-J Day. The percentage of total output taken for government and export purposes fell from above 44 in 1943 and 1944 to less than 15 in 1948. The percentage of total output available for private consumption and investment purposes rose from less than 56 percent in 1943-1944 to more than 85 percent in 1948. This was accompanied, of course, by a great rise in the absolute amount of output available for private purchase. The amount of real output available for these purposes during the postwar period after reconversion was never less than 40 percent above the levels in 1943 nor less than 60 percent above the levels of 1939. This fact alone should refute any contention that the cause of the postwar inflation was a decline in the absolute amount of available goods and services. The dynamic factor must be sought on the side of spendings.

CONCLUSIONS

It should be repeated that the measures of real output employed in this chapter are approximate at best and should be used only as indicators of general magnitudes. They do, however, warrant several conclusions that are important for later analysis. (1) The expansion of spendings was accompanied by a marked rise of real output above the levels prevailing in 1939. But the peak was reached during the war period. Real output declined in late 1945 and early 1946, and then rose again to a level about 60 percent above that of 1939 and somewhat below that of the war period. Further increases could be achieved only slowly. (2) The ability to expand real output was an important brake on inflation during the prewar period when there were millions of unemployed and plants were being underutilized; it could not be very helpful in the postwar period when a state of practically "full employment" had already been reached. (3) At no time during the war period was the volume of goods and services available to the private sectors of the economy for consumption and capital purposes as low as it was in 1939. The rise of total real output was greater than the increase in the amount used for net exports and for other governmental war and nonwar purposes. We had both "more guns and more butter." (4) Even in the war period the rate of private consumption of real goods and services, on an overall basis, was greater than in 1939. However, this rise was concentrated in nondurable goods and services, for durable goods were less available. (5) The amount of output available for private capital maintenance and expansion was lower during the war than in 1939. Yet our national capital stock, in real terms, was probably greater at the end of the war than in 1939 because of the high rate of private capital accumulation in 1940, 1941, and early 1942 and because of the large amount of government-financed investment. (6) At the peak of the war effort our people and business firms were receiving money incomes equivalent to the money value of our greatly expanded output, yet more than 44 percent of that output was being taken for net exports and governmental purposes. This was clearly inflationary to the extent that the government did not take away from the private sectors of the economy amounts of money income equivalent to the amounts of goods and services extracted for net export or for other governmental uses. (7) During most of the postwar period not more than 16 percent of our output was used for net export and governmental purposes; about 84 percent was available for private consumption and capital maintenance and expansion. (8) In most of the postwar period the output of real goods and services available for consumption was at least 50 percent above 1939 levels, and the amount of real output used by the private sectors of the economy for the maintenance and expansion of the stock of capital within the country was at least double the 1939 levels. (9) The inflation cannot be explained in terms of a scarcity of goods and services in any absolute sense; it must be explained in terms of the rise of spendings relative to the supply of goods and services.

These first three chapters have outlined the general course of the inflation. The following chapters will analyze in more detail the various policies that contributed to the inflation.

IV

||||||||||||||||||||||||||||||||||||||||||||||||||||||||||||||||||||||||||||||||||||||||||||||||||||||||||||||

Federal Fiscal Policy, 1940-1946

THERE can be no doubt that federal fiscal policies were the dynamic factor that initiated and reinforced the continuous rise of spendings during the period from early 1940 until the end of the war. The great rise of federal spendings directly contributed to the rise of total spendings for output, increased the flow of money income to the private sectors of the economy, and created demand conditions that were favorable to increased private investment spendings. The accompanying tax policy was far too mild to absorb these increases of money income, so that private disposable incomes and spending power were greatly enhanced. Federal deficits, the excess of government spendings over government revenue, measure the net contribution of the government to the disposable money incomes of the private sectors, and this increase of private disposable incomes was available for enhanced private consumption and saving.

Table 14 shows the tremendous magnitude of federal financial operations during these years. During the six years following June 1940 the federal government spent $383,372 million. This was more than twice as much as it had spent during the preceding 150 years, nearly 100 times as much as it spent during the Civil War, and 10 times as much as it spent during World War I. Its annual spendings at the peak of the war effort were greater than total spendings for output during any year between 1929 and 1940. Such huge increases of government spendings, adding directly to the demand for output and generating large increases in the money income received by persons and business firms, could not fail to create serious inflationary pressures. The increase of these pressures was retarded somewhat, but by no means neutralized, by the great increase in tax collections. Federal cash income during the six years following June 1940 amounted to $196,716 million. To collect this amount was no mean feat; it

TABLE 14.   Cash Operating Outgo, Income, and Deficits of the Federal
Government, 1940-1946
(In millions of dollars)[1]

Fiscal Year Ending June 30	Cash Operating Outgo	Cash Operating Income	Cash Operating Deficit
1941	$ 14,060	$ 9,371	$ 4,689
1942	34,585	15,291	19,294
1943	78,979	25,245	53,735
1944	94,079	47,984	46,095
1945	95,986	51,051	44,945
1946	65,683	47,784	17,899
Total	$383,372	$196,716	$186,656

was one and a half times as much as had been collected during the preceding 150 years and more than 10 times as much as was collected during World War I. But it was far from adequate; tax collections fell short of federal spendings during the period by $186,656 million. The total federal deficit for these six years was greater than total federal spendings during the preceding century and a half.

In short, the process of war finance was a great "pump-priming"

[1] SOURCE: *Treasury Bulletins*. The federal expenditure and receipt figures used in this chapter will be, unless otherwise indicated, those relating to cash operating outgo, cash operating income, and cash operating deficits. These differ somewhat from budget figures in that they include only cash payments to and collections from the public, ignoring transactions among various accounts within the government itself. Outgo figures exclude debt retirement, and income figures include receipts from social security taxes. The significance of these points will be brought out later.

operation whose dominant objective was not to assure economic stability but to secure the manpower and materials necessary to win the war. In the process of securing these, the government spent more than $383 billion into the income stream. A part of this injected money income was recaptured through tax collections from individuals and business firms, but these collections were so inadequate that the total deficit for the period amounted to more than $186 billion. This deficit was partially met by borrowing from individuals and businesses a part of the large savings made possible by their swollen money incomes; this proved inadequate, however, so that a considerable part of the increase of the federal debt was in effect paid for with money newly created by the Federal Reserve and commercial banks, and this new money was injected into the income stream through federal spendings. Such is the general outline of federal fiscal policy during the war. Let us now analyze it more closely.

FEDERAL EXPENDITURES DURING THE WAR

During the decade of the 1920's annual federal expenditures averaged about $3 billion. They began to rise slowly as the Great Depression deepened, and under the New Deal program they reached record peace time levels of about $8 billion a year. Some viewed even this level of government expenditures with alarm, forecasting an untrammelled inflation—a forecast that we now know could not have become a reality in the face of widespread unemployment and unused productive capacity. With the initiation of the defense program in early 1940 federal spendings began to rise still further. The increase was slow at first, reflecting the time needed for planning and the difficulty of adding rapidly to the armed forces. But the tempo rose. Lend-lease was instituted, the rearmament program was expanded, plans were translated into orders and orders into production, and the number of men in the armed forces grew. By the time of Pearl Harbor federal spendings had risen to an annual rate of nearly $30 billion and many believed that we had already approached the limit of our defense and war effort. This, too, proved erroneous. Faced with actual war rather than a mere threat, with a degree of national unity sadly lacking before the Pearl Harbor attack, and feeling

TABLE 15. Cash Operating Outgo, Income, and Deficits of the Federal Government, 1940-1946, Quarterly Averages at Annual Rates (In millions of dollars)[2]

Year and Quarter	Cash Operating Outgo	Cash Operating Income	Cash Deficit
1940—1 Q	$ 9,028	$ 8,004	$ 1,024
2 Q	9,480	6,912	2,572
3 Q	10,432	7,716	2,316
4 Q	12,728	7,644	5,080
1941—1 Q	15,536	11,352	4,180
2 Q	17,828	10,476	7,356
3 Q	21,240	10,188	11,052
4 Q	28,760	11,420	17,340
1942—1 Q	36,144	22,196	13,948
2 Q	52,744	17,692	35,028
3 Q	66,136	18,064	48,072
4 Q	76,352	18,608	57,744
1943—1 Q	82,116	30,724	51,392
2 Q	91,300	33,580	57,720
3 Q	89,880	48,496	45,384
4 Q	92,940	43,164	49,776
1944—1 Q	96,516	50,852	45,664
2 Q	96,988	53,432	43,556
3 Q	92,928	46,924	46,004
4 Q	94,448	43,208	51,240
1945—1 Q	95,712	61,180	34,532
2 Q	100,852	52,852	48,000
3 Q	89,620	48,912	40,708
4 Q	64,152	41,256	22,896
1946—1 Q	54,592	56,612	2,020[a]
2 Q	54,360	44,356	10,004

[a] Surplus.

that our very existence as a free nation was at stake, we devoted to the war effort an amount of manpower and materials that surpassed all previous expectations. This was reflected, as shown in Table 15, in the rise of federal spendings from an annual rate

[2] Computed from monthly figures in *Treasury Bulletins*.

of $28,760 million in the last quarter of 1941 to $100,852 million in the second quarter of 1945.

There is little to be said about federal spending "policy" during the war period. In general, the great volume of spendings merely reflected the decision to fight an all-out war not only with men but also with large amounts of the expensive equipment so effective in modern land, sea, and air warfare. Several things were done to keep down the level of government expenditures. (1) Many types of nonwar government spendings, such as public

TABLE 16. Spendings of the Federal Government, 1939-1945
(In millions of dollars)[3]

Purpose	1939	1940	1941	1942	1943	1944	1945
Net purchases from business	$1,649	$ 2,549	$11,547	$39,998	$58,557	$60,176	$43,239
Compensation of employees	3,444	3,537	5,046	10,836	21,255	27,905	30,614
Net interest payments	643	726	774	1,038	1,707	2,420	3,334
Transfer payments (Social security and veterans' benefits)	1,240	1,426	1,375	1,426	1,246	1,850	4,324
Net subsidies to business	927	915	666	769	861	1,371	1,516
Grants-in-aid to state and local governments	988	857	807	888	942	947	870
Net purchases from abroad	64	84	330	1,193	1,411	925	943
Total	$8,955	$10,094	$20,545	$56,148	$85,979	$95,594	$84,840

works, relief, and maintenance, were reduced. (2) Direct price and wage controls were introduced. (3) Attempts were made to improve purchasing methods and to recapture excessive payments through renegotiation. (4) Interest rates were kept at low levels. Additional savings could undoubtedly have been made by increasing the effectiveness of the actions listed above and by curbing the wasteful, or at least the inefficient, practices of the military. But as a practical matter it is doubtful that expenditures could have been curbed very much more without interfering with the war effort. In the midst of war when the prestige of the military is at its height, when many procurement officials are inexperienced

[3] SOURCE: *Survey of Current Business*, July, 1947, p. 23 and July, 1949, p. 13. These figures are not strictly comparable to those for "cash operating outgo" presented in the two preceding tables. The differences are not great enough, however, to detract significantly from the analysis.

if not untrained, when we want to minimize deaths and injuries among our fighting men, and when no one wants to jeopardize our chances of an early victory, it is very difficult to practice "economy."

It has already been noted that federal spendings inject money into the income stream flowing to business firms and individuals. Table 16 shows the various ways in which these spendings entered into income. Let us look at 1944, the peak year of federal spend-ing. About 63 cents of each dollar spent was used to purchase goods and services from business firms within the country, thereby supplying money income to the firms, their employees, and their suppliers. Another 29 cents out of each dollar spent went to the employees of the government—about three-quarters of this to military personnel—to pay for their services. Net interest pay-ments to individual and institutional creditors of the government accounted for 2.5 cents of each dollar; social security and veterans' benefits for 2 cents, and net subsidies to business for 1.5 cents. Thus, 98 cents out of each dollar, or $93.7 billion, of federal spendings entered into our business and personal incomes in 1944. Another 1 cent of each dollar was transferred to state and local governments as grants-in-aid, and the remaining cent was used for net federal purchases from abroad. Thus it is easy to see how the great rise in the rate of federal spendings from less than $9 billion in 1939 to more than $95 billion in 1944 contributed a continuously rising stream of money income to the private sectors of the economy. Such a rise of private money incomes was bound, unless fully recaptured through increased tax collections, to exert pressure toward increased private spendings, thereby adding to inflationary pressures. This brings us to federal tax policy.

FEDERAL TAX POLICY DURING THE WAR

Federal revenues during the late 1920's averaged about $4 billion a year. After falling somewhat during the early thirties as national income declined they rose markedly during the New

Deal, reflecting increases in tax rates as well as the partial recovery of national income. In 1939 they were nearly $6 billion, and many people were already complaining of the unbearable burden of taxes. But they could not foresee the heavier burdens to come. Federal tax collections rose to nearly $9.4 billion in the fiscal year ending in mid-1941 and then continued upward to more than $51 billion in the fiscal year 1945. For the six years following June 1940 they totaled, as we have seen, $196.7 billion. This

TABLE 17.   Federal Tax Receipts, Fiscal Years 1941-1946
(In millions of dollars)[4]

Source	1941	1942	1943	1944	1945	1946	Total for Period 1941-1946
Individual income taxes	$1,418	$ 3,263	$ 6,630	$18,261	$10,034	$18,705	$ 67,311
Taxes on corporate income, total	2,053	4,744	9,669	14,767	16,027	12,554	59,814
Excess-profits taxes	166	1,595	4,844	8,479	10,112	6,732	31,928
Other taxes on corporate income	1,887	3,149	4,825	6,290	5,915	5,822	27,888
Social Security taxes	925	1,186	1,498	1,739	1,780	1,701	8,829
Miscellaneous internal revenue taxes (mostly excise taxes on goods and services)	2,967	3,847	4,553	5,291	6,949	7,725	31,332
All other receipts[a]	907	674	1,240	3,723	3,838	3,928	14,310
Total	$8,269	$13,668	$23,385	$45,408	$47,740	$44,239	$181,618

[a] A considerable part of these "other receipts" represent amounts received from renegotiation of war contracts. Amounts received from this source were, in millions of dollars: 1943, $558; 1944, $2,235; 1945, $2,041; 1946, $1,063.

increase of revenues reflected not only a rise of effective tax rates but also a great rise of tax bases accompanying the increase of national money income. But large as they were, tax collections covered only 51 percent of federal spendings during the period, leaving a total deficit of $186.7 billion.

Table 17 shows the principal sources of federal revenues during the years included in the period, and Table 18 presents a summary for the period as a whole. Out of each dollar of tax col-

[4] SOURCE: *Annual Report of the Secretary of the Treasury*, 1946, pp. 398-399. Figures for totals are on a daily Treasury statement basis and are not strictly comparable to the figures on "cash operating income." Also, there are small discrepancies in this table because totals are on a daily Treasury statement basis while some of the figures for individual types of taxes are on a collection basis.

lections during the period 37.1 cents came from personal income taxes, thereby tending to curb the rise of disposable personal incomes and to retard the increase of personal spendings. Another 32.9 cents were paid out of corporate profits, more than half in the form of excess profits taxes and the remainder in the form of corporate income taxes based on the absolute size of profits rather than on their increase since the prewar period. These tax payments tended to limit the rise of money income remaining in

TABLE 18.   Summary of Federal Tax Receipts for the Fiscal Years 1941-1946

Source	Receipts (In millions of dollars)	Percentage of Total Receipts
Individual income taxes	$ 67,311	37.1
Taxes on corporate profits, total	59,814	32.9
Excess-profits taxes	31,928	17.6
Other taxes on corporate income	27,888	15.3
Social Security taxes	8,829	4.9
Miscellaneous internal revenue (mostly taxes on goods and services)	31,332	17.2
All other receipts	14,310	7.9
Total	$181,618	100.0

the hands of corporations. Another 4.9 cents came from social security taxes, and represented subtractions from the rising incomes of employers and workers. Still another 17.2 cents came from miscellaneous internal revenue taxes, mostly levies on the production or sale of goods and services. Nearly half of these were taxes on liquor and tobacco. All other receipts accounted for 7.9 cents out of each tax dollar collected.

Taxes have two principal functions. One is to supply the government with money. But taxes are not the government's only source of money; it can, for a time at least, secure the money that it needs by borrowing from the public or by having new money created for it by the central bank and the commercial banking system. There seems to be little doubt that we could have "financed" World War II without any increase of tax collections. The only disadvantage of this plan is that it would have heightened inflationary pressures during both the war and postwar periods. Thus the prime function of taxation by a government with the power to create money is to prevent, or at least to limit, inflationary pressures. It is to reduce, or at least to limit the rise of, the disposable money incomes of individuals and business firms in order to limit their spendings. If there were no fear that the rate of total spendings—government and private—would become excessive, there would be no reason to tax away any part of the money incomes of individuals and businesses. But this was obviously not the situation after our entrance into the war; there was more than a mere danger that the rate of total spendings would become excessive, and with the necessity for great increases in government spendings heavy tax collections could serve the useful purpose of limiting the rise of disposable personal and business incomes, thereby limiting the rise of private spendings.

With any given level of government spendings, the effect of collecting taxes is, of course, to make the disposable money incomes of individuals and business firms less than they would have been if the taxes had not been collected. But to understand developments during a period of rising government spendings it is necessary to distinguish clearly between (1) a tax policy that will prevent any increase in total spendings for output, and (2) a tax policy that will merely lessen the rise of total spendings. To prevent any increase in the rate of total spendings for output, each rise of government spendings for output would have to be offset by *an equal and simultaneous decrease* of private consumption and investment spendings. To achieve this result through tax policy it would be necessary, with each rise in government spendings, to increase tax rates to such an extent that *without any increase in the national money income* the disposable money incomes of individuals and businesses would be lowered enough to decrease private spendings as much as government spendings had risen. It must be emphasized that under such a policy (a) the decrease of private spendings for output would have to be equal to and simultaneous with the rise of government spendings, and (b) that the increased tax collections used to lower private disposable incomes and private spendings would have to result solely from increased effective tax rates rather than from increased national money income.

Federal tax policy during the defense and war periods was far too mild to prevent a rise in the rate of total spendings for output; it could only retard somewhat the rise of total spendings by lessening the rise of the disposable incomes of individuals and business. This is indicated by the figures relative to the size of federal deficits. In the 1941 fiscal year federal tax collections failed by $4.7 billion to subtract from private money incomes as much as federal spendings contributed to them. As government spendings continued to rise the amount of tax collections lagged farther and farther behind, even though national money income was rising, so that by 1943 the net contribution of the federal government to national money income—the excess of its spendings over its tax collections—was running at an annual rate of nearly $54 billion. From that time until after the middle of 1945 federal net contributions to private money incomes remained at a level well above $40 billion a year. Moreover, it should be remembered that a considerable part of the increase of federal tax collections was due not to the increase of tax rates but to the rise of private money incomes. For example, national money income, which can be used to indicate roughly the behavior of the various tax bases, rose from $72.5 billion in 1939 to $183.8 billion in 1944, an increase of 154 percent. To the extent that increased tax collections were themselves generated by a rise of private money incomes they could not prevent a rise of private spending power from occurring but could only decrease the extent of the rise.

The purpose of the preceding sections is not to argue that beginning in 1940 federal tax policy should have been such as to reduce private spendings by an amount equal to the rise of government spendings. At least in the earlier stages of the defense program while the actual rate of output was far below capacity levels there was a strong case for an expansionary fiscal policy. We could still expand both production for defense and production for civilian needs. Nor is it argued here that even after early 1943, when total output had reached capacity levels, federal tax collections should have been at least as great as federal spendings. It will be seen later that considerations relating to business and individual incentives may make it wise national policy to risk inflation rather than impose the extremely high tax rates that would be necessary to balance the budget at a rate of federal spendings approximating $100 billion a year. The purpose here is only to point out that the tax policy actually followed was so mild that, far from reducing private spending power in the face of increasing government spendings, it actually allowed private disposable incomes and spending power to rise markedly.

FEDERAL DEFICITS AND THEIR FINANCING

The size of federal deficits during the defense and war period and their expansionary effects on national money income and spendings have already been noted. This section will therefore limit itself to a description of the sources of the funds used to finance the deficits. The basic facts are shown in Table 19.

During the six years following June 1940 federal cash borrowings from individuals and institutions totalled $199 billion, raising the total federal interest-bearing debt held outside the government itself from $40.4 billion to $239.4 billion. The major part of this borrowing—$186.7 billion—was necessary to cover the government's cash deficit for the period. Another $12.3 billion, however, was borrowed to increase the Treasury's money balance as a protection against contingencies. What were the sources of these borrowings? Economists advised the Treasury that every effort should be made to borrow as much as possible from nonbank sources, thereby providing funds to the government without the creation of additional money, and draining off a part of private money incomes which might otherwise increase the upward pressure on private spendings. For a time a campaign was waged to introduce compulsory lending. In the end, however, those advocating reliance on voluntary loans won the battle. They preferred to rely on the techniques of modern salesmanship and advertising. Individuals and institutions other than banks did increase their holdings of federal obligations by $109 billion during the six years preceding June 1946, and it is undoubtedly

TABLE 19. Federal Borrowings, Their Use, and Their Sources, 1940-1946
(In millions of dollars)[5]

Fiscal Year Ending June 30	Federal Cash Operating Deficit	Increase or Decrease (—) of the Treasury's General Fund Balance	Net Cash Borrowing	By Nonbank Holders	Net Increase in Amount of Federal Interest-Bearing Debt Held		
					By Federal Reserve and Commercial Banks, Total	By Commercial Banks	By Federal Reserve Banks
1941	$ 4,689	$ 742	$ 5,431	$ 2,143	$ 3,318	$ 3,600	$ —282
1942	19,294	358	19,652	12,869	6,761	6,300	461
1943	53,735	6,515	60,250	28,498	30,757	26,200	4,557
1944	46,095	10,662	56,757	32,913	23,899	16,200	7,699
1945	44,945	4,529	49,474	27,173	22,691	15,800	6,891
1946	17,899	—10,460	7,439	5,431	2,191	200	1,991
Total increase for the period	$186,656	$12,346	$199,003	$109,027	$89,617	$68,300	$21,317

true that the prevailing patriotic fervor and the sales techniques playing upon it were important factors in creating a willingness to buy and hold these securities. But, as will be argued later, it seems likely that reliance on voluntary loans would have been far less effective in the absence of a price control and rationing program that limited private spendings for output and virtually

[5] Computed from various tables in *Treasury Bulletins*. It should be noted that the figures relating to debt reflect only the debt held outside the federal government itself; it does not include an increase of about $22 billion in federal debt held by government agencies and trust funds. These securities involved no borrowing from outside the government itself; as the Treasury collected and spent social security taxes it issued to the trust funds under its control government securities indicating a future obligation to pay social security benefits.

forced persons and business firms to save an abnormally large proportion of the swollen money incomes remaining in their hands after they had paid their taxes.

Even so, purchases by nonbank buyers were so inadequate that the government was forced to call upon the Federal Reserve and commercial banks to increase their holdings of the federal debt by $89.6 billion. Not all of these bank purchases of government securities involved an increase of the money supply in the form of currency or checking deposits; time and savings deposits with commercial banks increased by $17 billion during the six-year period, and much of this increase probably represented "voluntary" savings out of business and personal incomes. But Federal Reserve and commercial bank holdings of government securities increased $72.6 billion more than the increase of time and savings deposits with commercial banks; this was the major factor increasing the money supply—currency outside banks plus privately owned checking deposits—from $38.7 billion in June 1940 to $106 billion in June 1946, an increase of $67.3 billion or 174 percent.[6] In effect, the banking system monetized this part of the federal debt. In return for government securities the banks created new checking deposits for the Treasury, which then spent the money into the income stream to purchase goods and services or to make transfer payments into the hands of business firms and individuals.

In peace time it is sometimes difficult to show how new money gets created and how the increased money supply gets translated into an increased rate of spendings. The war period presents no such difficulty. Both the creation of new money and the injection of new money into the spending stream were integral parts of federal spending-taxing-borrowing policy. Committed to fighting a major war and to the rate of spending necessitated by this

[6] Several other factors also affected the supply of currency outside banks and privately owned checking deposits. The other principal factor tending to raise the money supply was an increase of about $13.9 billion in other commercial bank loans and investments. The principal factor tending to reduce the privately owned money supply was a $12.6 billion increase of federal deposits at banks.

decision, the federal government simply called upon the Federal Reserve and commercial banks to manufacture any money that it needed beyond the amounts acquired through taxes or through borrowing from nonbank lenders. And the new money, along with the money secured from taxes and other loans, was spent into private hands. The Federal Reserve System, whose principal peacetime function is supposed to be that of promoting economic stability, used its money-creating powers during the war period to assure the Treasury that it would at no time lack money with which to meet its needs.

FISCAL POLICY AND PRIVATE SAVING DURING THE WAR

The preceding sections have emphasized that federal fiscal policy exerted a tremendous inflationary effect on disposable private incomes as federal spendings contributed to private incomes much more than tax collections extracted from them, and that this deficit financing exerted a strong upward pressure on private spending. This section will show that the deficit spending program was largely responsible, both directly and indirectly, for the abnormally high rate of private saving during the war and for the tremendous private accumulation of liquid assets which proved to be a strong inflationary influence during both the war and the postwar periods.

Gross private saving during any period is, of course, equal to the disposable incomes of corporations and persons minus the amounts spent for consumption purposes. It is possible, therefore, to show that the huge deficit-spending program of the federal government generated an abnormally high rate of private saving by adding to disposable private money incomes so much more than could be spent for consumption goods and services in view of their limited availability and the presence of price ceilings. With the rise of total spendings for output, to which government spendings contributed so much both directly and indirectly, corporate net savings rose greatly, as is shown in Table 20. Corporate profits rose to about four times their 1939 level; only a part of this increase was absorbed by increased taxes, so that corporate profits after taxes doubled. Even after paying somewhat larger dividends, corporations were able to increase their rate of net saving from $1.2 billion in 1939 to more than $6 billion in 1943 and 1944. Total corporate net saving for the years 1940-1945 amounted to $28.5 billion. These, however, were only corporate savings out

TABLE 20.   Corporate Profits, 1939-1945
(In millions of dollars)[7]

Year	Corporate Profits Before Income and Excess-Profits Tax Liability	Corporate Income and Excess-Profits Tax Liability	Corporate Profits after Taxes	Net Dividend Payments by Corporations	Undistributed Corporate Profits (Net Corporate Savings)
1939	$ 6,467	$ 1,462	$ 5,005	$3,796	$1,209
1940	9,325	2,878	6,447	4,049	2,398
1941	17,232	7,846	9,386	4,465	4,921
1942	21,098	11,665	9,433	4,297	5,136
1943	25,052	14,406	10,646	4,493	6,153
1944	24,333	13,525	10,808	4,680	6,128
1945	19,717	11,215	8,502	4,699	3,803

of their net incomes; in addition corporations accumulated very large gross savings in the form of capital consumption allowances.

Personal saving also rose greatly. Reflecting the rise of spendings for output, personal income before taxes rose from $72.6 billion in 1939 to $171.9 billion in 1945 (Table 21). Personal taxes rose far less, so that disposable personal income rose from $70.2 billion in 1939 to $151.1 billion in 1945. Because of price

[7] SOURCE: *Survey of Current Business,* July, 1947, pp. 30-33 and July, 1949, p. 10. See the *Survey of Current Business,* July, 1947, p. 30 for a description of this series. These profit figures include profits on inventories which amounted (in millions of dollars) to:

1939—$ 714	1943—$773
1940— 148	1944— 287
1941— 2,617	1945— 564
1942— 1,204	

ceilings and the limited increase of consumer's goods and services available for purchase, only a part of this increase of disposable personal income could be used to swell consumption spendings, so that people were virtually "forced" to save unprecedentedly large amounts.

The effect of federal deficits on the rate of private gross saving can be shown more directly, however, by referring to the fact that the amount of private gross saving that can occur during a

TABLE 21.   Personal Income, Its Components and Its Utilization, 1939-1945
(In millions of dollars)[8]

	1939	1940	1941	1942	1943	1944	1945
Wage and salary receipts	$45,149	$48,929	$60,907	$ 80,721	$103,599	$114,881	$115,326
Other labor income	535	575	589	706	888	1,302	1,548
Proprietors and rental income	14,747	16,280	20,826	28,436	32,840	35,492	37,503
Dividends	3,796	4,049	4,465	4,297	4,493	4,680	4,699
Personal interest income	5,417	5,395	5,402	5,411	5,495	5,940	6,672
Transfer payments from government and corporations	2,963	3,119	3,119	3,150	2,971	3,597	6,179
Total Personal Income	$72,607	$78,347	$95,308	$122,721	$150,286	$165,892	$171,927
Less: Personal taxes	2,440	2,604	3,293	5,981	17,845	18,935	20,867
Equals: Disposable Personal Income	$70,167	$75,743	$92,015	$116,740	$132,441	$146,957	$151,060
Less: Personal Consumption Spendings	67,466	72,052	82,255	91,161	102,244	111,550	123,079
Equals: Personal Saving	$ 2,701	$ 3,691	$ 9,760	$ 25,579	$ 30,197	$ 35,407	$ 27,981

period is equal to the sum of (1) the federal deficit, (2) deficits of state and local governments, (3) net foreign investment, and (4) gross private domestic investment.[9] The sum of these four types of spendings represents the part of private gross incomes

[8] SOURCE: *Surveys of Current Business.*

[9] The validity of this equation can be shown as follows:

1. Disposable private gross income is equal to gross national income minus net tax collections by the government. That is,

Disposable private gross income = personal consumption + gross private domestic investment + net foreign investment + the government deficit

2. Gross private saving is equal to disposable private gross income minus personal consumption. That is,

Gross private saving = gross private domestic investment + net foreign investment + the government deficit

TABLE 22. Gross Private Savings and Gross Investment, 1940-1945
(In millions of dollars)[10]

	Gross Private Savings			
Calendar Year	Personal Saving	Corporate Net Saving[a]	Other Private Saving[b]	Total
1940	$ 3,691	$ 2,398	$ 9,916	$ 16,005
1941	9,760	4,921	8,270	22,951
1942	25,579	5,136	11,114	41,829
1943	30,197	6,153	11,031	47,381
1944	35,407	6,128	15,442	56,977
1945	27,981	3,803	16,750	48,534
Total for six years	$132,615	$28,539	$72,523	$233,677

	Gross Investment			
Calendar Year	Net Foreign Investment	State and Local Government Deficit or Surplus (−)	Gross Private Domestic Investment	Federal Deficit	Total
1940	$ 1,509	$ −862	$13,949	$ 1,409	$ 16,005
1941	1,124	−1,396	18,334	4,889	22,951
1942	−207	−1,786	10,873	32,949	41,829
1943	−2,245	−2,472	5,709	46,389	47,381
1944	−2,099	−2,642	7,714	54,004	56,977
1945	−1,438	−2,580	10,733	41,819	48,534
Total for six years	$−3,356	$−11,738	$67,312	$181,459	$233,677

[a] Undistributed corporate profits.
[b] Mostly business allowances for capital consumption.

that is not absorbed by consumption and tax collections and that is saved by the private sectors.

Table 22 shows the behavior of private savings during the period and also the types of "gross investment" spendings that created the ability of the private sectors to save such great amounts.

The first part of the table shows how greatly the rate of private saving rose during the war period. Total gross private savings

[10] Computed from data in *Survey of Current Business*, July, 1949, p. 11. "Other private saving" also includes for each year some statistical discrepancy, which is shown in the tables just cited.

for the six years, 1940-1945, amounted to the huge sum of $233.7 billion, of which $132.6 billion or 57 percent were personal savings, $28.5 billion or 12 percent were undistributed corporate profits, and $72.5 billion or 31 percent were other forms of private gross saving—mostly capital consumption allowances of business.

The second part of the table shows the contributions to gross private savings that were made by the various types of gross investment spendings for output. The ability of the private sectors to save tended to be reduced by net foreign disinvestment and by the current surpluses of state and local governments. Aside from our net gifts to foreigners, which are included in personal consumption and the federal deficit, we purchased more goods and services from foreigners than they purchased from us after 1941; this tended to reduce our ability to save. State and local governments, enjoying much larger revenues as the national income rose, largely relieved of the burden of providing unemployment benefits, and unable to secure the labor and materials necessary for large public works programs, actually showed a surplus of $11.7 billion for the period. This measures the excess of their tax collections from the public over their spendings to the public. All of the gross investment for the period as a whole represented gross private domestic investment and the federal deficit. The former was large in 1940-1941, but it dwindled during the war as labor and material for this purpose became less available, so that for the period as a whole it accounted for only 29 percent of gross investment. The federal deficit amounted to $181.5 billion or 78 percent of gross savings during the entire 1940-1945 period. For the war years 1942-1945 it amounted to 175.2 billion, or 90 percent of all gross savings during that period. This bears out the earlier statement that the huge federal deficits were the major factor enabling the private sectors of the economy to save such abnormally large amounts during the war.

The above facts cast light on several aspects of the inflation during both the war and the postwar periods. (1) The deficit financing program itself generated most of the increase of private saving by adding to private disposable incomes much more than could be spent for consumption in the face of shortages and price ceilings. (2) A major part of the increase of saving did not

TABLE 23. Estimated Liquid Asset Holdings of Individuals and Businesses, 1939 and 1945
(In millions of dollars)[11]

	End of 1939	End of 1945	Increase from End of 1939 to End of 1945	Holdings End of 1945 as Percentage of Holdings at End of 1939
Total	$69.0	$227.5	$158.5	330
Currency	5.8	25.5	19.7	440
Demand deposits	20.9	60.2	39.3	288
Time deposits	26.3	47.7	21.4	181
Savings and loan shares	4.0	7.2	3.2	180
U. S. Government securities	12.0	86.9	74.9	724
Business Holdings, Total	19.4	73.0	53.6	376
Currency	1.6	4.7	3.1	294
Demand deposits	12.5	33.7	21.2	270
Time deposits	2.0	3.1	1.1	155
Savings and loan shares	0.1	0.2	0.1	200
U. S. Government securities	3.2	31.3	28.1	978
Personal Holdings, Total	49.6	154.5	104.9	311
Currency	4.2	20.8	16.6	495
Demand deposits	8.4	26.5	18.1	315
Time deposits	24.3	44.6	20.3	184
Savings and loan shares	3.9	7.0	3.1	179
U. S. Government securities	8.8	55.6	46.8	632

represent the "free choice" of savers; the latter would almost certainly have spent much more for consumption if greater supplies had been available or if price ceilings had not held as well as they did. (3) Because of their huge accumulations of savings

[11] SOURCE: *Federal Reserve Bulletin*, July, 1949, p. 794. These figures exclude holdings of banks, insurance companies, savings and loan associations, nonprofit associations, foreigners, and government bodies and agencies. It should be noted that these figures understate the growth of liquid assets, and especially those in the form of bank deposits. For example, the table above indicates that privately owned bank deposits amounted to $107.9 billion on December 31, 1945 while bank statistics indicate that they amounted to $124.3 billion on that date.

during the war business firms and individuals ended the war far richer than they had been in 1939. (4) A major part of these private savings was used to increase greatly the amount of liquid assets held by individuals and business firms. Not all savings were used in this way; some were used to retire debt, to purchase houses or other durable goods, or to purchase other nonliquid assets. The greater part, however, was saved in highly liquid forms.

Table 23 presents an estimate of the liquid asset holdings by persons and business firms at the end of 1939 and the end of 1945. Though this estimate appears to understate the growth of these holdings it does indicate the general magnitude of the increase. It shows that business firms and individuals increased their total holdings of liquid assets by $158.5 billion, or 230 percent, during the six-year period. Of this total increase, $59 billion, or 37.2 percent, represented a rise of private holdings of money itself—currency and checking deposits. Another $21.4 billion, or 13.5 percent, was in the form of increased holdings of time deposits which were convertible into money on short notice at the option of their owners. Another $74.9 billion, or 47.3 percent, was in the form of increased private holdings of U. S. Government securities which were practically as liquid as money. Increased holdings of shares in savings and loan associations accounted for another $3.2 billion, or 2 percent of the total. In short, the huge government deficits of the period were largely responsible for the ability of the private sectors to add greatly to their accumulation of savings in some form, and a major part of these savings came to be represented by highly liquid assets. In terms of money values our people were not only much richer at the end of the war, but their added riches were held largely in the form of an increased supply of money and of other assets that were almost as liquid as money.

A later chapter will emphasize that the huge wartime accumulation of private savings was a major factor in producing the postwar increase in both the ability and willingness of the private sectors to spend for output. Individuals and business firms were easily able to increase their spendings because their holdings of money and "near money" were at least 3.3 times as great as in 1939. And they were willing to spend more for many reasons, one of which was that they were so much richer than in the pre-war period. And most of the increased riches were created by the federal wartime deficits. To the extent that federal spendings were met by taxes, our people and business firms were left with only their receipts for taxes to evidence their contribution to government financing. But to the extent that government spendings were financed by deficits, those excess spendings had to be matched by the issuance of government securities to the private sectors of the economy, and these were considered as assets by their holders. Some of the securities were bought and held by individuals and nonfinancial business firms. Others were sold to financial institutions, such as the Federal Reserve, commercial and savings banks, savings and loan associations, insurance companies, and so on. To the extent that this occurred individuals and nonfinancial business firms received increased claims against financial institutions, and these claims took the form of currency, checking deposits, time and savings deposits, shares at savings and loan associations, increased claims against life insurance companies, and so on.

CONCLUSION

This chapter has outlined the federal fiscal policy which provided the dynamic inflationary force during the defense and war periods and whose aftereffects constituted one of the principal inflationary forces during the postwar period. The great rise of government spendings contributed increasing amounts to spendings for output and to private money incomes. Coupled with this was a tax policy much too mild to prevent a great rise in private disposable incomes. This strongly impelled both individuals and business firms to increase their spendings, and the increase was partially and precariously held in check during the war only by a comprehensive system of direct controls over prices, wages, and the use of goods and services. A considerable part of the rise of disposable private incomes was used to raise the rate of private saving to an abnormally high level during the war years. Some of these huge savings were used to retire debt or to purchase non-liquid assets, but the major part of them was held in the form of liquid assets, such as government securities, currency, bank deposits, and claims against other financial institutions.

V

||||||||||||||||||||||||||||||||||||||||||||||||||||||||||||||||||||||||||||||||||||||||||||||||||||||||||||||||||||||||||||||||||||||||||||||||||||||

Federal Tax Policies, 1940-1945

SEVERAL aspects of federal tax policy during the 1940-1945 period have already been noted: (1) The great increase of tax collections, (2) the growing inadequacy of taxes relative to both government spendings and mounting private incomes, with the result that government deficits and disposable private money incomes mounted until the peak of the war effort was reached, and (3) the types of taxes yielding the greater part of federal revenue. The major revenue producers were personal income taxes, taxes on corporate income, levies on the production, sale, or use of goods and services, and social security taxes. The purpose of this chapter is to describe in nontechnical terms the most important taxes employed and the principal tax proposals that were not adopted.

INDIVIDUAL INCOME TAXES

The individual income tax was the most productive of all, yielding in the six years following June 30, 1940 more than $67 billion, or more than 37 percent of all federal revenues. Its yield rose from $1.4 billion in the fiscal year 1941 to $19 billion in the fiscal year 1945.[1] This marked increase of yield was traceable to three principal factors: (1) the very large rise of personal money incomes, (2) the decrease of personal exemptions, which

[1] See Tables 17 and 18 on pages 67 and 68 above.

subjected to taxes a much larger percentage of total personal incomes, both by adding to the tax rolls millions of people whose incomes had formerly been wholly exempt and by subjecting to taxes a larger part of the incomes of those already on the tax rolls, and (3) by raising the tax rates applicable to taxable incomes.

In 1939 the individual income tax applied to only a small part of total personal incomes, for personal exemptions were $1000 for a single person, $2500 for a married person, and $400 for each dependent. Only about 4 million persons paid any federal income tax at all, and many billions of income received by those

TABLE 24. Exemptions from the Federal Personal Income Tax[2]

	Single Person	Married Person	Each Dependent
In effect, 1939	$1000	$2500	$400
Revenue Act of 1940	800	2000	400
,, ,, ,, 1941	750	1500	400
,, ,, ,, 1942	500	1200	350
,, ,, ,, 1944	500	1000	500

who did pay the tax were exempt. It was clear that exemptions would have to be lowered markedly if the yield of this tax was to be increased greatly without extremely high effective rates on taxable income. There was, however, strong opposition to this move. Those previously exempt from the tax continued to believe that the best tax is one paid by someone else, and many of those already subject to the tax did not relish the idea of having a larger proportion of their incomes put into the taxable category. Moreover, many continued to believe that the principle of "ability to pay" meant that all income taxes should be paid by the upper-income groups; they did not fully appreciate the fact that the great rise of government requirements could not be fully met out of the incomes of those already subject to the income tax and that the lower-income groups would have to make

[2] SOURCE: *Annual Report of the Secretary of the Treasury,* 1944, p. 458.

larger sacrifices through increased income taxes, other taxes, larger savings, or a decreased purchasing power of their income dollars. These were some of the principal reasons why exemptions were lowered so slowly, reaching their lowest level only in the Revenue Act of 1944.

In addition to lowering personal exemptions under the regular income tax, Congress also introduced, in the Revenue Act of 1942, a special levy on personal incomes, called the Victory Tax. This was a tax of 5 percent on all personal net incomes in excess of $624 a year, regardless of the family status of the taxpayer. Apparently recognizing that this violated the principle of ability

TABLE 25. Taxable Individual Income Tax Returns Filed[3]

Fiscal Year	Millions of Taxable Returns	Fiscal Year	Millions of Taxable Returns
1940	4	1943	27
1941	7	1944	42
1942	17	1945	42

to pay, Congress provided for a postwar refund of a part of these taxes. Married persons were to get refunds of 40 percent of this tax, not to exceed $1000, plus 2 percent, not to exceed $100, for each dependent. Single persons were to get a refund of 25 percent of the tax, not to exceed $500, plus the above refund for each dependent. Thus the Victory Tax was in effect a combination of tax and compulsory lending to the government. In 1943, however, the postwar refund provision was eliminated and the tax was reduced to 3 percent of all personal net income in excess of $624 a year. In 1944 the Victory Tax as such was repealed and the 3 percent rate was integrated into the regular personal income tax.

With the general rise of money incomes, the lowering of

[3] These figures, which are only approximate, were computed from the reports of the Bureau of Internal Revenue contained in the *Annual Reports of the Secretary of the Treasury.*

personal exemptions, and the introduction of the Victory Tax, the federal personal income tax became for the first time a mass tax. The number of taxable returns rose from about 4 million in the fiscal year 1940 to about 42 million in each of the fiscal years 1944 and 1945 (Table 25).

The prewar methods of administering this tax became increasingly unsatisfactory as the tax became heavier and was extended to millions in the lower-income groups. In the first place, the methods and times of payment were unsatisfactory. In the prewar period the tax on a given year's income was not reported until March 15 of the following year and payment was made during the latter year. There was no provision for collection at the source, rising money incomes were not reflected in increased tax collections until the following year, evasion was facilitated, and a taxpayer who suffered a marked decrease of income might have difficulty in paying taxes on his higher income of the preceding year. There was obviously much to be gained by collecting taxes at the source, by making the tax paid during a given year depend on the amount of income received and the tax rates in effect during that year, and by providing methods for payment of taxes in installments on each payday rather than in a lump sum. On several occasions during 1941 and 1942 the Secretary of the Treasury asked Congress for authority to collect taxes at the source, but no action was taken until the passage of the Current Tax Payment Act of 1943.[4] This legislation provided for withholding at the source and for the payment of taxes on a given year's income during that year. The transition created difficulties, however, for taxpayers were faced with the prospect of having to pay in 1943 their tax liabilities on both their 1942 and 1943 incomes. To solve this problem Congress generously, to the annoyance of the Treasury, cancelled the major part of one year's tax liability. In general, the amount cancelled was based on the lower of the taxpayer's tax liabilities for 1942 or 1943, and was equal to 100 percent of the first $50 of tax plus 75 percent of the

[4] Except for the Victory Tax.

tax liability in excess of $50.[5] The Treasury's inflow of revenue was not interrupted by this change, but some taxpayers did receive large windfalls equal to the amount of their cancelled tax liabilities. The introduction of collection at the source and current tax payment was a marked improvement in tax administration and should have been introduced much earlier.

A second major deficiency of the income tax as a mass tax was its complexity, both in the provisions of the laws themselves and in the forms used for computing and reporting income. This complexity was increased by the earlier wartime revenue acts and reached a new high with the introduction of the Victory Tax. Not until 1944 was the tax effectively simplified, especially for the lower-income groups. It seems almost certain that much revenue was lost because of this delay in simplification, for many congress-men hesitated to extend such a complex tax to the lower-income groups.

In addition to lowering exemptions, income tax rates were raised markedly. In 1939 the progressive marginal rates on tax-able income ranged from 4 to 79 percent; by 1944 these ranged from 23 to 94 percent. The effects of lowered exemptions and increased tax rates on the income tax liabilities of the various income groups are indicated in Table 26, which shows the income tax liabilities of a married person without dependents in the various years from 1936 to 1945. This table brings out several facts, some of which have already been noted. (1) As column 1 suggests, the federal income tax in effect in 1939 was in truth a "rich man's tax"; the great majority of families paid no income tax at all, and few others paid large amounts. This tax took less than 1 percent of a $5000 income and only about 4 percent of a $10,000 income. With this background it is easy to understand why Congress was so slow in extending the tax to low-income groups and in imposing heavier burdens on the middle-income groups. (2) Even as late as 1942 the effective tax rate on a mar-

[5] For a short description of this legislation, see *Annual Report of the Secretary of the Treasury,* 1943, pp. 109-111.

TABLE 26. Federal Income Tax Liabilities of a Married Person Without Dependents, 1936–1945[6]

Col. 1 Net Income Before Personal Exemptions	Col. 2 1936–1939	Col. 3 1940	Col. 4 1941	Col. 5 1942	Col. 6 1943[a]	Col. 7 1944 and 1945	Col. 8 1944 tax as Percentage of 1939 Tax	Col. 9 Percentage of 1944 Income Paid as Tax[b]	Col. 10 Highest Marginal Rate Applicable (Percent)[c]
$ 600	—	—	—	—	$ 1	$ 2	—	0.3	3
750	—	—	—	—	6	6	—	0.8	3
800	—	—	—	—	8	7	—	0.9	3
1,000	—	—	—	—	15	12	—	1.2	3
1,200	—	—	—	—	21	36	—	3.0	23
1,500	—	—	—	48	79	98	—	6.5	23
1,800	—	—	23	103	144	160	—	8.9	23
2,000	—	—	42	140	188	202	—	10.1	23
2,500	—	11	90	232	297	305	—	12.2	23
3,000	8	31	138	324	405	411	5138	13.7	23
4,000	44	70	249	532	647	631	1430	15.8	25
5,000	80	110	375	746	894	844	1056	16.9	25
6,000	116	150	521	992	1,173	1,070	922	17.8	29
7,000	172	233	687	1,246	1,460	1,380	802	19.7	29
8,000	248	317	873	1,532	1,780	1,690	631	21.1	29
9,000	329	422	1,079	1,826	2,107	2,020	614	22.4	33
10,000	415	528	1,305	2,152	2,467	2,370	571	23.7	37
15,000	924	1,258	2,739	4,052	4,533	4,435	480	29.6	46
20,000	1,589	2,336	4,614	6,452	7,100	7,005	441	35.0	53
25,000	2,489	3,843	6,864	9,220	10,035	9,955	402	39.8	59
30,000	3,569	5,614	9,339	12,204	13,185	13,130	368	43.8	65
40,000	5,979	9,552	14,649	18,532	19,847	19,845	332	49.6	72

TABLE 26. Federal Income Tax Liabilities of a Married Person Without Dependents, 1936-1945 (Continued)

Col. 1 Net Income Before Personal Exemptions	Col. 2 1936-1939	Col. 3 1940	Col. 4 1941	Col. 5 1942	Col. 6 1943ᵃ	Col. 7 1944 and 1945	Col. 8 1944 tax as Percentage of 1939 Tax	Col. 9 Percentage of Highest 1944 Income Paid as Taxᵇ	Col. 10 Highest Marginal Rate Applicable (Percent)ᶜ
50,000	8,869	14,128	20,439	25,328	27,075	27,180	306	54.4	75
60,000	12,329	19,320	26,509	32,492	34,794	34,935	283	58.2	78
70,000	16,449	24,864	32,779	39,956	42,814	42,990	261	61.4	81
80,000	21,269	30,738	39,249	47,720	51,133	51,345	241	64.2	84
90,000	26,669	36,942	45,919	55,784	59,753	60,000	225	66.7	87
100,000	32,469	43,476	52,704	64,060	68,584	68,955	212	69.0	90
150,000	63,394	77,532	87,189	106,536	113,838	115,281	182	76.9	92
200,000	95,344	112,199	122,174	150,012	160,092	161,410	170	80.7	93
250,000	128,294	146,864	157,659	194,000	206,858	208,395	162	83.4	94
500,000	304,144	330,156	345,084	414,000	440,747	442,775	146	88.6	94
750,000	489,094	521,620	537,569	634,000	674,000	678,395	140	90.4	94
1,000,000	679,044	717,584	732,554	854,000	899,000	913,395	132	91.3	94
2,000,000	1,449,019	1,510,566	1,552,539	1,734,000	1,799,000	1,853,395	128	92.5	94
5,000,000	3,788,994	3,916,548	3,922,524	4,374,000	4,499,000	4,669,395	124	93.4	94

ᵃ Includes net Victory Tax.

ᵇ 1944 tax as a percentage of net income before exemptions.

ᶜ Sum of the 3 percent normal rate and the highest surtax rate applicable to the income.

⁶ Figures for the years 1936-1943 inclusive are from *House Report No. 871*, 78th Congress, First Session, p. 95. Other figures were computed by the writer. These do not include payments of unforgiven taxes under the 1943 act.

ried person without dependents was only 7 percent if his income was $2000, 11 percent if his income was $3000, and 15 percent if his income was $5000 (see column 5). (3) The Revenue Act of 1942, whose results are reflected in the tax liabilities for 1943, added markedly to the yield of this tax, but subsequent legislation in 1943 and 1944 added very little even though federal deficits continued to mount and the President pleaded with Congress for heavier levies. A majority in Congress contended that heavier income tax burdens were infeasible. (4) Columns 7 and 9 show the tax burdens of the various income classes under the legislation in effect during 1944 and 1945. The tax on income below $1000 consisted solely of the 3 percent normal tax on all income in excess of $500; the levies on income in excess of $1000 were made up of both the 3 percent normal tax and the graduated surtax applicable to net income in excess of deductions and after exemptions of $500 per person. The effective tax rate—the percentage of net income before exemptions taken by the tax—reached 10 percent at a $2000 income level, did not pass 20 percent until income had passed $7000, and did not exceed 40 percent until income reached $25,000. This was at a time when the government was taking more than 40 percent of national output for its uses. (5) Column 10 shows the highest marginal tax rates applicable to each income class—the percentage of the last dollar earned that was taken away by income taxes. This is useful in evaluating the oft-made argument that any further increase of tax rates would have destroyed, or at least would have reduced significantly, people's incentive to work and to perform other desirable economic functions. The figures cast doubt on this argument. The great majority of taxpayers, having incomes of $3000 or less, were subject to a marginal tax rate not in excess of 23 percent, and relatively few were in the income class above $5000 where the marginal rate exceeded 25 percent. In all likelihood the marginal rates could have been increased significantly for the income groups between, say, $1500 and $20,000 without any serious deterioration of incentives and without inequity. Moreover, considerations relating to ability to pay, if not to incentives, indicate that the progression of tax rates should have started at a lower level. As shown by Table 27, the surtax brackets applicable to lower and middle income groups progressed by $2000 intervals. As a result, within the income range from $1100 to $3300 all married persons without dependents were subject to the same marginal tax rate, 23 percent. Similarly, all within the income range between $3300 and $5500 had a marginal rate of 25 percent. Within these ranges the effective tax rate rose as income increased because a larger proportion of income

TABLE 27. Marginal Tax Rates Applicable to Lower- and Middle-Income Group Under the Individual Income Tax in Effect in 1944 and 1945[7]

Net Income Before Exemptions of Married Person Without Dependents	Brackets of Taxable Net Income	Marginal Tax Rate (Percent)
$ 1,100 to $ 3,300	$ 0 to $ 2,000	23
3,301 to 5,500	2,000 to 4,000	25
5,501 to 7,500	4,000 to 6,000	29
7,501 to 9,500	6,000 to 8,000	33
9,501 to 11,500	8,000 to 10,000	37
11,501 to 13,500	10,000 to 12,000	38
13,501 to 15,500	12,000 to 14,000	43

was subject to tax, but the marginal rate did not. A marginal rate of 23 percent on a married person's income of $1100 to about $1500 was probably at least adequate, but it appears that marginal rates might well have been higher above some figure near the $1500 level. A greater yield without sacrifice of equity could have been achieved by using $500 rather than $2000 intervals for increasing marginal tax rates in the medium-income range.

Though Table 26 shows in a general way the income tax liabilities of persons in the various income groups, it does not indicate the aggregate amount of income taxes collected from the

[7] The first column assumes a standard deduction of 10 percent of net income before exemptions and a $1000 personal exemption. The marginal tax rate is the normal 3 percent tax plus the surtax applicable to that bracket of income.

TABLE 28. Taxable Individual Income Tax Returns for 1944

(Number of taxable returns in thousands; money amounts in Col. 3 and following in millions of dollars)[8]

Col. 1	Col. 2 Number of Taxable Returns		Col. 3 Aggregate Income		Col. 4 Surtax Exemptions	Col. 5 Tax Liability[a]		Col. 6 Income after Federal Income Taxes		Col. 7 Income After Taxes and Above Surtax Exemptions	
Income Class	Number	% of Total	Amount	% of Total		Amount	% of Total	Amount	% of Total	Amount	% of Total
$ 500 and under	2,045	4.8	$ 1,338	1.1	$ 1,645	$ 29	0.2	$ 1,309	1.3	$ —336	—0.7
" 750	2,951	7.0	2,586	2.3	2,640	118	0.7	2,468	2.5	—172	—0.4
" 1,000	3,477	8.2	3,922	3.4	3,324	232	1.4	3,690	3.7	366	0.8
" 1,250	3,512	8.2	4,825	4.2	3,537	353	2.1	4,472	4.5	935	2.0
" 1,500	3,459	8.2	5,614	5.0	3,687	458	2.8	5,156	5.2	1,469	3.1
" 1,750	3,404	8.0	6,375	5.6	3,832	568	3.5	5,807	5.9	1,975	4.2
" 2,000	3,130	7.4	6,643	5.8	3,741	620	3.8	6,023	6.1	2,282	4.9
" 2,250	2,870	6.8	6,811	6.0	3,722	644	4.0	6,167	6.3	2,445	5.2
" 2,500	2,787	6.6	7,308	6.4	3,780	719	4.4	6,589	6.7	2,809	6.0
" 2,750	2,514	5.9	7,223	6.3	3,566	736	4.5	6,487	6.6	2,921	6.2
" 3,000	4,133	9.8	13,379	11.8	6,100	1,453	9.0	11,926	12.1	5,826	12.4
" 3,500	2,786	6.6	10,394	9.0	4,278	1,210	7.5	9,184	9.3	4,906	10.5
" 4,000	1,778	4.2	7,516	6.5	2,764	956	5.9	6,560	6.7	3,796	8.1
" 4,500	1,039	2.5	4,916	4.3	1,592	671	4.1	4,245	4.3	2,653	5.7
" 5,000	933	2.2	5,057	4.4	1,393	759	4.7	4,298	4.4	2,905	6.2
" 6,000	418	1.0	2,693	2.4	591	453	2.8	2,240	2.3	1,649	3.5
" 7,000	221	0.5	1,646	1.4	294	307	1.9	1,339	1.4	1,045	2.2
" 8,000	151	0.4	1,279	1.1	196	255	1.6	1,024	1.0	828	1.8
" 9,000	112	0.3	1,060	0.9	143	224	1.4	836	0.8	693	1.5
" 10,000	89	0.2	931	0.8	114	207	1.3	724	0.7	610	1.3
" 11,000	68	0.2	776	0.7	86	181	1.1	595	0.6	509	1.1
" 12,000	57	0.1	716	0.6	72	174	1.1	542	0.6	470	1.1
" 13,000	46	0.1	620	0.5	58	157	1.0	463	0.5	405	0.9
" 14,000	39	0.1	558	0.5	48	148	0.9	410	0.4	362	0.8
" 15,000	129	0.3	2,224	1.9	161	648	4.0	1,576	1.6	1,415	3.0
" 20,000	68	0.2	1,504	1.3	83	506	3.1	998	1.0	915	1.9
" 25,000	38	0.1	1,049	0.9	46	395	2.4	654	0.7	608	1.3
" 30,000	42	0.1	1,431	1.2	49	599	3.7	832	0.8	783	1.7
" 40,000	20	—	908	0.8	24	420	2.6	488	0.5	464	1.0
50,000 and over	37	0.1	3,458	3.0	40	2,025	12.5	1,443	1.5	1,394	3.0
Total	42,354	100.0	$114,761	100.0	$51,607	$16,225	100.0	$98,536	100.0	$46,930	100.0

[a] Tax liability before credits for tax paid at source on income earned abroad.

8 Computed from Table 1 of the Treasury Department Press Release (Press Service No. S-436), August 21, 1947.

various groups, for it shows neither the number of income recipients in each group nor the aggregate amount of income received by each group. This information, which is vitally needed as a basis for wise tax policy, was somewhat neglected during the war period. Congress itself either failed to compile it or failed to consider it seriously, and the Treasury's presentations of this information to Congressional committees were incomplete and in general not very effective. As a result, discussion of such questions as the following left much to be desired: What part of the national income was being received by the various income groups? What part of total income tax collections came from each group? How much income was left in the hands of each group after it had paid its income taxes? How much income was left with each group after taxes and after exemptions of an amount sufficient to cover minimum needs? What groups had the excess disposable income that was creating inflationary pressures?

Table 28 presents relevant information for the year 1944. Several facts must be kept in mind in interpreting this table. (1) The definition of "income" is that of the income tax laws rather than that of the Department of Commerce; in general, it is that "income" which after subtracting certain deductions and personal exemptions leaves taxable income. (2) The income classes shown in the first column are not family income classes, but are based on the amount of income—as defined above—shown on the tax returns. Some are returns from single persons, some are joint returns of husband and wife, some are separate returns of husband and wife, and the returns include varying numbers of personal exemptions. (3) This table includes only taxable individual returns. In 1944 there were also 4,757,000 nontaxable returns covering aggregate incomes of $1,703,580,000. There were also 92,369 taxable fiduciary returns covering an aggregate income of $656 million and yielding a tax of $131 million.

Column 2 presents the familiar fact that by far the greater number of income receivers were in the income groups below $5000; in 1944 only 6 percent of the income tax returns showed incomes of $5000 or more and only 0.1 percent showed incomes of $50,000 or more. In view, however, of the unfortunate wartime tendency to lump all incomes below $5000 into one group and to assume that none of the people in it could equitably be asked to pay more taxes it is worth noting that while 36.5 percent of all returns showed incomes of less than $1750 nearly 58 percent of the returns showed incomes between $1750 and $5000.

The distribution of income by income classes is indicated in column 3. Those with incomes of $5000 or more received 22 percent of all reported income, while those reporting incomes of $50,000 or more received 3 percent of the total. About 16 percent of all income went to those reporting incomes less than $1750, and 62 percent to those reporting incomes between $1750 and $5000.

Column 5 shows the sources of income taxes in 1944 by income groups. Reflecting the progressive nature of the tax, those reporting incomes of $5000 or more received 22 percent of all reported income and paid 46 percent of all income taxes, and those reporting incomes of $50,000 or more received 3 percent of all reported income and paid 12.5 percent of all income taxes. Only 7 percent of tax collections came from those reporting incomes of less than $1750, but 47 percent came from those with incomes between $1750 and $5000.

Columns 6 and 7 provide a basis for answering these crucial questions: Assuming that it was desirable during the war to collect much heavier taxes, from what income groups would they have had to come? One could answer this question by using the data in column 6, showing the aggregate amount of income remaining in the hands of the various income groups after their 1944 federal income taxes. It seems more appropriate, however, to use the data in column 7, which indicate the amount of income left in the hands of each income group after federal income taxes and after an exemption of $500 each for the taxpayer, his spouse, and his dependents. Equity demands that a certain minimum income per person be free, or virtually free, from tax. The figures give support neither to those extremists who favored a policy of making the very rich pay for the war nor to those who would have added greatly to the tax burdens of the very low income groups, whether in the form of income taxes or sales taxes. The fact is that income tax yields could not have been greatly enhanced by further increases of tax rates applicable to the highest income groups. After paying their 1944 income taxes and after an exemption of $500 per person, the aggregate amount of income left in the hands of those reporting incomes of $50,000 or more was less than $1.4 billion, and the aggregate amount left in the hands of those reporting incomes of $15,000 or more was only $5.6 billion. The point here is not that these groups could not and should not have paid more taxes; it is only that adequate increases of tax collections could not have been secured from these groups alone.

At the lowest end of the income scale little if any more taxes could have been collected without hardship and inequity. Because of the 3 percent normal tax from which there was only a $500 exemption regardless of marital status—unless the spouse also had an income—and regardless of the number of dependents, many in the lowest groups paid income taxes even though their incomes were less than $500 for each person in the family. Much heavier taxes in this area would have eaten into the minimum income per person which equitably should be left tax-free. The great bulk of income left after 1944 taxes and after an exemption of $500 per person was in the hands of those reporting incomes between $1750 and $8000; these groups accounted for 75 percent of the total, or $35.2 billion. If Congress and the Treasury had studied carefully the distribution of income and especially the distribution of income after 1944 taxes and after the $500 exemption per person, it would have been obvious that the major part of any further increase of tax collections would have had to come from this group, though some further revenues could have been secured from the higher income levels. It should also have been clear that it was in this area that a large reserve of taxpaying capacity was to be found. For a married person without dependents, an income of $2000 was subject to an effective tax rate of only 12 percent and a marginal rate of 23 percent; at $8000 the effective tax rate was only 21 percent and the marginal tax rate was only 33 percent. A more rapid progression of tax rates on income in excess of $500 per person would have yielded much more revenue without undue hardships on taxpayers and without a significant deterioration of incentives.

TABLE 29.   A Comparison of Income Tax Liabilities of a Married Person with Two Dependents at Selected Income Levels in the U.S., the U.K., and Canada During the Latter Part of the War[9]

Net Income Before Exemptions	The U. S.	Amount of Tax Liabilities in						Net Tax in the U. K. as a Percent of That in the U. S.	Net Tax in Canada as a Percent of That in the U. S.
		Total Tax	The U. K. Refund	Net Tax	Total Tax	Canada Refund	Net Tax		
$ 1,000	$ 12	$ —	$ —	$ —	$ —	$ —	$ —	—	—
2,000	39	304	114	190	275	138	137	487	351
5,000	645	1,655	225	1,430	1,747	600	1,147	222	178
10,000	2,095	4,300	260	4,040	4,698	1,091	3,607	193	172
20,000	6,535	11,020	260	10,760	11,366	1,091	10,275	165	157
50,000	26,505	36,250	260	35,990	34,985	1,091	33,894	136	129
100,000	68,130	83,900	260	83,640	80,198	1,091	79,107	123	116

Such a policy would also have been appropriate for reducing inflationary pressures. Further taxation of the highest income recipients could not reduce inflationary pressures significantly, for members of this group were few in number, had only a small part of total disposable income, and used a considerable part of their disposable income for saving rather than consumption. On the other hand, the objective of inflation control would not justify taxing away from the lowest groups so much of their incomes that they could not purchase enough goods and services to main-

[9] Figures for the U.K. and Canada are from R. A. Musgrave, "The Wartime Tax Effort in the United States, the United Kingdom, and Canada," *Proceedings of the National Tax Association*, 1943, p. 310. The U. S. figures were computed by the writer and reflect the taxes in effect in 1944 and 1945. See the Musgrave article for a discussion of the difficulties and significance of international tax comparisons.

tain their health and efficiency. A tax policy of exempting a necessary minimum of income per person and of applying rapidly progressive rates on income in excess of that level would minimize hardships and still act as a check on excessive increases of private spending.

Both the United Kingdom and Canada proved during the war that it is feasible to use personal income taxes considerably higher than those in effect here during the latter part of the war period. It is always difficult to make precise international comparisons of tax burdens and to assess their significance, and in this case there is the further difficulty that both the United Kingdom and Canada provided for a postwar refund of a part of their wartime income taxes. But even the net income taxes after refunds in those countries were considerably higher than those in effect here, except on the lowest groups where our income taxes exceeded theirs. And it was in the middle-income range, where such a large aggregate of disposable income was to be found, that their effective tax rates exceeded ours by the largest amount.

TAXES ON CORPORATE INCOME

The second most productive taxes during the war period were those on corporate profits. These yielded a total of $59.8 billion, or 32.9 percent of all federal revenues during the six years following June 1940. Of this total, $31.9 billion came from excess-profits taxes and $27.9 billion from other taxes on corporate income. Public opinion was highly in favor of these taxes, especially the high taxes on increases of corporate income, and not merely because stockholders make up only a small minority of our population. There were several reasons for this. The cases of scandalously high profits during World War I had been widely publicized, the Nye Investigation and the theory that business interests sometimes foment war to improve their profits had made a deep impression on some people, it was easy to see that both directly and indirectly increased government spendings would create increased corporate profits, it was inevitable that some business concerns would make excessive profits on government contracts, and there was a general feeling that it was immoral for business to profit by a national emergency. A great majority of the people undoubtedly sympathized with President Roosevelt's objective of "taking the profits out of war" and of avoiding the creation of "a new batch of war millionaires." The political question was not whether there should be higher taxes on corporate profits, but how high these taxes should rise, whether they should be based on the absolute amount of net income or on the increase of net income over prewar levels or over some reasonable rate of return on investment, and on the details of the taxes. Let us now look briefly at the tax based on the absolute size of corporate net income and then at the excess-profits tax, realizing that a full treatment of these complex taxes would fill volumes.

The yield of corporation income taxes which were based on the absolute amount of net income rose from $1.9 billion in the fiscal year 1941 to an average of about $6 billion during the fiscal years 1944 through 1946. This increase was due to both the increase of corporate profits and the increase of tax rates. The tax rate, which stood at 19 percent in 1939, was raised to 24 percent in 1940, to 31 percent in 1941, and to 40 percent in 1942. It remained at the 1942 level through the end of the war despite the Treasury's request that it be raised to 50 percent.[10]

The excess-profits tax was based not on the total amount of profits but on the "excess" over certain exemptions and credits.

[10] The lower tax rates on small corporate incomes—$50,000 or less under the 1942 law—are ignored here. The relation between the corporate income tax and the excess-profits tax was changed several times. Under the Revenue Act of 1940, the excess-profits tax could not be deducted in computing income subject to this tax. The Revenue Act of 1941 allowed deduction of excess-profits taxes in computing income subject to this tax. The Revenue Act of 1942 provided that this tax should apply only to that part of net income not subject to the excess-profits tax. This provision continued in effect during the remainder of the war. In this way corporate income was segregated into two categories for tax purposes; only "normal" income was subject to the corporation income tax, and only "excess income" was subject to the excess-profits tax.

These are shown in Table 30. In computing the amount of its income subject to this tax, a corporation was permitted to deduct from its net income (1) a specific exemption, which was first set

TABLE 30. Deductions in Computing Corporate Net Income Subject to the Excess-Profits Tax[11]

	Revenue Acts			
	1940	1941	1942	1943
Specific exemption	$5,000	no change	no change	$10,000
Credit (average income credit or invested capital credit, whichever is higher)	Average income base: 95% of average base-period (1936-1939) net income plus 8% of net capital addition or less 6% of net capital reduction[a]	no change	no change[b]	no change
	Invested capital base: 8% of invested capital	Invested capital base: 1st $5,000,000 of invested capital— 8%; over $5,000,000 —7%	Invested capital base; 1st $5,000,000 of invested capital— 8%; next $5,000,000 —7%; next $190,000,000 —6%; over $200,000,000 —5%.	Invested capital base: 1st $5,000,000 of invested capital 8%; next $5,000,000 —6%; over $10,000,000— 5%.

[a] The largest deficit in any base-period year might be dropped in computing base-period earnings. Also, those whose earnings in the second half of the base period were larger than in the first half were allowed to use a "growth formula" to increase their average income credit.

[b] The law was liberalized by providing that the net income during the lowest year in the base period might be computed at 75 percent of the average net income of the other three years in the base period.

at $5000, and raised to $10,000 in 1943; and (2) the larger of (a) an average income credit, or (b) an invested capital credit. The average income credit was, in general, equal to 95 percent of average annual earnings during the base period 1936-1939 plus

[11] SOURCE: *Annual Report of the Secretary of the Treasury*, 1944, p. 462.

8 percent of any net addition to capital or minus 6 percent of any net reduction of capital. (See notes to Table 30 for further allowances.) The invested capital credit was first set at 8 percent of invested capital and eventually lowered somewhat to 8 percent on the first $5,000,000 of invested capital, 6 percent on the next $5,000,000, and 5 percent on invested capital in excess of $10,000,000. The granting of this option to corporations reflected

TABLE 31.   Excess-Profits Tax Rates During World War II[12]

	Revenue Acts of			
	1940	1941	1942	1943
Gross rates on excess profits	1st $ 20,000—25% next 30,000—30% " 50,000—35% " 150,000—40% " 250,000—45% over 500,000—50%	1st $ 20,000—35% next 30,000—40% " 50,000—45% " 150,000—50% " 250,000—55% over 500,000—60%	90 percent flat rate	95 percent flat rate
Postwar refund	none	none	10% of excess-profits tax[a] paid	no change
Limitation upon excess-profits tax	none	none	The sum of corporation income tax and excess-profits tax is not to exceed 80% of corporate income. The EPT will be reduced to conform to this limitation	no change

[a] With certain limitations this postwar credit could be taken currently to reduce debt.

an inability to decide whether "excess profits" were to be defined as an "excessive rate of return on invested capital" or as an increase over average profits realized in a peacetime period. The result was that those corporations with poor earning records in the base period were able to raise their earnings to the indicated rates of return on invested capital before becoming subject to the excess-profits tax while those whose base period experience had been more favorable deducted the 95 percent of average base period earnings with adjustments.

[12] SOURCE: *Ibid.*, p. 463.

In the Revenue Act of 1940, which first established this tax, the rates were graduated from 25 percent on the first $25,000 of taxable excess profits to 50 percent on amounts in excess of $500,000 of taxable excess profits. These rates were increased by 10 percentage points in 1941, replaced by a flat rate of 90 percent in 1942, and raised in 1943 to a flat rate of 95 percent, where it remained until the tax was repealed as of the end of 1945. The last two acts provided, however, for certain postwar refunds and limitations of rates which are shown in Table 31, and which will be discussed later.

As the burden of corporate taxes was raised many people became concerned over the possible inequities and loss of incentives that might result. It was feared that (1) both the income and excess-profits taxes would bear too heavily on those corporations with widely fluctuating annual profits; (2) corporations would not be able to meet their debt obligations while such high taxes were in effect; (3) corporations would enter the postwar period without sufficient funds to finance reconversion and full employment; and (4) high marginal tax rates would reduce the wartime incentive of corporations to make necessary capital investments, to deplete exhaustible resources, to use plant capacity to the full, and to operate efficiently. Several measures, of which only the most important will be noted here, were taken to avoid or lessen these dangers. (1) The amount of tax payable was made to depend on average income over five years rather than on income during an annual period. Under the corporation income tax, net operating losses could be carried back two years, but not back of January 1, 1941, and the unused portion could be carried forward two years. Moreover, any unused portion of a corporation's excess-profits credit could be carried back two years, but not back of January 1, 1941, and any part not used in this way could be carried forward two years. This use of a five-year average had the double purpose of protecting firms with widely fluctuating incomes during the war period and of providing refunds to meet, at least in part, reconversion costs and losses.

(2) The laws of 1942 and 1943 provided for a postwar refund of 10 percent of excess-profits taxes. In this way the government currently collected 95 percent of excess profits under the 1943 law, but the marginal net tax rate was 85.5 percent. It was believed that this would serve the multiple purpose of draining off excess purchasing power from corporations, of reducing any deleterious effect on incentives toward production and efficiency during the war, and of providing corporations with liquid funds to finance postwar reconversion and employment. With certain limitations a corporation was allowed to take its postwar credit currently to reduce its indebtedness. (3) It was provided that the sum of a corporation's income tax and gross excess-profits taxes should not exceed 80 percent of its income and that the excess-profits tax was to be reduced to the extent necessary to conform to this limitation. This limitation came into operation when a corporation's income rose to about five times its base-period earnings or to five times its invested capital credit, whichever was larger. Beyond this level both the gross and net rates of the excess-profits tax were reduced. There is real doubt as to whether this limitation, which lost the Treasury a considerable amount of revenue, could be justified even on the basis of incentives. If a net marginal rate of 85.5 percent did not unduly reduce a corporation's incentive before its income reached five times its base-period earnings it is difficult to see why the same marginal net rate should become more deleterious at higher income levels. (4) In arriving at net income, corporations were allowed to deduct depreciation at accelerated rates on capital improvements certified as necessary to the defense and war economy and where normal depreciation rates appeared to overestimate the useful life of the project. Such a provision was clearly necessary if private enterprise was to finance projects that would be of doubtful value in the postwar period. There is evidence, however, that this provision was abused in some cases. (5) Special privileges were extended to corporations using exhaustible resources. Many mineral producers were allowed to deduct liberal depletion allowances,

excessively liberal in the view of many people, in computing net income; and the lumber industry was permitted to treat income from the cutting of timber, including selective logging, as a capital gain on which the tax rate was only 25 percent. It was argued that these allowances were necessary to make firms willing to deplete exhaustible resources in a period of high marginal tax rates, but they were granted on a highly arbitrary and discriminatory basis, they were probably more liberal than was necessary for the purpose, and it is at least arguable that directives rather than such liberal monetary incentives should have been used to assure supplies of these materials. Moreover, it is difficult to find adequate reasons for exempting from the excess-profits tax certain types of firms—such as pipeline companies transporting natural gas, and airlines with government contracts for transporting mail.

In summary, the yield of taxes on corporate income rose to high levels during the war, both because of the great rise of corporate profits and because of the increase of tax rates. But the rise of effective tax rates was still so small as to allow corporate profits after taxes to double. The principal considerations preventing further increases of these taxes related to incentives toward wartime production and efficiency, to the ability of corporations to meet their financial obligations during the war, and to the ability and incentives of corporations to finance reconversion to peacetime production and to provide full employment. It is interesting to note that in line with the American habit of considering a corporation as an entity separate from its owners, the position of stockholders received much less attention than corporations themselves as producing units with their own financial needs and obligations.

MISCELLANEOUS INTERNAL REVENUE TAXES

These composed the third most productive group of taxes during the war period, yielding a total of $31.3 billion during the six years following June 1940, or 17.2 percent of all federal revenues.

Their yield rose from $3 billion in the fiscal year 1941 to $7.7 billion in the fiscal year 1946. As can be seen in Table 32 most of this revenue came from levies on goods and services. Nearly 49 percent came from liquor and tobacco taxes, 13 percent from

TABLE 32.   Yields of Miscellaneous Internal Revenue Taxes,
Fiscal Years 1941-1946
(In millions of dollars)[13]

Type	1941	1942	1943	1944	1945	1946	Total, 1941-1946	Percent of Total
Liquor taxes	$ 820	$1,048	$1,423	$1,618	$2,310	$2,525	$ 9,744	31.1
Tobacco taxes	698	781	924	988	932	1,166	5,489	17.5
Manufacturers' excise taxes, total	617	768	504	503	782	922	4,096	13.0
Gasoline and lubricating oil	381	416	332	323	499	481	—	—
Autos, trucks, tires, and tubes	156	188	44	76	148	250	—	—
Other	80	164	129	104	135	191	—	—
Retailers' excise taxes, total	—	80	165	225	424	492	1,386	4.4
Jewelry	—	42	88	113	184	223	—	—
Furs	—	20	44	59	79	92	—	—
Toilet preparations	—	19	33	45	87	96	—	—
Luggage	—	—	—	8	74	81	—	—
Other taxes								
Telephone, telegraph, cable, etc.	27	75	158	231	342	380	1,213	3.9
Transportation	—	21	170	369	455	447	1,462	4.7
Admissions	71	115	154	205	357	415	1,317	4.2
Use of motor vehicles and boats	—	73	147	135	129	116	600	1.9
Sugar	75	68	54	69	73	57	396	1.3
Capital stock	167	282	329	381	372	352	1,883	6.0
Estate and gift	407	433	447	511	643	677	3,118	10.0
All other	85	103	78	56	130	176	628	2.0
Total	$2,967	$3,847	$4,553	$5,291	$6,949	$7,725	$31,332	100.0

other taxes on manufacturers' production or sales, 4.4 percent on retailers' sales of four "luxuries," and 16 percent from taxes on communications, transportation, admissions, the use of autos and boats, and sugar. Thus 82 percent of miscellaneous internal revenue, or 14.1 percent of all federal revenue during the period,

[13] SOURCE: *Ibid.*, 1946, pp. 398-399.

TABLE 33. Wartime Tax Rates on Selected Goods and Services[14]

	Unit	In effect Dec. 31, 1939	1940	Revenue Act of		
				1941	1942	1943
Distilled spirits, except brandy	Proof gallon	$2.25	$3.00	$4.00	$6.00	$9.00
Beer	Barrel	5.00	6.00	no change	7.00	8.00
Still wine, not more than 15% alcohol	Wine gallon	5¢	6¢	8¢	10¢	15¢
Cigarettes	1000	3.00	3.25	no change	3.50	no change
Admissions	Price	1¢ for each 10¢ or fraction thereof if 41¢ or more	1¢ for each 10¢ or fraction thereof if 21¢ or more	1¢ for each 10¢ or fraction thereof	no change	1¢ for each 5¢ or major fraction thereof
Rubber tires	Pound	2¼¢	2½¢	5¢	no change	no change
Inner tubes	Pound	4¢	4½¢	9¢	'' ''	'' ''
Auto chassis	Mfgrs' sale price	3%	3½%	7%	'' ''	'' ''
Use of autos	1 auto			$5.00 per year		
Electric light bulbs	Mfgrs' sale price			5%		20%
Electrical energy for domestic and commercial use	Sale price					no change
Jewelry, furs, and luggage	Retail price			10%	10%	20%
Local telephone service	Amount charged			6%	10%	20%
Transportation of persons	Amount paid			5%	10%	15%
Transportation of property	Amount paid			—	3%	no change

14 SOURCE: *Ibid.*, 1944, pp. 466–480.

came from levies on the production, sale or use of goods and services. The wartime increase in the yields of these taxes reflected increases of effective tax rates, increases of physical quantities produced or sold, and a rise of selling prices. Some of the most important increases of these tax rates are shown in Table 33.

This type of tax was one of the most controversial of all tax issues during the war period. At one extreme were those who ardently favored a general federal sales tax at a rate high enough to add several billions to revenues. At the other extreme were those who with equal ardor opposed a general sales tax and any increase of selective excise taxes above the prewar levels. Others in between were not opposed to increases of excises on "real luxuries" but did oppose increased taxes on necessities. Those favoring a heavy reliance on these taxes advanced several arguments in their behalf. (1) They would yield large revenues. This argument was usually coupled with the contention that it was infeasible to collect additional revenues through income taxes. (2) Everyone ought to contribute to the support of the government. (3) Sales taxes are relatively painless, for they are paid in installments each time a person makes a purchase. (4) They would absorb large amounts of purchasing power from the masses and reduce inflationary pressures. (5) They would reduce the production incentives to a smaller extent than would income taxes with the same yield. (6) Substantial taxes on scarce items would reduce the effective demand for them to the level of available supplies. This argument was used to justify the 1941 tax increases on such things as tires, tubes, and autos. The increases were far too small, however, to be very effective for this purpose.

Opponents of general federal sales taxes and of increases of at least some of the selective taxes on goods and services offered a number of counter-arguments. (1) Taxes on goods and services are inequitable and violate the principle of ability to pay, for they cannot take into consideration the total income of the purchaser, or his increase of income since some base period, or the number of his dependents. Levies on necessities are especially odious from this point of view. In this respect such taxes are much inferior to income taxes, which can take into consideration the major factors relating to ability to pay. (2) The lowest income groups were already subject to a heavy burden of indirect taxes, such as the existing federal levies on goods and services and state sales taxes. (3) Federal levies of this type high enough to yield substantial revenues would necessitate increases in OPA ceiling prices, raise the cost of living, make it impossible to prevent further wage increases that would at least equal the yield of the sales taxes, raise farm-parity prices, increase the cost of goods and services purchased by the government, and add appreciably to the flow of income payments. (4) General sales taxes, especially those collected at the retail level, would raise serious administrative problems.[15]

OTHER TAXES

A few remarks will suffice for the other major revenue producers during the war. Estate and gift taxes were increased somewhat by lowering exemptions and raising rates, but these taxes yielded less than 2 percent of all federal revenue. Tax rates on the declared value of corporation capital stock were increased but this tax yielded only about 1 percent of total revenue. Employment taxes—chiefly contributions under the old-age insurance system but also including contributions for unemployment insurance and insurance of carrier employees—yielded about 5 percent of federal receipts. The rise of these receipts during the period resulted solely from increased payrolls for the scheduled rise of these rates was postponed by Congress beyond the end of the war despite the Treasury's repeated requests that the rates be allowed to rise and that compensation be given to workers in the form of improved

[15] One of the best treatments of sales taxes is to be found in a memo by the Division of Tax Research of the Treasury Department, "Considerations Respecting a Federal Retail Sales Tax." This is included in *Hearings Before the Ways and Means Committee of the House of Representatives on Revenue Revision of 1943,* pp. 1095-1258.

social services after the war. Renegotiation of war contracts contributed $5.9 billion to federal receipts during the period. Legally these were not taxes but were downward adjustments of original contract prices in the light of actual production experience. They did, however, serve the dual purpose of helping to meet government financial needs and of reducing the amount of purchasing power left in the hands of business.

In summary, we find that during the six years following June, 1940, the federal government relied mainly on three general types of taxes to provide it with money and to reduce the purchasing power of the private sectors of the economy: (1) personal income taxes, which accounted for 37.1 percent of total receipts; (2) corporation income and excess-profits taxes, which accounted for 32.9 percent of total receipts; and (3) levies on the production, sale, or use of a number of goods and services, which as a group yielded 14.1 percent of total receipts. The remaining 16 percent of all receipts were of a wide variety, including employment taxes, estate and gift taxes, capital stock taxes, customs, stamp taxes, renegotiation of war contracts, and so on.

TAX PROPOSALS THAT WERE NOT ADOPTED

No less interesting than the tax policies that were adopted were some of the tax proposals, made by the Treasury or by others, that failed to win the approval of Congress. Most of these will be mentioned only briefly at this point. Congress failed to enact considerably higher tax rates on both individual and corporate incomes as proposed by the Treasury, and it also reacted unfavorably toward certain other Treasury proposals that would have increased the revenues from these levies. Among these were compulsory joint returns of husband and wife, designed to increase effective tax rates on incomes above the low levels; the ending of tax exemption on income from state and local securities; and reduction of allegedly excessive depletion allowances. Proposals for heavy general federal sales taxes were disapproved, to the satisfaction of the Treasury.

The latter was also pleased by the unfavorable Congressional response to proposals for a tax on increases of individual incomes. This proposal was supported by several arguments: (1) Individuals as well as corporations should not be allowed to profit by a national emergency; the same ethical arguments that support an excess-profits tax are equally applicable to a general "excess-income tax." (2) Ability to pay taxes depends not only on the absolute level of one's income, but also on the recent increase of his income. Those whose incomes have been stable at a given level for some time are likely to have established habitual consumption standards and to have committed themselves to recurring financial obligations of such a magnitude as to make the payment of significantly higher taxes very burdensome. On the other hand, one whose income has risen markedly since the prewar period is less likely to have raised his financial commitments correspondingly, and is more likely to have uncommitted income out of which to pay taxes without an acute sense of hardship. (3) Such a tax is most appropriate for reducing inflationary pressures, for excessive increases of private spendings are traceable to the increases of private incomes.

Congress was more impressed, however, by the Treasury's arguments against such a tax. (1) It is very doubtful that persons with wartime increases in income have greater ability to pay taxes than those whose incomes have not increased. Some of those who experienced the largest wartime increases of income had been in very low income groups before the war and had contracted debts, and many would experience serious decreases of income as the boom in war industries receded. Moreover, increases of income associated with changes in location were often accompanied by marked increases of living expenses. (2) It would be difficult to establish an equitable base from which to measure income increases, for many had been wholly or partially unemployed, had entered the labor force only during the war, or for other reasons had received only abnormally low incomes in the prewar period. (3) Such a tax would impinge on income increases resulting from normal advancement as well as from the war. (4) It would seriously impair the incentive to work by reducing the reward for overtime and more intensive work, by eating up a part of the wage differentials used to entice workers into war industries and away from more convenient, secure, and pleasant jobs, and by reducing the incentive for women to enter the labor force. (5) If large exemptions were granted in the interest of equity the rates of the tax would have to be very high if they were to reduce inflationary pressures very much. (6) It would present difficult administrative and compliance problems, and not only because of the lack of information as to the base-period incomes of millions of people.[16]

Another group of tax proposals that led to little actual legislation concerned further methods of inhibiting private spendings and enhancing savings and of compelling people to lend to the government in accordance with a prescribed formula. Some concentrated on the first objective of inhibiting spending and of increasing saving; they would not prescribe the use to be made of savings. Others concentrated on compulsory lending to the government, though they pointed out that people would have less income to spend after the compulsory loans. Little official attention seems to have been given to the Kalecki type of plan for general expenditure rationing, which would have established a ceiling on family spendings depending on the number of members, thereby limiting effective current demand for goods and services and forcing people to save the remainder of their incomes.[17] In 1942, however, the Treasury did recommend to Congress a spendings tax, which would have been based not on the amount of income but on the amount of expenditures. To protect minimum living standards an amount

[16] For a more complete evaluation of this proposal, see a memo by the Division of Tax Research of the Treasury Department, "Taxation of Increases in Individual Incomes," *ibid.*, pp. 90-107.

[17] See Ralph E. Hoblen, "General Expenditure Rationing with Reference to the Kalecki Plan," *American Economic Review*, September, 1942, pp. 513-523.

of spendings equal to $500 for a single person, $1000 for a married person, and $250 for each dependent would have been exempt from the tax. The next $1000 of spendings would have been subject to a 10 percent tax, to be refundable after the war. Spendings above this level would have been subject to nonrefundable progressive taxes ranging up to 75 percent on spendings in excess of $10,000 a year. Several advantages were claimed for this plan. (1) It would yield additional revenue, though the revenue would vary inversely with the effectiveness of the tax in checking spendings. (2) The 10 percent refundable tax would be in effect a compulsory loan to the government which would help to meet its financial needs during the war and which would be subject to repayment after the war on terms consistent with inflation control. Moreover, refundable collections would have a less deleterious effect on incentives than would a straight income tax increase with the same yield. (3) The tax would act as a penalty on spending and as a reward for saving. This would be particularly true of the nonrefundable graduated tax on spending. It would not be required that the induced increase of savings be lent to the government, but it was assumed that in fact a large amount of them would be. (4) This tax would be superior to sales taxes in that it would exempt minimum necessities and would progressively penalize those spending more than the minimum amounts.[18] The principal reason for Congressional rejection of this tax seems to have been its alleged complexity.

Many people were in favor of introducing compulsory lending to the government during the war period. After raising tax rates to the feasible limit, they would compel people to lend additional amounts of their incomes to the government on a graduated basis. They believed that these compulsory loans should cover a large

[18] For further discussions of this proposal, see Randolph Paul, *Taxation for Prosperity*, The Bobbs-Merrill Company, 1947, pp. 92-95; and *Annual Report of the Secretary of the Treasury*, 1943, pp. 93-94, 410-420. Milton Friedman, "The Tax As a Wartime Measure," *American Economic Review*, March, 1943, pp. 50-62. Kenyon E. Poole, "Problems of Administration and Equity," *American Economic Review*, March, 1943, pp. 63-73.

part of the government's deficit. Several advantages were claimed for this method of finance. (1) It would reduce people's disposable incomes and lessen the upward pressure on spendings during the war without such deleterious effects on incentives as would result from tax rates high enough to accomplish the same purposes. Each dollar taken by compulsory loans need not, of course, reduce spendings by a corresponding amount. Some of the loans would represent amounts that would have been saved anyway, and some people would probably dispose of capital assets or borrow in order to maintain their rate of spendings. This second difficulty could have been avoided by forcing each person to lend a prescribed portion of his current income plus any reduction of his net capital during the year. (2) Any sacrifices involved in lending to the government could be distributed among the various income classes more equitably than by voluntary loans. (3) The government would be enabled to finance its deficits without asking the banking system to create so much new money and without issuing so many securities that were in effect cashable at the option of the holder, for the compulsory loans could be made repayable after the war on terms consistent with the maintenance of economic stability. It should be recognized, however, that the greater the limitation on the freedom of the lender to cash his claims, the greater would be the danger that compulsory lending would lessen incentives toward production.

The general principle of compulsory loans was used to only a very limited extent. When the excess-profits tax rate was raised to 90 percent in 1942 it was provided that 10 percent of these taxes should be refunded after the war, and the 1942 Victory Tax included refund provisions which, however, were repealed by the 1943 amendments. In the earlier part of the war the Treasury was stoutly opposed to any extensive use of the compulsory lending principle, but in 1943 it relented to the point of "suggesting the possibility" that a considerable part of its proposed increases of personal income taxes, especially of the increases on the medium income groups, might be made refundable after the war.[19] Congress rejected this suggestion for a postwar refund as well as most of the Treasury's proposed tax increases, so the compulsory lending idea was actually used only in the excess-profits tax and for a short time and to a limited extent under the Victory tax.

[19] See the *Annual Report of the Secretary of the Treasury,* 1944, pp. 384-390, 393-395, 398-415.

VI

Some Comments on Wartime Tax Policies

THE preceding chapter presented a general outline of wartime tax policy. This one will deal with the principal factors that shaped tax policy and will offer a brief criticism and evaluation of the policies followed.

PRINCIPAL FACTS AND CONSIDERATIONS AFFECTING WARTIME TAX POLICY

Though the primary interest here is in the relationship of tax policies to both wartime and postwar inflation, we must not assume that these policies were shaped only by the objective of reducing inflationary pressures. Many other factors, including inertia, lack of knowledge, institutional factors affecting the functioning of the government and the orientation of political forces, and conflicting objectives, exerted powerful influences on the formulation of policy.

UNDERESTIMATE OF EXPENDITURES

One important factor in explaining the slow increase of effective tax rates was the difficulty of predicting the timing and the extent of the increases of government expenditures. During the period before our entrance into the war no one could predict whether or when we would become an active belligerent, what our military and economic role in the war would be, and what level of expenditures would be necessitated by that role. It was clearly evident after Pearl Harbor that war expenditures would rise considerably above the levels previously anticipated, but even the President seems at first to have underestimated both the speed and the extent of the rise that would occur. In his January 1942 budget message he estimated expenditures during the fiscal year ending in June 1943 at $50 billion, in April he raised the estimate to $73 billion, and in October he raised it to $80 billion. Actual expenditures during the year turned out to be $79.7 billion. This underestimate of both the speed and extent of the rise of expenditures, coupled with the usual slowness of Congress in dealing with tax legislation, was an important factor in delaying the enactment of higher effective tax rates.

PREWAR UNEMPLOYMENT

The long period of serious unemployment preceding the war and the persistence of some unemployment even beyond the time of Pearl Harbor served in several ways to delay increases of effective tax rates and to limit their ultimate rise. (1) During the defense period, and especially during the period before mid-1941, there seemed to be no valid reason for raising effective tax rates to levels high enough to balance the budget and further restrict private disposable incomes, for there were still unemployed labor and other productive resources available to produce more munitions and more civilian goods as well. It was difficult to forecast when an expansionary fiscal policy would cease to result primarily in increased real output and would create progressively more serious dangers of price inflation. (2) During the Great Depression, characterized by an excessively low rate of spendings for output, it came to be widely accepted that the attainment and maintenance of prosperity demanded that the spending power of the masses should not be reduced by heavy taxes. As the danger shifted from deflation to inflation it was difficult for public officials as well as those who would pay the higher taxes to appreciate the fact that a reversal of tax policy was indicated. (3) Throughout the war many continued to fear that with the return to peace our economy would again sink into a depression of the prewar type. To avoid such an event they looked not unkindly on a tax program light enough to enable both business and individuals to accumulate large savings for postwar use.

THE PREWAR PATTERN OF FEDERAL TAXES

Despite the revolutionary rise of the government's fiscal requirements federal tax authorities found it difficult to break away from prewar patterns of taxes and methods of tax administration. The individual income tax is a good example. Only with difficulty was Congress persuaded to lower exemptions and transform this from "a rich man's tax" to a mass tax, to introduce collection at the source, to provide for current payment of tax liabilities, and to simplify tax returns, especially for the lower income groups. If before the war the income tax had been a mass tax with these improved methods of administration, its effective rates might have been increased more quickly and to higher levels, and there might not have been so many who contended, even early in the war, that its ability to produce revenue had already reached its maximum so that further increases of revenue would have to be sought from other levies, such as sales taxes.

THE SLOWNESS OF THE LEGISLATIVE PROCESS

Another important factor in explaining the lag of revenues is one that even in peacetime causes so much unhappiness to those who would like to see fiscal policy used as a flexible instrument of economic stabilization—the slowness of congressional action on revenue measures. Though the President asked Congress for additional taxes in January 1942, the Revenue Act of 1942 did not become law until the following October, and his January 1943 request for more revenue was not finally acted upon by Congress until February 1944. The expeditious methods utilized in so many other fields of wartime economic control were conspicuously absent in the formulation of tax policy. One hesitates to suggest that Congress should under any conditions throttle debate on important issues or delegate a large part of its taxing authority to an administrative agency, but the wartime experience certainly casts doubt on the wisdom of holding almost interminable hearings and permitting almost endless debate in a time of national emergency. Wartime experience also underlined the need for more efficient working relations between the Treasury and the tax committees of Congress.

ECONOMIC CONFLICTS AND PRESSURE GROUPS

Even in the midst of war the various economic groups tried to protect and even to improve their income positions, both before and after taxes. As competitive controls were supplemented or replaced by government controls the economic conflicts which normally occurred in the market arena shifted to Congress and to administrative agencies. Many of the rank and file members of these economic groups were more public-spirited and less selfish than their more vociferous colleagues and official spokesmen, but the latter were constantly exerting pressure on Washington. The various economic groups wanted not only to get but also to retain liberal amounts of money income, so they turned their pressure on the tax authorities. The attitude of each group seemed to be, "More taxes, yes, but collect them from someone else." For example, representatives of such organizations as the National Association of Manufacturers, Chambers of Commerce, Boards of Trade, and the National Retail Dry Goods Association were in general favorable to heavy sales taxes and increased income taxes on the lower income groups, but they opposed such things as "excessively high" income surtaxes, compulsory joint returns by husband and wife, taxation of income from state and local government securities, "undue" increases of the corporate income tax, and failure to allow "adequate" deductions in computing corporate income subject to the excess-profits tax.[1] On the other hand, CIO representatives fought against sales taxes and reduction of personal exemptions below $1500 and $750 levels, but gave their blessing to higher corporate income and excess-profits tax rates, to compulsory joint returns, to ending exemptions on income from state and local securities, to higher estate and gift taxes, and to closing loopholes available to the higher income groups.[2] Brewers opposed higher taxes on beer. Proposals for higher taxes on gasoline and lubricating oils brought protests from refiners, truckers, bus operators, rural mail carriers and state tax authorities. One disgusted observer remarked that the congressional hearings appeared to be an annual meeting of the Amalgamated Association of Tax Dodgers.[3]

It is not suggested here that the activities of these economic pressure groups are improper or are not a useful part of the whole governmental process, but it is clear that compromise solutions that merely succeed in keeping peace among the contending groups are not necessarily those that will most promote the general public interest. In this case each group seemed much more keenly interested in avoiding or limiting taxes on its own members than in increasing the taxes to be borne by others, so that the net effect of pressure group activities was toward delaying and limiting tax increases. As Professor Newcomer has concluded:

. . . the fact that most of the evidence presented at the hearings and elsewhere is in the form of complaints concerning taxes from individuals with specific grievances tends to warp the judgment of the committee members. Hardships are overemphasized, and the presentation of specific cases is always more impressive than generalizations.

[1] For examples of these statements, see *Hearings Before the Ways and Means Committee of the House of Representatives on Revenue Revision of 1942*, 77th Congress, 2nd Session, Vol. 1, pp. 133 ff., 236 ff., 269 ff., 509 ff., 618 ff.
[2] *Ibid.*, Vol. 2, pp. 2120 ff.
[3] *Ibid.*, pp. 1884.

Consequently, Congress is more influenced by evidence against taxes than by evidence in their favor. The CIO's plea for higher individual income surtaxes, higher estate and gift taxes, and higher corporation taxes fell on deaf ears; but their opposition to a general sales tax and to reduced exemption for the income tax was successful. The occasional individual or organization who comes to speak in the interests of the general public, such as the Consumers Union, the National Lawyers Guild, or the Union for Democratic Action, is apt to be met with indifference, or even suspicion. It is expected that witnesses will have some axe to grind.[4]

PROTECTION OF PRODUCTION INCENTIVES

One of the most powerful and effective arguments used to delay and limit tax increases was that taxation should not be so heavy as to interfere with wartime production. This is, of course, a sound and important consideration in tax policy, but it was abused during the war period and permitted to limit unduly the amount of taxes collected. It was invoked indiscriminately by every group seeking to avoid taxes, whether or not it had a basis in fact. Moreover, the argument was usually "fuzzy"; those employing it typically did not describe clearly the precise way that production was allegedly being threatened. If the constituent parts of the production incentive problem had been more carefully analyzed in official quarters it would probably have been possible to tailor the tax laws in such a way as to secure more revenue and still protect production incentives. Let us look at some of the possible effects of taxes on wartime production and some of the ways in which any deleterious effects of taxes on production might have been remedied or obviated.[5]

(1) Tax collections can be so heavy as to leave the private sectors of the economy with such small disposable incomes that they will not be able to buy at profitable prices all the goods

[4] Mabel Newcomer, "Congressional Tax Policies in 1943," *American Economic Review*, December, 1944, p. 753.

[5] For an enlightening discussion of this issue, see Carl Shoup, "Problems in War Finance," *American Economic Review*, March, 1943, pp. 75-87.

and services that the economic system can produce and that are not needed for governmental purposes, thereby causing unemployment. This was a valid argument against marked increases of effective tax rates during much of the defense period, but it was clearly inapplicable during the war when people's disposable incomes were so large that they were not only buying all the available consumption goods and services, but were also exerting strong upward pressure on price levels and saving unprecedentedly large sums. In fact, there was a constant danger that these large disposable private incomes would lessen total production by setting off rapid price increases, thereby diverting an excessive amount of attention to speculative activities, making fixed-price contracts infeasible, and inducing an increase of labor disputes. Moreover, the very large private demand, and the attendant high profitability of civilian production, tended in some cases to inhibit the shift of productive resources to war purposes. (2) High marginal tax rates on the net income of business may make enterprises unwilling to replace and add to the supply of capital equipment, especially where the investment is risky. This argument was less broadly valid during the war than it is in peacetime. We did not want large amounts of capital construction in all industries during the war; labor and materials had to be conserved for only the most essential purposes. The appropriate solution of this problem was not, therefore, to hold down tax rates on the incomes of all business firms, but rather to have the government finance the essential projects or else to grant special concessions, such as accelerated depreciation allowances, only to those firms making essential capital investments. (3) Excessive taxation may reduce aggregate savings to undesirably low levels and make adequate investment funds unavailable to business. It was clearly improper to use this argument to oppose taxes higher than those actually employed during the war. Aggregate savings were unprecedentedly high, a high rate of private investment was undesirable, there is no evidence that essential investment suffered from any lack of funds, and in case of necessity the government itself could have financed essential projects either directly or by lending. (4) Very high marginal tax rates may make the extractive industries unwilling to deplete their exhaustible resources. This problem was met, as we have seen, by such devices as liberal depletion allowances and treatment of earnings as a capital gain. Some concessions of this general nature were probably required, but it is also probably true that more revenue could have been gained without a loss of either equity or production through less liberal tax concessions and a judicious use of directive powers. (5) Very high marginal tax rates may reduce the efficiency of business, for a large part of any increase of profits goes to the government rather than to the business firm. This argument alone probably accounts for the fact that excess-profits tax rates were not raised to 100 percent without any provision for a postwar refund. It is difficult to know whether the 85.5 percent marginal net rate in effect during the latter part of the war could have been significantly increased without excessively deleterious effects on efficiency; we know too little about the strength of the various nonpecuniary incentives of management during a war period and too little about the effectiveness and general desirability of direct controls over business efficiency. But if the 85.5 percent net marginal rate did not exert too deleterious an effect on a corporation's efficiency while its profits were not more than five times its base-period earnings, there appears to be little or no justification for the overall 80 percent limitation, which—for corporations with the largest increases of profits— lowered the net marginal rate of the excess-profits tax well below 80 percent.[6] This loss of revenue appears to have been unjustified by considerations relating to either efficiency or equity. (6) High marginal rates may discourage labor from working overtime and from working more intensively to secure bonuses for greater than standard output. But this argument does not justify the failure to collect more income taxes from the medium-income groups. It is probable that marginal rates could have been raised somewhat above the 23 to 25 percent levels, the highest to which most

[6] See p. 102 above.

workers were subject, without much additional deleterious effects on their willingness to work longer and harder. And even if this was not true, it would not have been difficult to work out devices for increasing revenues from these groups while still protecting incentives to work long and hard. For example, the regular tax rates could have been raised and workers given the option of paying these regular taxes on all of their income or of segregating their overtime and bonus pay and paying on it a flat tax rate of, say, 25 percent. Alternatively, all income might have been subjected to higher marginal rates with a postwar refund of at least some of the tax increase on overtime and bonus pay. If the administrative difficulty of separating out overtime and bonus pay proved too great, and it should not have proved so, tax rates in the medium-income area should have been increased with provision for a refund of a part of the increase in the postwar period. (7) High marginal rates may interfere with the movement of labor from civilian to war industries, for with a given wage structure they would narrow the net wage differentials after taxes. Several devices could have been used to assure the mobility of labor despite higher taxes on the medium-income groups. (a) Expenses of moving to the proximity of a war plant could have been made deductible in computing taxable income. (b) Direct manpower controls could have been used to a greater extent to limit employment in nonwar industries. And (c) the allocation of materials and supplies to nonwar industries could have been used to a greater extent to limit employment opportunities there. (8) High marginal rates may inhibit the entrance of wives into the labor force. It is doubtful that marginal rates considerably higher than those used in the medium income range during the war would have been very deleterious in this respect. If, however, this was a real danger, it could have been reduced by allowing married women, at their option, to pay a flat rate of 25 percent on their incomes from work, or a minimum amount of their labor income could have been exempted from taxes.

In summary, the protection of production incentives is a highly important objective of tax policy in time of war as well as in time of peace; the objective of controlling inflation could not justify tax policies that would interfere with war production or seriously impede production for essential civilian needs. Moreover, it is admittedly difficult to evaluate the effects of higher tax rates on production incentives, for the wartime motivations of people, whether enterprisers or laborers, vary widely. Highly conscientious people and those with close relatives and friends in the armed forces probably needed little pecuniary incentive to work long, hard, and efficiently. Others may have been activated primarily by the amount of money they could get and keep. The protection of production incentives probably made it infeasible to levy tax rates high enough to balance the budget, but the writer believes that effective tax rates could have been increased considerably above the highest levels reached during the war, even in the medium-income area, without serious deleterious effects on incentives.

ABILITY TO PAY AND EQUITY IN TAXATION

We may dismiss at the outset the contention that the American people as a whole did not have the ability to pay more taxes during the war. This argument is wholly refuted by the fact that disposable private income was so large as to permit people to buy all the goods and services that could be made available for nongovernmental purposes, to exert a strong upward pressure on prices, and still to save huge amounts. There can be no doubt that much more revenue could have been collected without making our people unable to purchase, at stable prices, all the available goods and services and also to save normal amounts. A more difficult problem was how to distribute higher tax burdens equitably among the various groups. At least two concepts of equity came into conflict with each other. According to one, increased taxes should come primarily from those whose incomes had increased over prewar levels. It was argued that wartime was not the time to alter relative income positions, that no one should seek to profit by the war, that the danger of inflation emanated from the increases of disposable money income and that those whose incomes had not risen above prewar levels should not suffer marked reductions of their customary living standards. According to this theory, tax policies should leave the various groups in the same relative income positions after taxes that they had occupied in the prewar period. The excess-profits tax and the proposed tax on increases of individual incomes were in line with this principle. Practically, the latter would probably have called for much higher taxes on such groups as farmers, workers, and proprietors of unincorporated businesses.

According to the other concept of equity, tax burdens should be graduated with the absolute level of personal income after adjustments for other factors relating to ability to pay, such as the number of members in the family. An amount of income per person sufficient to cover minimum necessities should be exempt and incomes above this level subjected to rates graduated quickly enough and to high enough levels to yield the required revenues. In periods of rising tax burdens such a policy would, of course, tend to decrease the inequality of incomes after taxes.

The controversy between those who believed that increased tax burdens should be allocated on the basis of increases of income since the prewar period and those who would allocate them on the basis of the absolute amount of income helped to delay and limit tax increases. But even among those who agreed that taxes should be based on the absolute amount of income there were wide differences of opinion as to how high personal exemptions should be, how high the first bracket tax rate should be, and how rapidly and to what limit surtax rates should progress. Representatives of labor and others who favored the low-income groups asserted that equity required high exemptions and tax rates that rose slowly but reached high levels toward the top end of the income scale. The writer is in agreement with those who would not have imposed further burdens on the very lowest income groups and for that reason disapproves of the proposals for a heavy general sales tax and for additional selective levies on goods and services purchased by this group. Nevertheless, he believes that personal exemptions should have been lowered to not more than $500 per person earlier in the war and that tax rates should have been graduated more rapidly on incomes in excess of this amount. In 1941, a prosperous year, 60 percent of all American families had incomes below $2000 and nearly 45 percent had incomes below $1500. It therefore seems likely that at least half of the families had incomes of less than $500 per member. It surely does not seem unreasonably severe in wartime to define "a necessary minimum" as the median income per capita in the immediately preceding period and to tax incomes in excess of that amount at rapidly progressive rates.[7]

Higher effective tax rates on "the middle class" and higher-income groups were opposed by many on the ground that they would unduly lower customary standards of living and make it impossible for people to meet fixed financial commitments, such as large life insurance premiums. This argument was much overdone. In the first place, the highest effective tax rates reached during the war left the middle-class groups with disposable incomes far in excess of the amounts needed to purchase necessities and minimum comforts, and most of the members of this and the higher-income groups could pay considerably higher taxes by sacrificing such things as vacations, travel, domestic servants, luxury types of clothing, and durable goods. Hardships in specific cases were widely publicized and erroneously made to appear to be the rule rather than the exception. In the second place, not enough stress was placed on the fact that these groups could properly be asked to make large financial sacrifices in time of war. In the third place, comparable attention was not given to the hardships imposed by inflation on fixed-income groups—hardships that were magnified by the inadequate tax program. In the fourth place, if

---

[7] The writer believes this is true even though the cost of living during the war rose somewhat above 1941 levels, so that the dollars of the war period did not represent as much purchasing power as the dollars of 1941.

Congress was really convinced that further net taxes would impinge too sharply on those whose incomes had not risen it should have found ways of extracting more money from the people as a whole without excessive hardships on this group. For example, it could have raised gross tax rates to higher levels and provided that a part of the increase would be refunded after the war under conditions consistent with economic stability. But those who could show that their incomes had not risen might have been allowed to take some or all of the refund currently.

THE OBJECTIVE OF LIMITING INFLATION

Wartime tax policy was also greatly influenced by the objective of keeping inflationary pressures under control. This purpose was repeatedly emphasized by the Treasury and was accepted "in principle" by Congress. But the effectiveness of tax policy for this purpose was reduced by the prevailing inability to forecast the probable duration of inflationary dangers and by differences of opinion as to the proper methods of dealing with them. Would the postwar period be inflationary or deflationary? Even during the war period, what should be the relative roles in the anti-inflation program of taxation, borrowing out of current income, and direct controls such as price and wage ceilings? Could price and wage controls succeed if disposable incomes were not reduced by higher taxes or the draining off of money through an aggressive program of borrowing current income? Vacillating attitudes toward questions of this type served to limit the increase of wartime taxes.

As price ceilings were extended in early 1942 to cover almost all important goods and services, OPA officials repeatedly warned that the price control program would be endangered and might fail if it was not supplemented by wage ceilings and an aggressive program for draining off private spending power through much higher taxes and a borrowing program aimed at increasing the propensity to save and to lend current income to the government.

At first this emphasis on the necessity for higher taxes to supplement the price control program probably helped to secure the enactment of higher effective tax rates. Later, however, as direct price controls continued to be highly successful despite mounting government deficits and private disposable incomes, many came to believe that the OPA could be relied upon to hold inflation in check and that further increases of taxes were not necessary for the purpose. Moreover, the rise of effective tax rates was inhibited by an excessive faith in the efficacy of the government's borrowing program as a device for reducing the propensity to spend and increasing the propensity to save. It is undoubtedly true that the Treasury's dramatic borrowing program did to some extent increase people's willingness to save and decrease their propensity to spend, but its effectiveness for this purpose was overestimated by the Treasury. In the congressional hearings on the Treasury's 1943 proposals for $10.5 billion of additional taxes Secretary Morgenthau seems to have made a tactical error in reporting so enthusiastically on the success of his borrowing program.[8]

CONCLUSION

Wartime tax policies were highly inadequate for the purpose of inflation control and were one of the basic factors in the war and postwar inflation. Higher effective tax rates would have lessened inflationary pressures during both the war and the postwar periods. It is not suggested, however, that taxes should have been increased to the level that would have been required to balance the federal budget during the war period. An expansionary fiscal policy during most of the defense period assisted in bringing output up toward capacity levels, and tax rates high enough to wipe out federal deficits during the years 1942-1945 would probably have damaged production incentives to an unbearable extent. The magnitude of the further tax increases that would have been

[8] See E. D. Allen, "Treasury Tax Policies in 1943," *American Economic Review*, December, 1944, p. 722.

required to balance the budget is indicated by the federal cash deficits during this period (Table 34). Some additional revenue could probably have been secured from corporations without serious effects on incentives, but it is highly doubtful that this

TABLE 34.   Federal Cash Deficits, 1941-1945[9]

Calendar Year	Federal Cash Deficit (In billions of dollars)
1941	$10.0
1942	38.7
1943	51.1
1944	46.6
1945	36.5

TABLE 35.   Effective Tax Rates Required to Balance the Federal Budget, 1941-1945, Under Certain Assumptions
(In billions of dollars)[10]

Calendar Year	Col. 1 Personal Income	Col. 2 Actual Federal, State, and Local Taxes on Persons	Col. 3 Additional Personal Taxes Necessary to Balance the Federal Budget[a]	Col. 4 Col. 2 plus Col. 3	Col. 5 Total Personal Taxes (Col. 4) as a percentage of Personal Income
1941	$ 95.3	$ 3.3	$ 6.0	$ 9.3	9.8%
1942	122.7	6.0	34.7	40.7	33.2
1943	150.3	17.8	47.1	64.9	43.2
1944	165.9	18.9	42.6	61.5	37.1
1945	171.9	20.9	32.5	53.4	31.1

[a] The figures in column 3 are the federal cash deficit for the year less the $4 billion assumed to be covered by increased taxes on corporate income.

would have amounted to more than about $4 billion a year and it might have been less. Let us assume for the sake of illustration that an extra $4 billion a year could have been secured from corporations and that the remainder would have had to be collected from individuals. Table 35 shows the impact of such a policy on

[9] SOURCE: *Treasury Bulletins.*

[10] Figures for personal income and actual personal taxes are from the *Survey of Current Business*, July, 1949. It should be noted that the concept of personal income used here is that of the Department of Commerce rather than that of the income tax laws and is somewhat more inclusive than the latter.

personal incomes. Column 5 indicates that, on the average, individuals would have had to pay well over 30 percent of their total incomes as taxes during the war period if, in addition to existing federal, state, and local taxes, they had been required to pay the indicated further amounts to balance the federal budget. It is to be noted that these are the average tax rates that would have been required on total personal income before any exemptions. To the extent that the lowest income groups were protected by

TABLE 36. Effect of Minimum Exemptions on Average Tax Rates
Required to Balance the Federal Budget
(In billions of dollars)

Calendar Year	Col. 1 Total Necessary Tax Collections[a]	Col. 2 Aggregate Personal Income in Excess of $500 per Person[b]	Col. 3 Col. 1 as a Percentage of Col. 2	Col. 4 Aggregate Personal Income in Excess of $300 per Person	Col. 5 Col. 1 as a Percentage of Col. 4
1941	$ 9.3	$ 28.7	32.4	$ 55.3	16.8
1942	40.7	55.3	73.6	82.3	49.5
1943	64.9	82.0	79.1	109.3	59.4
1944	61.5	96.8	63.5	124.5	49.4
1945	53.4	102.1	52.3	130.0	41.1

[a] Column 4 of Table 35 above.
[b] This is equal to personal income as shown in column 1 of Table 35 above minus $500 times the population during the year. Column 4 was computed in a comparable way.

allowing exemptions, the average tax rate on taxable incomes would have had to be higher. This is shown in Table 36. Column 3 indicates that with exemptions of $500 per person average tax rates on taxable income would have had to be above 65 percent during the years 1942-1945 in order to meet state and local needs and balance the federal budget. And Column 5 shows that with exemptions of only $300 per person average tax rates on taxable income would have had to be in excess of 50 percent to meet this objective.[11] These are, of course, average rates on taxable income

[11] These figures are highly approximate for several reasons. (1) The income figures used are those of the Department of Commerce and are somewhat higher than those corresponding to the definition of income under the tax laws. (2) With much higher effective tax rates, spendings for output and personal incomes would not have risen as much as they actually did. (3) With much

and could have been achieved through lower marginal rates on the first amount of income above exemptions with progressively higher marginal rates on additional amounts of income. But, in view of the fact that the great bulk of income in excess of these exemptions was in the hands of those with incomes not in excess of $5000 it is clear that very high marginal rates would have had to be imposed on the first bracket of taxable income in order to balance the federal budget.

To have raised tax rates to the levels that would have been necessary to balance the federal budget would have been unwise, even in 1942 or 1943, for it would undoubtedly have had excessively damaging effects on the incentive to work. This may be an unfair reflection on the patriotism of our people; perhaps they should have been willing to work long, hard, and efficiently for a net reward after taxes just sufficient to cover their minimum needs, and they should have responded satisfactorily to nonpecuniary disciplines and incentives. But farm, mine, and factory jobs are often monotonous, especially after long hours, and in many cases appear to be only remotely related to the success of the war effort, so that as a practical matter it was probably necessary to use the added incentive of permitting workers to keep a considerable part of the extra dollars earned for their last hours of work even though this added to inflationary pressures. Nevertheless, tax rates on taxable income should have been raised considerably above the highest levels actually attained during the war.[12]

---

higher tax rates and lower private spendings the government might not have had to spend so much for the goods and services that it required. These and several other considerations counsel use of these estimates only for the purpose of illustrating the general magnitude of the problem.

[12] See pp. 94-97 above.

VII

||||||||||||||||||||||||||||||||||||||||||||||||||||||||||||||||||||||||||||||||||||||||||||||||||||||||||||||||||||||||||

Some Aspects of Federal Borrowing
Policies, 1940-1946

B ETWEEN June 30, 1940 and June 30, 1946 the total federal debt rose from $48.5 billion to $269.9 billion, an increase of $221.4 billion or 456 percent.[1] But a part of this debt differs so greatly from the remainder that it should be treated separately. This is the part held within the government itself by U. S. Government agencies and trust funds, the principal of which are the

TABLE 37.   U. S. Securities Held by U. S. Government Agencies and
Trust Funds, 1940-1946
(In millions of dollars)[2]

June 30	Absolute Amount Held	Increase During Year Ending
1940	$ 7,080	$ —
1941	8,495	1,415
1942	10,622	2,127
1943	14,332	3,700
1944	19,097	4,775
1945	24,940	5,843
1946	29,130	4,190
Total increase, 1940-1946		$22,050

[1] *Federal Reserve Bulletin*, February, 1949, p. 162. This is the gross Federal debt, including both direct and fully guaranteed securities.
[2] SOURCE: *Federal Reserve Bulletin*, February, 1949, p. 162. For figures showing net purchases by the various trust funds, see *Treasury Bulletin*, February, 1949, p. 8.

Federal Old-Age and Survivors Insurance Trust Fund, the Railroad Retirement Account, the Unemployment Trust Fund, the Government Life Insurance Fund, and the Federal Employees Retirement Funds. The increase in the federal debt held by these funds differs in two major respects from increases in the debt held outside the federal government. (1) This part of the increase in the debt was in general offset by collections of money from the public in the form of taxes or other deductions from private income to finance retirement, insurance, or unemployment benefit plans. These deductions from income served to hold down the increase of private spendings, much as do other types of taxes, and for that reason were included in our earlier figures showing the government's "cash operating income" for the period.[3] (2) This part of the debt rise does not increase the amount of federal securities held outside the government. It does, of course, represent an increase in the government's future obligations to pay retirement, unemployment, and life insurance benefits in accordance with the governing contracts, but it does not increase the assets which people hold in the form of government securities and which they may cash or sell at will. For these reasons we shall not deal further with this part of the federal debt but shall concentrate on federal debt held outside the government itself. Most of this is held within the country.

In considering the government's borrowing policy during the war it is useful to keep in mind a fact that was emphasized in Chapter IV: that the abnormally high rate of private saving during the war period was largely due to federal deficit spending. It was the size of the cash deficit, which was roughly equal to the amount borrowed outside the government, that largely determined the total amount of private savings. And the savings generated by deficit spending were in the first instance received by individuals and business firms in the form of money. The government's

[3] These deductions from income may not, however, reduce private spendings as much as would an equal amount of other taxes, for people do receive in return the right to future benefits.

TABLE 38.   Ownership of U. S. Government Securities Held Outside U. S. Government Agencies and Trust Funds, 1940-1946
(In millions of dollars)[4]

June 30	Total	Held by Nonbank Investors						Held by Banks		
		Total	Individuals	Mutual Savings Banks	Insurance Companies	Other Corporations and Associations	State and Local Governments	Total	Federal Reserve Banks	Commercial Banks
1940	$ 41,416	$ 22,850	$10,300	$ 3,100	$ 6,500	$ 2,500	$ 400	$ 18,566	$ 2,466	$16,100
1941	46,837	24,953	11,500	3,400	7,100	2,400	600	21,884	2,184	19,700
1942	66,369	37,724	18,400	3,900	9,200	5,400	900	28,645	2,645	26,000
1943	126,474	67,072	31,700	5,300	13,100	15,500	1,500	59,402	7,202	52,200
1944	183,529	100,228	46,500	7,300	17,300	25,900	3,200	83,301	14,901	68,400
1945	234,175	128,183	59,800	9,600	22,700	30,900	5,300	105,992	21,792	84,200
1946	240,768	132,585	64,100	11,500	25,300	25,300	6,500	108,183	23,783	84,400
Percent of total held June 30, 1946	100.0	55.1	26.6	4.8	10.5	10.5	2.7	44.9	9.9	35.0

[4] Computed from *Federal Reserve Bulletin*, February, 1949, p. 162. The figures include both direct and fully guaranteed securities.

Table 39. Net changes in the Ownership of U. S. Government Securities Held Outside the Federal Government, 1940-1946
(In millions of dollars)[5]

Net Change During Year Ending June 30	Total Change	Net Changes in Holdings by Nonbank Investors						Net Changes in Bank Holdings		
		Total	Individuals	Mutual Savings Banks	Insurance Companies	Other Corporations and Associations	State and Local Governments	Total	Federal Reserve Banks	Commercial Banks
1941	$ 5,421	$ 2,103	$ 1,200	$ 300	$ 600	$ -100	$ 200	$ 3,318	$ -282	$ 3,600
1942	19,532	12,771	6,900	500	2,100	3,000	300	6,761	461	6,300
1943	60,105	29,348	13,300	1,400	3,900	10,100	600	30,757	4,557	26,200
1944	57,055	33,156	14,800	2,000	4,200	10,400	1,700	23,899	7,699	16,200
1945	50,646	27,955	13,300	2,300	5,400	5,000	2,100	22,691	6,891	15,800
1946	6,593	4,402	14,300	1,900	2,600	-5,600	1,200	2,191	1,991	200
Increase during the six-year period	$199,352	$109,735	$53,800	$8,400	$18,800	$22,800	$6,100	$89,617	$21,317	$68,300
Percent of total increase during the six-year period	100.0	55.0	27.0	4.2	9.4	11.4	3.0	45.0	10.7	34.3

[5] Computed from data in Table 38 on page 133.

borrowing policies relating to the sources of its loans and to the form of the securities issued determined not the total amount of private savings but only the form in which these savings would be held by the private sectors. But borrowing policy was nevertheless important, for by affecting the form and liquidity of privately held assets, both during and at the end of the war, it could thereby affect private spending policies.

Tables 38 and 39 bring out a number of facts that will be useful in the later analysis. (1) During the six years ending June 30, 1946, the federal debt held outside the government itself rose from $41.4 billion to $240.8 billion, an increase of $199.4 billion or 482 percent. As noted earlier, $12.3 billion of these net borrowings were used to increase the Treasury's general fund balance, but the major part, or $186.7 billion, was required to cover the cash operating deficit for the period. This involved, of course, an equal increase in assets held by the private sectors in the form of government securities. (2) Table 39 shows the net increase in the volume of governments in the hands of the various classes of holders. These figures reflect not only purchases from and sales to the Treasury but also the effects of transfers within the market. One striking fact is the relatively small proportion of the securities that were bought and held by individuals and nonfinancial corporations. Individuals increased their holdings by $53.8 billion, an amount equal to only 27 percent of the net increase of these securities outstanding, and this despite total personal savings that must have amounted to more than $130 billion during the period. Nonfinancial corporations increased their holdings by $22.8 billion, or by 11.4 percent of the total increase of outstanding governments, but this was equal to only a fraction of corporate gross savings which must have aggregated upwards of $90 billion. It appears that Treasury efforts to place most of its new securities solidly in the hands of individuals and nonfinancial business firms were only partially successful; these groups elected to hold a major part of their savings in the form of currency, checking deposits, and other claims against financial institutions rather than in governments. (3) Mutual savings banks and insurance companies increased their holdings by $27.2 billion, an amount equal to 13.6 percent of the total increase of these securities outstanding. They were able to do this largely because of the large amounts of private savings that flowed to them during the war. (4) State and local governments used their current surpluses of tax collections to increase their holdings by $6.1 billion, an amount equal to 3 percent of the net increase of these securities outstanding. (5) The Federal Reserve and commercial banks increased their holdings by $89.6 billion, which was equal to 45 percent of the increase in the federal debt. A part of this increase represented an increase of time and savings deposits left at commercial banks by depositors. The major part, however, was purchased through the creation of new currency and checking deposits and most of this increased money came to be held by individuals and business firms.

In summary, individuals and nonfinancial corporations increased their holdings of governments by an amount equal to only 38.4 percent of the total increase of federal securities outside the government itself. Nearly 59 percent of the total increase was purchased by financial institutions, and 45 percent of the total was taken by the Federal Reserve and commercial banks. This increase of bank holdings was largely responsible for the great increase of the money supply during the war period.

The above facts will serve as a useful background for the following study of the principal considerations that shaped wartime borrowing policy.

SOME CONSIDERATIONS IN BORROWING POLICY

As soon as the government made its decision to undertake large defense and war expenditures and to follow an inadequate tax policy it was, of course, committed to a heavy borrowing program. The success of the war effort was not to be endangered by any lack of money, even if a large part of the deficit had to be covered by the creation of new money. There still remained, however, the problem of determining the type of borrowing policy to be employed. This was an important problem, for different types of borrowing policies could exert highly differing influences on the operation of the economy during both the war and the postwar period. It is therefore desirable to look at some of the most important considerations in wartime borrowing policies.

EFFECTS ON THE PRIVATE PROPENSITY TO SPEND DURING THE WAR

One of the prime considerations in borrowing policy was the effect of the borrowing program on the propensity of individuals and business concerns to spend for consumption and capital purposes during the war. Ideally, a borrowing program with inflation control as one of its objectives would supplement the anti-inflationary effects of taxation. Tax collections would reduce, or at least restrict the rise of, disposable private incomes, thereby limiting the amounts that the private sectors would feel that they could spend. Borrowing policy would then be such as to force, or at least to encourage, the private sectors to save very large parts of their disposable incomes and to reduce the amounts that they would be able or willing to spend for consumption or capital purposes. This would limit the rise of total spendings for output by holding down private spendings and perhaps also, to the extent that this reduced the current rise of prices, by holding down the amounts that the government had to spend to acquire the desired quantities of goods and services.

It must be emphasized that the objective of preventing a rise of inflationary pressures during the war demanded that the propensity to save be increased and that the propensity to spend be reduced to such an extent that the private sectors of the economy would not try to bid up the prices of available civilian goods. Two points in this statement are important. (1) The emphasis is on an increased propensity to save rather than on the willingness to lend to the government. A greater willingness to lend to the government out of previously idle money balances or out of savings that would have been made anyway does not reduce inflationary pressures if the propensity to spend remains unabated. On the other hand, the purpose of inflation control during the war period could be served if the private sectors of the economy increased their propensity to save even though the increased savings were not lent to the government. (2) A borrowing policy is successful as an anti-inflationary device during the war period itself only to the extent that it prevents inflationary pressures from arising; it falls short in this respect to the extent that it merely diverts into the purchase of government securities the residual large volume of private savings that remain after the private sectors have already exerted as much spending pressure as they can in view of the shortage of goods and services and the effectiveness of price ceilings. This is the crucial question here: Did the Treasury borrowing program effectively lower the private propensity to spend during the war, thereby contributing significantly to the success of the OPA price control program? Or was the Treasury program largely ineffective in this respect, with the OPA and allied programs nevertheless succeeding in forcing large amounts of savings, some of which were borrowed by the Treasury?

As mentioned earlier, there was a considerable amount of support during the war for two fiscal devices that would have tended to lower the private propensity to spend, especially for consumption purposes, and to raise the propensity to save. The first was a graduated tax on consumption spending, which would have penalized spending and rewarded saving. The second was compulsory lending of a part of current income to the government. The spendings tax was wholly rejected, and compulsory lending was employed only in conjunction with the excess-profits tax and for a short period in the Victory Tax. Thus the Treasury relied primarily on voluntary loans to cover its wartime deficits. These loans were secured from five principal types of lenders: (1) individuals, (2) nonfinancial business concerns, (3) financial institutions other than the commercial and Federal Reserve banks, (4) commercial banks, and (5) the Federal Reserve banks.

The Treasury considered borrowing from individuals to be the least inflationary of all, for it would "mop up excess purchasing power and reduce the inflationary demand for scarce goods and services," and it would also enable the Treasury to secure the required amount of funds without such extensive recourse to the banking system. Several devices were used to reduce the desire of individuals to spend for consumption as well as to increase their willingness to exchange their money savings for government securities. Publicity materials proclaimed the necessity of saving in order to fight inflation as well as to provide money with which to win the war, and people were constantly reminded of the postwar usefulness of a backlog of savings to protect them from the hardships of unemployment and to enable them to purchase the many things that would then be available. Payroll deduction plans were widely instituted to facilitate purchases of securities and to intercept income before it reached the hands of workers who might otherwise be tempted to spend it. Group competitions and 100 percent clubs were formed to bring informal pressure on people to buy government securities. Attempts were made to create and strengthen the feeling that one should cash his securities during the war only to meet an emergency. The Treasury offered individuals a wide choice of securities, all of which were highly liquid and safe and some of which yielded more than other securities of comparable liquidity and safety. These devices did tend to increase the propensity of individuals to save and to surrender money savings for federal securities. It is difficult, however, to assess the degree of their effectiveness for either purpose or the role that they played in damping inflationary pressures during the war period. Just how much greater would have been the propensity of individuals to spend for consumption during the war period in the absence of these measures? And if the propensity of individuals to save was not much increased by these measures, just how much greater would inflationary pressures have been during the war period itself if people had bought a smaller quantity of the debt and more had been sold to the banks so that people would have held more money and fewer securities? We can not answer these questions, but we shall throw more light on them later.

The Treasury also concentrated on borrowing large amounts from nonfinancial business concerns as the next least inflationary method of borrowing. It succeeded, as is shown by Table 39, and in this way reduced the amount that it had to borrow from the banking system. It is doubtful, however, that Treasury efforts to promote this type of lending had any significant effect on the propensity to spend during the war period itself. To lower private spendings, borrowings from nonfinancial business concerns would have had to (1) decrease the amount of profits distributed to the owners of business—that is, increase business savings; or (2) decrease business spendings for goods and services. I believe that the decision of business concerns to follow conservative dividend policies and to save large amounts during the war was due almost entirely to a desire to accumulate large liquid funds for postwar contingencies and that it was little affected by the Treasury's plea for loans. Moreover, I believe that the low rate of business spending during the war was due not to the Treasury's borrowing campaign but to price ceilings and the limited supply of labor and materials made available for the maintenance and net accumulation of capital goods. In short, it is doubtful that Treasury borrowing from this source either decreased the outpayment of business profits to individuals or reduced business spending during the war. It merely meant that business concerns ended the war with many of their liquid assets in the form of government securities rather than money balances. This may have affected the rate of business spendings after the war but it probably exerted very little anti-inflationary effect during the war period itself.

As a third type of borrowing from nonbank lenders, the Treasury promoted vigorously its campaign to secure loan funds from financial institutions other than the commercial and Federal

Reserve banks. Borrowings from this source could decrease the private propensity to spend during the war only in the following ways: (1) By enlisting the aid of financial institutions in stimulating more saving by individuals and business concerns. It is true that savings banks and others did advertise widely the virtues and patriotic purposes of thrift, but the effectiveness of this campaign is difficult to assess. (2) By causing these institutions to require repayment of loans previously made to private borrowers, which might in some cases lead to a higher rate of private saving. This device seems to have been used very little. (3) By causing financial institutions to be less liberal in making new loans to private borrowers. The campaign to curb lending for "nonessential" private purposes was of some importance in this respect, and its effectiveness was probably enhanced by the availability of income-yielding federal securities. On balance, however, it is doubtful that the Treasury's campaign to secure loans from these financial institutions materially increased the private propensity to save during the war period. Its principal effect was to assure that these institutions would, at the end of the war, hold most of their liquid assets in the form of government securities rather than money balances.

Though the Treasury repeatedly stated that one of its prime objectives was to borrow as much as possible from nonbank lenders and to minimize its recourse to the commercial and Federal Reserve banks, its inability to secure an adequate amount of funds from other sources forced it to borrow heavily from the banking system, most of these funds being supplied through the purchase of governments by the banks themselves, though some of them represented bank loans to others for the purchase of governments. To the extent that this expansion of bank credit exceeded current increases of time and savings deposits at commerical banks and current decreases of other bank loans and investments, it created a corresponding increase of the money supply in the form of currency and checking deposits. This type of borrowing certainly did nothing to curb the private propensity to spend.

Federal Reserve purchases of government securities served not only to increase the money supply in the hands of the public but also to provide additional reserve funds to the commercial banking system. We shall see later that the wartime function of the Federal Reserve was to supply the banking system with all the reserve funds that it needed to absorb the amount of government securities that the Treasury wished to sell to it and to prevent a rise of interest rates. Because the banking system suffered no limitation on its total lending power, Treasury borrowing from the Federal Reserve did not itself exert any limiting effects on the private propensity to spend.

We must conclude that the Treasury borrowing program left much to be desired as an instrument for increasing the propensity to save and for reducing the propensity to spend during the war period itself. Compulsory fiscal devices for this purpose were largely rejected. Congress refused to enact a spending tax, which would have penalized consumption spending and rewarded saving. Compulsory lending to the government was employed only in the excess-profits tax and in the short lived Victory Tax. Compulsory loans on a scale large enough to cover most of the federal deficit might have lowered markedly the propensity to spend, especially for consumption purposes. It is true that some people who were compelled to lend to the government might have maintained their rate of spending by liquidating other assets or by borrowing. This is not, however, a convincing argument against the plan. In the first place, even with this defect the plan would probably have been more effective than voluntary loans in checking private spending. And in the second place, the defect could have been remedied by controls over consumer credit and by making the amount of compulsory lending depend on not only current income but also on the net amount of other assets liquidated during the period. The Treasury's appeal to individuals to save and lend voluntarily to the government probably did increase somewhat the propensity of individuals to save rather than to spend. The campaign to borrow large amounts from nonfinancial business concerns and from financial institutions other than the Federal Reserve and commercial banks was probably largely ineffectual in this respect. Though recognizing that the Treasury's plea to individuals to save and lend did reduce to some extent their propensity to spend, this writer would still ascribe most of the credit for preventing an even greater inflation during the war itself not to the Treasury campaigns to borrow large amounts from nonbank lenders but to the effectiveness of direct wage and price controls buttressed by rationing and other controls over the purchase and use of goods and services. Selective controls over the volume of credit extended to private borrowers also helped, though probably to only a small extent, in holding private spendings in check.

EFFECTS ON THE FORM AND LIQUIDITY OF ASSETS HELD AT THE END OF THE WAR

Of comparable importance were considerations relating to the effect of Treasury borrowing policies on the form and liquidity of the assets that the private sectors of the economy would hold as they entered the postwar period. With most of current private savings attributable to the federal deficit and most of the increase of liquid assets traceable directly or indirectly to the sale of additional government securities, the Treasury was in a position to influence greatly the form and liquidity, as well as the amount, of privately held assets. In this way the Treasury's policy could exert an influence on the postwar behavior of private spendings, employment, output, and prices. If individuals and businesses were permitted to hold their huge wartime savings in a completely liquid form capable of being spent directly or cashed quickly and without penalty, a serious postwar inflation might occur. This danger might be diminished, however, to the extent that wartime savings were exchanged, voluntarily or involuntarily, for illiquid assets which could be cashed only under government control.

The Treasury could reduce the liquidity of assets held by individuals and business concerns at the end of the war in two principal ways: (1) By borrowing from individuals and non-financial business concerns rather than from banks, so that these private sectors would hold government securities rather than an increased supply of money to represent their wartime savings. And (2) by issuing illiquid types of securities that could be cashed only under government control. But how could the Treasury borrow such large amounts from nonbank sources if the potential lenders knew that the government securities would be illiquid? Compulsory lending would have been the only practical solution of this problem. Individuals and business concerns could have been forced to lend to the Treasury enough or nearly enough, to cover wartime deficits, and the Treasury obligations issued to them in exchange for their savings could have been made cashable after the war under conditions consistent with the maintenance of economic stability. This is not to imply that a compulsory lending scheme would have been simple to administer or wholly effective in preventing postwar inflation. Care would have had to be taken to assure that compulsory lending did not unduly injure wartime incentives to produce and earn higher incomes. Individuals whose large wartime savings were frozen might still have felt free to spend for consumption an abnormally large part of their postwar incomes. It might have been difficult to prevent people from borrowing against their frozen wartime savings or from liquidating other assets in order to increase their consumption spendings. There would have been very strong political pressures for a premature release of these funds. And the limitations of economic forecasting would have made it difficult to determine when and at what rate wartime savings should be released. Nevertheless, an adequate compulsory lending program during the war would have enabled the Treasury to borrow much more from nonbank lenders and still to maintain more control over the postwar use of wartime savings.

When the government decided to use compulsory loans to only a very limited extent and to rely almost exclusively on voluntary

loans it threw away its only chance of achieving the double objective of minimizing its recourse to borrowing from the commercial and Federal Reserve banks and of retaining control over the
postwar use of wartime savings. The objective of limiting liquidity
in the postwar period was sacrificed in order to make government
obligations more attractive to buyers. All federal securities issued
during the war were made almost completely liquid; they could
be redeemed or sold whenever their holders wished at prices
which were, in general, at least as high as their original issue price.
A large part of the securities were redeemable on demand, another
sizeable part matured within 90 days, and still another part matured
within a year. And the prices of all the marketable federal debt,
including even the longest-term issues, were supported by the
Federal Reserve at or above the original sale price. Even after all
these concessions, however, nonbank lenders failed by a wide
margin to buy enough securities to cover the federal deficit, so
the Treasury had to borrow large amounts from the Federal Reserve
and commercial banks, thereby enabling the private sectors of the
economy to enter the postwar period with an increased money
supply to represent a large part of their wartime savings. Thus,
reliance on voluntary lending, with the accompanying necessity of
appealing to the lenders' desire for liquidity, meant that the
private sectors of the economy entered the postwar period with a
considerable part of their wartime savings in the form of money
itself which they could spend as and when they wished, and with
their large holdings of government securities practically as liquid
as money. Even the great accumulations of accounts at savings
and loan associations and of time and savings deposits were highly
liquid.

With government securities practically as liquid as money, these
questions arise: "Did the Treasury's wartime campaign to sell
securities to nonbank buyers accomplish anything in holding down
postwar spendings? Were the private sectors of the economy any
less willing to cash their governments and spend than to spend
money balances? Would postwar spendings have been any larger

if the government had borrowed almost exclusively from the banks, so that the increase of private assets would have been largely in the form of money at the end of the war?" It is certainly true that the distinction between money and other liquid assets becomes quite blurred when the latter are made almost completely liquid. Nevertheless, it seems likely that increased individual and business holdings of government securities, even though they are almost as liquid as money, had a somewhat smaller inflationary effect on postwar spendings than would an equal increase in money holdings. In the first place, the inflationary potential inherent in large accumulations of highly liquid governments was not widely understood, so it created less fear of inflation—and perhaps also less fear-inspired spending—than would an equal increase of the money supply. In the second place, many people are probably less likely to cash their governments in order to spend than they are to spend a money balance. Most of us know, if we have been in that happy position, that a sizeable amount of idle money in our pockets or in a checking account is a constant temptation to spend, and that our strongest puritanic resolutions may yield to a whim or to the eloquence of a salesman. But savings represented by a security are less vulnerable. We have a sense that they are "committed" and we are less likely to take the positive action of liquidating them in order to get money to spend. This reluctance to spend may be increased by a vague feeling that it "isn't quite right" to withdraw loans from the government. In the third place, the fact that government securities yield interest whereas money balances do not tends to inhibit the cashing of them in order to spend. The cost of securing money is equal to the interest sacrificed by cashing the government obligation. This is true whether the proceeds are used for consumption, for the purchase of capital goods, or for lending to others. Interest rates might have been even lower and the availability of loan funds to private borrowers even greater in the early postwar period if individuals, corporations, insurance companies, savings banks, and other institutions had held much larger idle money balances and fewer income-yielding government securities.

In view of these considerations it seems likely that the Treasury's wartime campaign to maximize its security sales to nonbank borrowers did, to the extent that it was successful, tend to inhibit somewhat the rise of postwar spendings. The extent of this influence is impossible to estimate, however.

Why did the government fail to adopt compulsory lending during the war? To some extent this was due to a reluctance to use an unfamiliar fiscal device. All the possible objections to compulsory lending were cited: its administrative difficulties, the possible damage to production incentives if a part of income were frozen in government obligations rather than received as currently disposable money income, the hardships that might be imposed on some people by any lending formula, and the difficulties of releasing savings at appropriate times and at an appropriate rate after the war. Moreover, the Treasury seems to have oversold itself on the efficacy of its dramatic voluntary lending program. The failure to adopt compulsory lending was also due in part to the current underestimate of the danger of postwar inflation and of the contribution that a huge stock of privately owned liquid assets could make to that danger. A large supply of highly liquid assets in private hands would be helpful if the end of the war should usher in deflation and unemployment rather than still more inflation, and government officials could not decide which to expect.

INTEREST RATES ON FEDERAL BORROWINGS

For several years before our entrance into the war interest rates in general, and especially short-term rates, had been at very low levels. This was attributable primarily to the combination of a depressed private demand for investable funds and an easy money policy that kept the banks supplied with billions of dollars of excess reserves. Throughout the war period the Treasury maintained interest rates on its obligations close to the low levels prevailing early in 1942. In fact, yields on the longer-term issues showed a slight downward trend during the latter part of the war. In view of the frequent charges that the low-interest policy of the Treasury was an important factor in the inflation it will be useful to look at some of the principal considerations in Treasury policy relative to interest rates.[6]

One of the prime objectives of the Treasury was to keep interest rates at low levels in order to hold down carrying charges on the federal debt. Secretary Morgenthau was happy to report that the average interest rate on the federal debt was less than 2 percent, and pointed to the tax savings effected by this low rate. This cannot, however, be the sole objective of interest-rate policy in wartime. If it were the government should finance its deficits by printing paper money which yields no interest, or by having the central bank purchase all the new obligations and then repay to the Treasury any interest received on them.

Another consideration in interest-rate policy was the effect on private spendings during the war. We are accustomed to the idea that in peacetime an increase of interest rates tends to reduce private spendings and a decrease of interest rates to increase these spendings. But this is not necessarily true in wartime, when private spendings are subject to so many direct controls. Higher interest rates during the war would not have reduced government spending and could have decreased private spendings in only two ways: (1) By inducing larger private savings at each level of national income. It is doubtful that moderately higher interest rates would have been very effective for this purpose. Corporate policy as to savings—undistributed profits and capital consumption allowances—was probably dominated by considerations relating to postwar needs rather than by current interest rates. The effect of interest rates on personal saving is more difficult to assess. Some people might have saved more if rewarded by a higher rate of return, but in general personal decisions relative to saving were

---

[6] At this point we shall deal only with the general level of interest rates and neglect temporarily the more technical problem of the structure of the rates.

probably little affected by the height of interest rates; the propensity of individuals to save would probably have been little greater if rewarded by a return of, say, 4 percent rather than slightly less than 3 percent. The dominant factors in personal decisions as to savings were probably the shortages of desirable consumption goods and services, price ceilings, a patriotic urge to contribute to the winning of the war and to the prevention of inflation, and a desire to accumulate funds to meet future needs and contingencies. (2) By reducing private investment spendings. It is doubtful that private spendings for capital maintenance and accumulation during the war were significantly greater under the policy of low interest rates than they would have been if interest rates had been higher. With the profitability of new investment at very high levels the effective limiting factor on private investment was in most cases not the cost of investable funds, but direct government limitations on capital spendings—price ceilings, allocations of materials, limitations on inventories, and orders preventing or restricting the purchase or use of scarce materials. These were supplemented by pleas to lenders to refuse loans for nonessential purposes. In view of these facts, the Treasury was probably right in asserting that higher interest rates would not have lessened wartime inflationary pressures significantly.[7]

Another related consideration was the effect of interest rates on the willingness to purchase and hold government securities through the end of the war period. Though higher interest rates would probably have increased very little the propensity to save, they might have exerted more of an influence on the willingness of individuals and businesses to exchange their money savings for government securities. The amount of interest paid was not, of course, the only determinant of the willingness to purchase and hold government securities. Also important were appeals to patriotism and the degree of liquidity and safety attached to the governments. The Treasury used these other appeals as a supplement to interest payments, and to some extent perhaps as a substitute for

[7] *Annual Report of the Secretary of the Treasury,* 1945, pp. 413-414.

higher interest rates, to promote the sale of its securities. All were told that lending to the government was a patriotic duty. All the new securities were made highly liquid and safe. A wide variety of securities was offered in order to appeal to the tastes of the various types of investors. Those designed especially for sale to individuals were not only completely safe and liquid but also yielded more than other government securities with the same maturity. These noninterest concessions undoubtedly helped greatly in the sale of securities. But the crucial question is this: "How much could the Treasury have increased its sales to nonbank buyers if in addition to its appeals to patriotism, its issue of a wide variety of securities, and its endowment of all securities with a very high degree of safety and liquidity it had also paid higher interest rates?" A policy of allowing interest rates to move up gradually during the war might actually have reduced total purchases of governments by nonbank lenders, for these lenders might have felt that they would gain more by waiting.[8] On the other hand, if the Treasury had raised the general structure of interest rates to a higher level and then succeeded in the very difficult task of convincing potential buyers that no further increase of rates would occur it might have been able to sell more securities to nonbank buyers. How many more no one can say, but it appears unlikely that a moderate increase of interest rates would have increased nonbank purchases very much.

If the above conclusions are correct, the low-interest policy, as compared with a policy of only moderately higher rates, did not markedly increase wartime inflationary pressures. It did not, to any great extent, lower the private propensity to save, increase private investment spendings, decrease the amount of securities purchased by nonbank lenders, or increase the amount that had to be borrowed from the banking system. Of course, very much higher interest rates might have been somewhat more effective in these respects.

[8] See *Federal Reserve Bulletin,* November, 1943, pp. 1054-1055; Board of Governors *Annual Report,* 1942, p. 9 and 1945, pp. 9-10.

In formulating its wartime interest policy the Treasury also had in mind the level of interest rates that it believed would be appropriate during the postwar period. It did not, of course, want to commit itself to a level of interest rates on its long-term obligations that would be higher than necessary to maintain these securities at or near their par values after the war. On the other hand, difficulties might arise if interest rates on the debt issued during the war should prove to be considerably below the appropriate level of interest rates after the coming of peace. In such a case, the Treasury would either have to bring pressure on the Federal Reserve to prevent interest rates from rising to their appropriate levels; or it would have to refund, in a market characterized by rising interest rates, a very large volume of short-term debt and also, perhaps, many of the nonmarketable issues—such as savings bonds—that nominally had longer maturities but were in effect redeemable on demand. Moreover, the rise of interest rates would, of course, be accompanied by a decline in the prices of the longer-term marketable issues, so the Treasury would either have to refund them at higher interest rates or allow their holders to suffer capital depreciation. Treasury officials appear to have believed that their wartime interest policy was consistent with this objective, for they stated repeatedly that they did not expect a rise of interest rates in the postwar period and that there was no reason to expect a postwar depreciation of government bonds.[9] They contended that continued low interest rates in the postwar period were not only likely but also highly desirable as a stimulus to production and employment. According to Secretary Morgenthau,

After the completion of the transition from war to peace, the continuation of low interest rates will be a definite factor in the stimulation of full employment. This is because those very sectors of the economy which are potentially sensitive to interest rates—housing and producers' expenditures for capital goods—bear just the reverse relationship to the economy in peace as in war. In war, they are small; and they are

[9] See *Annual Reports of the Secretary of the Treasury,* 1944, p. 7; 1945, pp. 5-6, 411-414; 1946, p. 3.

limited in amount, not by interest rates, but by the Spartan necessity of conserving our resources for the war effort. In peace, they must be large in order to insure full employment, and will be larger at low interest rates than at high ones. The benefits of a low-interest policy, therefore, will carry through from the wartime to the peace-time economy.[10]

The accuracy of this forecast as it applies to the early postwar period will be assessed later.

ADAPTATION OF SECURITIES
TO THE NEEDS OF LENDERS

One of the important aspects of borrowing policy most fre-quently mentioned by the Treasury was the issue of a wide variety of securities tailored to meet the needs of the various classes of purchasers.[11] In line with this objective it issued securities with maturities ranging from 90 days to 25 years and bearing yields ranging from 3/8 of 1 percent to 2.9 percent, and it varied widely the terms of redemption of the various issues, though in fact, if not by legal obligation, all were made almost completely liquid and safe. This policy of diversifying its issues offered several ad-vantages to the Treasury itself. (1) It facilitated sales of securities. (2) It increased the chance that purchasers would continue to hold them after the war rather than offer them for sale or redemption. And (3) it enabled the Treasury to offer lower interest rates on a considerable part of its debt while paying more to secure funds that otherwise might not be lent. But this policy also had other purposes. One was to protect the small investor. Secretary Morgen-thau stated,

. . . the Treasury felt—and Congress agreed with us—that the small investor is entitled to more than merely the expectation of a

[10] *Ibid.*, 1945, p. 414. For other similar statements, see *ibid.*, pp. 5.6; 1944, p. 7; 1946, p. 3.

[11] See, for example, *Annual Report of the Secretary of the Treasury*, 1945, pp. 410-412.

stable market after the war. He is entitled to a legal guarantee. This is the reason why our sales appeal to small investors has been confined to savings bonds—which have guaranteed cash redemption values that assure the investor of getting at least his money back.[12]

Another purpose was to insure the continued liquidity of the commercial banking system and to limit its earnings on the monetized debt. To these twin ends banks were forbidden, with some exceptions, to buy securities with a maturity beyond 10 years, and in practice most bank purchases were of shorter maturities.

[12] *Ibid.,* p. 411.

VIII

||||||||||||||||||||||||||||||||||||||||||||||||||||||||||||||||||||||||||||||||||||||||||||||||||||||||||||||||||||||||

Federal Security Issues, 1940-1946

THE preceding chapter brought out some of the most important considerations in federal borrowing policy during the war and emphasized the wide variety of obligations utilized. The purpose of this chapter is to describe the borrowing process in more specific terms—the types of securities offered, the methods used to sell them, the types of buyers appealed to by each type of security, the techniques used to limit bank purchases, and, finally, the composition of the federal debt at the conclusion of the war.

TYPES OF FEDERAL SECURITIES
OFFERED FOR SALE

To cover its deficits the Treasury offered for sale two broad categories of securities: nonmarketable and marketable. The principal nonmarketable securities, which could not be transferred but, with certain limitations, were redeemable on demand at the Treasury or its agencies, included (1) U. S. Savings Bonds, (2) U. S. savings stamps, and (3) Treasury Tax Savings Notes. The principal marketable issues were (1) bills, (2) certificates of indebtedness, (3) notes, and (4) bonds. Each of these will be described briefly.

U.S. SAVINGS BONDS

On May 1, 1941 the Treasury began to sell three series of non-marketable securities which were called at first Defense Savings Bonds and later U. S. Savings Bonds.[1] The most popular of these were the Series E bonds, which were especially designed and promoted for sale to the small individual saver. They could be purchased only by individuals, the amount that could be purchased in any year was limited to $3,750 on the basis of purchase price, and they were issued in denominations of $25, $50, $100, $500, and $1000.[2] They were sold on a discount basis at 75 percent of face value and matured in 10 years. They were, however, redeemable on demand after they had been held 60 days at prices so arranged that their yield would be quite low if cashed soon after purchase, but would rise gradually to 2.9 percent if held to maturity. The yield on marketable 10-year bonds was only about 2 percent. Thus, in line with its objective of protecting the small investor and of borrowing his savings, the Treasury offered him a security that would be completely safe and completely liquid after 60 days and would also give him a yield nearly one and a half times that on marketable bonds of comparable maturity and without a comparable guarantee of safety and liquidity.

Series F bonds were somewhat similar, though slightly less attractive. They too were discount bonds which were sold at 74 percent of their face value and matured in 12 years. They were redeemable on demand at any time after they had been held six months, and the redemption prices were so arranged as to produce yields ranging from 0.45 percent if cashed at the end of a year to 2.53 percent if held to maturity. They were eligible for purchase not only by individuals but also by anyone else except commercial banks, though the combined amount of these and of Series G bonds

---

[1] These replaced similar securities, the Series A-D Bonds, which had been offered for sale between March 1935 and May 1941.

[2] In June 1944 a $10 denomination was authorized for sale only to the armed forces, and in October 1945 a $200 denomination was authorized. Sales of these were very small, however.

that might be purchased in any year was limited to $100,000.[3] They were issued in denominations ranging from $100 to $10,000.

We have seen that the Series E and F bonds were discount bonds which yielded income only when redeemed. It was believed, however, that some buyers preferred securities paying a current income, so Series G bonds were offered. These were the same as Series F bonds as to eligibility for purchase, limitations on annual purchase, denominations, maturity, and redeemability, but they were sold at par value and paid 2.5 percent interest currently. In order to reduce this yield if cashed before maturity they were redeemable

TABLE 40.   U. S. Savings Bonds Outstanding, 1941-1946
(In millions of dollars)[4]

June 30	Total Amt. Outstanding	Increase During Year Ending	Series E Amt. Outstanding	Increase During Year Ending	Series F Amt. Outstanding	Increase During Year Ending	Series G Amt. Outstanding	Increase During Year Ending
1941	$ 664	$ 664	$ 203	$ 203	$ 67	$ 67	$ 394	$ 394
1942	6,584	5,920	3,671	3,468	499	432	2,414	2,020
1943	17,648	11,064	11,287	7,618	1,242	743	5,119	2,705
1944	30,981	13,333	21,125	9,838	1,996	754	7,861	2,742
1945	42,000	11,019	29,097	7,972	2,604	608	10,299	2,368
1946	45,670	3,670	30,358	1,261	2,895	291	12,416	2,117

on earlier dates at prices somewhat below their par value, though the sum of redemption price plus interest received would always equal or exceed the purchase price.

In summary, in order to appeal to individuals and other smaller nonbank investors the Treasury offered these U. S. Savings Bonds, which, though nonmarketable, were redeemable on demand after an initial period, were thereafter completely liquid, and yielded significantly more than marketable bonds of comparable maturity. As shown in Table 40, the amount of these bonds outstanding had risen to $45.7 billion by June 1946. Of these, 66.5 percent were Series E, 27.2 percent Series G, and only 6.3 percent Series F.

[3] During 1941 the limitation was $50,000. It will be seen later that under certain limitations commercial banks were permitted to acquire the F and G Series.
[4] SOURCE: *Treasury Bulletin,* February, 1947, pp. 36-37.

It will be noted that sales of these securities started slowly, rose to a peak later in the war as the rate of private savings rose, and then receded as the war ended. Table 41 suggests that Series F and G bonds were purchased largely by individuals in the well-to-do group and by businesses and eligible financial institutions, for 60 percent of their sales were in denominations of $5000 and $10,000, and 90 percent were in denominations of $1000 or more. Individuals in the lower income groups bought

TABLE 41.   Percentage Distribution of U. S. Savings Bond Sales by Denominations, May 1, 1941–June 30, 1946[5]

Denomination	Series E	Series F and G
$ 10	0.3	—
25	32.7	0.1
50	13.6	—
100	20.6	3.0
200	0.5	—
500	12.3	6.8
1,000	20.0	29.8
5,000	—	19.1
10,000	—	41.2
Total	100.0	100.0
Total sold (millions)	$42,113	$16,334

more of the Series E, as is suggested by the fact that 33 percent of the sales were in denominations of $25 or less and 67 percent were in denominations of $100 or less. Nevertheless, nearly a third of the purchases of Series E bonds were in denominations of more than $100 and many of these must have been by higher-income individuals.

The Treasury utilized fully the modern techniques of selling and advertising to promote sales of these securities. They were not only included in the big war loan drives but were also kept on sale and promoted vigorously at all times. Issuing and selling agencies were established everywhere. For example, in June 1943 there were 51,150 qualified issuing agents, including 15,342

[5] SOURCE: *Ibid.*, August, 1946, p. 40.

commercial and savings banks, 3,684 building and loan associations, 2,753 credit unions, 9,240 other corporations, and 20,140 postoffices. In addition, hundreds of thousands of volunteer workers peddled savings bonds in offices, plants, theaters, street corners, and elsewhere. Payroll savings plans were widely instituted and various sorts of informal pressure were applied to employees to permit at least 10 percent of their pay to be withheld for savings bond purchases. In mid-1944 there were 27,600,000 participants in these plans, with monthly purchases of $540 million, equal to 10.6 percent of the pay of those participating.[6] These selling methods were supplemented by advertising appeals, pleas by movie and radio stars, and so on. People were asked not only to buy these securities, but also to hold them unless money was urgently needed. That these pleas were less than wholly successful is suggested by Table 42. The redemption rate was highest for Series E bonds. Though many of the redemptions were necessary to meet urgent financial needs of bondholders, many more of them probably were not.

U.S. SAVINGS STAMPS

Another type of redeemable nonmarketable security issued to secure money from people of small means, including children, were U. S. savings stamps. These were issued in denominations ranging from 10¢ to $5. Though the amount of them outstanding never rose above $214 million they were a useful method of enabling low-income groups to accumulate sums large enough to purchase savings bonds. Their sales aggregated $1.7 billion during the war, and more than 75 percent of this amount was exchanged for savings bonds.

TREASURY TAX SAVINGS NOTES

The other principal type of nonmarketable securities offered by the Treasury was its tax savings notes, which were first sold

[6] *Annual Report of the Secretary of the Treasury,* 1945, p. 55.

TABLE 42. Sales and Redemptions of U. S. Savings Bonds, 1941-1946
(In millions of dollars)[7]

Fiscal Year Ending June 30	Total			Series E			Series F			Series G		
	Sales	Redemptions	Redemptions as Percentage of Sales	Sales	Redemptions	Redemptions as Percentage of Sales	Sales	Redemptions	Redemptions as Percentage of Sales	Sales	Redemptions	Redemptions as Percentage of Sales
1941	$ 664	1	—	$ 203	—	—	$ 67	—	—	$ 395	1	—
1942	5,993	75	0.1	3,526	60	0.2	435	3	—	2,032	12	0.6
1943	11,789	760	6.4	8,271	689	8.3	758	17	2.2	2,759	55	2.0
1944	15,498	2,292	14.8	11,820	2,100	17.8	802	58	7.2	2,876	134	4.7
1945	14,891	4,156	27.9	11,553	3,846	33.3	679	89	13.1	2,658	220	8.3
1946	9,612	6,408	66.7	6,739	5,912	87.7	407	149	36.6	2,465	348	14.1

[7] SOURCE: Treasury Bulletin, February, 1947, pp. 36-37.

in August 1941. These issues had three principal purposes: (1) to supply the Treasury with money in advance of tax collections; (2) to provide a convenient method for individuals and business concerns to save in order to meet future tax payments—an objective of some importance to individuals before the enactment of the Current Tax Payments Act of 1943; and (3) to absorb funds that might otherwise create inflationary pressures. Though the various issues differed somewhat they had the following general

TABLE 43. Treasury Notes—Tax and Savings Series, 1941-1946
(In millions of dollars)[8]

June 30	Amount Outstanding	Change During Fiscal Year Ending
1941	$ 0	$ —
1942	3,015	3,015
1943	7,495	4,480
1944	9,557	2,062
1945	10,136	579
1946	6,711	−3,425

characteristics: they were nonmarketable, they matured in not more than three years, their yield if held to maturity was a little more than 1 percent, they were acceptable at par plus accrued interest in payment of taxes, and they were redeemable in cash at their purchase price.[9] Table 43 shows the amounts of these notes outstanding on various dates. The great bulk of them was purchased by business concerns, mostly by corporations.

Let us now turn our attention to the principal marketable issues —those that could be freely bought and sold but that carried no legal obligation by the Treasury to redeem them before their maturity dates.

[8] SOURCE: *Treasury Bulletin*, February, 1947, p. 20.
[9] There were three series of these notes. Series A and B were on sale from August 1, 1941 to June 22, 1943. For a description of these, see *Annual Report of the Secretary of the Treasury*, 1942, pp. 207-212. Series C Notes were first offered on September 14, 1942. For a description of these, see *ibid.*, 1943, pp. 298-307.

TREASURY BILLS

Treasury bills are three-month obligations sold on a discount basis. Yields on these bills were at very low levels in 1940 and 1941 as banks held several billions of excess reserves, but they were allowed to rise somewhat until early 1942 when they were stabilized at ⅜ of 1 percent, at which level they continued through the end of the war. Small quantities of these low-yield securities were purchased by well-to-do individuals, but their principal purchasers were, in the order of their importance, the Federal

TABLE 44.   Treasury Bills Outstanding, 1940-1946
(In millions of dollars)[10]

June 30	Amount Outstanding	Net increase or decrease (−) During Year Ending
1940	$ 1,302	
1941	1,603	$ 301
1942	2,508	905
1943	11,864	9,358
1944	14,734	2,870
1945	17,041	2,307
1946	17,039	−2

Reserve banks, commercial banks, and other business concerns. Unlike most other marketable securities, they were on almost continuous sale with large offerings every week. Table 44 shows the large extent to which these shortest-term obligations were used. The Treasury liked them because their interest rate was so low, and they appealed to some investors, mostly institutional, who were willing to accept low yields in order to secure the highest degree of liquidity and safety.

CERTIFICATES OF INDEBTEDNESS

These securities, whose maturity is limited to one year, had not been used since 1934 but were again issued after March

[10] SOURCE: *Annual Report of the Secretary of the Treasury, 1946*, p. 457.

1942. They are not discount securities but are sold at par plus any accrued interest, and interest on them is paid at the time of their maturity. The first issue yielded ½ of 1 percent, but with subsequent issues the rate was raised to ⅞ of 1 percent, at which level it was stabilized through the end of the war. Like the bills, these securities did not appeal primarily to individuals, but to banks, other financial institutions, and businesses. The large amounts of these short-term securities employed by the Treasury are indicated in Table 45.

TABLE 45.   Certificates of Indebtedness Outstanding, 1941-1946
(In millions of dollars)[11]

June 30	Amount Outstanding	Net Increase During Year Ending
1941	$ 0	$ —
1942	3,096	3,096
1943	16,561	13,465
1944	28,822	12,261
1945	34,136	5,314
1946	34,804	668

TREASURY NOTES

These securities mature in from one to five years after issue and are sold at par plus any accrued interest. Interest rates on them during the war ranged from about 0.90 percent on those with maturities of slightly more than a year to 1.25 percent on those maturing in about three years, and to 1.5 percent on those maturing in about five years. The amounts of these securities outstanding on various dates are shown in Table 46.

[11] SOURCE: *Ibid*. Neither the statistics nor the discussion includes small amounts of one- to seven-day certificates issued by the Treasury to the Federal Reserve banks to secure temporary funds to be used while other funds were being collected.

TABLE 46.   Treasury Notes Outstanding, 1940-1946
(In millions of dollars)[12]

June 30	Amount Outstanding	Net Increase or Decrease (−) During Year Ending
1940	$ 6,383	$ —
1941	5,698	− 685
1942	6,689	991
1943	9,168	2,479
1944	17,405	8,237
1945	23,497	6,092
1946	18,261	−5,236

TREASURY MARKETABLE BONDS

The longer-term issues were Treasury bonds. The maturities of these issues were all more than 5 years and most of them ranged from 10 to 25 years. They were sold at par plus any accrued interest, and the interest rate carried by them varied with their maturity. For example, those maturing in 10 years and callable in 8 years by the Treasury bore coupon rates of 2 percent; those maturing in 15 years and callable in 12 years bore 2¼ percent coupon rates; and those maturing in 25 years and

TABLE 47.   Treasury Marketable Bonds Outstanding, 1940-1946
(In millions of dollars)[13]

June 30	Amount Outstanding	Net Increase During Year Ending
1940	$ 26,555	$ —
1941	30,215	3,690
1942	38,085	7,870
1943	57,520	19,435
1944	79,244	21,724
1945	106,448	27,204
1946	119,323	12,875

[12] SOURCE: *Ibid.*
[13] SOURCE: *Ibid.* These figures do not include small amounts of Panama Canal Bonds, Conversion Bonds of 1946-1947, and Postal Savings Bonds.

TABLE 48. The Federal Debt in the Form of Interest-Bearing Public Issues, 1940-1946
(In millions of dollars)[14]

Type of Security	June 30, 1940		June 30, 1946		Net Increase June 30, 1940 to June 30, 1946	
	Amount	% of Total	Amount	% of Total	Amount	% of Total Increase
Nonmarketable, total	$ 3,166	8.4	$ 56,173	22.9	$ 53,007	25.5
U. S. Savings bonds	2,905	7.7	49,035	20.0	46,130	22.2
Treasury Notes— tax and savings series	0	0	6,711	2.7	6,711	3.2
Other	261	0.7	427	0.2	166	0.1
Marketable, total	34,436	91.6	189,606	77.1	155,170	74.5
Treasury bills	1,302	3.5	17,039	6.9	15,737	7.6
Certificates of indebtedness	0	0	34,804	14.2	34,804	16.7
Treasury notes	6,383	17.0	18,261	7.4	11,878	5.7
Treasury bonds[a]	26,752	71.1	119,503	48.6	92,751	44.5
Grand total	$37,602	100.0	$245,779	100.0	$208,177	100.0

a This includes, in addition to the amounts listed under "Treasury bonds" in the source table, small amounts of other bond obligations of the U. S.
14 SOURCE: *Annual Report of the Secretary of the Treasury*, 1946, p. 457.

callable in 20 years bore coupon rates of 2½ percent. The highest rate borne by any marketable bond issued during the war was 2½ percent. Table 47 shows the amounts of bonds outstanding at various times during the period.

COMPOSITION OF THE FEDERAL DEBT IN MID-1946

Having looked briefly at the principal types of securities offered by the Treasury during the war, let us now turn our attention to the composition of the debt at the end of the war and to some

TABLE 49. Distribution of the Marketable Federal Debt by Maturities, June 30, 1946
(In millions of dollars)[15]

	Amount	Percent of Total
Treasury bills	$ 17,039	9.0
Certificates of indebtedness	34,804	18.4
Treasury notes and bonds due or callable		
Within 1 year	10,119	5.3
Between 1 and 5 years	35,055	18.5
Between 5 and 10 years	32,847	17.2
Between 10 and 20 years	37,189	19.6
After 20 years	22,372	11.8
	$189,649	100.0

of its implications. Table 48 supplies information relevant to the interest-bearing public issues.[16] One of the striking facts brought out by the table is the heavy reliance on nonmarketable securities which were not transferable and were nominally not short-term but which were in fact redeemable on demand at

[15] SOURCE: *Federal Reserve Bulletin*, February, 1949, p. 162. These figures include guaranteed as well as marketable debt.

[16] We are neglecting here some components of the total federal debt (1) Special issues, which amounted to $4.8 billion in June 1940 and $22.3 billion in June 1946. These were all held in U. S. Government agencies and trust funds. (2) Securities guaranteed by the federal government. These declined in amount during the war. (3) Noninterest bearing debt, which was quite small.

guaranteed prices at or above their original sale price. These rose during the six years from 8.4 to 22.9 percent of the total debt and accounted for 25.5 percent of the total increase. Another important fact is the heavy reliance on issues with short maturities. In 1940 only 8.4 percent of the total debt was in nonmarketable securities which were redeemable on demand, and only 3.5 percent was in securities with an original maturity of less than a year; 71.1 percent was in marketable bonds. By June 1946, however, the debt was 22.9 percent in nonmarketable bonds redeemable on demand, 21.1 percent in Treasury bills and certificates, 7.4 percent in Treasury notes, and only 48.6 percent in Treasury

TABLE 50.   Interest Rates on Federal Marketable Securities Issued
During the War

Type of Security	Maturity	Interest Rates
Treasury bills	3 months	⅜ of 1%
Certificates of indebtedness	not over 1 year	⅞ of 1%
Treasury notes	1 to 5 years	0.90% to 1½%
Treasury bonds	10 years	2%
	15 years	2¼%
	25 years	2½%

bonds. The maturities of the marketable debt are shown more clearly in Table 49. Nearly $62 billion of these securities were due or callable within a year, and if the redeemable nonmarketable issues are included the total is raised to $118.1 billion.

The Treasury policy of issuing such large amounts of "floating debt" had some severe critics who believed that more of it should be "funded" into long-term obligations on which payment could not be demanded until their maturity. The Treasury answered its critics with several arguments. (1) The issue of short-term marketable obligations decreased interest charges on the federal debt. This is shown clearly in Table 50. The interest cost on the longest-term marketable bonds was 6.6 times that on Treasury bills and 2.9 times that on certificates of indebtedness. The decline of the average interest rate on the public debt from about 2.5 percent in 1940 to less than 2 percent in 1946 was due more to the shift toward shorter maturities than to a decline in the interest rates applicable to each maturity. (2) To protect their liquidity commercial banks should buy principally the shorter-term issues. Moreover, banks were not entitled to high interest rates on governments, for in general they paid for them by creating deposits.[17] (3) Small individual holders are entitled to the guarantee of safety and liquidity afforded by nonmarketable but redeemable issues.[18] And, of course, such securities were easier to sell to individual investors. (4) Highly liquid short-term and redeemable securities will serve a very useful purpose in the reconversion period, for they can be liquidated in an orderly manner to secure the money needed at that time for business and personal spending.[19] (5) The idea that the government should "fund" its debt by issuing most of it in the form of long-term obligations and then sit idly by regardless of fluctuations in the market prices of these securities is false. A private debtor, whose obligations make up only a small part of total debt and who is not charged with responsibility for general credit conditions, may properly do this. But the government, whose debt is a major part of the total and who has a high degree of responsibility for conditions in the entire credit market, cannot properly wash its hands of developments after its securities are issued. It must bear in mind the fact that

. . . the time which the original purchaser of a security will hold it will depend principally upon his own future needs and convenience, and to a very minor extent upon the nominal maturity of the security. The indiscriminate issuance of long-term securities to all classes of investors would not insure their being held to maturity by their original purchasers, but would result merely in premature market liquidation. . . . The funding of a major part of the short-term debt into longer-term securities . . . would serve merely to increase the

---

[17] *Annual Report of the Secretary of the Treasury*, 1943, p. 392.

[18] *Ibid.*, 1943, p. 6, and 1945, p. 411.

[19] *Ibid.*, 1944, p. 8.

interest cost to the Government and to shift the risk of future changes in interest rates (and corresponding movements, in the opposite direction, of bond prices) from the Government to private investors. Such a policy would increase, rather than reduce, the factors making for instability in the post-war economy, as the Government is in a better position to bear the risk of changes in interest rates than most classes of investors, and—unlike any class of investors—is also in a position to minimize it.[20]

It was considered wiser policy, therefore, to issue short-term or redeemable securities to those types of purchasers who were not likely to continue to hold government debt for a long period. Several related advantages were claimed for this policy. It would contribute to liquidity in the postwar period; it would reduce the possibility of panicky liquidations and in general reduce the instability of the prices of both government and private obligations, which can adversely affect not only security holders but also private firms attempting to raise money for investment purposes; and it would enable the government to refund its short-term and redeemable obligations in the future by issuing securities well adapted to prevailing conditions in the money markets.[21]

The above argument is very revealing, not only as a justification of such a large volume of "floating" federal debt, but also as an indication that even during the war the Treasury was thinking of "maintaining an orderly market" for all federal obligations in the postwar period. We shall see later that during the war all marketable federal securities—the longest-term as well as the shortest-term—were in fact redeemable on demand, for the Federal Reserve stood ready to buy them at or above their issue prices. This policy continued during the postwar period, though with some modifications after mid-1947. The implications of such a policy will be considered in some detail in a later chapter, but one major point should be emphasized here: All federal securities issued during the war were *de facto* redeemable on

[20] *Ibid.*, 1944, pp. 7-9.
[21] *Ibid.* See also *Annual Reports of the Secretary of the Treasury*, 1943, p. 7 and 1945, pp. 411-412.

demand by either the Treasury or the Federal Reserve. The Treasury legally contracted to redeem on demand all nonmarketable issues after they had been held a short time. And as a matter of policy, though not of legal contract or obligation, the Federal Reserve purchased at support prices at least equal to their issue prices all Treasury bills, certificates, notes, and marketable bonds that other buyers were unwilling to hold. So long as this arrangement between the Treasury and the Federal Reserve continued, even the longest-term governments were payable on demand and did not protect the government as a whole, including the Federal Reserve, against large demands for repayment. Under such a policy the issue of nominally short-term rather than nominally long-term securities increased the danger to the government as a whole only to the extent that yields on the short-term issues were lower and that these lower yields decreased the willingness of the public to hold governments.

METHODS USED TO SELL
GOVERNMENT SECURITIES

Let us now look briefly at some of the most important aspects of the selling methods employed by the Treasury. We have already noted that the principal nonmarketable securities—savings bonds and tax saving notes—were kept on continuous sale and promoted vigorously at all times as well as being included in the big war loan drives. Treasury bills were offered weekly throughout the war period, and certificates of indebtedness at somewhat less frequent intervals. Marketable bonds were also offered almost continuously up to November 1942, but by that time the Treasury had become dissatisfied with this program, for it felt that too large a proportion of its funds was coming from commercial banks. It therefore made plans for a series of major war loan drives, of which there were eight between November 1942 and the end of 1945. The techniques employed in these drives varied somewhat, but in general they were as follows: (1) A complex nationwide organization was set up to promote sales during the drives. This included not only members of the Treasury, but also the Board of Governors of the Federal Reserve System, the Federal Reserve banks, commercial banks, and representatives of many other organizations. (2) Sales goals were set by types of securities, by types of purchasers, and by geographic areas, and vigorous attempts were made to reach or surpass these goals. (3) Each of the earlier drives lasted for three or four weeks and each of the later drives for six or seven weeks, though the counting period for sales of nonmarketable issues was somewhat longer.

TABLE 51.   Dates of the Eight War Loan Drives[22]

Loan	Formal Period of the Drive (Sales period for marketable issues)	Counting Period of the Drive (Sales period for nonmarketable issues)
First	Nov. 30–Dec. 23, 1942	Dec. 1–Dec. 31, 1942
Second	Apr. 12–May 1, 1942	Apr. 1–May 8, 1942
Third	Sept. 9–Oct. 2, 1943	Sept. 1–Oct. 16, 1943
Fourth	Jan. 18–Feb. 15, 1944	Jan. 1–Feb. 29, 1944
Fifth	June 12–July 8, 1944	June 1–July 31, 1944
Sixth	Nov. 20–Dec. 16, 1944	Nov. 1–Dec. 31, 1944[a]
Seventh	May 14–June 30, 1945[b]	Apr. 9–July 7, 1945[a]
Victory	Oct. 29–Dec. 8, 1945[b]	Oct. 29–Dec. 31, 1945

[a] The final dates for processing these subscriptions were extended to January 2, 1945 in the sixth loan, and to July 9, 1945 in the seventh loan.
[b] These represent the periods for individuals only. The periods for other eligible investors were somewhat shorter, running from June 18 through June 30, 1945 in the seventh loan, and from December 3 through December 8, 1945 in the Victory loan.

(See Table 51.) (4) The drives included a wide variety of securities, as is shown in Table 52. Every drive included all the nonmarketable issues, certificates of indebtedness, and the longest-term 2½ percent marketable bonds. Each drive also included some other issue of shorter-term bonds. Treasury bills were included only in the first two drives, and Treasury notes only in the fifth and sixth. It is worth noting that of the total sales during these drives 27.4 percent were of nonmarketable issues, and nearly 47 percent were of marketable bonds; sales of the nominally shorter-term bills,

[22] SOURCE: *Annual Report of the Secretary of the Treasury*, 1946, p. 507.

TABLE 52. Securities Sold in the Eight War Loan Drives
(In billions of dollars)[23]

	1st	2nd	3rd	4th	5th	6th	7th	Victory Loan	Total	Sales of Each Type of Security as % of Total Sales of All Securities in the Eight Drives
Nonmarketable, total	$ 2.3	$ 3.8	$ 5.8	$ 6.4	$ 6.4	$ 6.0	$ 7.7	$ 4.5	$ 43.0	27.4
Series E savings bonds	0.7	1.5	2.5	3.2	3.0	2.9	4.0	2.2	19.9	12.7
Series F and G savings bonds	0.3	0.7	0.8	1.0	0.8	0.7	1.0	0.7	6.0	3.8
Tax Savings Notes	1.3	1.7	2.5	2.2	2.6	2.4	2.7	1.7	17.1	10.9
Marketable, total	10.6	14.8	13.1	10.3	14.2	15.6	18.6	16.6	113.8	72.6
Treasury bills	0.9	0.8							1.7	1.1
Certificates	3.8	5.3	4.1	5.0	4.8	4.4	4.8	3.7	35.9	22.9
Notes					1.9	1.6			3.5	2.2
Bonds, with interest @ 1½%							1.7		1.7	1.1
" @ 1¾%	3.1								3.1	2.0
" @ 2 %		4.9	5.3		5.2	6.9			22.4	14.3
" @ 2¼%				3.4			5.1	3.0	11.5	7.4
" @ 2½%	2.8	3.8	3.8	1.9	2.3	2.7	7.1	9.8	34.2	21.8
Grand total	$12.9	$18.6	$18.9	$16.7	$20.6	$21.6	$26.3	$21.1	$156.9	100.0

[23] SOURCE: *Treasury Bulletin*, February, 1946, pp. 19-20.

certificates, and notes accounted for 26 percent of the total. (5) Sales efforts during these drives were, in general, concentrated on nonbank investors, and especially on individuals. To this end, individual quotas were fixed at what was considered high levels, and in several of the drives the period for individual subscriptions was longer than that for other eligible investors. Nevertheless, as shown in Table 53, individuals accounted for only 27.6 per-

TABLE 53. Percentage Distribution of Purchases During the Eight War Loan Drives, by Class of Purchaser[24]

Loan	Total	Individuals	Corporations and Other Investors	Commercial Banks[a]
First	100.0	12.3	48.4	39.3
Second	100.0	17.7	54.9	27.4
Third	100.0	28.4	71.6	
Fourth	100.0	31.7	68.3	
Fifth	100.0	30.8	69.2	
Sixth	100.0	27.2	72.8	
Seventh	100.0	33.0	67.0	
Victory	100.0	32.0	68.0	
Total for eight loans	100.0	27.6	65.9	6.5

[a] Commercial banks were limited to purchases of approximately $5 billion in each of the first two loans and were excluded from direct participation in later drives.

cent of total subscriptions during the eight drives. (6) Efforts were made to limit commercial bank purchases. This point will be considered in some detail in the following section.

LIMITATION OF COMMERCIAL BANK PARTICIPATION IN LOANS TO THE TREASURY

The Treasury faced a difficult problem in determining the relationship of commercial banks to its borrowing program. On the

[24] SOURCE: *Ibid.,* February, 1946, p. 9. For a more complete breakdown of purchases by class of investor and by type of security purchased, see *ibid.,* pp. 19-20.

one hand, it repeatedly stated that one of its major objectives was to borrow as much as possible from nonbank lenders and to borrow from banks only on a residual basis; it did not want banks to provide any funds that could be secured from others. On the other hand, it knew that it would have to borrow very large amounts from the banks and it wanted to secure these funds at low interest rates. To achieve both of these objectives through general credit policy was almost impossible. A restrictive Federal Reserve policy that would limit the total lending power of the commercial banks would promote the first objective but endanger the second. A liberal Federal Reserve policy of supplying the banks with a very large volume of reserves at little or no cost to them would promote the second objective but endanger the first. The Treasury attempted in the following ways to achieve both objectives simultaneously. (1) To insure that it would be able to borrow the necessary amounts from commercial banks at very low interest rates it secured the coöperation of the Federal Reserve in keeping the commercial banking system more than amply supplied with lending power. (2) At the same time, it applied several direct limitations on commercial bank purchases of governments and on commercial bank loans to other purchasers of governments. The next chapter will describe the various measures adopted to assure an almost unlimited ability of the commercial banks to lend at low interest rates. Only the direct limitations placed on commercial bank purchases of governments and on bank loans to others on the basis of governments will be discussed here.

LIMITATIONS ON COMMERCIAL BANK LOANS ON GOVERNMENT SECURITIES

During World War I very large amounts of money were created through commercial bank loans to other purchasers of government securities. All investors were implored to buy governments with borrowed funds as well as with their own savings, and

banks were encouraged to make loans for this purpose. During
World War II the Treasury viewed this type of lending with less
favor. It still wanted banks to lend to "legitimate" investors who
could pay for their governments within a short period, but it did
not want an "excessive" expansion of bank credit for this purpose,
and it wished to discourage "free riders" who bought securities
only for the purpose of selling them shortly thereafter at a profit.
The guiding principle for these loans was jointly announced by
all bank supervisory authorities on November 22, 1942:

> In connection with Government financing, individual subscribers
> relying upon anticipated income may wish to augment their subscrip-
> tion by temporary borrowings from banks. Such loans will not be
> subject to criticism but should be on a short-term or amortization basis
> fully repayable within periods not exceeding six months.[25]

No adequate statistics as to the volume of bank loans on governments are available, but total bank loans to others than brokers
and dealers for the purchasing or carrying of securities increased
nearly $3 billion between 1941 and the end of 1945. Some banks
appear to have violated the official principle applying to these
loans. They did not conscientiously refuse loans to speculators,
and in some cases they lent to buyers with an understanding that
the banks themselves would later, when they became eligible,
acquire the securities at a price which would yield a profit to
the speculator.

LIMITATIONS ON BANK PURCHASES
OF GOVERNMENT SECURITIES

The Treasury employed two general methods of limiting commercial bank purchases of governments. The first was to issue
certain types of securities which were ineligible for commercial
bank purchase. These banks were not permitted to hold any Series
E bonds, and with small exceptions they could not acquire Series

[25] *Federal Reserve Bulletin,* December, 1942, p. 1174.

F and G bonds or marketable bonds with maturities exceeding 10 years and with interest rates in excess of 2 percent. The only exception was that during three of the war loan drives commercial banks were allowed to subscribe to Series F and G bonds and to the longer-term marketable bonds in a limited amount based on the volume of their time and savings deposits. Under these exceptions banks acquired about $1.8 billion of bank-restricted marketable bonds and small amounts of Series F and G bonds. This policy of issuing bank-restricted securities had a multiple purpose: to limit total bank purchases of governments, to prevent banks from taking advantage of the higher interest rates offered to induce other types of investors to lend to the government, to facilitate Treasury borrowing from the banks at low rates of interest, and to preserve the liquidity of the banking system.

The second method of limitation was to restrict bank purchases of newly-issued securities, even though the securities were eligible for holding by banks, by limiting the amount that banks could purchase at the time of issue, by giving preference to subscriptions by nonbank buyers, or by outright prohibition of bank purchases at the time of issue. This policy evolved slowly. In late 1941 and early 1942 bank subscriptions to certain issues were limited to 50 percent of their combined capital and surplus. During each of the first two war loan drives banks were permitted to subscribe to certain issues, but their subscriptions were limited to $5 billion in each drive. In each of the subsequent war loan drives banks were prohibited from subscribing during the drive itself to any of the securities included in the drive except to the limited extent noted above. In this way the Treasury could insure that the securities included in the drive would in the first instance be purchased by nonbank subscribers, though the banks could, of course, acquire the bank-eligible issues after a drive was over.

It is impossible to evaluate accurately the success of these measures in maximizing the amount of securities bought and held by nonbank investors and in minimizing the net increase of

TABLE 54. Outstanding Marketable Governments Eligible for Commercial Bank Purchase and Actual Commercial Bank Holdings, 1941-1946

(In millions of dollars)[26]

June 30	Outstanding Issues of Marketable Governments (Direct and Fully Guaranteed)	*Less:* Bank Restricted Issues	*Equals:* Outstanding Marketable Governments Eligible for Commercial Bank Purchase	*Less:* Holdings of Bank-Eligible Issues by the Federal Reserve and U. S. Govt. Agencies and Trust Funds	*Equals:* Eligible Securities Available for Commercial Bank Purchase	*Less:* Actual Commercial Bank Holdings	*Equals:* Excess of Available Eligible Securities Over Actual Amount Held by Commercial Banks
1941	$ 44,073	$ 0	$ 44,073	$ 4,332	$ 39,741	$19,700	$20,241
1942	55,122	882	54,240	4,591	49,649	26,000	23,649
1943	99,403	8,711	90,692	9,331	81,361	52,200	29,161
1944	141,917	21,161	120,756	16,784	103,972	68,400	35,572
1945	181,728	36,756	144,972	23,771	121,201	84,200	37,001
1946	190,073	53,459	136,614	25,377	111,237	84,400	26,837

[26] Computed by the writer from tables in various *Treasury Bulletins* and *Annual Reports of the Secretary of the Treasury*. These figures understate somewhat the additional securities eligible for bank purchase, for the last column is computed by subtracting total commercial bank holdings of governments from the available bank-eligible marketable issues, and the banks in fact held some nonmarketable issues and some bank-restricted marketable issues. These probably amounted, in late 1945 and early 1946, to about $2 billion.

bank holdings, for we do not know to what extent bank competition for securities decreased the amounts held by others. It is clear, however, that these devices were far from perfect as limitations on total bank acquisitions. In the first place, the issue of bank-restricted securities did not place an inflexible limit on total bank purchases, for the amount of outstanding bank-eligible issues far exceeded actual bank holdings. This is shown in Table 54. And in the second place, the limitation or prohibition of bank purchases of new issues did not prevent banks from increasing their total holdings of governments either during the time that new issues were being sold or after the sales had been made. Banks purchased older issues even during the periods in which war loan drives were occurring, and after the drives had been completed they purchased some of the issues from other types of holders. The Treasury found it necessary to ask the coöperation of banks "in declining to make loans for the purpose of acquiring the drive securities later for your own account . . . and in declining to purchase outstanding securities from nonbank investors on the understanding or condition that a subscription for a substantially like amount of Treasury securities offered during the drive will be made through your bank. . . ."[27]

In view of the limited effectiveness of the measures actually employed, it appears that the Treasury probably should have placed stricter limitations on the types and amounts of securities eligible for bank acquisition. For example, in coöperation with the banking authorities it could have forbidden banks to increase their holdings of the regular public issues above the levels of some base date and provided that any additional acquisitions would have to be in the form of special issues available only for holding by the banks. Then by pushing to the utmost its sales of regular issues to nonbank buyers and by issuing only the minimum required amounts of special bank-eligible obligations the Treasury could indeed have assured that it was borrowing from the banks on only a residual basis.

[27] *Annual Report of the Secretary of the Treasury,* 1945, p. 327.

TYPES OF GOVERNMENT SECURITIES HELD BY VARIOUS TYPES OF INVESTORS

We have already seen that one of the major aspects of the Treasury's borrowing policy was to issue a wide variety of securities tailored to meet the needs of the various classes of investors. It is therefore worthwhile to look briefly at the types of investors to whom the various securities appealed. Let us consider first the

TABLE 55.   Type and Maturity Distribution of Marketable Governments Held by the Principal Types of Investors, June 30, 1946[28]

Security	Federal Reserve Banks	Commercial Banks	Mutual Savings Banks	Insurance Companies	Others
Treasury bills	60.8	1.5	0.1	0.1	3.0
Certificates	28.7	21.8	2.2	2.4	22.3
Bonds and notes due or					
callable within 1 year	6.0	7.4	1.0	2.0	5.2
in 1-5 years	3.4	33.0	6.3	6.2	13.5
in 5-10 years	0.6	28.7	14.3	11.6	12.0
in 10-20 years	0.3	4.3	53.7	51.7	25.2
after 20 years	0.2	3.3	22.4	26.0	18.8
Total	100.0	100.0	100.0	100.0	100.0
Total amount reported (in millions)	$23,783	$76,578	$11,220	$24,285	$47,015

nonmarketable issues. All the Series E bonds were purchased by individuals. A major part of the Series F and G bonds were also purchased by individuals, and most of the remainder by nonfinancial corporations, though limited amounts were taken by commercial banks, state and local governments, savings banks, and insurance companies. Nonfinancial corporations were the principal buyers of the tax saving notes, followed by individuals, state and local governments, and other investors. Though we do not have complete statistics as to the total amounts of each

[28] Computed from data in the *Federal Reserve Bulletin*, February, 1949, p. 162.

marketable security held by the various classes of investors, we do have sample data indicating the percentage of their total marketable governments—in the form of each type and maturity—held by the various classes of investors. The distribution as of June 30, 1946 is shown in Table 55.

In mid-1946 more than 95 percent of Federal Reserve holdings of governments had maturities of a year or less. This was a result, as will be seen later, of the Treasury policy of issuing such a large volume of short-term securities, of the very low yields on the short maturities, and of the Federal Reserve policy of acting as residual buyer in order to prevent a rise of yields above the pattern agreed upon with the Treasury. With the longer-term securities given a degree of safety and liquidity close to that of the shorter-term issues, other holders came to prefer the higher-yield longer-term securities and to shift the lower-yield shorter-term obligations to the Federal Reserve banks.

Commercial banks held only a small percentage of their governments in the form of the lowest-yield bills, but 31 percent in securities due or callable within a year and more than 92 percent in securities due or callable within 10 years. This was due in part to bank policy and in part to Treasury restrictions on their acquisition of maturities beyond 10 years. Mutual savings banks and insurance companies, on the other hand, concentrated their holdings in the longer-term issues. The category labelled "others" is too broad to reveal much about its various components. We can, however, shed some light on the preference of individuals, non-financial corporations, and state and local governments by looking at their subscriptions during the eight war loan drives, as shown in Table 56. Of individual purchases during the drives, 58.5 percent were nonmarketable securities, most of these being Series E bonds. The 41.5 percent in marketable securities was largely of the longer-term obligations. Less than a third of the purchases by nonfinancial corporations were of nonmarketable securities, and most of these were of tax saving notes. About two-thirds of their purchases of marketable issues were of certificates and notes and about a third were of bonds. States and local governments purchased small amounts of Series F and G bonds and somewhat larger amounts of tax saving notes, but more than 90 percent of their purchases were of marketable securities. More than 40 per-

TABLE 56.   Subscriptions by Individuals, Nonfinancial Corporations, and State and Local Governments in the Eight War Loan Drives[29]

| Securities Purchased | Percent of Total Subscriptions by Each Type of Investor | | |
	Individuals	Nonfinancial Corporations	State and Local Governments
Nonmarketable, total	58.5	31.5	8.8
Series E	46.1	0	0
Series F and G	9.4	3.0	2.1
Tax saving notes	3.0	28.5	7.7
Marketable, total	41.5	68.5	91.1
Certificates	6.1	41.7	42.3
Notes	1.3	3.2	3.9
Bonds—10 years or less	14.1	9.4	10.0
" —more than 10 years	20.0	14.2	34.8
Grand total	100.0	100.0	100.0
Total subscriptions (in millions)	$43,256	$53,464	$8,161

cent of their total purchases were of certificates, and well over a third were of bonds maturing in more than 10 years.

To round out our survey of Treasury borrowing policy, the next chapter will describe Federal Reserve credit policy during the war. Whatever may be the case in peacetime, Federal Reserve credit policy and Treasury debt policy were inseparable during World War II.

[29] SOURCE: *Treasury Bulletin,* February, 1946, pp. 19-20. These figures are not, of course, an accurate index of holdings at any one time. They do not reflect purchases outside the drives, they do not reflect sales or redemptions by these holders, and they tend to overstate the importance of the short-term obligations.

IX

|||||||||||||||||||||||||||||||||||||||||||||||||||||||||||||||||||||||||||||||||||||||||||||||||||||||||||||||||||||||||||||

Federal Reserve Credit Policies
During the War

AFTER Pearl Harbor the dominating objective of Federal Reserve policy was to facilitate Treasury borrowing. Monetary policy became subservient to fiscal policy. The principal function of the Federal Reserve was to assure that the Treasury would not at any time lack money—that it would be able to borrow from the commercial or Federal Reserve banks all the funds that it needed beyond those secured from taxation and nonbank borrowing. Moreover, interest rates were to be kept at low and stable levels throughout the war and the prices of government securities were to be prevented from declining. In line with these objectives the Federal Reserve itself bought large amounts of governments, kept the commercial banks amply supplied with low-cost or no-cost reserves, and assured them that it would provide, on attractive terms, any further reserve funds that they might need. In short, the creation of new money was not limited either by a shortage of bank reserves and bank lending power or by a rise in the cost of additional reserve funds from the Federal Reserve banks. This policy was such an integral part of the inflationary process that it must be analyzed closely. We shall first describe the situation prior to Pearl Harbor and then analyze Federal Reserve policy during our participation in the war as a belligerent.

MONETARY CONDITIONS AND
CREDIT POLICY, 1939–1941

With a few exceptions, the Federal Reserve did not have to take positive actions during this early period to maintain low interest rates and ample loan funds for borrowers with a good credit rating. Continued easy credit was assured by the combination of a relatively low private demand for loan funds and a very large volume of excess bank reserves, the latter resulting mainly from increases in our monetary gold stock rather than from Federal Reserve contributions. Between February 1934 and the outbreak of war in 1939 our monetary gold stock more than doubled, rising from $7.4 billion to $16.6 billion. A part of this increase represented domestic gold production, but most of it reflected our large export balance and the net inflow of foreign capital, much of it fleeing from uncertainty abroad. With the outbreak of war gold imports accelerated, so that our monetary gold stock at the end of 1941 had reached $22.7 billion, or $15.3 billion above the February 1934 levels. The excess reserves of member banks amounted to more than $5 billion in late 1939 and climbed to nearly $7 billion in late 1940. The great potential expansion of bank credit represented by these excess reserves did not constitute an immediate inflationary danger so long as government and business demands for loan funds remained at low levels. But as defense expenditures, federal deficits, and business spendings mounted, bank credit began to expand rapidly and Federal Reserve officials became alarmed. In an unprecedented action the Board of Governors, the presidents of the twelve Federal Reserve Banks, and the twelve members of the Federal Advisory Council, in December 1940, submitted a special joint report to Congress, pointing out that the existing powers of the Federal Reserve to deal with inflation were not adequate and asking for a number of additional powers.[1] Congress ignored the plea. In November, 1941 the Federal Reserve raised member

[1] Board of Governors, *Annual Report,* 1940, pp. 68-70.

bank reserve requirements to the highest level permitted by the Federal Reserve Act, but even after this action the banks still had more than $3 billion of excess reserves. Except for certain selective controls, which will be discussed later, the Federal Reserve adopted no other restrictive measures during this period.

The evolution of Federal Reserve open-market policy during this period is very interesting, for it represented a departure from traditional central bank practice and constituted a long step toward the type of open-market policy followed during the war and the postwar period. Before this time students of central banking were well agreed on these two points: (1) Of all the types of Federal Reserve credit, the one whose quantity was subject to the most accurate control was Federal Reserve holdings of U. S. Government securities. The Federal Reserve itself retained the initiative and decided exactly how many securities it would buy or sell, the rate at which it would buy or sell, and the timing of its purchases or sales. And (2) Federal Reserve open-market operations affected not only the quantity of credit but also interest rates and yields, primarily—in fact, almost exclusively—through their effects on the reserve positions of commercial banks and on the volume of member bank indebtedness to the Federal Reserve. Open-market purchases by the Federal Reserve tended to increase bank reserves, or to enable banks to reduce their debts to the Reserve banks, thereby encouraging banks to increase the supply of loan funds, and this tended to lower interest rates and to raise the prices of outstanding bonds. On the other hand, open-market sales of securities by the Federal Reserve tended to lower bank reserves or to increase bank indebtedness to the Reserve banks; this tended to decrease the supply of bank loans, thereby tending to raise interest rates and to lower the prices of outstanding bonds. The direct effect of Federal Reserve purchases and sales on the prices and yields of governments, and through them on the prices and yields of other securities, had never been put forth as a major consideration in open-market policy.

In 1937, however, this aspect of open-market policy began to receive more emphasis. After reaching high levels in late 1936 the prices of long-term governments and high-grade corporate bonds began to decline early in 1937. This decline did not extend to treasury bills and notes. The Federal Open Market Committee thereupon purchased more than $200 million of the longer-term bonds and reduced its holdings of the shorter-term notes and bills by about $150 million. The decline of government bond prices was stopped and reversed.[2] By these operations the Federal Reserve System influenced directly—not merely through its effects on bank reserves—the yields on both long- and short-term government securities, and indirectly the yields on others.

Though the System continued to be interested in the prices of government securities no further extensive operations were necessary until just before the outbreak of war in 1939, when bond prices again began to decline.[3] To stop this movement the System did two things: (1) It announced that all the Reserve banks stood ready to lend on government securities at par value to nonmember as well as to member banks, the discount rate to be the one applicable to such loans to member banks. The rate at Boston and New York was 1 percent, and five other Reserve banks instituted a preferential rate of 1 percent on loans secured by governments. And (2) it purchased $473 million of governments in the open market.[4] Again the decline of bond prices was arrested. During the rest of 1939 and most of 1940 the Federal Reserve was a net seller of governments in order to retard the rise of their market prices, though it did make net purchases in the spring of 1940 to cushion the decline of bond prices accompanying the invasion of Norway and Denmark and later the Low Countries.[5] The next extensive operations came just after Pearl Harbor, when

[2] *Ibid.,* 1937, pp. 5-7.
[3] For evidence that the Federal Open-Market Committee continued to be concerned with maintaining an orderly market in governments, see *Ibid.,* 1938, pp. 77-79.
[4] *Ibid.,* 1939, pp. 5-7.
[5] *Ibid.,* 1940, pp. 3-4.

the system purchased $60 million of bonds and $10 million of bills in order to end the price break.

Official statements made it clear that the primary purpose of these operations was not to affect the volume of member bank reserves and member bank indebtedness to the Reserve banks, but to exert a direct influence on the prices and yields of governments and, through them, on the prices and yields of other securities. In its 1939 annual report the Board stated,

> In earlier years changes in the System portfolio had been made with reference to their effect on member bank indebtedness or the volume of excess reserves. With bank reserves at an unprecedented and constantly mounting level, and with a vast amount of funds in the hands of individual and institutional investors seeking outlets, such changes in member bank reserves as are caused by System open-market operations are no longer a major factor in easing or tightening credit conditions. On the other hand, such operations exert an influence on conditions in the capital market. The entry or withdrawal of the System as an active buyer or seller has an influence not only on prices of the particular issues that the System buys or sells, but also on the market for Government obligations as a whole and to some extent on the capital market in general. In view of the fact that member banks held a large volume of Government and corporate bonds, the endeavors of the System to contribute to the maintenance of an orderly bond market tend to stabilize banking conditions and, through their effect on the capital markets, they contribute to general economic recovery.[6]

Federal Reserve officials justified on two principal bases their attempts to "maintain an orderly market in governments." With regard to their large-scale purchases in 1939, they stated,

> . . . the System was guided principally by the following considerations:
>
> (1) By helping to maintain orderly conditions in the market for United States Government securities the System can exert a steadying influence on the entire capital market, which is an essential part of the country's economic machinery, and disorganization in which would

[6] *Ibid.,* 1939, p. 9.

be a serious obstacle to the progress of economic recovery. The market for United States Government securities is the only part of the capital market in which the System is authorized by law to operate, and Government securities occupy a vital place in that market.

(2) The System also has a measure of responsibility for safeguarding the large United States Government portfolio of the member banks from unnecessarily wide and violent fluctuations in price. The System cannot and does not guarantee any current prices of government obligations, nor does it undertake to preserve for member banks such profits as they may have on their government securities, or to protect them against losses in this account. The Government security market, however, has become in recent years the principal part of the money market, and member banks are in the habit of adjusting their cash positions through sales and purchases of United States government securities. This practice has arisen partly because of a shrinkage in the availability of other liquid assets, such as Street loans and bankers' acceptances, which in earlier years were in much larger volume and were the medium through which banks were likely to adjust their positions. In the enhanced importance of the Government portfolio to member banks, the System sees an additional reason for exerting its influence against undue disturbances in Government security prices.[7]

Thus, by the time of Pearl Harbor the "maintenance of an orderly market for government securities" had already become an important consideration in Federal Reserve policy. This was a long step toward wartime policy, but it still differed significantly from the policies followed later. (1) The professed purpose was not to facilitate Treasury borrowing but to protect member bank portfolios and to maintain an orderly bond market in the interest of general economic recovery. This failure of Federal Reserve officials to mention Treasury needs in their policy pronouncements does not, of course, prove that their actions were not at all influenced by the Treasury's interest as a borrower. (2) The Federal Reserve had not yet committed itself to a policy of maintaining an inflexible structure of bond prices and yields; it still professed a willingness to allow these to move in an "orderly

[7] *Ibid.*, 1939, pp. 5-6 and 1937, pp. 6-7.

manner" and considered its purposes to be only that of preventing fluctuations of a "speculative," "panicky," "violent," "temporary," or "disorderly" nature.

While the System has neither the obligation nor the power to assure any given level of prices or yields for Government securities, it has been its policy in so far as its powers permit to protect the market for these securities from violent fluctuations of a speculative, or panicky nature. Prices of fixed-interest rate securities, including those of the Government, inevitably adjust to changes in long-time interest rates. Consequently, an orderly rise or fall in United States bond prices in response to changes in underlying credit conditions, as expressed in interest rates, does not call for action by the System. Violent temporary movements, however, caused by such circumstances as the shock of the outbreak of European hostilities, make it in the public interest for the System to use its influence toward preventing a disorganized condition in the market.[8]

During the war, however, the Federal Reserve proceeded to the more inflexible policy of preventing yields on governments from rising above the levels agreed upon with the Treasury. We shall see that as soon as it did this the Federal Reserve lost its control over the supply of money; it had to buy, with newly created money, all the governments that others were not willing to hold at yields which did not exceed the inflexible established pattern.

FEDERAL RESERVE POLICY AFTER
PEARL HARBOR

On the day after Pearl Harbor, the Board of Governors assured the public that the Federal Reserve could and would see that the Treasury was supplied with all the money that it needed for war finance.

The existing supply of funds and bank reserves is fully adequate to meet all present and prospective needs of the Government and of

[8] *Ibid.,* 1939, p. 5.

private activity. The Federal Reserve System has powers to add to these resources to whatever extent may be required in the future.

The System is prepared to use its powers to assure that an ample supply of funds is available at all times for financing the war effort and to exert its influence toward maintaining conditions in the United States Government security market that are satisfactory from the standpoint of the Government's requirements.[9]

Then in March 1942 the Federal Open Market Committee agreed with the Treasury that the general market for goverments "should be maintained on about the then existing curve of rates" and pledged the coöperation of the System in preventing a rise of rates.[10]

The Federal Reserve used many measures during the war to assure the Treasury of plenty of money at continued low interest rates.[11] (1) It joined with all other supervisory authorities in assuring banks that they would not be criticized for providing large amounts of funds to the Treasury. As promised in the November 1942 statement,

1. There will be no deterrents in examination or supervisory policy to investments by banks in Government securities of all types, except those securities made specifically ineligible for bank investment by the terms of their issue.

2. In connection with Government financing, individual subscribers relying upon anticipated income may wish to augment their subscriptions by temporary borrowings from banks. Such loans will not be subject to criticism but should be on a short term or amortization basis fully repayable within periods not exceeding six months.

3. Banks will not be criticized for utilizing their idle funds as far as possible in making such investments and loans and availing themselves of the privilege of temporarily borrowing from or selling Treas-

---

[9] *Ibid.*, 1941, p. 1.
[10] *Ibid.*, 1942, p. 104.
[11] We shall not describe here the invaluable service rendered by the Federal Reserve as fiscal agent for the Treasury, nor its usefulness in the bond-selling campaigns.

ury bills to the Federal Reserve Banks when necessary to restore their required reserve positions.[12]

(2) The Federal Reserve Act was amended to permit the Reserve banks to buy limited amounts of securities directly from the Treasury.[13] In general this power was used only to supply the Treasury with temporary funds while it awaited collections from others. Most of the Federal Reserve purchases were made in the open market. (3) In 1942 it lowered the reserve requirements of central reserve city banks from 26 to 20 percent, at which level they remained through the end of the war. (4) In April 1943 the Federal Reserve Act was amended to exempt from reserve requirements and also from assessments for deposit insurance all U. S. Government deposits "arising solely as a result of subscriptions by or through" the banks for government securities.[14] Since banks had previously been required to hold reserves against these so-called "war loan deposits" this represented a decrease of reserve requirements and an increase in bank lending power. In fact, during the big war loan drives banks tended to accumulate excess reserves, for—to the extent that purchases were made by nonbank lenders—deposits were transferred from categories against which reserves were required to war loan deposit accounts which were free of reserve requirements. It was partly because of this process that banks tended to acquire so many securities during the periods of the drives, or soon thereafter, before the Treasury had drawn down its war loan deposits. Then later, as the Treasury checked its deposits out to private owners and these became subject to reserve requirements, the banks would sell governments to the Federal Reserve to repair their reserve positions. (5) The Federal Reserve set low interest rates on its loans to both member and nonmember banks and, as was noted above, assured them that they would not be criticized for temporary borrowing. At the

[12] *Federal Reserve Bulletin*, December, 1942, pp. 1174-1175.

[13] Board of Governors, *Annual Report*, 1942, p. 55. This amendment was approved in March 1942. The limit on the amount purchased directly from the Treasury and held by the Reserve banks at any one time was set at $5 billion.

[14] *Federal Reserve Bulletin*, May, 1943, pp. 372-373, 378.

time of Pearl Harbor seven of the Reserve banks had discount rates of 1 percent on loans collateralled by government securities, and in March and April 1942, the other five Reserve banks lowered their rates to this level. Then in October all the Reserve banks established a preferential discount rate of 0.5 percent on their loans secured by government obligations maturing or callable within a year. This became the effective rate on most loans, for very few banks lacked a sufficient supply of short-term governments. But even these low rates elicited little borrowing by member banks; the banks could secure Federal Reserve funds more cheaply and without the onus of having borrowed by selling the 0.38 percent Treasury bills to the Reserve banks. This contrasts sharply with the policy employed during and immediately following World War I. At that time the Reserve banks bought only small amounts of government securities and extended their funds to member banks primarily by making loans to them. The Reserve banks' holdings of governments did not rise above $300 million, but their outstanding loans to member banks rose to $1.8 billion at the end of 1918, to $2.2 billion at the end of 1919, and to $2.7 billion in late 1920. But during World War II the Federal Reserve supplied funds primarily by purchasing governments. While its loans to banks remained under $1 billion it increased its government holdings from $2.2 billion in 1941 to about $24 billion in late 1945 and early 1946. (6) As indicated above, the Federal Reserve relied primarily on its open-market operations to assure an ample supply of loan funds at continuing low levels of interest rates. To accomplish these purposes it followed a policy of buying, without any limitation as to quantity, all the governments that others were not willing to hold at the pattern of yields agreed upon with the Treasury. In April 1942 the Reserve banks began their policy of purchasing at a 0.38 percent discount all Treasury bills offered to them, and in August they began to offer to sellers of bills the option to repurchase an equal quantity at the same rate. By these means the yield on bills was not only effectively stabilized at 0.38 percent, but the bills were also made as liquid as money. In a similar way, the Reserve banks stood ready to buy all 12-month certificates of indebtedness offered to them at their 0.88 percent posted buying rate. Though no rates on the longer-term marketable notes and bonds were formally posted and publicized, the Federal Reserve nevertheless purchased these issues in whatever quantities were necessary to prevent their yields from rising above the established pattern, and it sometimes sold them as their yields fell below the pattern levels. It will be noted that the treatment of bills was somewhat different from that of the other marketable issues. The bill rate was held completely constant by granting to others the option to sell to or buy from the Federal Reserve at a fixed yield. In the case of the certificates, notes, and bonds, the Federal Reserve stood ready to buy all that was necessary to prevent their yields from rising above the agreed-upon levels, but it did not formally commit itself to a policy of selling these securities freely in order to prevent their yields from declining below the pattern. It often did sell these obligations as their prices tended to rise above these levels, but sometimes it allowed the prices of some of the medium- and longer-term issues to rise.

It is clear that so long as the Federal Reserve stood ready to buy all governments offered to it at a stable pattern of yields, the actual level of yields on these obligations could not rise, and the Treasury was assured of a market for its securities. But it must be emphasized that this represented a radical departure from the traditional theory of monetary policy. As soon as this fixed-yield policy was adopted the Federal Reserve lost its initiative and its control over the money supply; it had to be a party to creating all the money that the public wished to hold at the fixed pattern of yield rates. Its holdings of goverments were determined not by itself but by the Treasury as the issuer of securities and by others as buyers and sellers. The Federal Reserve became in effect a slot machine that would always pay off; anyone could insert into it an unwanted government obligation and receive in return an amount of money equal to the support price. Such a policy put us on a type of monetary standard that might accurately be called a "low-yield government security standard," for the central bank stood ready to monetize unlimited amounts of these obligations at virtually fixed prices.

Three other points about this policy should be noted. (1) The Federal Reserve lost control not only over the total amount of its government holdings but also over the types and maturities of its holdings; this, too, was determined by the Treasury and by other buyers and sellers. Though the Federal Reserve freely offered its advice to the Treasury, it was the Treasury that decided the quantity of each type of security that it would issue. And other buyers and sellers, retaining complete freedom to determine not only the total amount of their holdings but also the types to be held, bought and sold as they saw fit, leaving the Federal Reserve to take the residual. (2) The maintenance of low interest rates on governments also assured very low interest rates on private obligations. Investors retained complete freedom to shift at will from one type of security to another, and with yields on governments held at a low level they were willing to offer very attractive terms to private borrowers. If need be, they could sell their governments to the Federal Reserve to get money for private loans. The failure of banks and others to lend more to private borrowers was not due to any Federal Reserve limitation on total bank lending power. (3) With the adoption of this policy direct access to Federal Reserve funds was no longer limited to banks. The Reserve banks had traditionally been considered a system of "bankers' banks"; the guiding principle had been that they should lend primarily, if not exclusively, to banks; and even their open-market purchases were supposed to be primarily for the purpose of providing more bank reserves. But under this new policy every holder of governments was given access to Federal Reserve funds; for to hold prices at support levels the Federal Reserve had to purchase securities sold not only by commercial banks, but also by individuals, nonfinancial businesses, and all types of financial institutions. Moreover, it had to purchase securities from all types of holders regardless of the purpose for which the new money was to be used—for consumption, for the purchase or construction of capital goods, for the purchase of other securities, or for additions to idle balances.

AMOUNTS AND TYPES OF GOVERNMENT SECURITIES PURCHASED BY THE FEDERAL RESERVE

We have already seen that prior to Pearl Harbor the Federal Reserve did not have to take positive actions to assure the maintenance of easy credit. In fact, even after the increase of reserve requirements in November 1941 member banks still held more than $3 billion in excess reserves. Beginning in 1942, however, the situation changed rapidly and the Federal Reserve had to increase greatly the amount of its outstanding credit, principally by purchasing governments, in order to prevent any tightening of credit. As shown in the latter part of Table 57, the Federal

TABLE 57. Outstanding Federal Reserve Credit and Some Related Items, 1941-1945

(In millions of dollars)[15]

A. *Absolute Amounts on Selected Dates*

End of Year	Total Federal Reserve Credit	Monetary Gold Stock	Money in Circulation	Member Banks' Reserves
1941	$ 2,361	$22,737	$11,160	$12,450
1942	6,679	22,726	15,410	13,117
1943	12,239	21,938	20,449	12,886
1944	19,745	20,619	25,307	14,373
1945	25,091	20,065	28,515	15,915

B. *Changes During the Period*

Change During Calendar Year	Funds Supplied by the Increase of Federal Reserve Credit	Principal Uses of Funds Supplied by the Increase of Federal Reserve Credit		
		To Offset Decrease of Monetary Gold Stock	To Supply Additional Coin and Currency for Circulation	To Increase Member Bank Reserve Balances
1942	$ 4,318	$ 11	$ 4,250	$ 667
1943	5,690	788	5,039	—231
1944	7,506	1,319	4,858	1,487
1945	5,346	554	3,208	1,542
Total for 4 years	$22,730	$2,670	$17,355	$3,465

[15] SOURCE: *Federal Reserve Bulletins.* For other relevant factors see tables in the Bulletins labelled, "Member Bank Reserves, Reserve Bank Credit, and Related Items."

Reserve increased the volume of its outstanding credit by $22.7 billions during the four years preceding the end of 1945. These additional funds contributed by the Reserve banks were utilized for three principal purposes: (1) To offset the $2.7 billion drain due to the gold outflow during the war. (2) To meet the public's demand for an additional $17.4 billion of coin and currency as money incomes and aggregate money savings grew. And (3) to increase member bank reserve balances by $3.5 billion. Thus, the contributions of the Reserve banks, made almost wholly by pur-

TABLE 58. Types of Governments Held by the Reserve Banks, 1941-1946
(Last Wednesday of the month; in millions of dollars)[16]

Date		Total	Treasury Bills	Certificates of Indebtedness	Treasury Notes	Bonds
Dec.,	1941	$ 2,254	$ 10	$ 0	$ 777	$1,467
June,	1942	2,583	219	34	716	1,612
Dec.,	1942	5,989	823	1,033	1,344	2,789
June,	1943	7,202	3,816	1,092	797	1,498
Dec.,	1943	11,61,	6,906	2,407	677	1,625
June,	1944	15,081	9,052	3,382	1,183	1,464
Dec.,	1944	19,064	11,521	4,732	1,568	1,243
June,	1945	21,692	12,972	5,924	1,686	1,113
Dec.,	1945	24,037	12,802	8,167	2,120	947
June,	1946	23,385	14,399	6,482	1,748	755

chasing governments, were large enough to supply all the increased demand for coin and currency, to offset the drain of gold, and to provide the banking system with an expanded reserve base. This increase of their total reserves combined with utilization of their excess reserves and some reduction of their average reserve requirements (as a percentage of deposits) enabled the banking system to create a huge volume of additional deposits.

The excess reserves of member banks averaged only about a billion dollars from the middle of 1943 until well into the postwar period. Before the war such a reduction of excess reserves would ordinarily have been accompanied by some tightening of credit.

[16] SOURCE: *Federal Reserve Bulletins.*

That this did not occur during the war is eloquent testimony that the new open-market policy of the Federal Reserve had completely changed the significance of excess reserves. With very large holdings of governments, especially of the shorter maturities, and with the Reserve banks willing to buy these on demand at stable prices, banks had no reason to hold a large volume of reserves beyond their legal requirements. Their governments not only yielded some income but were as liquid as money and fully as satisfactory as

TABLE 59.   Maturities of Governments Held by the Reserve Banks, 1941-1946
(Last Wednesday of the month; in millions of dollars)[17]

| | Maturities | | | | | |
Date	Within 90 Days	90 Days to 1 Year	1 Year to 2 Years	2 Years to 5 Years	Over 5 Years	Total
Dec., 1941	$ 96	$ 97	$247	$ 477	$1,337	$ 2,254
June, 1942	286	202	287	353	1,455	2,583
Dec., 1942	1,199	886	242	1,408	2,254	5,989
June, 1943	3,981	1,347	240	752	882	7,202
Dec., 1943	7,256	2,457	224	488	1,190	11,615
June, 1944	10,181	2,739	18	1,022	1,120	15,081
Dec., 1944	12,703	4,064	760	620	918	19,064
June, 1945	14,752	4,780	907	508	747	21,963
Dec., 1945	15,839	7,000	0	508	691	24,037
June, 1946	17,877	4,436	46	449	582	23,385

a protection against future contingencies. Banks could not count their government holdings as legal reserves, but they certainly did consider them as "potential reserves."

It is also interesting to note the types of governments acquired by the Reserve banks. At the end of 1941, as shown by Table 58, Reserve bank holdings were almost entirely in bonds and notes; their bill holdings were almost negligible. During 1942 the Reserve banks acquired further amounts of all types of marketable governments, but in 1943 another trend began. From that time until well after the end of the war the Reserve banks actually reduced their bond holdings to quite small amounts while ac-

[17] SOURCE: *Federal Reserve Bulletins.*

quiring very large amounts of the shorter-term issues—primarily bills and certificates. By the end of 1945 their holdings were distributed as follows: 53.3 percent in bills, 34.0 percent in certificates, 8.8 percent in notes, and only 3.9 percent in bonds. Table 59, indicating the maturities of the governments held by the Reserve banks, shows the same picture. At the end of 1941 less than 5 percent of the Federal Reserve holdings had maturities of less than 90 days and less than 9 percent had maturities of less than a year; nearly 60 percent matured beyond 5 years. But by the end of 1945 nearly 66 percent had maturities within 90 days and 95 percent had maturities of less than a year; less than 3 percent had maturities beyond 5 years.

It is not at all difficult to understand why the Federal Reserve, as a passive residual buyer, had to concentrate its purchases in the short maturities. This was due to a combination of three things. (1) The shape of the yield pattern agreed upon with the Treasury. It will be remembered that this pattern was represented by a smooth upward-rising curve starting at 0.38 percent for maturities within 3 months and passing through 0.88 percent for 12-month maturities, 2 percent for 10-year maturities, and 2.5 percent for the longest maturities. These yields were equal to the nominal interest rates on new issues with these maturities. But as outstanding issues approached maturity, market competition drove their prices up to a level that would reduce their yield to that of new issues having the same or a comparable maturity date. And as a part of its support program the Federal Reserve had to stand ready to buy the outstanding issues at prices which would reduce their yields to the levels maintained for new issues of comparable maturity. (2) The Treasury policy of issuing very large amounts of the shorter-term securities. And (3) the freedom of other investors to buy and sell at will, and to arbitrage among the various issues of governments. Before the war the holding of longer-term governments did involve a degree of risk considerably above that on short-term issues. There was always the danger of a rise in basic long-term interest rates with an accompanying decline of bond prices, and the possibility that a general wave of selling would reduce the liquidity of these securities during an emergency. But under the new Federal Reserve support policy the distinction between long and short maturities lost most of its significance. *At their support prices and so long as Federal Reserve support was continued,* the longer maturities were just as safe and just as liquid as the shortest maturities. They could have a higher degree of risk and illiquidity only to the extent (1) that their prices rose above support levels and there was danger they would later decline to support levels, and (2) that there was a danger the Federal Reserve would discontinue or lower its support prices without adequate notice to investors. It is no wonder, therefore, that as the new Federal Reserve policy came to be understood and as its continuance for an indefinite period came to be expected, other investors bought and held the longer-maturity higher-yield securities and sold the shorter-term lower-yield obligations to the passive but willing Reserve banks.

In fact, preference for the long-maturity issues became so great that bond prices were bid up to levels considerably above par in the late war and early postwar period. After remaining only fractionally above par through 1944 they rose to nearly 3 percent above par by the end of 1945 and more than 6 percent above par in early 1946.

SELECTIVE CREDIT CONTROLS DURING THE WAR

The preceding section emphasized that the general credit policy of the Federal Reserve placed no effective limit on the expansion of bank credit. Instead, the Reserve banks said in effect, "We stand ready to supply the banking system with all the reserve funds that it may desire. These funds may be secured at the option of banks or others by selling to us government securities with any maturity. The cost of these funds will be only the yield sacrificed on the governments sold to us, which is only $\frac{3}{8}$ of 1 percent on maturities of 90 days or less and $\frac{7}{8}$ of 1 percent on 12-month maturities. Moreover, we will lend to either member or non-member banks at very low discount rates. Come one, come all!" This raises a very interesting question: Why, in the face of this extremely liberal Federal Reserve policy, did the volume of bank credit fail to expand much more? Why did the banks fail to buy many more governments and to expand very greatly their loans to private individuals and business firms for consumption and investment purposes?

The major part of the answer is to be found in factors that have already been mentioned: (1) The tremendous rise of disposable money incomes resulting primarily from the large and rising volume of government expenditures and an inadequate tax program; and (2) the combination of a shortage of goods and services for private purposes and price control to prevent a bidding up of the prices of these things. This both limited the amount that the private sectors could spend and forced them to save huge amounts. Individuals had little reason to borrow from the banks; their disposable incomes were far greater than the available supply of consumption goods and services, and they were saving very large amounts. The supply of durable goods, such as autos and new houses, which usually account for so much of personal borrowing, was especially short. Business concerns were in a similar position. As a group they were saving very large amounts, and their capital spendings were limited by price control, the general shortage of goods and services for capital maintenance and accumulation, and a whole series of direct limitations on the purchase and use of these scarce items. Thus, shortages and the direct control of prices and goods held private spendings below private disposable incomes, so there was little private demand for bank credit. Moreover, nonbank investors had a very large amount of current savings with which to bid governments away from the banks.

Nevertheless, it should be noted that the credit authorities employed several selective controls to limit the expansion of bank credit. The most important of these were the following. (1) As noted in the preceding chapter, the Federal Reserve and the Treasury coöperated in trying to limit bank loans on governments and bank purchases of governments.[18] (2) Limitations were placed on consumer credit. Beginning in September 1941, Regulation W prescribed minimum down payments and maximum maturities on installment credit for the purchase of a number of listed articles, and also placed limitations on other cash loans of $1000 or less repayable in installments.[19] The volume of outstanding consumer credit actually declined from about $10 billion in August 1941 to $5.5 billion in the late war period, and part of this decline was attributable to Regulation W. A more important factor, however, was probably the scarcity of consumer durable goods combined with the high level of disposable personal incomes and savings. (3) Margin requirements on loans for the purchase and carrying of securities were continued in effect. From 1937 until February 1945, purchasers of securities were required to put up a cash margin of at least 40 percent; they could borrow not more than 60 percent of the market value of a security. These margin requirements were raised during 1945 and early 1946. By the end of January 1946 they had reached 100 percent; purchases of securities were purely "on a cash basis" and loans could not be made for the purpose. (4) All the Federal bank supervisory authorities joined together in requesting banks and other lenders to curtail loans for nonproductive purposes and to refuse loans for the accumulation of inventories of consumer goods beyond minimum requirements. Federal bank examiners were instructed to watch inventory loans with special care and "to urge full coöperation" by the banks.[20]

It is impossible to assess the net effectiveness of these selective credit controls which were designed to limit the amount of credit demanded or supplied, for we do not know how much more bank credit would have expanded if these controls had not been

---

[18] See pp. 173-177 above.
[19] Board of Governors, *Annual Report,* 1941, pp. 8-10.
[20] *Ibid.,* pp. 112-114.

TABLE 60.   The Money Supply and Its Determinants, 1939-1945 (In billions of dollars)[21]

	1939	1940	1941	1942	1943	1944	1945	Net Increase 1939-1945
Sources								
Monetary gold stock	$17.6	$22.0	$22.7	$22.7	$21.9	$20.6	$20.1	$ 2.5
Treasury currency outstanding	3.0	3.1	3.2	3.6	4.1	4.1	4.3	1.3
Total Federal Reserve credit outstanding	2.6	2.3	2.4	6.7	12.2	19.7	25.1	22.5
Commercial bank loans and investments—total	40.7	43.9	50.7	67.4	85.1	105.5	124.0	83.3
U. S. security holdings	16.3	17.8	21.8	41.4	59.8	77.6	90.6	74.3
Other investments	7.1	7.4	7.2	6.8	6.1	6.3	7.3	9.2
Loans	17.2	18.8	21.7	19.2	19.1	21.7	26.1	8.9
Total sources=Total amounts used	$63.9	$71.3	$79.0	$100.4	$123.3	$149.9	$173.5	$109.6
Less:								
Amounts absorbed by competing uses: U. S. government deposits and cash holdings	$ 2.0	$ 1.4	$ 3.1	$ 9.5	$ 11.4	$ 21.6	$ 25.9	$ 23.9
Time deposits at commercial banks	15.1	15.6	15.7	16.2	19.1	23.9	29.9	14.8
Other competing uses	10.6	12.1	11.6	11.9	13.2	14.0	15.3	4.7
Total	$27.7	$29.1	$30.4	$37.6	$43.7	$59.5	$71.1	$ 43.4
Equals: the money supply: Privately owned demand deposits	$29.8	$34.9	$39.0	$48.9	$60.8	$66.9	$75.9	$ 46.1
Currency outside banks	6.4	7.3	9.6	13.9	18.8	23.5	26.5	20.1
Total money supply	$36.2	$42.2	$48.6	$62.8	$79.6	$90.4	$102.4	$ 66.2

[21] SOURCE: Computed by the writer from data in the *Federal Reserve Bulletins*. For a comparable and somewhat more accurate but more complex formulation, see Morris A. Copeland and Daniel H. Brill, "Banking Assets and the Money Supply Since 1929," *Federal Reserve Bulletin*, January, 1948, pp. 24-32. Some of the data in Table 60 were taken from this source.

employed. It seems probable that they were much less effective than the direct control of prices and commodities. In any case, we should remember that during the war the credit authorities relied on these selective controls rather than any limitation of total bank lending power to check the expansion of bank credit and the money supply.

THE INCREASE OF THE MONEY SUPPLY

Having surveyed both fiscal and credit policy during the war period, we are now in a position to deal more fully with the behavior of the money supply. Economists differ somewhat in their definition of this term, but it shall be used here to include only privately owned checking deposits and currency outside the banks. If the reader prefers to include time deposits at commercial banks and government deposits and cash holdings he may do so by adding in these amounts as shown in Table 60.

Table 60 indicates that the money supply, as defined above, rose from $36.2 billion at the end of 1939 to $102.4 billion at the end of 1945, an increase of $66.2 billion or 183 percent. It also uses a balance sheet approach to show the determinants of the money supply at any given time and changes in its magnitude over a period of time. At any given time the money supply is equal to the total amount of funds supplied by the sources indicated in the table minus the amounts absorbed by competing uses. For example, at the end of 1939 the money supply ($36.2 billion) was equal to the total amount supplied by these sources ($63.9 billion) minus the amounts absorbed in government deposits and cash holdings, time deposits at commercial banks, and certain other competing uses ($27.7 billion). And the net increase of the money supply during any period is equal to the net increase of the amounts supplied by these sources minus the net increase of the amounts absorbed in competing uses.

The last column of Table 60 accounts for the $66.2 billion increase in the money supply during the six years preceding the end of 1945. The total increase in the amounts supplied by these sources was $109.6 billion. Only $3.8 billion of this came from increases in the monetary gold stock and outstanding Treasury currency; the other $105.8 billion represented an increase of outstanding Federal Reserve and commercial bank credit. All of the increase of Federal Reserve credit and $74.3 billion of the increase of commercial bank credit represented net increases in their holdings of governments; only $9.1 billion was attributable to the increase of other commercial bank investments and loans. Thus, $96.7 billion or 88 percent of the total increase represented funds supplied by Federal Reserve and commercial bank net purchases of governments. Not all of these additional funds were added to the money supply; $23.9 billion was added to government deposits and cash holdings, $14.8 billion was used to increase time deposits at commercial banks, and $4.7 billion was absorbed by other competing uses. But, as we have seen, $66.2 billion was added to the supply of privately held money.

These statistics bear out the conclusions reached earlier. Monetary policy was dictated by fiscal considerations, and the tremendous increase of the money supply during the war period was due primarily to the large purchases of governments by the Federal Reserve and commercial banks.

X

||||||||||||||||||||||||||||||||||||||||||||||||||||||||||||||||||||||||||||||||||||||||||||||||||||||||||||||||||||||||||||||||||||||||||||||||||||

The Role of Direct Controls Over Prices, Wages, and Goods and Services During the War

THE preceding chapters have emphasized that fiscal and mone-
policy during the defense and war period were highly inflationary and that direct controls over prices, wages, and the production
and use of goods and services constituted the principal bulwark
against inflation. This chapter cannot present a complete description
and evaluation of this system of direct controls. It can, however,
indicate some of the principal effects that these controls exerted on
the rate of total spendings for output, national money income,
private savings and spendings, the shift of output to war purposes,
and the distribution of both money and real income among the
various sectors of the economy.

The principal types of direct controls employed during the war
were the following. (1) Price ceilings on almost all important
goods and services. (2) Wage ceilings. (3) Subsidies to limit
or prevent price increases while maintaining output. (4) Rationing
of many consumer goods, such as foodstuffs, tires, gasoline, and
shoes. (5) A whole series of limitations and regulations on the
production, use, and distribution of goods and services at the producer and dealer levels. These included limitations on business
inventories, production directives, limitation orders prohibiting or
limiting the use of scarce goods and services for "nonessential"

purposes, priorities for the use of materials, and allocations. (6) Export and import controls. And (7) government purchases and sales of goods produced either abroad or in this country. The relationships between these controls and the course of the inflation will be analyzed after we have looked at the types of economic problems that had to be solved during the war.

The basic economic problems of the war economy were the same as those of any economic system which cannot turn out enough goods and services to meet all needs: (1) To achieve and maintain "full production." (2) To secure an "optimum" composition of output—that is, to produce the most important goods and services in the most desirable proportions. In more specific terms, this required, during the war period, the diversion of a large part of our productive capacity into the production of goods and services that would help win the war, and the use of the remainder in turning out the most essential civilian goods and services. And (3) to secure an "equitable" distribution of real income among the various sectors of the economy. There is, however, an almost unlimited number of techniques for solving these problems.

Some believed strongly that even during the war we should have relied upon a laissez-faire competitive system of controls. No direct controls over prices, wages, and goods and services should have been employed; we should have relied solely on the profit motive to solve these problems. Everyone should have retained his freedom to utilize his disposable money income as he saw fit, and production and prices should have been allowed to adjust themselves, as in peacetime, to the pattern of effective demand in the market. Theoretically it might have been possible to employ this system of economic controls without a large amount of inflation if taxation had been heavy enough and had been tailored to the purpose. In general outline this method of control would have worked as follows: At some stage early in the war, tax rates would have been raised to such high levels that private persons and business firms would have had to reduce their spendings as much as government spendings rose. This reduction of private demands would have freed resources from the production of civilian goods, and the increased government spendings would have attracted resources into the production of war goods. Thus, at least in principle, production could have been diverted to war goods and away from civilian goods to the necessary extent without general inflation if taxation had been heavy enough to hold private money incomes and private spending power in check.

Even if taxes had been increased far more than they were, this system of competitive controls without the use of direct controls would have had serious shortcomings during the war. (1) In practice, it would have been very difficult if not impossible to change tax policy as fast as the rate of government spendings was changed. (2) Marginal tax rates would have had to be so high as to interfere seriously with production incentives and with the necessary shifts of productive factors. (3) Faced with extremely high marginal tax rates and wishing to protect their peacetime markets, many business firms would have been reluctant to shift to war production. (4) If private buyers had retained their freedom of choice large amounts of scarce materials and services badly needed for war purposes would have gone into civilian uses. (5) Competition among government procurement agencies would have driven up prices. (6) The great shifts in relative prices and relative money incomes would have led to widespread discontent and to competitive attempts to improve both money and real income positions. (7) National unity would have been seriously endangered by the resulting controversy over the distribution of income both before and after taxes. These shortcomings would have been evident even if attempts had been made to prevent any rise of disposable private incomes above the levels prevailing in the early war period.

This was not, of course, the kind of tax policy that was followed. As has already been seen, tax policy was so inadequate that private disposable incomes rose continuously. Some critics of direct controls believed that even in the face of this inadequate tax policy we should have relied solely on competitive controls and rejected all direct controls over prices and goods. What would have been the consequences of such a policy? We probably would have won the war and the government probably would have secured the goods and services needed for war purposes, but only at the cost of a galloping inflation that would have reached very high levels before V-J Day. Several factors would have contributed to this accelerating inflationary spiral. (1) The government's demand for output was, or at least should have been, a price-inelastic demand. To assure an early victory without sacrifice of our men the government needed at least 40 percent of our real output for war purposes, and every increase in the prices of the things it needed would have been accompanied by an equivalent increase of its spendings. In the absence of direct controls government spendings would have been higher. Without direct limitations on private purchases, the government would have had to bid goods and services away from private sectors, thereby contributing large amounts to private money income, and private spendings would also have been much larger. (2) The private propensity to consume would have been higher. We know that even with relatively stable prices during the war, people wanted to buy more consumption goods and services than they did, and that they would have done so if they had not been deterred by price ceilings, rationing, and a shortage of the most desirable goods. If this was true with relatively stable prices, how much greater would have been the propensity to spend if prices had started rising rapidly and people had retained their freedom to spend as they wished. Only the uninformed or the most highly patriotic would have been willing to save and hold money or government securities; there might well have been a rapid flight to goods and equities. (3) Private investment spendings would have been higher. Undeterred by either price ceilings or direct restrictions on labor and materials and frightened by the current depreciation of money, business firms would have spent much larger amounts for capital maintenance and accumulation. (4) Wage increases would have been much greater. Favored by an acute labor shortage, workers would have demanded much higher wages and competing employers would have been willing to pay them and pass the burden along in the form of higher prices. In fact, labor would have attempted to secure wage increases to offset, or more than offset, every increase in the cost of living. At the same time farmers, mine operators, manufacturers, and dealers would have been attempting to maintain or actually improve their real purchasing power by increasing their selling prices. In short, to reject all direct controls in the face of such an inadequate tax policy would have assured a spiralling inflation.

Let us now see how the various direct controls, individually and collectively, influenced the course of the inflation.

PRICE CEILINGS

By the end of April 1942 almost all important prices had been placed under ceilings. After that time prices could be increased only with government permission, and this was given only to elicit increased supplies of specific commodities or services, to "correct gross inequities," or to meet certain other minimum standards laid down in the enabling legislation. This does not mean, of course, that the OPA prevented any further price increases after early 1942. Many upward price adjustments were approved, black markets appeared in some areas and in some commodities, there were cases of quality deterioration without a corresponding reduction of prices, low-profit items disappeared in some lines and production was concentrated on higher-profit goods, and new items were in many cases granted prices somewhat above those prevailing before the war on comparable items. Because of these factors the "actual" rise of prices was somewhat greater than that registered in the official indexes. But even after full allowance for "hidden increases," the OPA program was remarkably successful in the face of constantly increasing upward pressures from swollen money incomes.

It would be a mistake, however, to consider the OPA as merely an instrument for holding down a very large number of individual prices, and only in this way limiting the degree of inflation. It also had a number of other effects. (1) It made wage controls politically feasible. Labor submitted to wage ceilings only on the assurance that the cost of living would be held down and that other types of money income would be kept within bounds by price ceilings, taxation, and renegotiation of war contracts. (2) It also represented a compromise among other groups competing to improve their relative income positions. Though there was a considerable amount of dissatisfaction with the levels at which ceilings were set, each group was much less reluctant to keep its prices down when it knew that others were subject to the same general type of regulation. (3) By reducing expectations of rapid price increases it reduced speculation and hoarding of goods. (4) Both directly by holding down the prices of war goods and indirectly by reducing private bidding, it held down the money cost of the war and the size of federal deficits. (5) As noted earlier, it greatly increased private savings out of each level of disposable income. With the physical supply of goods and services limited and with ceilings over their prices, people were virtually forced to save abnormally large proportions of their swelling money incomes after taxes. They almost certainly would not have done so if prices had been allowed to move up rapidly. And (6) it lessened the expansion of the money supply by holding down the size of the federal deficit, by increasing private saving out of any given level of money income, by lessening the rise of private spendings for both consumption and investment purposes, and by discouraging speculation in inventories and stocks.

WAGE CEILINGS

Though wage ceilings were instituted later than price ceilings and were not wholly effective, they nevertheless were an important factor in holding down the extent of the inflation. (1) By holding down cost levels they prevented the breaking of price ceilings. (2) They prevented wage rates from rising to much higher levels, thereby avoiding still larger increases in private money incomes and private spending power. (3) Both directly by holding down labor costs on war goods and indirectly by limiting private money incomes they held down the money cost of the war and the size of federal deficits. And (4) in the above ways they limited the expansion of the money supply and of other private holdings of liquid assets.

SUBSIDIES

In a limited number of cases the government employed subsidy payments to hold down the prices of goods and still maintain their output. The immediate and direct effect was, of course, to hold down the applicable price indexes, for the subsidy payments were not included in them. Some contended, however, that the longer-term net effect of these subsidies was to enhance inflation, for the subsidy payments increased federal deficits, private money incomes, and private spending power. This argument is too simple and, in general, misleading. A more realistic analysis requires that these subsidies be considered by categories. Some clearly reduced total federal spendings. The copper subsidy is an outstanding example. Here the technique was to pay a standard price for the great bulk of copper production, but to grant a subsidy on the high-cost marginal output which was vitally needed. This was in effect a differential-pricing scheme which greatly reduced the total cost of copper. The government, as principal purchaser of the metal, actually saved money through this type of subsidy and lessened its total payments to the private sectors of the economy.

The net effect of subsidies on consumer goods is more difficult to analyze. What would have happened in the absence of these subsidies? Some assume that money wage rates would have remained unaffected and that one of two things would have happened. The cost of living would have risen to the necessary extent, thereby shifting money income from consumers to producers and dealers and also lowering the purchasing power of wages; or no such increase in the cost of living would have been allowed, with the result that the money incomes of producers and dealers would have been reduced. In either case government spending would have been lessened. But these assumptions ignore the difficult problems faced by the government during the war: (1) Congress had stipulated minimum levels below which ceilings could not be set; (2) the rise in the prices of farm products had in some cases squeezed processors' and dealers' margins; and (3) workers contended that wage rates would have to be raised if the cost of living were allowed to increase to any greater extent. At several points during the war, wage ceilings were in serious danger. Perhaps the government should have taken a stronger stand against these groups, lowering the net realization of farmers, forcing more absorption by processors and dealers, and holding wage ceilings despite some further increases in the cost of living. In this way it might have avoided consumer subsidies. This, however, would have endangered the delicate wage-price balance. Wage ceilings might not have held, many price ceilings might have had to be increased, and an upward wage-price spiral might have been started. Though one may deplore the responsiveness of the government to pressure group demands during the war he must recognize its existence. The writer believes that given these conditions, consumer subsidies tended to reduce both the war and postwar inflation. They prevented further wage increases, they probably prevented even larger increases of government spendings by holding down the cost of war goods, and they prevented even larger increases of private money incomes.

CONSUMER RATIONING

In peacetime we ordinarily rely on the limitation of consumer incomes and the free movement of prices to ration output among the various claimants. Prices rise to the level at which the effective demand for each product is lowered to the level of the forthcoming supply. But this technique of rationing was inadequate during the war while prices were held down in the face of rapidly rising disposable incomes and less rapidly increasing supplies for civilian use. At the established price ceilings the demand for most commodities was far above the supplies available. Or to put it another way, disposable money income was not scarce enough to ration supplies at prevailing price levels. In this situation consumer rationing of such scarce things as foodstuffs, shoes, tires, and gasoline served a multiple purpose. (1) It reduced greatly the amount of time and effort spent in looking around for scarce items and standing in line. (2) It assured a fairer distribution of goods necessary for the maintenance of health and efficiency. And (3) it assisted greatly in preventing price increases. It did this in several ways. (a) It held down the effective demand for rationed items by forbidding people to buy more than the quantity indicated by their ration coupons. (b) It helped create a general feeling that essential scarce items were being fairly distributed and that purchases beyond the rationed amounts were unpatriotic. And (c) it reduced hoarding both by consumers and by producers and dealers. Price control would probably have been far less effective during the war if rationing had not been used to limit demand and create a feeling that scarce essentials were being fairly distributed.

OTHER DIRECT CONTROLS OF
GOODS AND SERVICES

Many other direct controls at the producer, dealer, and industrial-user levels helped to limit inflation and to divert productive power and materials into the most essential uses. Limitations on inventories lessened speculative purchasing and hoarding, promoted a smooth flow from producer to user, limited the demand for bank credit, and maximized the volume of goods available for current use. Limitation orders prohibiting or limiting the use of scarce goods and services for "nonessential" ends served a multiple purpose. (1) They deterred inflation by eliminating or reducing demands for less essential purposes. (2) They kept down the money cost of the war by making producers more willing to shift to war production. By forbidding or restricting the production of nonessential civilian goods, the government put itself in a more favorable bargaining position. (3) They prevented the use of scarce materials, facilities, and services in relatively unimportant products. Priority orders, which gave preference to some products and in effect suppressed other, and direct allocations of materials and shipping space had somewhat the same effect. Production directives, though not widely employed, were useful in shifting production to war purposes, from less important to more important civilian goods, and from higher-profit to lower-profit items.

Taken as a whole these direct controls, like consumer rationing, were of great assistance in protecting price ceilings as well as in determining the pattern of production and distribution of goods and services. They served to hold down the money cost of the war, to lessen private investment spendings, and to reduce the rise of private money incomes.

EXPORT AND IMPORT CONTROLS

The most obvious purposes of government regulation of exports and imports were to conserve shipping space, to prevent our products from falling into the hands of the enemy, to conserve our output for the most useful purposes of ourselves and our allies, and to confine our limited imports to the most useful items. They also served, however, to lessen somewhat the degree of inflation here. Export limitations held in check the foreign demand for our products, and import controls were used to some extent to hold down the prices charged by foreign sellers and to bring in those goods whose production costs would be highest here.

GOVERNMENT PURCHASES AND SALES
AND RELATED MEASURES

The extent of inflation was also reduced somewhat by large government purchases and sales of goods produced abroad and at home. (1) In the case of several commodities, the government entered into agreements with our allies to purchase jointly, or at least not to bid up prices, in foreign countries, thereby not only reducing the money cost of the war but also preventing larger price increases on imported civilian goods. (2) For some commodities the government became the sole purchaser for this country in foreign markets thereby eliminating competitive bidding among our importers, lessening the price increase on imports, and inhibiting the growth of black markets. (3) It entered into a number of agreements with foreign countries, fixing the prices at which we would buy as well as the quantities of their products that we would take. And (4) in several cases where the various parts of the supply of a commodity had widely varying costs, government agencies purchased the entire output, or a large part of it, and resold it at or below its average cost so that existing price ceilings could be maintained or price increases minimized.

CONCLUSIONS

The above discussion of direct wartime controls over prices, wages and goods and services is admittedly incomplete and in many respects superficial. It will, however, serve as an introduction to some important conclusions.

At no time during the war did the various economic groups become so patriotic as to forget their desires to maintain or improve their relative income positions. Farmers were determined to secure money incomes that were higher not only in absolute amounts but also in relation to urban incomes. Manufacturers fought for prices high enough to yield profit margins per dollar of sales at least equal to those in the most favorable prewar years. Dealers demanded gross margins at least as high as those in favorable years. At the same time workers demanded increases in money wage rates at least large enough to offset each increase in the cost of living. In the absence of direct controls a price-wage-price spiral with accelerating money incomes and spendings would have been an inevitable result in view of the great rise of government requirements and the inadequate tax policy. The system of direct controls represented a politico-economic compromise and greatly decreased the extent of the price rise. Like so many compromises it was far from ideal and left each contending group with at least apparent gains. Price ceilings on farm products were set at such high levels as to permit very large increases in farm incomes. Manufacturers' profits rose greatly with the permitted increase of prices, the great rise of volume, the decline of overhead costs and selling expenses, and the shift toward higher-margin items. Dealers' profits also reflected the great rise of volume, the disappearance of special sales, the decline of selling expenses, and so on. Wage earners, too, enjoyed not only higher average hourly earnings but even greater increases in average weekly earnings as a result of permitted increases of hourly rates, overtime pay rates, upgrading, movement from low-wage to high-wage industries and increased hours of employment. Perhaps, however, it was the very laxity of the compromise solution that made it workable and that forestalled an even more serious inflation; though each group continued to complain about its treatment it knew that in terms of money income it was doing very well indeed and that its purchasing power was being protected by price ceilings on the things it bought. The various groups made scurrilous remarks about the OPA and the War Labor Board but fortunately did not seriously upset the delicate wage-price balance.

Consumer rationing and other direct controls, though far from perfect, also played an important role in the wartime success of price control. They effectively reduced the demand for many commodities by limiting the amounts that each buyer could purchase, by eliminating demands for proscribed purposes, and by assuring buyers that they could secure the amounts to which they were entitled without resorting to black markets. These controls would have assisted the price control authorities even more if ration coupons had not been issued in excessive quantities in some cases and if authorizations and high priorities had not at times been issued in quantities considerably in excess of the available supplies. The premature relaxation of rationing and of many other direct controls over goods and services at the end of the war was a potent factor in lessening the effectiveness of price controls.

A few critics of direct controls have argued that the price control program did not at all decrease the total amount of inflation between 1940 and 1948 but merely postponed a major part of it to the postwar period. This is not the case. As noted earlier, we cannot assume that all other elements in the situation would have remained unchanged without price control. Wage controls would not have been feasible, government spendings would have had to be much higher, federal deficits would have been much larger, private money incomes and spendings would have been much greater, and the money supply would have expanded much more. In short, the degree of inflation before V-J Day would probably have been much greater than that which actually occurred between 1940 and 1948, and it is impossible to estimate how much more inflation would have come after V-J Day.

XI

An Outline of the Postwar Inflation

We now turn our attention to the postwar period. By V-J Day the cost of living had already risen 30 percent above 1939 levels and wholesale prices had risen 37 percent.[1] But larger increases were still to come. Between August 1945 and August 1948 the cost of living rose another 35 percent and wholesale prices 61 percent. In short, more than 60 percent of the entire increase in the cost of living between 1939 and late 1948, and nearly 70 percent of the total rise of wholesale prices, occurred after the end of the war when government spendings had fallen far below their wartime levels and federal deficits were changed to surpluses. Despite a liberalization of OPA policies and the weakening or withdrawal of many supporting direct controls, the rise of prices was slow until the end of June 1946. By the latter date the cost of living had risen only 3 percent and wholesale prices only 7 percent above their V-J Day levels. But as direct controls were first weakened and then removed prices surged rapidly upward.

The renewed upsurge of spendings and prices after the end of the war was quite unexpected by many economists, government officials, and others. They believed that the rapid and drastic decline of government spendings would not be offset by a rise

[1] These are the increases shown by the price indexes. As noted earlier, the "actual" rise was probably somewhat larger if black markets, quality depreciation, and the disappearance of low-end items are taken into account.

of private spendings, and that the transition period would be characterized by large amounts of unemployment that would continue for a considerable period. Immediately after V-J Day a division within the Office of War Mobilization and Reconversion offered both a "more favorable" and a "less favorable" projection of output, income, and employment during the transition period.[2] Even the "more favorable" projection indicated that the average number of unemployed might be 6,300,000 in the last quarter of 1945, about 7,400,000 in 1946, and 5,700,000 in the first half of 1947. The "less favorable" projection indicated that unemployment might average 6,300,000 in the last quarter of 1945, about 8,300,000 in 1946, and 9,000,000 in the first half of 1947. These forecasts were, of course, erroneous. To some extent the error was due to an overestimate of the postwar labor force; for some returning veterans took unpredicted vacations before seeking jobs, and unexpectedly large numbers of others withdrew from the labor force at the end of the war. But the major mistake was in underestimating private demands for output. These forecasts actually overestimated government spendings during the transition period, but they seriously underestimated the percentage of disposable personal incomes that would be spent for consumption goods and services, the volume of private investment, and the postwar effective demand for our exports.

Basically, the postwar inflation reflected the fact that the sum of all demands for output—demands for consumption, for private investment purposes, for exports, and for government use—exceeded the total amount of output that could be made available. In a sense this is always true; our desires for goods exceed the available supply. But in the postwar period the various classes of purchasers not only had an intense desire and a willingness to spend for large amounts of output; they also either had, or demanded and were able to get, large and increasing amounts of

[2] For a description and discussion of these projections, see Everett E. Hagen and Nora Kirkpatrick, "Forecasting Gross National Product and Employment During the Transition Period," in *Studies in Income and Wealth,* National Bureau of Economic Research, 1947, vol. 10.

money with which to attempt to bid goods and services away from each other. And these competitive attempts to buy more goods and services than were available drove prices up continuously. An integral part of this spending-income-price spiral was the insistence of the various groups on maintaining or improving their real incomes by securing increases in their money incomes at least sufficient to offset increases in the prices of the things they bought. Many groups were highly dissatisfied with their income positions at the end of the war. Though price ceilings on agricultural products had been set at liberal levels, farmers in general insisted that their prices should be higher relative to other prices; and in support of their position, pointed to the low levels of farm incomes relative to those in urban areas. Manufacturers admitted that they had done well during the war but insisted that their prices should be raised to offset the expected loss of volume and the attendant rise of unit costs as volume fell, overhead costs rose, and selling expenses increased. Dealers also wanted higher margins to offset predicted declines of volume and higher selling and service expenses. Workers and their unions were highly dissatisfied; they claimed that wages had been too low during the war and maintained that both their own welfare and the maintenance of full employment and production required an increase of basic wage rates at least sufficient to offset the loss of income resulting from the discontinuance of overtime, downgrading, and the return of workers to lower-paying civilian industries. Thus, even at the end of the war, various groups were demanding improvement in both their absolute and relative income positions, and as controls were relaxed and withdrawn higher money incomes were demanded and in great numbers of cases received. Then, as prices rose, each group fought for still further increases in its money income. If the money demand for output had been less insistent, many of these demands for higher money income would have been successfully resisted; or, if the demands had been granted, unemployment might have occurred. But so great was the demand for output that the demands for higher wages and other money incomes could be granted and the full added cost passed on to buyers without reducing physical output, sales, and employment.

This upward spiral of spendings, incomes, and prices required an equivalent increase of money payments which could be provided by an increase in the money supply, an increase in the velocity of money, or both. The expansion was not hindered by any scarcity of the means of payments. Individuals, business firms, and foreigners drew upon their large idle balances built up during the war, the money supply expanded further by several billion dollars, and general credit policy assured the easy availability of money at low interest rates.

Before analyzing more thoroughly the policies related to these movements it will be useful to look at the statistical facts concerning total spendings for output, gross national income, and their components.

GROSS NATIONAL PRODUCT, 1945–1948

Table 61 shows the behavior of GNP and its components from the beginning of 1945 to the end of 1948. Table 62 shows (1) the percentages of GNP contributed by the various types of spendings for output, and (2) the percentages of the total value of output that were utilized for various purposes. Several important facts stand out. The first is the further rise of total spendings for output, as shown in Table 61. The decline of government spendings for output during 1945 and early 1946 was not fully offset by the current increase of private spendings, so that GNP in the first quarter of 1946 was about 11 percent below its level of a year earlier. This was not, however, accompanied by any significant lessening of inflationary pressures. Purchasers were still both willing and able to spend much larger amounts, and their spendings were held in check only by the continuance of price control and by the limitation of physical output during the period of reconversion from war to civilian production. But the relaxation and abandonment of price control, and to a lesser extent the expan-

TABLE 61. Gross National Product and Its Components, 1945-1948,
Quarterly Figures at Annual Rates Seasonally Adjusted
(In billions of dollars)[3]

Period	Gross National Product	Personal Consumption	Gross Private Domestic Investment	Net Foreign Investment	Government Purchases of Goods and Services		
					Total	Federal	State
1945—1Q	$222.6	$119.0	$ 7.7	$—2.7	$98.6	$90.8	$ 7.8
2Q	225.0	120.5	9.9	—2.7	97.3	89.5	7.8
3Q	213.0	123.3	10.4	—1.0	80.2	72.1	8.1
4Q	200.3	129.5	14.9	.6	55.2	46.8	8.5
1946—1Q	199.1	137.6	23.6	2.8	35.1	26.2	8.9
2Q	206.3	143.0	28.8	5.3	29.2	19.8	9.4
3Q	221.1	153.0	32.9	5.6	29.6	19.3	10.3
4Q	224.0	157.5	32.6	4.9	29.0	17.9	11.1
1947—1Q	228.2	160.5	31.5	8.9	27.3	15.4	11.9
2Q	233.6	165.6	29.5	10.2	28.3	15.8	12.6
3Q	232.4	168.1	26.5	8.7	29.1	15.6	13.5
4Q	248.6	173.5	36.9	7.8	30.4	16.0	14.4
1948—1Q	251.4	175.2	40.7	3.9	31.5	17.0	14.6
2Q	261.6	178.7	44.2	2.8	35.9	20.4	15.5
3Q	266.5	180.3	47.1	—.1	39.2	22.8	16.4
4Q	270.3	180.9	48.0	1.0	40.3	23.4	16.9

TABLE 62. Percentages of Gross National Product Utilized for Various
Purposes, 1945-1948 (or Percentage of GNP Contributed by Various
Types of Spendings), Quarterly Figures at Annual Rates Seasonally
Adjusted (In percentages)[4]

Period	Gross National Product	Personal Consumption	Gross Private Domestic Investment	Net Foreign Investment	Government Purchases of Goods and Services		
					Total	Federal	State
1945—1Q	100.0	53.5	3.5	—1.2	44.3	40.8	3.5
2Q	100.0	53.6	4.4	—1.2	43.2	39.8	3.5
3Q	100.0	57.9	4.9	—.5	37.7	33.8	3.8
4Q	100.0	64.7	7.4	.3	27.6	23.4	4.2
1946—1Q	100.0	69.1	11.9	1.4	17.6	13.2	4.5
2Q	100.0	69.3	14.0	2.6	14.2	9.6	4.6
3Q	100.0	69.2	14.9	2.5	13.4	8.7	4.7
4Q	100.0	70.3	14.6	2.2	12.9	8.0	4.9
1947—1Q	100.0	70.3	13.8	3.9	12.0	6.7	5.2
2Q	100.0	70.9	12.6	4.4	12.1	6.8	5.4
3Q	100.0	72.3	11.4	3.7	12.5	6.7	5.8
4Q	100.0	69.8	14.8	3.1	12.2	6.4	5.8
1948—1Q	100.0	69.7	16.2	1.6	12.5	6.8	5.8
2Q	100.0	68.3	16.9	1.1	13.7	7.8	5.9
3Q	100.0	67.7	17.7	a	14.7	8.6	6.2
4Q	100.0	66.9	17.8	.4	14.9	8.7	6.3

a A negative figure, less than —0.1.

[3] SOURCE: *Surveys of Current Business* and *Federal Reserve Bulletins.*
[4] Computed from data in Table 61.

TABLE 63. Gross National Product in Money and Real Terms, 1945-1948, Quarterly Figures at Annual Rates Seasonally Adjusted (Money figures in billions of dollars)[5]

Period	Col. 1 GNP in Current Dollars	Col. 2 Index of GNP in Current Dollars First Quarter of 1945=100	Col. 3 Cost-of-Living Index 1939=100	Col. 4 GNP in 1939 Dollars	Col. 5 Index of GNP in 1939 Dollars, First Quarter of 1945=100	Col. 6 GNP in 1939 Dollars Excluding Amounts Paid for Services of the Military	Col. 7 Index of (Col. 6), First Quarter of 1945=100
1945—1Q	$222.6	100.0	126.9	$175.4	100.0	$157.2	100.0
2Q	225.0	101.1	128.1	175.6	100.1	157.1	99.9
3Q	213.0	95.7	129.2	164.9	94.0	146.4	93.1
4Q	200.3	90.0	129.4	154.8	88.3	139.6	88.8
1946—1Q	199.1	89.4	129.9	153.3	87.4	144.2	91.7
2Q	206.3	92.7	132.0	156.3	89.1	150.3	95.6
3Q	221.1	99.3	143.7	153.9	87.7	149.3	95.0
4Q	224.0	100.6	151.3	148.1	84.4	144.4	91.9
1947—1Q	228.2	102.5	154.3	147.9	84.3	145.1	92.3
2Q	233.6	104.9	156.4	149.4	85.2	146.9	93.4
3Q	232.4	104.4	160.8	144.5	82.4	142.2	90.5
4Q	248.6	111.7	165.2	150.5	85.8	148.2	94.3
1948—1Q	251.4	112.9	167.7	149.9	85.5	147.6	93.9
2Q	261.6	117.5	170.5	153.4	87.5	151.2	96.2
3Q	266.5	119.7	174.2	153.0	87.2	150.7	95.7
4Q	270.3	121.4	172.4	156.8	89.4	154.4	98.2

[5] Computed by the author from data in *Surveys of Current Business.*

sion of output, again allowed spendings to increase. By late 1948, GNP had risen to $270.3 billion, 20 percent above the high levels of early 1945 and 196 percent above 1939 levels.

Real output increased far less than spendings for it. As noted earlier, we have no accurate measure of real output for the period, but Columns 4 to 7 of Table 63 present rough approximations arrived at by deflating the GNP figures by the cost-of-living index.[6] Column 6 presents what are perhaps the most meaningful figures, showing the value in 1939 dollars of GNP exclusive of the amounts paid to military personnel for their services. These indicate that real output in this sense declined about 10 percent between early 1945 and early 1946, and then recovered somewhat to range between 90 and 96 percent of the early 1945 level during the postwar period up to the third quarter of 1948.[7] These factors are highly important in understanding the postwar inflation. Though real output in this sense seems to have been about 60 percent above 1939 levels, it expanded very little during the two years following June 1946. With unemployment at virtually an irreducible minimum, with a tendency toward shorter work-weeks and longer vacations, with both management and labor apparently somewhat lax in the midst of prosperity, and with the growth of the labor force, capital accumulation, and technological advance being a slow process, it was indeed difficult to achieve significant further increases in real output during a short period. These facts emphasize two points. (1) In this situation an increase in the rate of total spendings had to be reflected almost completely in price rises. But (2) the very high rate of real output relative to prewar levels probably made the postwar inflation less serious than it would have been if our postwar productivity had been seriously reduced by damages from land or air warfare.

[6] For a longer discussion of this problem, see Chapter III.

[7] As shown in columns 4 and 5 of Table 63, the level of real output in the postwar period was even lower relative to the early 1945 level if we include in the GNP the value of services rendered by military personnel as indicated by their compensation.

TABLE 64. Gross National Income and Its Components, 1945-1948,
Quarterly Figures at Annual Rates, Seasonally Adjusted
(In billions of dollars)[8]

| Period | Gross National Income (=GNP) | Less | | Other Deductions and Statistical Error[a] | Equals Net National Income[b] | Compensation of Employees | Proprietors and Rental Income | Corporation Profits[c] | Net Interest |
		Indirect Business Taxes	Capital Consumption Allowances						
1945—1Q	$222.6	$15.0	$12.7	$3.0	$191.8	$127.5	$37.8	$23.5	$3.1
2Q	225.0	15.3	13.0	5.7	190.9	126.9	37.6	23.5	3.1
3Q	213.0	15.6	13.3	4.7	179.4	123.0	36.9	16.5	3.0
4Q	200.3	16.1	10.7	4.8	168.6	114.8	37.7	13.2	2.9
1946—1Q	199.1	16.5	11.2	3.4	167.9	111.6	38.9	14.5	2.9
2Q	206.3	17.1	11.7	1.8	175.7	114.5	39.4	18.8	3.0
3Q	221.1	17.7	12.2	7.0	184.2	119.6	43.2	18.4	3.0
4Q	224.0	18.0	12.6	3.2	190.2	122.1	43.5	21.6	3.0
1947—1Q	228.2	18.0	12.9	3.7	193.6	124.1	44.9	21.4	3.2
2Q	233.6	18.2	13.6	3.3	198.7	125.3	43.2	26.7	3.4
3Q	232.4	18.8	13.9	-2.9	202.7	128.1	44.5	26.5	3.5
4Q	248.6	19.7	14.4	2.7	211.8	132.8	47.6	27.8	3.5
1948—1Q	251.4	19.6	14.9	1.8	215.1	135.1	48.0	28.5	3.6
2Q	261.6	20.2	15.6	1.0	224.9	137.7	50.4	33.0	3.7
3Q	266.5	20.6	15.9	0	230.4	143.3	49.9	33.3	3.9
4Q	270.3	20.7	16.4	-1.1	234.3	144.9	49.7	35.7	4.1

a Reflects statistical discrepancy, business transfer payments, and subsidies less current surplus of government enterprises.
b All the net national income figures are before any taxes except indirect business taxes.
c After inventory valuation adjustment.
8 SOURCE: Surveys of Current Business and Federal Reserve Bulletins.

A study of Tables 61 and 62 brings out the behavior of the various types of spendings making up the GNP. Government purchases declined markedly until early 1947, when they again began to rise, reflecting both increased federal spendings and the continued increase of state and local expenditures. Though inflationary pressures would have been lessened by still further decreases of government spendings, the dynamic upward thrust came from the other types of spendings. The increase of consumption expenditures was by far the greatest single contributor to the rise of the GNP, followed in order by private spendings for capital maintenance and accumulation and by net foreign investment.

The rise of spendings for output created a corresponding increase in the gross national income received by the various sectors of the economy. By the last quarter of 1948, gross income receipts were at a rate 35 percent above the level in early 1946, 20 percent above early 1945, and 196 percent above 1939. Those who blithely stated that price increases were bound to decrease the amount of goods and services that could be sold apparently ignored the accompanying increases in money incomes and spending power. Table 64 shows the dollar amounts of gross incomes received by the various claimants, and Table 65 indicates the percentage shares received.

The preceding sections have outlined the postwar upsurge of total spendings for output and have indicated the types of spendings contributing to the rise. It will now be useful to see why the various types of spenders were both willing and able to spend such large and increasing amounts. This section will emphasize the factors producing the desire and willingness to spend. The pivotal importance of this question is obvious when one compares the postwar period with the decade of the 1930's when the effective demand for output was so low as to produce deflation and widespread unemployment.

TABLE 65. Percentage Distribution of the Gross National Income, 1945-1948 Quarterly Figures, Seasonally Adjusted
(In percent of gross national income)[9]

Period	Gross National Income (=GNP)	Indirect Business Taxes	Capital Consumption Allowances	Other Deductions and Statistical Error	Net National Income	Compensation of Employees	Proprietors and Rental Income	Corporation Profits	Net Interest
1945—1Q	100	6.7	5.7	1.3	86.2	57.3	17.0	10.6	1.4
2Q	100	6.8	5.8	2.5	84.8	56.4	16.7	10.4	1.4
3Q	100	7.3	6.2	2.2	84.2	57.7	17.3	7.7	1.4
4Q	100	8.0	5.3	2.4	84.2	57.3	18.8	6.6	1.4
1946—1Q	100	8.3	5.6	1.7	84.3	56.1	19.5	7.3	1.5
2Q	100	8.3	5.7	0.9	85.2	55.5	19.1	9.1	1.5
3Q	100	8.0	5.5	3.2	83.3	54.1	19.5	8.3	1.4
4Q	100	8.0	5.6	1.4	84.9	54.5	19.4	9.6	1.3
1947—1Q	100	7.9	5.7	1.6	84.8	54.4	19.7	9.4	1.4
2Q	100	7.8	5.8	1.4	85.1	53.6	18.5	11.4	1.5
3Q	100	8.1	6.0	-1.2	87.2	55.1	19.1	11.4	1.5
4Q	100	7.9	5.8	1.1	85.2	53.4	19.1	11.2	1.4
1948—1Q	100	7.8	5.9	0.7	85.6	53.7	19.1	11.3	1.4
2Q	100	7.7	6.0	0.4	86.0	52.6	19.3	12.6	1.4
3Q	100	7.7	6.0	0	86.5	53.8	18.7	12.5	1.5
4Q	100	7.7	6.1	-0.4	86.7	53.6	18.4	13.2	1.5

[9] Computed from data in Table 64.

EXPORTS AND IMPORTS

An important, though not the major, factor in the high postwar demand for our output was the high foreign demand. As shown in Table 66, the excess of our exports over our imports was $7.8 billion in 1946, $11.3 billion in 1947, and $6.3 billion in 1948. A number of factors contributed to the intense desire of

TABLE 66.   U. S. Exports and Imports, and the Means of Financing
Net Exports, 1945-1948
(In millions of dollars)[10]

	1945	1946	1947	1948
Exports of goods and services	$16,273	$14,966	$19,751	$16,826
Imports of goods and services	10,232	7,167	8,463	10,491
Net exports	$ 6,041	$ 7,799	$11,288	$ 6,335
Means of financing net exports				
Net gold inflow	−548	623	2,163	1,532
Liquidation of dollar assets	−2,085	1,345	2,350	−671
U. S. Government net grants and loans	7,659	5,053	5,713	4,735
Dollars disbursed by the International Monetary Fund and the World Bank	—	—	761	385
Net U. S. private remittances	473	598	568	603
Net U. S. private capital exports	550	335	727	876
Errors and omissions	−8	−155	−1,004	−1,125

other countries to buy from us: (1) The wartime damage to productive capacity and the postwar social and economic disorganization in many countries. We are all familiar with the destruction of dwellings, railroads, factories, and animals; the impoverishment of farm land because of the lack of fertilizer; the shortages of fuel, raw materials, and foodstuffs at the end of the war; the malnutrition of millions of people; and the general social and economic disorganization that retarded the recovery of production. These countries urgently needed supplies for the multiple purpose of feeding their people, repairing productive

[10] SOURCE: *Survey of Current Business,* March, 1949, pp. 16-18.

facilities, securing raw materials for their industries, inhibiting inflation, and stemming the rise of communism. Moreover, low production in many of these areas diverted demand from other countries to the American markets. For example, the low output of steel in Britain and Germany diverted to our market many other European and South American demands; the low production of foodstuffs in Eastern Europe and the virtual cessation of East-West trade increased the demand for our agricultural output; and so on. (2) The great rise of money incomes abroad, the rise of prices there, and the support of exchange rates at levels that were "too high" relative to the dollar. Not only in belligerent countries but also in other areas, such as South America, money incomes expanded greatly during the war and in many the expansion continued in the postwar period. Price increases occurred everywhere, but in many areas price controls were retained so that people had large amounts of spending power in excess of the amounts they could spend for available goods and services at existing legal price levels. "Suppressed inflation" was widespread. At the same time, these foreign moneys were in general not allowed to depreciate in terms of the dollar. This country therefore became a relatively cheap country in which to buy, and the relative cheapness of our products, as well as their availability, diverted world demand to our markets. In fact, the desire to buy here was so large that it was held in check only by our export controls, by foreign restrictions on imports and exchange operations, and by the shortage of dollars. This factor also contributed to our inflation in another way. The greater increases of prices abroad without an offsetting decline of foreign exchange rates raised the cost of our imports. (3) The accumulation of gold and dollar balances by certain countries during the war and their postwar willingness to spend them. We have already noted that during the war period this country paid out gold and dollar balances to some countries, mostly in Latin America, to buy more goods than we exported to them. In the postwar period these countries, wanting a high level of imports with which to maintain or increase consumption standards and to carry out a high rate of capital construction, took large amounts of our exports.

If other countries desired large amounts of our output, we were willing for a number of reasons to permit large exports. (1) The humanitarian motive of relieving suffering abroad, both directly by providing means of subsistence and indirectly by restoring foreign productive capacity. (2) The desire to curb the rise of communism abroad. (3) The desire to reestablish worldwide productivity and trade as a means of securing a stable peace and assuring ourselves of an expanding export market in the long-run. (4) The desire to avoid depression and unemployment here during the early postwar period. It is doubtful indeed that we needed an export surplus to avoid depression but this seems to have been an important, though not the dominant, consideration. And (5) the desire of American exporters to get a firm foothold in foreign markets in order to make immediate profits and develop markets for the longer-term.

Thus, foreigners wanted large amounts of our output, and our government was willing not only to permit large exports but also to help finance them. Table 66 shows how other countries were able to finance such a huge volume of net imports from us. During the three years 1946-1948 these totalled $25.4 billion. About 60 percent of them were financed by federal grants and loans under such programs as the British loan, UNRRA, aid to China, aid to Greece and Turkey, civilian supplies for occupied countries, and the European Recovery Program. These amounts are included in our figures for government spendings and were fully covered by tax collections in this country. Another 17 percent of our net exports was covered by foreign payments of gold to us out of their accumulated stocks and current production. This tended to increase both our money supply and bank reserves. Nearly 12 percent of our net exports were paid for by the net transfer of dollar deposits from foreign to American ownership and by selling other dollar assets here. Dollar loans by the International Monetary Fund and the World Bank financed another 4.5 percent, and the remaining

14 percent was covered by private remittances and net private capital exports.

There can be no doubt that the large net purchases of our output by other countries contributed to postwar inflation here. It is impossible, however, to measure precisely the net contribution of foreign demand to the magnitude and duration of our inflation, for we do not know what other policies would have changed in the absence of the big export surplus. If one wishes to emphasize the inflationary pressures from this source he can point out that this can be considered a "marginal demand" that may make the difference between price stability and inflation; that the concentration of foreign demand on foodstuffs, steel, and certain other items that were in greatest demand here accentuated their scarcity and the rise of their prices; that an export surplus tends to exert a multiplier effect on domestic spendings and money income; and that the export surplus contributed to the increase of our money supply by increasing our monetary gold stock, by transferring dollar deposits from foreign to American ownership, by causing the sale here of dollar assets that directly or indirectly enhanced the expansion of bank credit, and by reducing the Treasury's surplus during these years.

Though they contain much truth, the above arguments should not be overemphasized. In the first place, our net exports, though large in absolute amounts, did not in any of these years exceed 5 percent of our GNP; they amounted to 3.7 percent in 1946, to 4.9 percent in 1947, and to 2.5 percent in 1948. Domestic purchasers accounted for by far the largest part of both total spendings and the increase of spendings. In the second place, there seems to be no particular reason, other than to gratify nationalistic feelings, why the foreign demand rather than some part of our own demand for output should be labelled "marginal demand." After all, the satisfaction of this foreign demand need not have had a net inflationary effect if measures had been adopted to lower domestic demands concurrently. And in the third place, we do not know how different the federal government's fiscal policy would have been in the absence of its large foreign aid program. One might assume that both its tax policy and its other expenditures would have been unaffected, so that its current cash surpluses would have been larger. But it is probably more realistic to assume that the government would have cut tax rates considerably more, or would have spent more for military or domestic programs, or that is would have done both of these things.

These uncertainties must not, however, be allowed to obscure the fact that our large net exports were a factor in the postwar inflation, and that they might have been even more important if our government aid to other countries had not been fully financed by tax collections from the private sectors of the economy.

GOVERNMENT PURCHASES OF GOODS AND SERVICES

A later chapter will deal more fully with federal fiscal policy. At this point we shall make only a few comments on the behavior of government spendings for output, neglecting transfer payments which were large in amount and treating separately federal expenditures and state and local expenditures.

As indicated in Tables 61 and 62 above, federal purchases of goods and services in early 1945 were at an annual rate of nearly $91 billion and accounted for 41 percent of total spendings for output. They began to taper off about the time of V-E Day, fell precipitately for a time after V-J Day, and then declined more slowly to reach, in 1947, an annual rate of less than $16 billion, or less than 7 percent of total spendings for output. But by the end of 1948 they had again risen to a rate of $23.4 billion and were accounting for 8.7 percent of GNP. The continuance of federal spending for output above prewar levels was due primarily to three factors—increased compensation of government employees and increased prices of goods and services purchased from industry, the large foreign aid program, and the larger military establishment. To a lesser extent, however, this was supplemented by an expanded domestic program.

While federal spendings for output showed first a downward and later an upward trend, state and local purchases advanced steadily throughout the period. During the war they had fallen to low levels as compensation of state and local employees lagged behind, and as the shortage of labor and materials precluded public works programs and even major repairs. In early 1945 they were contributing only 3.5 percent of total spendings for output. But from that time they rose steadily as state and local employees achieved higher rates of pay, as the prices of goods and services rose, as durable goods such as autos and trucks again became available, and as school construction, road building, and other public works expanded. By late 1948 these spendings had risen to an annual rate of $16.9 billion, or 6.3 percent of total spendings for output. It is interesting to note that though the absolute amount of output used for state and local purposes was considerably above prewar levels, the percentage of GNP being used for these purposes even at the end of 1948 was still not above the prewar levels. This figure was 8.7 percent in 1929, 7.7 percent in 1940, and 6.2 percent in 1941.

GROSS PRIVATE DOMESTIC INVESTMENT

One of the major dynamic factors in the postwar inflation was the high and rising rate of private spendings for goods and services with which to maintain and increase the supply of capital goods. As shown in Tables 61 and 62, they were quite low in early 1945, running at an annual rate of $7.7 billion and accounting for only 3.5 percent of total spendings for output. But they expanded steadily as materials, labor, and other productive facilities were freed from war uses and as prices rose. By late 1948 they had reached an annual rate of $48.0 billion and were accounting directly for more than 17 percent of total spendings for output.

This raises a crucial question: "Why, in contrast to the situation in the 1930's, were private enterprisers willing and able to spend such large amounts and to use such a large percentage of our expanded output for the purpose of capital maintenance and accumulation?" Such investment can occur, of course, only if two conditions are met: (1) Entrepreneurs believe that large amounts of new investment will yield "acceptable" profits, and (2) sufficient amounts of investible funds are available on attractive terms. Both of these conditions were met in the postwar period. We shall

TABLE 67.   Gross Private Domestic Investment and Its Components, 1945-1948, Quarterly Figures at Annual Rates Seasonally Adjusted
(In billions of dollars)[11]

Period	Gross Private Domestic Investment, Total	Residential Construction- Nonfarm	Other Construction	Producers' Durable Equipment	Net Change in Business Inventories
1945—1Q	$ 5.9	$0.4	$2.1	$ 6.0	$ −2.5
2Q	7.8	0.5	2.4	6.5	−1.6
3Q	11.0	0.7	2.6	7.7	−0.1
4Q	12.2	1.2	3.4	8.8	−1.3
1946—1Q	21.3	2.3	4.9	8.8	5.3
2Q	25.1	2.9	5.8	12.3	4.1
3Q	28.1	3.6	6.0	13.9	4.6
4Q	31.3	3.9	6.2	16.2	5.0
1947—1Q	32.6	4.5	6.3	16.6	5.2
2Q	26.4	4.3	6.0	17.9	−1.8
3Q	25.6	5.2	6.3	17.6	−3.5
4Q	35.4	7.0	6.9	18.9	2.5
1948—1Q	38.0	16.9		19.8	3.9
2Q	38.0	18.1		21.0	2.6
3Q	40.2	18.7		21.9	3.5
4Q	42.8	17.9		22.7	5.3

see later that the easy availability of low-cost investible funds was assured by the large wartime accumulation of idle money balances and other assets that were easily convertible into money, by a liberal Federal Reserve credit policy, by large corporate savings, and by several other related factors. The means of payment for capital goods were in ample supply at low cost. But we still must explain why there was such a great willingness to spend for capital pur-

[11] SOURCE: *Survey of Current Business.*

poses. To do this it is necessary to break down investment spendings, as is done in Table 67.

RESIDENTIAL CONSTRUCTION

Many factors combined to produce a high rate of residential construction. (1) The low rate of housing construction not only during the war itself but also during most of the 1930's. Our population increased about 15 percent between 1930 and 1946, and it is unlikely that the number of habitable dwelling units rose proportionally. (2) The large wartime migration from rural to urban areas and among urban areas. This increased sharply the housing shortage in the areas of net in-migration and also raised the total demand for new housing. (3) The return of veterans and the high marriage rate. During the war there was much "doubling up" of families as the wives of veterans lived with their parents, "in-laws," other relatives, or friends. As demobilization progressed these groups, as well as large numbers of newly-weds, sought separate quarters. The large increase in the birth rate also increased the demand for more living space. (4) The prevailing high income levels. With higher incomes many people sought better and larger living quarters. This movement was probably accentuated by the maintenance of rent controls that made shelter cheap relative to other commodities whose prices were rising. Moreover, the combination of very high wartime incomes and the limited availability of many other things probably led numerous people to increase their demand for housing space. (5) The wartime accumulation of personal savings. Having saved considerable amounts during the war, many felt more willing and able to make the necessary down-payment on new houses. It is common knowledge that large numbers of people purchased houses not because they considered them a "good investment" at prevailing prices but because of their desperate need for living quarters. (6) The easy availability of housing credit. Interest rates were kept at low levels; credit for housing was available in large amounts;

the government mortgage-insuring agencies required only very small down-payments, appraised properties at liberally high levels, and permitted amortization over long periods; veterans were granted loans on even more favorable terms.

OTHER CONSTRUCTION AND PRODUCERS' DURABLE GOODS

Though some of the new dwelling units were purchased by investors whose purpose was to rent them to others and make profits, many were purchased for occupancy by their owners, whose motive was to secure not profits but living quarters. But the expectation of profits was the primary motive behind most of the investment in other private construction and in producers' durable goods. Enterprisers wanted to use large amounts of current output to maintain and increase the supply of capital in these forms because they expected to reap high profits on their new investments. Here again many factors combined to produce expectations of high profits and to make enterprisers both willing and able to spend for investment purposes. (1) The high and rising demand for business output. Enterprisers as a group expected a rising sales volume because of higher consumer demands, high net exports, and continuing large government spendings. Moreover, large private investment spendings in some lines both directly and indirectly increased the profitability of investment in other lines. For example, large investments in automobile manufacturing plant and equipment directly stimulated investment in wider areas by increasing national money income. With a rising volume of sales, industry saw a good chance of utilizing at a high rate not only existing capacity but also large additions to it. Even the lurking fear of a future depression was not sufficient to offset this optimism. (2) The low rate of private investment during the war and also during much of the 1930's. It is true, as noted in Chapter III, that during 1940, 1941, and the earliest stage of our participation in the war, private investment recovered from its low depression levels and the government itself financed many new facilities. In some industries, such as steel, aluminum, magnesium, and electronics manufacturing, productive capacity at the end of the war was considerably above prewar levels. But this did not mean that large amounts of new capital were not needed. The government-financed facilities tended to be concentrated in war industries, and many of them were not well located or were difficult to convert to peacetime products. Many shipbuilding facilities, shell loading plants, powder factories, and airplane plants were in this category. Machine tool installations had been made in huge volume during the war, but a considerable part of these had to be replaced for peacetime production. In many industries productive capacity at the end of the war was probably below the levels of 1939, and in many more it was insufficient to meet the enlarged postwar demands. (3) Innovations, changed patterns of demand, and changes in the relative prices of productive factors. The contributions of these factors to the high demand for capital are difficult to evaluate, but they must have been very large. Much of the existing plant and equipment had been made obsolete by innovations that had occurred since the capital was originally constructed, which in some cases was long ago. For example, large expenditures were considered necessary to modernize stores to give them "the new look," to increase the extent of "self service," to provide a better display of merchandise, and so on. Many manufacturing plants were operating with worn and inefficient equipment and plants without adequate lighting, ventilation, and space. Thousands of farms were still without electricity, the most efficient tractors and machinery, and efficient work and storage buildings. Railroads needed more and better equipment. Many other such cases could be cited. Changed patterns of demand, as well as the generally higher levels of income and spendings, also helped to swell investment. For example, the shift toward electrical energy, as well as the development of more efficient steam generating methods and the great rise of fuel prices, called for large investments in expanded and more efficient electric generating plants and equipment.

The postwar upsurge of the demand for housing created profitable investment opportunities in the building materials industries. And the postwar bulge in the demand for autos and other consumer durables opened additional investment opportunities in those lines. In some cases this movement was supplemented by changes in the relative prices and availability of the various productive factors. The continuance of low interest rates while wage rates were rising rapidly and labor was in short supply undoubtedly contributed to the rapid increase of mechanization in farming, manufacturing, and various other lines. The rise of coal prices and the sporadic interruption of coal production speeded up the shift of railroads to Diesel power. There were numerous other cases of this type. (4) The large wartime savings and the high postwar earnings of business enterprises. Economists sometimes assume that in making their investment decisions business enterprisers look solely at the prospective net earnings on additional capital and at the level of interest rates in the market. They seem to assume that investment decisions are not at all influenced by the amount of accumulated liquid assets in the hands of business, and that the current level of net earnings is influential only in so far as it affects estimates of future earnings on additional capital. This appears to the writer to be a serious error. Presumably an investment will not be made unless it is expected to yield some positive return, but given this expectation enterprisers are more likely to spend for capital purposes if they can finance the expenditure out of their own accumulated funds or out of current earnings than if they have to seek the funds in the market. In the first place, many a prospective enterpriser is more sanguine as to his probable success than are his potential creditors or suppliers of equity funds. He will invest his own accumulated funds or current income, if he has them,whereas he could not secure funds from others. In the second place, it seems likely that many firms invest their own funds in their enterprise without carefully considering the "opportunity cost" of this money. Do corporation boards reinvest their depreciation allowances and undistributed profits in their own firms only if the prospective return promises to be at least equal to the return that could be secured by lending the funds to others? Do they always first make their investment decisions and then find the means of financing them or do they sometimes look at the easy availability of funds from internal sources and then decide to make capital expenditures to utilize them? Do smaller enterprisers always know of existing alternative uses for their money? The answer to these questions appears to be in the negative. In the third place, many smaller enterprisers, such as farmers and storekeepers, seem to dislike going into debt or sharing their ownership equity, so they allow their investment decisions to be greatly influenced by the amount of their accumulated liquid assets and by their current incomes. Some corporation officials appear to share this feeling. For these reasons the writer believes that the large accumulation of wartime savings by business and the high level of postwar profits increased not only the ability but also the willingness of business to spend for capital purposes. (5) The large influx of new business firms. The number of operating businesses actually declined during the war period as the number of new business starts declined more than the number discontinued, but it began to surge up again as the war drew to a close. Many factors contributed to this rise of the business population—the current profitability of business, the ease of finding markets, the wartime accumulation of savings by veterans and others, the desire of many a veteran or worker to "be his own boss," the easy availability of credit, and the especially liberal loans to veterans. Though most of these new firms were small they probably accounted for a large aggregate amount of capital spendings. (6) The easy availability and low cost of credit. The factors noted above were the principal ones accounting for the willingness of enterprisers to spend for large amounts of nonresidential construction and for producers' durable equipment. The ability of enterprisers to spend was assured not only by their large accumulated savings and current earnings but also by a very liberal general credit policy.

BUSINESS INVENTORIES

Another significant factor in the high rate of private investment spending was the accumulation of business inventories. In this case, too, there were several contributing factors. (1) The depletion of inventories during the war. In many lines inventories were almost nonexistent at the war's end. This was true of autos, household electrical equipment, metal toys, many hardware items, and so on. In numerous other lines inventories at the end of the war were inconveniently low relative to current production and sales. (2) The high and rising volume of sales. Larger inventories were needed to assure uninterrupted production and to maintain a variety of products for purchasers. (3) The expectation of further price increases. During much of the period producers and dealers wanted more inventories in order to realize inventory profits or to avoid losses on forward contracts if the costs of supplies rose. (4) The ease of financing larger inventories out of accumulated business savings, current earnings, or low-cost credit.

That there was not an even larger accumulation of inventories and more inventory speculation seems to have been due to a number of factors: the very large final demand for products which drained inventories away, the public disapproval of inventory hoarding, fear in some cases that the price rise might be reversed, informal rationing by producers and wholesalers, and pressure by the banks to avoid "undue" inventory accumulation.

SUMMARY

This section has emphasized that the large and insistent demand for output to be used for the maintenance and increase of private capital was a very important factor in the postwar inflation. It is interesting to note, therefore, that their underestimate of these demands was one of the reasons why some of the forecasts relating to the postwar period proved to be so erroneous. In the "more favorable" OWMR projection, to which reference was made earlier in this chapter, gross private domestic investment, stated in first half of 1945 dollars, was assumed to be the amounts shown in Column 1 of Table 68. But, as indicated by Columns 2 and 3, the amounts of real output used for this purpose during 1946 and the first quarter of 1947 ranged between 26 and 87 percent above the projected levels. Private investment spendings in current dollars, which reflected the rise of wages and prices, exceeded the projected estimates by even larger amounts.

TABLE 68.   "Projected" and Actual Gross Private Domestic Investment, 1945-1947
(In billions of first half of 1945 dollars)[12]

Period	Col. 1 The OWMR "More Favorable" Projection	Col. 2 Actual	Col. 3 Actual Investment as Percentage of the Projected Amounts
1945—4Q	$12.8	$14.7	114.8
1946—1Q	12.3	23.0	187.0
2Q	15.1	27.6	182.8
3Q	17.1	29.0	169.6
4Q	19.2	27.3	142.2
1947—1Q	20.6	26.0	126.2
2Q	21.9	23.9	109.1

PERSONAL CONSUMPTION

Personal spendings for consumption goods and services were by far the largest contributor to the postwar expansion of the GNP. Between early 1945 and late 1948 they rose from an annual rate of $119 billion to $181 billion, an increase of $62 billion or 52 percent. This was nearly $14 billion more than the total rise of GNP during the period. Why did consumption rise so much? It is clear that a part of the answer lies in the marked increase of disposable personal incomes. As shown in Table 69, the amount

[12] For the projected figures, see Everett E. Hagen and Nora Kirkpatrick, *op. cit.*, p. 95. Actual figures are those of the Department of Commerce deflated by the cost-of-living index with the first half of 1945=100.

TABLE 69. Personal Income, 1945-1948, Quarterly Figures at Annual Rates Seasonally Adjusted (In billions of dollars)[13]

Period	Compensation of Employees[a]	Proprietors and Rental Income	Dividends and Personal Interest Income	Transfer Payments from Business	Transfer Payments from Government	Total Personal Income	Less: Personal Taxes	Equals: Disposable Personal Income
1945—1Q	$121.7	$37.8	$11.1	$ .5	$ 3.5	$174.4	$21.3	$153.1
2Q	120.8	37.6	11.1	.5	4.2	174.2	21.2	153.0
3Q	116.7	36.9	11.6	.5	5.0	170.7	20.7	150.0
4Q	108.5	37.7	11.9	.5	10.0	168.6	20.3	148.3
1946—1Q	105.5	38.9	12.4	.5	12.0	168.5	17.8	150.6
2Q	108.4	39.4	13.0	.6	11.1	173.5	18.7	154.8
3Q	113.6	43.2	13.4	.6	10.6	181.4	19.2	162.2
4Q	116.3	43.5	13.7	.6	9.7	183.8	19.6	164.2
1947—1Q	118.0	44.9	14.2	.6	10.1	187.8	21.2	166.6
2Q	119.3	43.2	14.6	.6	9.9	187.6	21.2	166.4
3Q	122.8	44.5	15.0	.6	13.7	196.6	21.6	175.0
4Q	127.6	47.6	15.2	.6	10.7	201.7	22.1	179.7
1948—1Q	130.0	48.0	15.6	.6	11.0	205.1	23.2	181.9
2Q	132.7	50.4	15.8	.6	10.8	210.3	20.7	189.6
3Q	138.1	49.9	16.3	.6	10.4	215.4	20.2	195.2
4Q	139.6	49.7	16.9	.6	9.9	216.6	20.4	196.2

[a] Less Contributions for Social Insurance.

[13] SOURCE: Various tables in *Survey of Current Business*, July, 1949.

of money income remaining at the disposal of persons after they had met all their tax liabilities had risen by late 1948 to an annual rate of $196.2 billion, a level 179 percent above that of 1939, and 30 percent above the levels prevailing in late 1945 and early 1946. This reflected the fact that a major part of the increased spendings for output accrued to persons as increased income receipts in the form of increased compensation for their labor, as larger rentals and earnings of farmers, professional people, and other unincorporated enterprisers, as higher dividends and to a lesser extent as higher interest receipts, and as larger transfer payments from the government, most of the latter being veterans' benefits. Thus a considerable part of the increase in consumption spendings was due to the rise of disposable personal incomes, which in turn reflected the rising spendings for output.

We must be careful, however, to avoid circular reasoning here; we must avoid saying that consumption rose because disposable incomes rose and that the rise of disposable incomes was largely caused by the rise of consumption spendings. We can avoid this difficulty by stating that the rise of disposable personal incomes was due to the high rate of spendings for output in the form of private investment spendings, net foreign investment, and government spendings, and to the rise in the propensity of people to spend their disposable incomes for consumption goods and services. And it is important to emphasize the dynamic role played by this marked rise in the propensity to consume and the decline in the propensity to save as compared with the wartime situation.

The statistical facts concerning the propensities to consume and to save are shown in Table 70. For the reasons indicated earlier, people used an unusually low proportion of their disposable incomes for consumption and devoted an unusually high proportion to saving during the war period. In early 1945 the average propensity to consume was only about 78 percent while the average propensity to save was at the high level of about 22 percent. But as war production tapered off and more consumption goods became available, and later as price controls were relaxed and

TABLE 70. The Propensity to Consume and to Save, 1945-1948, Quarterly Figures at Annual Rates Seasonally Adjusted
(In billions of dollars)[14]

| Period | Disposable Personal Income | Personal Con-sumption | Percentage of Disposable Income Spent for Consumption | Percentage of Disposable Income Saved | Changes from Preceding Quarter | | |
					in Disposable Income	in Consumption	in Saving
1945—1Q	$153.1	$119.0	77.7	22.3	$ —	$ —	$ —
2Q	153.0	120.5	78.8	21.2	—0.1	1.5	—1.6
3Q	150.0	123.3	82.2	17.8	—3.0	2.8	—5.8
4Q	148.3	129.5	87.3	12.7	—1.7	6.2	—7.9
1946—1Q	150.6	137.6	91.4	8.6	2.3	8.1	—5.8
2Q	154.8	143.0	92.4	7.6	4.2	5.4	—1.2
3Q	162.2	153.0	94.3	5.8	7.4	10.0	—2.5
4Q	164.2	157.5	95.9	4.1	2.0	4.5	—2.6
1947—1Q	166.6	160.5	96.3	3.7	2.4	3.0	—0.6
2Q	166.4	165.6	99.5	.5	—0.2	5.1	—5.4
3Q	175.0	168.1	96.1	3.9	8.6	2.5	6.3
4Q	179.7	173.5	96.5	3.5	4.7	5.4	—0.9
1948—1Q	181.9	175.2	96.3	3.7	2.2	1.7	0.6
2Q	189.6	178.7	94.3	5.7	7.7	3.5	4.1
3Q	195.2	180.3	92.4	7.6	5.6	1.6	4.2
4Q	196.2	180.9	92.2	7.8	1.0	0.6	0.3

[14] SOURCE: Computed from data in *Surveys of Current Business.*

abandoned, people returned to more normal consumption-saving habits. In fact, as shown in Table 70, consumption spendings rose during the last three quarters of 1945 despite the contemporary decline of disposable incomes, and in the first half of 1946 they rose considerably more than disposable incomes. Then from mid-1946 to mid-1948, despite the continued rise of money incomes, people never spent as little as 94 percent of their disposable incomes for consumption; they never saved as much as 6 percent. This was a very important element in the inflationary spiral. The

TABLE 71. Actual and "Projected" Average Propensity to Consume Personal Disposable Income, 1945-1947[15]

Period	The OWMR Projection	Actual
1945—4Q	80.2%	87.3%
1946—1Q	82.3	91.4
2Q	85.4	92.4
3Q	87.5	94.3
4Q	89.7	95.9
1947—1Q	89.9	99.5
1947—1Q	89.9	96.3
2Q	90.9	99.5

upsurge of consumption while government spendings for war purposes declined served to cushion the decline of total spendings for output in 1945 and early 1946, and the continued rise of consumption spendings after mid-1946 competed for output with rising spendings from other sources. At the very time that large amounts of output were being demanded for private domestic investment and net foreign investment, consumers were electing to use only a small part of their incomes for saving, preferring to spend a very large part of it for consumption goods and services.

It is worth noting here that another important error in the OWMR "projections" for the transition period was their under-

15 The OWMR projection is computed from the data included in the "more favorable" projection by Hagen and Kirkpatrick, *op. cit.*, p. 95.

estimate of the propensity to consume. As shown in Table 71, the percentage of disposable personal incomes actually channeled back into the market as demand for consumption goods and services was considerably above the forecasted levels; though disposable incomes rose considerably above the projected levels, the propensity to save was much lower than had been expected by these forecasters.

TABLE 72. Disposable Personal Income, Consumption, and Savings in 1939 Dollars, Quarterly Figures at Annual Rates, Seasonally Adjusted (In billions of 1939 dollars)[16]

Period	Disposable Income	Consumption	Savings
1945—1Q	$120.6	$ 93.8	$26.9
2Q	119.4	94.1	25.4
3Q	116.1	95.4	20.7
4Q	114.6	100.1	14.5
1946—1Q	115.9	105.9	10.0
2Q	117.3	108.3	8.9
3Q	112.9	106.5	6.5
4Q	108.5	104.1	4.4
1947—1Q	108.0	104.0	4.0
2Q	106.4	105.9	0.4
3Q	108.8	104.5	4.4
4Q	108.8	105.0	3.7
1948—1Q	108.5	104.5	4.0
2Q	111.2	104.8	6.3
3Q	112.1	103.5	8.6
4Q	113.8	104.9	8.9

Why was the propensity to consume so high and the propensity to save so low during the postwar period? In answering this question we must distinguish clearly between money income and consumption on the one hand, and real income and consumption on the other. The facts concerning these items in terms of money have already been noted. The movement of real income and consumption was somewhat different, as is shown in Table 72.

[16] Computed from data in *Surveys of Current Business*. These figures were arrived at by dividing the current dollar values by the cost of living index converted to a 1939 base.

Measured in 1939 dollars, consumption rose 15 percent between early 1945 and the second quarter of 1946 despite the fact that disposable income in 1939 dollars actually fell somewhat. But these figures, inaccurate as they probably are, indicate that after mid-1946 neither disposable real income nor real consumption rose significantly and that they may have declined slightly. People as a whole spent more in a vain attempt to secure larger aggregate amounts of real consumption goods and services, but they were largely unsuccessful because of the limited expansibility of total output and the larger amounts used for private investment, net foreign investment, and government uses. In effect, their larger consumption spendings succeeded only in offsetting the current price increases of consumption goods and in preventing aggregate real consumption from falling below the levels attained in 1946.

There still remains the problem of explaining why the propensity to consume rose far above wartime levels and even above the levels of 1941. Here again there were many relevant factors. (1) The release of output from war uses, the relaxation and withdrawal of price controls, and the lessened effectiveness of admonitions to save. People regained their freedom to spend; they were no longer subject to "forced saving" of the wartime types. This alone accounts for a considerable part of the marked rise in the propensity to consume above wartime levels, but it does not explain why it rose above the prewar level when direct controls had not yet been imposed. (2) Limitations of many types of civilian output during the war and the resulting postwar "vacuum." No automobiles were produced between early 1942 and the end of the war, so that the number of registered vehicles declined by more than a million and many of the remaining ones needed replacement or extensive repairs. The same was true of many other durable goods, such as stoves, refrigerators, washing machines, radios, pianos, metal toys, cameras, watches, toasters, and so on. Many people had taken little or no vacation during the war and felt entitled to one after the war's end. Millions of tires needed replacement. The low quality and limited availability of furniture during the war created a backlog of demand in that field. Many men found that they needed replacements for their hats, over-coats, suits, and shoes. Numerous other examples could be listed. In many cases the feeling of wartime deprivation was greater than was justified by the facts. Because their incomes had been so much larger than the amounts of desirable and available goods and services, many people felt that they had sacrificed greatly during the war and were justified in going on a spending spree after the return of peace. (3) The accumulation of large personal savings during the war. As noted earlier, personal savings during the six years 1940-1945 aggregated nearly $133 billion. Some of these were used during the war to reduce consumer indebtedness and some to acquire illiquid assets, but a major part of them was held in highly liquid forms. These large accumulations of personal savings could raise the postwar propensity to consume in two principal ways: (a) by making those who had reduced their debts or accumulated assets both more able and more willing to consume beyond their current incomes by borrowing or by disposing of assets, and (b) by making people who had reduced their indebted-ness or increased their assets feel freer to consume a larger part of their postwar incomes and save a smaller proportion even though they did not borrow or sell assets. Both of these influences were undoubtedly present, though we have no statistical measurement of their importance. There are, however, ample statistics to show that large numbers of families did consume more than their cur-rent incomes during one or more years in this period. Federal Reserve surveys indicated that of all spending units, 27 percent dissaved in 1946 and 28 percent dissaved in 1947. In each of the years another 8 percent were zero savers. These dissavers and zero savers were not concentrated in the lowest income groups but were to be found at all income levels. The most common method of financing spendings in excess of current incomes was by reducing liquid assets. The percentage of all dissavers using this method was 55 percent in 1946 and 52 percent in 1947. Next most common was the increase of consumer indebtedness.

Of all dissavers 25 percent used this method in 1946 and 30 percent in 1947.[17] These conclusions are borne out in a general way by certain other statistics. Redemptions of Series E bonds were very high in the postwar period. In 1946 they amounted to $5.4 billion, or nearly a billion more than current sales. They also amounted to $3.9 billion in 1947 and $3.7 billion in 1948, though current sales of these securities were slightly in excess of these figures.[18] It is true, of course, that not all the money secured by cashing E bonds was used for consumption spendings, but much of it undoubtedly was. As positive savers bought Series E bonds with a considerable part of their current savings, a large part of these funds was transferred to those who were cashing bonds and spending some of the proceeds for consumption purposes. The postwar increase in the velocity of money indicated that some previously idle money balances were being spent, some of them for consumption. And consumer debt increased $3.5 billion in 1946, $3.3 billion in 1947, and $2.5 billion in 1948.[19] (4) The return of veterans and the high marriage rate. As a group the returning veterans must have had a considerably higher propensity to consume than did other elements in the population. They felt the need for a spree; they needed new clothing and many other supplies; they married in large numbers and had to make the numerous purchases necessitated by the establishment of new households; and large benefits from the government helped them finance their purchases. In general these transfer payments were covered by tax collections, but it seems likely that the veterans' marginal propensity to consume was higher than that of the taxpayers. (5) The rise of nutritional standards during the war. We have already noted that during the war period per capita food consumption rose considerably above prewar levels. The food was available, money incomes were very high, many competing products were unobtainable in large amounts, and

[17] See *Federal Reserve Bulletins*, August, 1947, pp. 951-962 and August, 1948, pp. 914-932.
[18] *Treasury Bulletin*, February, 1949, p. 26.
[19] *Federal Reserve Bulletin*, March, 1949, p. 300.

rationing permitted a more nearly equal distribution of foods. Under these conditions millions of people in the lower income groups ate more and better food than ever before, and there is some indication that they carried over into the postwar period their higher estimation of what constitutes a "satisfactory diet." At the same time they were reluctant to reduce their other consumption standards below the most favorable levels they had attained at any time. (6) The tendency toward less inequality in the distribution of income. This was probably not a very impor-

TABLE 73. The Distribution of Income by Family Income Groups, 1941 and 1947, Percent of Total Income After Federal Personal Income Tax[20]

Family Units Ranked from Lowest to Highest Income[a]	Cumulative Percent of Total Money Income After Federal Personal Income Tax	
	1941	1947
Lowest fifth	3.7	4.3
Lowest two-fifths	13.2	14.7
Lowest three-fifths	29.1	30.9
Lowest four-fifths	52.3	53.7
All family units	100.0	100.0

[a] Includes single-person families.

tant factor in raising the propensity to consume, but it may have exerted some upward influence. The extent of this change in distribution is indicated in Table 73.

The rise of the propensity to consume seems to have been largely attributable to the types of factors just mentioned. It may be well, however, to mention briefly a few of the reasons why the rise was not even larger, for some had feared that with the coming of peace and the abandonment of direct controls a major part of the huge personal savings accumulated during the war would come tumbling into the consumption goods markets. That this did not occur to a greater extent was probably attributable to factors of this sort: (1) The desire of some people to maintain the higher degree of security accompanying avoidance

[20] SOURCE: *The President's Economic Report*, January, 1949, pp. 15, 91-95.

of debt and the holding of savings. They liked the feeling, new to many, of having their "heads above water" or higher above water. (2) The tendency for liquid asset holdings to be concentrated in the hands of the higher-income groups. In early 1946 the Federal Reserve conducted a survey to discover, among other things, the distribution of liquid assets among income classes. Some of these results are shown in Table 74. In this study "liquid assets" are defined as savings bonds and bank deposits; currency

TABLE 74. Liquid Asset Holdings by Income Classes, Early 1946[21]

Income Class of Spending Unit (Based on 1945 income)	Percent of All Spending Units	Percentage of Total Percent Holding Some Liquid Assets	Percent of Total Liquid Assets Held
under $1000	20	54	7
$1000–$1999	27	71	14
$2000–$2999	23	87	17
$3000–$3999	15	92	16
$4000–$4999	7	95	10
$5000–$7499	5	98	13
$7500 and over	3	100	23
All classes	100	78	100

holdings are excluded. For this and perhaps other reasons the holdings by the lower-income groups were probably underestimated. But the study indicated that the top 15 percent of income receivers held 43 percent of all liquid assets while the lowest 20 percent of income receivers held only 7 percent of the total. The spending of accumulated assets was probably lessened by the fact that such a large part of them was held by people who were accustomed to holding savings and whose current incomes were high enough to permit them to purchase liberally without dipping into past savings. (3) The fact that many savings were in effect earmarked for the purchase of specific types of durable goods

[21] SOURCE: *Federal Reserve Bulletin*, July, 1946, p. 717. A "spending unit" is defined as all persons living in the same dwelling unit and belonging to the same family who pool their income to meet their major expenses.

whose prices were "administered" and did not rise freely. Some people who were willing to spend their accumulated savings or to go back into debt for consumption purposes were not willing to do so to purchase just any type of consumption goods, but only to buy specific types of things, such as automobiles, refrigerators, or furniture. And the prices of these things were, in general, administered prices which were not raised to the maximum levels possible under the circumstances. Many people therefore placed their names on waiting lists and held their savings or delayed going into debt until the durable goods became available to them. (4) The expectation of lower prices later. Though some undoubtedly hastened to spend their money in fear of still further price increases, others delayed purchases expecting more favorable prices later. Throughout the period of inflation there was a strong sentiment that the boom would have to bust soon, yielding to price declines and possibly to widespread unemployment. Some people probably felt in a rather vague way that it would be a good idea to hold their savings against a rainy day and that they could get more for their money later. The response of others was much more specific; they were annoyed by the fact that they could buy cars only through used car lots at "absurdly high prices," that they had to take several hundred dollars worth of allegedly "optional equipment" to get a car, that trade-ins were seriously undervalued, that radio prices had risen "excessively," and so on. They therefore delayed their purchases until they could get a "more reasonable deal." (5) Limitations on consumer credit. Though the volume of consumer credit rose greatly during the period, its increase would probably have been even larger in the absence of Regulation W.

SUMMARY

The postwar inflation was much more complex than that occurring during the defense and war period. In the earlier period the dynamic upward thrust unquestionably came from the rise of government spendings, and private spendings rose only as a response. But the postwar inflation occurred despite a marked reduction of government spendings below their wartime levels. It was due not to any one factor but to a combination of circumstances which produced at the same time: (1) A willingness and ability of our people and business firms to spend very large and increasing amounts for housing and other forms of new capital goods, (2) a very high propensity to consume and a low propensity to save out of current disposable incomes, (3) a very large export demand, and (4) a level of government spendings which was below wartime levels but far above prewar levels. The sum of these demands exceeded the total amount of goods and services that could be made available, and the competitive attempts to secure more real output by spending more money could only bid up prices.

Among the important factors accounting for this great ability and willingness to spend were the following: (1) The huge wartime accumulation of savings by individuals and business firms, the major part of which was being held at the end of the war in the form of money balances and other liquid assets. (2) The relaxation of numerous direct controls which during the war had suppressed spendings for consumption and for capital maintenance and accumulation. (3) A backlog of unsatisfied demand due to the limited wartime production of consumer durables, of some nondurables, and of capital goods. In some lines, as in housing, the shortage was partially due to the low level of capital formation during the 1930's. (4) Dissatisfaction on the part of workers, farmers, and others with their wartime incomes. Each insisted on trying to improve both his absolute and relative income position by demanding increases in his money income. (5) A fiscal policy that allowed the private sectors to keep a larger part of their rising money incomes. (6) A monetary policy that assured the easy availability of credit at low interest rates. And (7) economic and political conditions abroad that created a large foreign demand for our products, a large foreign aid program by our government, and large military expenditures.

The following chapters will explore the relationship of fiscal, monetary, and wage policies to the inflationary process.

XII

||||||||||||||||||||||||||||||||||||||||||||||||||||||||||||||||||||||||||||||||||||||||||||||||||||||||||||||||||||||||||||

Federal Fiscal Policy in the
Postwar Period

THE earlier chapters dealing with the war period described the dynamic role of fiscal policy in the creation of inflationary pressures, pointing out the expansionary effects of the large and mounting deficits and the subordination of monetary policy to fiscal needs. This situation changed somewhat as the peak of government spendings was passed early in 1945 and as federal expenditures began to fall below receipts in 1946. Even so, however, fiscal policy continued to be of major importance during the postwar period. This was inevitable so long as the federal budget amounted to as much as $40 billion a year and the national debt exceeded $250 billion. This chapter will examine federal taxation, spending, and debt policies and then proceed to show the close relationship between fiscal and monetary policies during the period.

FEDERAL TAX POLICIES

When it came to reducing taxes, Congress displayed an alacrity that was noticeably absent in its consideration of tax increases during the war period. In July, even before V-J Day, it passed the Tax Adjustment Act of 1945.[1] This legislation had little effect

---

[1] For a general description of this legislation, see *Annual Report of the Secretary of the Treasury*, 1945, p. 101 and 1946, p. 89.

on the total amount of tax liabilities; its principal purpose was to make more readily available to business during the transition period some of the benefits provided by earlier legislation. It provided that the specific exemption from excess-profits taxes should be raised from $10,000 to $25,000, that the 10 percent postwar credit under the excess-profits tax might be taken currently for 1944 and subsequent years, that postwar refund bonds under the excess-profits tax should be made cashable at any time after January 1, 1946, and that certain other refunds to business should be speeded up.

The Revenue Act of 1945, which was approved in November, enacted tax reductions which would, it was estimated, lower tax collections by nearly $6 billion a year. It did this in several ways.[2] (1) It repealed the excess profits tax as of January 1, 1946 but continued the carryback of any unused excess-profits tax credit for one more year. (2) It repealed the capital-stock tax and the declared value excess-profits tax. (3) It lowered the rates of the corporation income tax; for larger corporations the reduction of the rate was from 40 to 38 percent. (4) It reduced individual income taxes. The 3 percent normal tax, which had applied to all income in excess of $500 regardless of the marital status or number of dependents of the taxpayer, was eliminated, and other personal income taxes were reduced about 5 percent. Special reductions were granted to veterans and members of the armed forces. (5) It repealed the use tax on automobiles and boats. And (6) it deferred for another year the automatic increase in tax rates under the old-age insurance plan.

To some extent, of course, the 1945 tax legislation reflected the usual opposition to taxes and the desire of legislators and other government officials to give something to everybody. But more important was the fear of deflation and unemployment. To avoid this it was believed that individuals and businesses should be allowed to keep a larger part of their incomes; any refunds due to business should be made quickly; and any factors that would weaken the incentive to reconvert, make capital investments, and

[2] For a brief description of this legislation, see *ibid.*, 1946, pp. 92-93.

hire men should be removed. The elimination of the excess-profits tax was considered especially desirable for this reason as well as to provide the maximum incentive to efficiency.

No important tax legislation was enacted in 1946, but in the following year tax reduction became a burning political issue. The year started out amicably as Congress, in response to the President's request, extended indefinitely the wartime excise tax rates. The trouble started in June 1947 when Congress passed a bill which would reduce individual income taxes about 20 percent.[3] The President vetoed this bill, stating that it represented "the wrong kind of tax reduction at the wrong time." Undaunted by this veto, Congress passed another similar bill in July 1947, and this too received the President's disapproval. In each case Congress failed to secure the two-thirds majority necessary to override the veto. In April 1948, however, it overrode a presidential veto to put into effect the Revenue Act of 1948.[4] This provided tax reductions which were estimated at $5 billion a year if national income averaged $200 billion. Most of the reduction was in personal income taxes. Exemptions were raised from $500 to $600 per person, a special exemption of $600 was introduced for those more than 65 years old, the special exemption for the blind was raised from $500 to $600, income tax rates were reduced at all levels, and married persons were permitted to split their incomes for tax purposes. Estate and gift taxes were modified in such a way as to reduce their annual yield by an estimated $250 million.

The behavior of total budget receipts during this period is indicated in Table 75. At this point we shall make only a few comments on these statistics. In the first place, the rise of total tax yields was not due to any increase of tax rates; it occurred despite the elimination of certain taxes, such as the excess-profits taxes, and the reduction of some other tax rates and was wholly due to the rise of national money income and price levels. The effect of the tax reductions was to allow the private sectors of the economy to keep a larger proportion of *any given level* of national

[3] *Ibid.*, 1947, pp. 56-58.
[4] For a general description of this legislation, see *ibid.*, 1948, pp. 50-54.

money income. A part of each increase of national money income was channeled into the hands of the federal tax collectors, but both individuals and business firms were left with rising money incomes after taxes. And in the second place, a significant part of federal receipts did not represent a subtraction from private disposable incomes. For example, about $2.9 billion in fiscal 1947

TABLE 75. Federal Budget Receipts, Fiscal Years 1946-1948
(In millions of dollars)[5]

	1946	1947	1948
Individual income taxes	$18,705	$19,343	$20,998
Corporation income and profits taxes	12,554	9,677	10,174
Miscellaneous internal revenue:			
Liquor taxes	2,526	2,475	2,255
Tobacco taxes	1,166	1,238	1,300
Manufacturer's excises	923	1,425	1,649
Retailers' excises	492	514	470
Estate and gift taxes	677	779	902
Other	1,941	1,618	1,725
Employment taxes and other social security contributions	1,714	2,038	2,396
Customs	435	494	422
Other receipts:			
Renegotiation of war contracts	1,063	279	162
Surplus property	501	2,886	1,929
Other	1,953	1,666	1,981
Total receipts	$44,276	$44,718	$46,362

and $1.9 billion in fiscal 1948 came from sales of surplus property. These purchases by the private sectors were on capital account rather than income account.

FEDERAL EXPENDITURES

We have already noted the general behavior of federal expenditures. After exceeding $100 billion in fiscal 1945, total budget expenditures fell to $63.7 billion in fiscal 1946, to $42.5 billion

[5] SOURCE: *Ibid.*, 1948, pp. 428, 431-436. Items may not add to exact totals, partly because of rounding and partly because totals are on a daily Treasury statement basis while some of the items are on a collection basis.

in 1947, and to $36.3 billion in fiscal 1948. After mid-1948 they again began to rise somewhat. They were still, however, much above the $9.3 billion level of fiscal 1940. By far the largest part of these expenditures were war-connected, as is indicated by spendings for national defense and related activities, international finance and aid, interest on the public debt, and expenses of the veterans'

TABLE 76. Federal Budget Expenditures, Fiscal Years 1946-1948
(In millions of dollars)[6]

	1946	1947	1948
National defense and related activities	$48,870	$17,279	$11,524
International finance and aid	727	4,415	3,983
Interest on the public debt	4,722	4,958	5,211
Veterans' administration	4,253	7,259	6,469
Aid to agriculture	−203	1,229	812
Social security program	845	1,066	1,619
Public Works	373	702	1,137
Housing and home finance	−246	183	−68
Refunds of taxes and duties	3,034	3,050	2,326
Miscellaneous	1,340	2,365	3,312
Total budget expenditures[a]	$63,714	$42,505	$36,326
Total receipts	$44,276	$47,718	$46,362
Budget surplus or deficit (−)[b]	−$19,438	$ 5,213	$10,036

[a] Excludes transfer of $3 billion from 1948 surplus to the European Cooperation Administration Trust Fund to be used in fiscal 1949.
[b] This is equal to total budget receipts minus budget expenditures.

administration. As a group these accounted for 80 percent of total budget expenditures in fiscal 1947 and 75 percent in fiscal 1948. (See Table 76.) These continued large federal expenditures reflected the large amount of goods and services used for government purposes, the increased prices of these goods and services, and large transfer payments made to veterans and others. The form of these payments to the private sectors of the economy and to state and local governments is shown more clearly in Table 77. Reflecting the demobilization of the armed forces and of wartime agencies and the tapering off of purchases for war purposes, federal spendings for labor and for the output of business fell drastically

[6] *Annual Report of the Secretary of the Treasury,* 1948, pp. 428-429.

despite the current increase of wages and commodity prices. But some other spendings into national money income rose. Federal transfer payments increased from $1.8 billion in 1944 to $4.3 billion in 1945, $9.2 billion in 1946, and $8.9 billion in 1947. Some of this increase represented larger social security benefits but more of it was attributable to the very large benefits to veterans.

TABLE 77.   Federal Expenditures in the Calendar Years 1945-1948
(In millions of dollars)[7]

	1945	1946	1947	1948
Compensation of employees	$30,614	$14,721	$ 9,232	$ 8,869
Net purchases from business	43,239	7,064	6,611	10,266
Net purchases from abroad	943	—993	—150	1,762
Transfer payments				
Social security benefits	1,336	2,359	2,139	2,246
Veterans' benefits	2,748	6,618	6,366	4,977
Other	240	232	375	403
Grants-in-aid to state and local governments	870	1,108	1,738	2,016
Net interest paid	3,334	4,164	4,115	4,168
Subsidies less current surplus of government enterprises	1,516	1,619	571	681
Total	$84,840	$36,892	$30,997	$35,388

These payments were so large as to cushion considerably the decline of disposable personal incomes in late 1945 and early 1946 and they continued to provide this group of people with large amounts of spending power. There were also large increases in federal grants to state and local governments and some increase in net interest payments.

FEDERAL DEFICITS AND SURPLUSES

Having surveyed briefly the general pattern of federal taxation and spendings in the postwar period, we come now to a crucial quantitative relationship—the relative sizes of federal receipts and

[7] *Survey of Current Business*, July, 1949, pp. 13, 25. It will be noted that these figures differ markedly in their coverage from the budget expenditure figures.

spendings, and the resulting deficits or surpluses. To show these quantitatively we shall use the Treasury series on cash operating income, cash operating outgo, and net cash operating income or outgo. This series has the double advantage of being available on a monthly basis and of eliminating transactions within the federal government itself; it shows only cash payments from and to the public—that is, cash payments (excluding debt operations) between the federal government and individuals, corporations, financial institutions, state and local governments, etc.[8]

As shown in Column 3 of Table 78, the federal government's cash spendings far exceeded its cash income during the first eight months of 1945, so that its cash deficits averaged well over $3 billion a month. As spendings declined after V-J Day, the size of the deficit also declined; but, except for two months' deficits it persisted through July 1946. In fact, the total deficit for the period from August 1945 through July 1946 amounted to $9.2 billion. Deficit spending did not end with the Japanese surrender. But in mid-1946, for the first time since early in the Great Depression, the Treasury's cash income began to exceed its spendings. Its surplus of cash income over cash outgo amounted to only $236 million for 1946 as a whole, but it rose to $5.7 billion for 1947 and to $8 billion for 1948.

These are the statistical facts concerning federal cash deficits and surpluses. But what was their economic significance? How did they affect the behavior of total spendings for output, prices, and related factors? To answer these questions we must divide the effects of federal deficits or surpluses into (1) direct income effects and (2) monetary effects.

DIRECT INCOME EFFECTS OF FEDERAL DEFICITS OR SURPLUSES

Treasury surpluses exert an effect on disposable private incomes that is just the opposite of the effects of deficits. As tax collections

[8] For a brief description of this series, see *Treasury Bulletin*, September, 1947, p. 14.

TABLE 78. Cash Operating Outgo and Income of the Federal Government,
1945-1948
(In millions of dollars) [9]

Period	Cash Operating Outgo	Cash Operating Income	Cash Surplus or Deficit (—)	Increase or Decrease (—) in Gen. Fund	Net Cash Borrowing or Repayment of Borrowing (—)
1945—Jan.	$ 7,781	$ 3,776	$ —4,005	$ —2,630	$ 1,375
Feb.	7,218	4,375	—2,843	—2,292	551
Mar.	8,929	7,144	—1,785	—2,036	—251
Apr.	7,799	3,198	—4,601	—3,911	690
May	8,469	3,883	—4,586	—1,741	2,845
June	8,945	6,132	—2,813	15,073	17,886
July	7,973	2,987	—4,986	—2,615	2,371
Aug.	7,829	3,688	—4,141	—3,451	690
Sept.	6,603	5,553	—1,050	—2,497	—1,447
Oct.	5,985	2,881	—3,104	—3,321	—217
Nov.	4,786	3,062	—1,724	1,632	3,356
Dec.	5,267	4,371	896	11,558	12,454
Total	$87,584	$51,050	$ —36,534	$ 3,769	$ 40,303
1946—Jan.	$ 5,605	$ 3,960	$ —1,636	$ —577	$ 1,059
Feb.	3,887	4,255	368	534	166
Mar.	4,156	5,929	1,773	—1,593	—3,366
Apr.	4,146	2,912	—1,234	—3,433	—2,199
May	4,358	3,470	—888	—2,398	—1,510
June	5,086	4,707	—379	—4,298	—3,919
July	2,745	2,332	—413	—2,209	—1,796
Aug.	2,760	2,803	43	—989	—1,032
Sept.	2,944	4,585	—1,641	—868	—2,512
Oct.	2,844	2,683	—161	—2,101	—1,940
Nov.	2,269	2,813	544	—1,405	—1,949
Dec.	3,578	4,156	578	—3,163	—3,743
Total	$44,378	$44,605	$ 236	$ —22,500	$ —22,736
1947—Jan.	$ 2,715	$ 3,821	$ 1,106	$ 1,210	$ 104
Feb.	3,487	4,947	1,460	622	—838
Mar.	2,961	5,585	2,624	—224	—2,848
Apr.	3,063	2,228	—835	—2,598	—1,761
May	2,781	2,746	—35	—245	—209
June	4,784	4,886	102	—758	—859
July	3,272	2,446	—827	—239	587
Aug.	3,073	3,112	41	332	291
Sept.	3,943	4,666	723	552	—201
Oct.	2,570	2,589	18	155	136
Nov.	2,490	3,305	816	—172	—987
Dec.	3,476	3,987	510	—838	—1,348
Total	$38,616	$44,319	$ 5,703	$ —2,203	$ —7,933
1948—Jan.	$ 2,497	$ 4,482	$ 1,986	$ 1,551	$ —435
Feb.	2,726	4,548	1,824	—330	—2,153
Mar.	3,418	6,019	2,601	1,035	—1,567
Apr.	2,397	2,402	4	—740	—744
May	2,507	2,969	462	334	—128
June	4,129	4,877	748	—14	—762
July	2,630	2,268	—361	141	502
Aug.	2,941	3,162	221	—241	—463
Sept.	3,229	4,667	1,438	751	—687
Oct.	2,769	2,280	—516	—781	—265
Nov.	3,466	3,190	—275	—417	—142
Dec.	4,224	4,106	—118	—177	—59
Total	$36,957	$44,971	$ 8,014	$ 1,113	$ —6,903

[9] SOURCE: *Treasury Bulletins.*

extract more money from the public's income than government spendings contribute to it, the net direct effect is to lower private money incomes after taxes. The surplus measures the net amount extracted from disposable incomes and spending power. And it must be emphasized that Treasury surpluses exert this antiexpansionary direct effect on the public's disposable income regardless of the way that the Treasury disposes of its surplus.

Through its net extractions from disposable money incomes, the Treasury surplus during the period from mid-1946 to mid-1948 probably lessened somewhat the rise of private spendings for output, especially consumption spendings. The collection of the surplus did not actually reduce disposable private money incomes and spendings; it was far too small for that, and a considerable part, if not all, of the surplus was itself due to the expanding tax base resulting from the rise of national money incomes and prices. At best it could only reduce the rise of private disposable incomes and inhibit somewhat the rise of total spendings. The antiexpansionary influence would have been stronger if higher effective tax rates had been retained. There was a case for the elimination, or at least a marked reduction, of the excess-profits tax, and perhaps also for eliminating the 3 percent individual normal tax which did not take into account the number of the taxpayers' dependents. But in this inflationary situation there was no justification for other tax reductions, least of all for reductions of other personal taxes.

MONETARY EFFECTS OF FEDERAL SURPLUSES

The preceding section emphasized that federal surpluses can exert a contractionary, or at least an antiexpansionary, effect on the public's disposable money income and spending power regardless of the way that the Treasury utilizes the surplus funds. This effect results from the process of *collecting* the surplus out of private incomes. But this is by no means the entire story; by altering the ways these surplus money inflows are *utilized* the Treasury can exert an important influence on bank reserves, the money supply, and general credit conditions, though it is obvious that other counteracting forces may be more powerful.

The Treasury can utilize an excess of cash income over cash outgo in three principal ways: (1) to retire securities held by individuals and institutions other than the Federal Reserve and commercial banks; (2) to retire securities held by commercial banks; and (3) to build up Treasury cash holdings, to increase Treasury deposits at the Federal Reserve banks, or to retire securities held by the Federal Reserve banks. Let us compare the monetary effects of these various methods of utilizing excess cash income. In each case we shall assume that the surplus is "government saving"—the excess of government income over government spendings.

The simplest case to trace through is that in which the current cash surplus is used to retire securities held by individuals, corporations, or institutions other than banks. The net direct effect here is to transfer money which was extracted from some taxpayer's income to the former holder of a government security. The taxpayer suffers a reduction of his disposable income, but the money received by the former security holder represents to him not income but merely a conversion of a part of his capital from securities into "cash." There is no direct effect on the total money supply or on the volume of bank reserves. Indirectly, however, a surplus used in this way may avoid or lessen an increase of the money supply if the "government saving" does indeed increase the total amount of saving out of a given level of national income. The surplus funds transferred to the former security holders may be used to meet a part of the demand for investment and consumption funds so that only a smaller part will be supplied through an expansion of bank credit. For example, surplus funds used to retire government securities held by insurance companies may then be lent to finance residential construction, thereby lessening the amount of mortgages purchased by the commercial banks.

The *direct* effect of using surplus tax receipts to retire government securities held by the commercial banks is to reduce the money supply by an equivalent amount. In substance, the tax-payers' checks representing the Treasury's surplus are deducted from demand deposits, thereby reducing bank liabilities, and the banks surrender to the Treasury an equivalent amount of securities, thereby reducing their total assets. Though the *direct* effect is to reduce the total money supply, probably in the form of checking deposits, the total volume of bank reserves remains unchanged by these transactions. As a result of the decrease of outstanding deposits and an unaffected volume of bank reserves, such a trans-action tends to produce excess reserves in the banking system, so that the banks can, if they wish, extend new loans or purchase additional securities equal to the amount of those retired, without any net deterioration of their reserve position.

Many economists and public officials appear to believe that it is much more anti-inflationary to use a current Treasury surplus to retire securities held by the commercial banks than it is to use the same surplus to retire securities held by individuals and nonbanking institutions. This is an error which is traceable to an excessive attention to the immediate direct effect on the money supply and to an inadequate amount of attention to effects on the rate of total spendings and to indirect effects on the money supply. To make this point, the effects of collecting and utilizing a current Treasury surplus should be divided into two categories: (1) The effects exerted by the *collection* of the surplus on disposable in-comes, spendings, and total saving, including both private and government saving. This effect depends on the size of the surplus and other relevant aspects of the government's taxing-spending policy; it is not dependent on the way the surplus funds are used. (2) The effects of the *utilization* of the surplus funds. Whether the surplus funds are transferred to individuals and nonbanking institutions or whether they are transferred to commercial banks the result is to provide the receiver with money on *capital account* which he may use to finance capital investment or consumer dis-saving. If the surplus is transferred to nonbank security holders the latter receive money (checking deposits) which formerly belonged to taxpayers. If the surplus is used to retire securities held by commercial banks, the latter experience a decrease of their reserve requirements sufficient to enable them to make new loans or security purchases equal to the amount of the government securities retired. Excess reserves are created in the banking system and these are indeed considered "loanable funds." Thus the amount of lending power transferred to the former owner of government securities is the same whether the surplus is used to retire securities held by the commercial banks or to retire those belonging to nonbank holders. One might argue, however, that the retirement of bank-held debt is still the more anti-inflationary because the banks as a group will be less likely than other types of investors as a group to increase their loans and security holdings in order to replace those that were retired. There is no particular reason why this should be true.

We can conclude, therefore, that in any given situation there is no reason to believe that the use of a given Treasury surplus to retire debt held by the commercial banks is any more anti-inflationary than the use of the same surplus to retire debt held by nonbank groups. In fact, the total effects on not only total spendings but also on the money supply are likely to be about the same in the two cases, and in neither case is this *utilization* of a surplus, as distinct from its *collection*, likely to be very antiexpansionary. This conclusion is of more than theoretical importance; it would appear that the Treasury overestimated the anti-inflationary effects of its retirement of securities held by commercial banks and used too large a part of its available funds for this purpose rather than for uses that would have drained off bank reserves.

The direct effect is to reduce both the money supply and commercial bank reserves when the Treasury uses its current surplus to build up its actual cash holdings, to increase its deposits at the Reserve banks, or to retire securities held by the Reserve banks. The public's checking deposits are reduced by an amount equal to the Treasury's surplus collections; and bank reserves are drawn down as the checks are cleared by deducting them from the banks' reserve accounts at the Reserve banks and as the Treasury uses the money to build up its cash holdings, or its deposits at the Reserve banks, or to retire securities held by the Reserve banks. The longer-run effects of such a policy depend upon the ease with which the banks can replenish their reserves and upon their willingness to do so. If the banks are without excess reserves and find it impossible, or even very onerous, to secure a replenishment of their reserves at the Reserve banks, they may reduce their outstanding credit by a multiple of the amount of reserves lost. But if the Reserve banks stand ready to supply reserve funds freely and on very attractive terms the credit policy of the banks is likely to be much less affected by the Treasury's use of its current surplus in these ways. This, as we shall see, was the situation in the postwar period. The Federal Reserve stood ready to supply any desired amount of funds through the purchase of government securities, and banks had large amounts of these securities that they were willing to sell to replenish their reserves and to restore and increase their lending power. This Federal reserve policy greatly reduced the restrictive effects of the Treasury's use of its current surplus in the ways we are considering here, but it seems likely that this Treasury policy did tend to inhibit the expansion of bank credit. Without implying that such a course would have been very effective, the writer contends that the Treasury should have used a larger part of its current surplus in ways that would have drained off bank reserves.

In short, we find that the Treasury surplus from mid-1946 to mid-1948 did inhibit to some extent the rise of spendings and prices. The Treasury's collection of receipts in excess of its expenditures reduced the rise of the public's disposable money income; tended to reduce private spendings; and tended to raise the amount of savings at each level of national income, though the "government saving" was probably offset to some extent by an induced reduction of private saving. The surplus also supplied the Treasury with large amounts of funds that it could use to influence the money supply and general credit conditions. From mid-1946 through 1948 the Treasury collected a total cash surplus of about $14 billion which it could use for this purpose. For this and other reasons the Treasury possessed central-banking powers which were at least comparable to those of the Federal Reserve.

OTHER SOURCES OF THE TREASURY'S POWER IN THE MONETARY FIELD

The preceding sections pointed out that the Treasury's cash surplus during this period provided it with a large amount of money which it could use in various ways to influence the behavior of the money supply and general credit conditions. But this was by no means the only source of the Treasury's monetary powers; there were also several others. Let us look at three of these: (1) the Treasury's general fund balance, (2) purchases and sales of securities in the market by government agencies and trust funds, and (3) attempts to increase net sales of securities to some types of investors in order to retire debt held by others.

THE TREASURY BALANCE

When the federal debt held outside the government itself reached its peak of $251.8 billion at the end of February 1946, the Treasury held a balance of nearly $26 billion in its general fund. This balance had been kept at a high level during the war period, but it was greatly increased as a large part of the proceeds of the Victory Loan was added to it in late 1945 and early 1946. It was solely the result of Treasury overborrowing. About $1.7 billion of this balance was held in the form of Treasury cash and deposits at the Federal Reserve, but the bulk of it, $24.4 billion, was in the form of Treasury deposits at commercial banks. Virtually all of the latter were war loan deposit accounts against which the banks were not required to keep reserves. This large Treasury balance represented a potentially important restrictive power if used for this purpose, but some of it could actually be expansionary if used in other ways. Let us, therefore, look at the effects of various methods of utilizing the Treasury balance in the form of (1) cash and deposits at the Federal Reserve, and (2) deposits at commercial banks.

The use of a previously accumulated Treasury balance in the form of cash and deposits at the Federal Reserve can never be anti-inflationary. At best it is neutral, as when these funds are used to retire debt held by the Reserve banks. It is actually expansionary when used otherwise. When such funds are used to build up Treasury deposits at commercial banks or to retire securities held by these banks, the effect is to increase the volume of bank reserves. And when such funds are used to retire debt held by nonbank investors the effect is to increase both the public's money supply and bank reserves. This sort of thing actually happened during the last nine months of 1946, as the Treasury, in its debt retirement program, drew down its balance of cash and deposits at the Reserve banks by $1.5 billion. This underlines the fact that debt retirement is not necessarily anti-inflationary.

What are the effects of utilizing an accumulated Treasury balance in the form of deposits at commercial banks? There is one type of use that clearly tends to be antiexpansionary. When such funds are used to build up Treasury cash and deposits at the Federal Reserve or to retire debt held by the Reserve banks, the effect is to reduce the volume of bank reserves, just as would Federal Reserve sales of securities in the open market. The potential force of such an action is indicated by the fact that at the end of February 1946 Treasury deposits at commercial banks amounted to $24.4 billion while total member bank reserves were only $15.6 billion.

There is no reason to believe that other uses of an *already accumulated* Treasury balance at commercial banks has any anti-inflationary effect. The use of such balances to retire bank-held debt does not at all affect the public's money supply, the volume of bank reserves, or the banks' reserve position. The Treasury merely cancels a certain amount of its debt due the banks in the form of government securities and the banks cancel an equivalent amount of Treasury-owned deposits, which the Treasury had no intention of spending. The banks' reserve position remains unaffected, for no reserves were required against the war loan accounts.[10] And this, it is to be noted, is the way that the major part of the Treasury's balance was drawn down in 1946. Virtually all the debt reduction during that year had no anti-inflationary effects. The use of such a Treasury balance to retire debt held by nonbank investors actually increased the money supply as deposit credits were transferred from the account of the Treasury to those of others. At the same time, however, the banks' reserve position was tightened somewhat as deposits were shifted from accounts against which no reserves were required to accounts which required reserves. It is therefore impossible to say whether such actions were expansionary, contractionary, or neutral.

We shall see later that most of the debt retirement that occurred in 1946 was not anti-inflationary for it merely represented the use of the Treasury balance *accumulated at commercial banks in an earlier period* to retire debt held by the commercial banks and by nonbank investors.

OPEN-MARKET PURCHASES AND SALES OF SECURITIES BY GOVERNMENT AGENCIES AND TRUST FUNDS

Largely because of our large social security program, these government agencies and trust funds receive considerable amounts of income each year and hold even larger amounts of government securities, some of which are special issues and some of types eligible for holding by others. In early 1946 the volume of securities

---

[10] It is true, of course, that this operation reduced the banks' holdings of governments that could have been sold to the Federal Reserve in exchange for added reserve balances. But because the banks were left with such a great volume of these securities and were relieved of such great deposit debts to the Treasury it is doubtful that this was antiexpansionary.

held by these agencies and funds amounted to nearly $28 billion and by mid-1948 they had reached almost $36 billion. The income of these funds in the form of taxes and other social security contributions has already been included in the Treasury's cash operating income, so we shall deal here only with the open-market purchases and sales of securities by these funds.

It should be clear that open-market purchases and sales of government securities by these funds have effects similar to open-market operations by the Federal Reserve if the funds received or disbursed are added to or subtracted from the Treasury balance in the form of cash or deposits at the Federal Reserve.[11] For example, suppose these accounts sell securities to purchasers other than the Reserve banks and add the receipts to the Treasury's balance at the Federal Reserve; the direct effect is to drain off bank reserves. On the other hand, bank reserves are increased to the extent that these accounts buy securities from sellers other than the Federal Reserve and pay for them out of Treasury cash or Treasury deposits at the Reserve banks. Because of the large volume of securities at their disposal, these funds can play an important role in the money market.

Their open-market operations were not large in this period. There were occasions, however, when they sold securities in the market to lower their prices, or to absorb funds into the Treasury, or both. And on other occasions they bought securities to produce the opposite effects. For example, from the first of April through the end of September 1947 Treasury investment accounts sold $1.8 billions of their securities in the market to help stop an unwanted rise of bond prices. Then during November and December of that year they purchased $917 millions in the market to cushion the current decline of bond prices. These techniques might well have been used to good effect on other occasions.

[11] This is also true if receipts from security sales are used to retire debt held by the Federal Reserve or if money disbursed is secured by borrowing from the Federal Reserve.

TREASURY ATTEMPTS TO MAKE NET SALES OF
SECURITIES TO SOME INVESTORS IN ORDER TO REDUCE
HOLDINGS BY OTHERS

As noted earlier, the Treasury wanted very much during this postwar period to reduce security holdings by the Federal Reserve and commercial banks. To this end it not only used a considerable part of its current cash surplus and its accumulated balance to retire bank-held debt but it also tried in various ways to persuade other investors to hold their governments and it attempted to sell larger amounts of new securities to nonbank investors in order to secure money with which to retire bank-held debt. Eligible investors were implored to hold their savings bonds and to buy as many more as possible. To promote this purpose, the Treasury continued its campaign to sell savings bonds, including the payroll savings plans, and in 1947 it raised the limit on annual purchases of Series E bonds from $5000 to $10,000 maturity value.[12] It also liberalized somewhat the restrictions on purchases of Series F and G bonds and in September 1947 offered an attractive issue of 2½ percent investment bonds.[13]

It is difficult to evaluate the anti-inflationary effect, if any, of the Treasury's efforts during the postwar period to persuade individuals and nonbank institutions to buy and hold government securities. In the first place, it is doubtful that these efforts succeeded in increasing very much the amounts of governments bought and held by these investors. The Treasury had to rely largely on moral suasion, and people's responsiveness to these appeals deteriorated rapidly after the end of the war. The increased availability of the more attractive issues, such as E bonds and the 2½ percent investment bonds, may have increased somewhat the total amount of governments held by nonbank investors, but there is some evidence that it merely led some investors to sell more or buy fewer of the other government securities. And in the second place, this

[12] *Annual Report of the Secretary of the Treasury,* 1948, pp. 191-192.
[13] *Ibid.,* pp. 180-187.

TABLE 79. A Summary of Treasury Dept. Operations and Related Factors, 1946-1948
(In millions of dollars)[14]

	March 1, 1946-June 30, 1946	June 30, 1946-June 30, 1947	June 30, 1947-June 30, 1948	Total for Period March 1, 1946-June 30, 1948
Sources of funds used to retire debt				
Treasury cash surplus or deficit (−)	$ −728	$ 6,659	$ 8,903	$14,834
Net reduction or increase (−) of Treasury balance[a]				
In Treasury cash and deposits at the F. R.	298	−1,047	−858	−1,607
In deposits at other banks	11,454	12,031	−811	22,674
Total	10,994	10,930	−1,624	20,300
Net Market sales by government agencies and trust funds	100	1,200		1,300
Total of all sources	$10,366	$18,789	$ 7,279	$36,434
Net amounts of debt retired by the Treasury (Treasury redemptions minus Treasury sales)				
From nonbank holders	$ 3,800	$ 3,600	$ 2,900	$10,300
From commercial banks	5,700	10,700	900	17,300
From Federal Reserve banks	1,600	4,000	5,000	10,600
Total	$11,100	$18,300	$ 8,800	$38,200
Discrepancy (amounts retired less amounts available from sources)	734	−489	1,521	1,766

[a] The two balances do not add to the total because the latter is equal to the total assets of the Treasury's general fund less its liabilities, whereas the two items listed here are only the two major assets of the fund. The statistics on the net amounts retired from each class of holder reflect only transactions between these holders and the Treasury; they do not include market purchases and sales by these holders. The figures in the latter part of the table are Treasury estimates and are somewhat too high. The amount of the gross debt held outside the government actually declined only $35.2 billion during the period.

[14] This table was computed by the writer. Data on the sources of funds are from *Treasury Bulletins*. Those on debt retirements by the Treasury are from *Annual Report of the Secretary of the Treasury*, 1946, p. 56; 1947, p. 44; and 1948, p. 38.

campaign was not necessarily anti-inflationary even if it did succeed in increasing the total amount of governments held by nonbank investors. The campaign could be anti-inflationary only if it succeeded in raising the private propensity to save, in lowering private investment spendings, or in doing both. These questions are relevant: Did the campaign succeed in increasing the proportion of disposable incomes used for saving by individuals and business firms, and in decreasing the proportion spent for consumption? Did it decrease the desire of the private sectors to spend for investment purposes? Did it make lenders less willing to supply funds for private investment and raise the cost or decrease the availability of funds for this purpose? The answers to these questions would appear to be largely in the negative, though the continuance of the payroll savings plan probably increased total saving to some extent.

CONCLUSIONS

What are we to conclude about postwar federal fiscal policy? The most important conclusion is that popular opinion was seriously in error in assuming that all debt reduction was anti-inflationary. It was not. The *collection* of the current cash surplus from mid-1946 to mid-1948 was anti-inflationary, for it represented extractions from disposable private incomes and spending power. But, as shown in Table 79, the current surplus provided only about 40 percent of the funds used for debt retirement during the period from March 1, 1946 to June 30, 1948. Most of the remainder was secured by drawing down the Treasury balance *accumulated in an earlier period* at commercial banks, and we have seen that the *use* of such funds for debt retirement can be antiexpansionary only if debt is retired from the Federal Reserve banks. But only $10.6 billion of the $36.4 billion of available funds were used for this purpose. The major part was used to retire debt held by commercial banks and others, and it is doubtful that the *retirement* of this debt, as opposed to the collection of the necessary funds from the public, exerted any anti-inflationary effect.

Discussion of fiscal policy during the period would have been much more intelligent if it had deemphasized debt retirement as such and had concentrated on the securing of a large current cash surplus by the Treasury and on the building up of Treasury deposits at the Federal Reserve banks and the retirement of Federal Reserve-held debt. Especially to be emphasized is the direct income effect of *collecting* a large current cash surplus.

Possibly the greatest criticism to be made of the postwar fiscal policy is its failure to achieve a larger current cash surplus during the period of inflation. This could have been done through greater reductions of federal spendings or through lesser tax reductions, or both. To the extent that greater reductions of expenditures could have been achieved through increased government efficiency and postponement or abandonment of less essential projects, it should have been done. It should not have occurred at the expense of the foreign aid program or of national security, though there were probably large economies to be effected in the military establishment. The conduct of Congress was similar to that during the war; it was characterized by much talk about the possibility of expenditure reduction but very little action.

XIII

||||||||||||||||||||||||||||||||||||||||||||||||||||||||||||||||||||||||||||||||||||||||||||||||||||||||||||||||||||||||||||||||||||||||||

Federal Reserve Policy in the
Postwar Period

A S THE war ended, the Federal Reserve was still pursuing its
wartime objective of assuring that the Treasury could borrow
at low interest rates all the funds that it needed. And the principal
way that it accomplished this objective was by surrendering control
over the volume of its security holdings and standing ready to buy
all the governments that others were not willing to hold at the
selected pattern of yields. For nearly two years after V-J Day this
policy was continued almost without change. In July 1947, however, the Federal Reserve began to allow rates to rise somewhat,
especially on shorter-term obligations, but the rise was at all times
controlled and rates were not allowed to rise above what have
usually been considered depression levels. The maintenance of
low yields on the huge volume of the federal debt assured that
credit for private purposes would continue to be highly available
at low interest rates.

The term "Federal Reserve policy" will be used here merely
to denote the policies actually administered by the System; it will
not necessarily imply that Federal Reserve officials took the initiative in formulating the policies, for the Treasury was dominant.
The levels of prices and yields on governments that the System
maintained was in most cases agreed upon by Federal Reserve
and Treasury officials. On many occasions there was no disagree-

ment between the two agencies; on other occasions they disagreed, usually with the Treasury wanting lower interest rates than those favored by the Federal Reserve. It seems almost certain that in the absence of Treasury influence the Federal Reserve would have raised interest rates, especially those on the shorter maturities, somewhat earlier and to somewhat higher levels. At no time, however, did Federal Reserve officials indicate a desire to tighten credit to an extent anywhere near comparable to that in 1920.

REASONS FOR MAINTAINING LOW INTEREST RATES AND "AN ORDERLY MARKET FOR GOVERNMENTS"

Why was the Treasury so insistent on the maintenance of low interest rates and the prevention of a decline in the prices of outstanding governments, and why did the Federal Reserve coöperate so fully with the Treasury, sometimes reluctantly but often willingly? Why, after February 1946 when the federal debt had already reached its peak and the Treasury had begun to retire a part of it, did not the Treasury cease to press for the maintenance of low interest rates, and why did the Federal Reserve fail to restrict credit to check the current inflation? It is always difficult to answer such questions relating to human motivations, for official statements may be rationalizations rather than a description of actual motivating considerations. Moreover, many officials were involved and their motivations seem to have varied considerably even when they arrived at the same policy decisions. Nevertheless, official statements as to the reasons for this policy are worth noting: (1) Increased rates on the federal debt would add greatly to the already large interest burden.[1] Both Federal Reserve and Treasury officials pointed out that with interest charges already amounting to about $5 billion a year and averaging 2 percent, every increase of one-half of a percentage point in the average rate would add

[1] Board of Governors, *Annual Report*, 1945, pp. 5-6; *Hearings Before the House Banking and Currency Committee*, November 25, 1947, p. 50; and *Hearings Before the Joint Committee on the Economic Report*, November 28, 1947, pp. 246-247.

about $1.25 billion per year to federal interest charges. It is important to note here that the Treasury could follow either of two general lines of action if it decided to terminate the policy of maintaining low interest rates. The first would be to refund, at higher interest rates, only the maturing debt, allowing the remainder of the outstanding debt to decline in price. This would postpone the full increase of interest charges, but it would impose capital depreciation on banks, insurance companies, and other holders. The other line of action would be to refund the entire debt at whatever rates of interest were required to prevent government securities from falling below par in the face of tightened credit conditions. This would protect holders against capital depreciation, but it would increase the Treasury's interest costs immediately to the full extent. Neither Federal Reserve nor Treasury officials were willing to follow either course of action except to the limited extent of raising somewhat the shorter-term rates of interest. (2) Fluctuating prices and yields on governments would greatly complicate the Treasury's refunding operations—a serious matter with about $50 billion of the debt maturing within a year and nearly $100 billion within five years.[2] (3) An increase of the yield on governments, which without an increase of coupon rates would mean a decline of their prices, would impose capital depreciation on financial institutions and other holders and might lead to panicky selling and loss of confidence in financial institutions.[3] Officials recalled the drastic decline of bond prices in 1920 when the federal debt was only $26 billion and pointed to the greater current possibilities of panic with this debt ten times as large and representing about 60 percent of all debt in the country. Marriner Eccles stated that with this larger federal debt a free market was out of the question if this was taken to mean an

[2] *Hearings Before the House Banking and Currency Committee on S. J. Res. 157*, August 3, 1948, p. 183.

[3] Board of Governors *Annual Report*, 1945, p. 7; *Federal Reserve Bulletin*, January, 1948, p. 11; *Hearings Before the Joint Committee on the Economic Report*, November 25, 1947, p. 140; *ibid.*, December 10, 1947, p. 620; and *ibid.*, May 12, 1948, pp. 101-102.

unmanaged, unsupported market. The real question could not be whether yields should be free or pegged; it had to refer to the levels at which pegging would occur. "There is no natural level. . . ."[4] There was also fear that a decline in the prices of marketable bonds might lead to wholesale redemptions of non-marketable savings bonds, which are, in effect, demand obligations. (4) A moderate rise of yields on government securities would not be effective as an anti-inflation measure.[5] Federal Reserve officials argued that a rise of rates so small that it would not greatly increase interest costs to the Treasury or impose serious capital depreciation on bondholders would not be a strongly restraining factor. (5) Low interest rates and generally easy credit conditions facilitated the process of reconversion and would continue to help maintain high levels of employment and production.[6] As late as May 1948 President Sproul, of the New York Federal Reserve Bank, contended that allowing long-term governments to decline more than fractionally below par would interfere with private flotations of loans and might have deleterious effects on production and employment.[7] It was argued that not only low interest rates but also stability of interest rates and bond prices were conducive to prosperity.

In summary, these were the principal reasons offered by officials for the policy of maintaining low interest rates and relatively stable government bond prices: to keep down interest costs to the Treasury and facilitate its large refunding operations, to protect investors against capital losses in terms of money if not in terms of purchasing power, to maintain confidence in financial institutions, and to maintain low interest rates and an orderly bond market for private obligations as a means of maintaining a high level of employment and production. Federal Reserve

[4] *Federal Reserve Bulletin,* November, 1946, pp. 1231-1232.
[5] *Ibid.,* January, 1948, pp. 15-16; *Hearings Before the Joint Committee on the Economic Report,* November 25, 1947, p. 139.
[6] *Annual Report of the Secretary of the Treasury,* 1946, p. 3.
[7] *Hearings Before the Joint Committee on the Economic Report,* May 12, 1948, pp. 101-102. See also his testimony on pp. 94-95.

open-market operations were the principal means of assuring this result. In fact, we shall see later that all other Federal Reserve instruments for credit control, except possibly some selective controls, became largely ineffective for restrictive purposes in the face of the Federal Reserve policy of buying all governments that others wished to sell to it at the official structure of yields. Holding very large amounts of governments which they could redeem or sell, not only banks but also all other investors could convert their securities into money at their own option, the only cost being the sacrifice of yield on the securities converted. And the Federal Reserve, by buying freely at the official yield pattern, held down the cost of converting governments into money.

FEDERAL RESERVE OPEN-MARKET POLICY

The Reserve System's open-market policy during the postwar period up to July 1947 was the same as that followed during the war. It continued to stand ready to buy at a yield of 0.38 percent all Treasury bills offered to it and to grant repurchase options to sellers of bills. It also continued its 0.88 percent posted rate on certificates of indebtedness. Thus the emphasis during this period was on keeping down interest rates on the shortest-maturity obligations, and such purchases as were made by the Federal Reserve were almost exclusively in this category. In fact, with the yields on the shortest maturities held to such low levels no other Federal Reserve actions were necessary to prevent a rise of yields on the longer maturities. Just as in the later stages of the war, investors continued to "play the pattern of the rates," tending to shift from the shorter-maturity, low-yield obligations to longer-maturity, higher-yield issues. Federal Reserve officials worried constantly about this process and tried to devise ways of stopping it and of lessening the upward pressure on the prices of longer-term bonds. In early 1946 the market prices of the longest-term marketable issues were more than 6 percent above par, and in mid-1947 they were still about 3 percent above par.

Marriner Eccles has testified that the Federal Reserve wanted to increase short-term rates soon after the end of the war but this proposal was vetoed by the Treasury.[8]

The first departure from the wartime pattern of yields came in July 1947, nearly two years after V-J Day, when the Federal Open Market Committee eliminated the 0.38 percent posted buying rate on Treasury bills; terminated the granting of repurchase options to the sellers of bills; and announced that the yield on bills would thereafter be expected to find its proper position relative to the rate on certificates, which for the time continued to be pegged at 0.88 percent. The Committee emphasized, however, that the System would continue to purchase and hold bills to the extent necessary to maintain an orderly market.[9] The second departure from the wartime pattern came in August 1947 when the Federal Open Market Committee discontinued its 0.88 percent buying rate on certificates and embarked on a policy of preventing yields on these obligations from rising above the Treasury issuing rate on new certificates. The Treasury thereafter gradually raised the rate on newly issued certificates, so that by December 1947 it had reached 1.13 percent. This permitted the yield on Treasury bills to move up to about 1 percent. These levels prevailed until the late summer of 1948. In August, however, the fourth departure occurred when the Secretary of the Treasury announced that on October 1 the rate on new certificates would be raised from 1.13 to 1.25 percent. Thus, by the end of 1948

---

[8] *Hearings Before the House Banking and Currency Committee on S. J. Res. 157*, August 3, 1948, pp. 187-188.

[9] Board of Governors, *Annual Report,* 1947, p. 93. Rumor has it that the Treasury continued to be unreceptive to higher interest costs on its short-term debt and that its consent to this move was at least partially due to the Board's action in April 1947 imposing a tax on outstanding Federal Reserve notes which would transfer to the Treasury about 90 percent of all Reserve bank earnings in excess of dividend requirements. The Board argued, it is said, that such a rise of rates on short-term Treasury obligations would have little net effect on the Treasury, for most of the bills were owned by the Federal Reserve and the higher interest would be returned to the Treasury through increased Federal Reserve contributions. For a description of this Federal Reserve action to pay its "excess earnings" to the Treasury see *ibid.,* pp. 83-84.

the certificate rate had risen from the wartime level of 0.88 percent to 1.25 percent, and the rate on bills had risen from 0.38 percent to about 1.15 percent.

In the meantime, in December 1947, the Federal Reserve as a third step had lowered somewhat its support prices of longer-term governments. As already noted, the prices of these securities were considerably above par in 1946 and early 1947. Believing that long-term yields had fallen too much, the Treasury sold about $1.8 billion of bonds out of its own investment accounts between April and the end of October 1947, and in October offered for sale a new issue of nonmarketable 2½ percent bonds.[10] These sales, coupled with the rise of short-term rates and the attending rise of uncertainty regarding the future of yields in general, large flotations of corporate securities, and a general rise of the private demand for loan funds, caused the prices of long-term governments to fall and yields on the longest-term issues to rise from 2.19 percent in April to 2.37 percent in November. This decline of bond prices was apparently considered too rapid, however, for the Federal Reserve stepped in and increased its holdings of bonds by about $2 billion during November and up to December 24, and Treasury investment accounts purchased another $917 million. Then, the day before Christmas, the Federal Open Market Committee lowered its support prices for the longer-term issues. No government security was allowed to fall below par, however, and the Federal Reserve purchased vigorously to support the new pattern of prices.[11] No further price declines were allowed to occur in 1948.

[10] Federal Reserve Bank of Boston, *Monthly Review,* January, 1948, p. 7.

[11] The Federal Open Market Committee's decision to take such action was made at its meeting on December 9, 1947. Action, however, was to be deferred until after the Treasury's January refunding operations had been completed unless market selling increased substantially. "It was understood that . . . the executive committee would continue the existing prices at which government securities were being supported until after the Treasury January refunding had been completed, at which time prices of bonds should be permitted to decline rapidly, if the market did not support itself, to a level not more than 100½ and not less than par on the longest restricted 2½ per cent issue and to not less than par on 1⅛ per cent one-year certificates. It was also understood that if, before

This, then, is the general outline of Federal Reserve open-market policy in the postwar period. (1) Up to July 1947, for nearly two years after V-J Day, the Federal Reserve allowed no increase of the yields on marketable governments. By keeping the yields on the shortest-maturities at their very low wartime levels the Federal Reserve had to take no further action to prevent an increase of the longer-term yields. In fact, the latter actually fell below the level that had prevailed during most of the war period and Federal Reserve officials were constantly concerned with the problem of preventing further declines. (2) Beginning

TABLE 80. Maturity Distribution of Federal Reserve Holdings of U. S. Government Securities, 1946-1948

(In millions of dollars)[12]

Date	Total Holdings	Within 90 Days	90 Days to 1 Year	1 to 5 Years	Over 5 Years
Feb. 27, 1946	$22,972	$15,847	$6,074	$ 360	$ 691
June 26, 1946	23,385	17,877	4,436	489	582
June 25, 1947	21,582	16,262	4,335	444	542
Dec. 31, 1947	22,559	14,357	5,565	198	2,439
June 30, 1948	21,366	11,634	3,527	1,146	5,060
Dec. 29, 1948	23,347	6,658	5,125	2,610	8,954

in July 1947 the Federal Reserve took a series of actions that permitted the structure of yields on governments to rise some-what, the yields on short maturities rising more than those on longer maturities. Between June 1947 and late 1948 the yield on bills rose from 0.38 to about 1.15 percent, that on certificates from 0.88 to 1.25 percent, and that on the longest-term bonds from 2.22 to 2.44 percent. Largely because of this rise of yields on short maturities relative to longer-term yields but also because of a growing public doubt as to the future of long-term rates, the

completion of the January refunding, market selling should increase substantially, the executive committee would be authorized to permit prices to decline to the level stated above as rapidly as was consistent with the maintenance of orderly market conditions." Board of Governors, *Annual Report*, 1947, p. 97.

[12] SOURCE: *Federal Reserve Bulletins.*

Federal Reserve as a passive buyer found its portfolio shifting to the longer-maturities. This is shown in Table 80. In June 1947 about 75 percent of all Federal Reserve holdings had maturities of not more than 90 days, and 95 percent had maturities of not more than a year. By the end of 1948, however, only 29 percent had maturities within 90 days and only 50 percent had maturities within a year; 38 percent had maturities beyond 5 years. (3) These actions represented a shift of stabilizing operations away from short-term rates and toward long-term rates. We have seen that from early 1942 until July 1947 the Federal Reserve pegged the short-maturity yields at very low levels with the result that yields on long-term governments tended to be depressed below their 1942 levels. But the 1947-1948 actions showed a tendency toward concentrating attention on preventing the longest-term rate from rising above 2.5 percent while allowing shorter-term rates to rise relative to it. In late 1947 and in 1948 several officials, including the chairman of the Board of Governors, the former chairman, and the president of the Federal Reserve Bank of New York, stated emphatically their determination to prevent the long-term rate from rising above 2.5 percent. Said Chairman McCabe, "I have a very strong conviction that it is vitally necessary to support the 2½ percent bonds . . . I would not say it is our policy forever. I say for the foreseeable future."[13]   Marriner Eccles, former chairman, agreed with this view: "The one thing you cannot do is to have confidence shaken in that 2½ percent rate. If you let that go below par, there is always a question, where does it go? Because people remember, a great many of them, what happened after the last war when they let those securities go below par."[14] The Secretary of the Treasury agreed; said Mr. Snyder, "I think we are definitely committed to a support of the 2½ percent rate."[15] Though short-term rates had been allowed

[13] *Hearings Before the Joint Committee on the Economic Report*, August 2, 1948, p. 101.

[14] *Ibid.*, December 10, 1947, p. 620.

[15] *Hearings Before the House Banking and Currency Committee on S. J. Res. 157*, August 4, 1948, p. 250. For a similar view by President Sproul of the New York Bank, see *Hearings Before the Joint Committee on the Economic Report*, May 12, 1948, pp. 101-102.

to rise in the preceding year and a half, further significant increases in them seemed unlikely at the end of 1948. Most officials seemed to agree with Marriner Eccles' view that, "Clearly you can't let the short-rate go up to a point where pressure on the long-term rates result, so you have to support the long-term market";[16] and with Secretary Snyder's statement that, "We feel there are very narrow limits in which you can can consider increased interest rates."[17] (4) The Federal Reserve during this period employed what were popularly and somewhat derisively known as "open-mouth operations." By leaving doubt as to its future course of action and creating some fear of a future rise of rates, it hoped to lessen the shift from short-term to longer-term issues and to make long-term credit somewhat less available to private borrowers. (5) The 1947-1948 permitted increases in the yields on governments did increase somewhat the cost of securing money by liquidating these securities, and they were accompanied by roughly equivalent increases of yields on comparable private securities. This was a step in the right direction, but two facts should be borne in mind. The first is that even the rates reached in 1948 were indeed very low relative to rates in other prosperous peacetime periods, and that current profits on investment were much higher than in most other prosperous periods. Interest rates as low as these in the face of very high profits were bound to be ineffectual in limiting the amounts of funds demanded for private investment purposes. And the second is that the Federal Reserve still stood ready to buy all the governments that others were unwilling to hold at the official pattern of yields in effect at any given time. The option as to the amount of money created at the selected yield patterns still remained with other security holders. In the following section it will be pointed out that this continued passive open-market policy of the Federal Reserve reduced the effectiveness of other credit control instruments that had traditionally been used to restrict the supply of

[16] *Hearings Before the House Banking and Currency Committee,* November 25, 1947, p. 50.

[17] *Hearings Before the Joint Committee on the Economic Report,* April 13, 1948, p. 18.

credit and make it more expensive. These other instruments might still be used to reduce interest rates below the pattern set by the Open Market Committee, but market rates could not be raised above this pattern, for individuals, corporations, and financial institutions could secure money at their option by selling securities to the Federal Reserve.

The Federal Reserve did not directly support the prices of all governments. It did not support nonmarketable bonds, and it did not operate on all the marketable issues. This does not alter our conclusion, however. The nonmarketable issues were redeemable on demand at the Treasury, and the Federal Reserve had to support the marketable obligations issued to redeem these securities. And by supporting the bulk of the marketable issues the Federal Reserve in effect supported all governments, for private arbitrage kept the yields on all government issues in line with one another.

OTHER ASPECTS OF FEDERAL RESERVE POLICY

Let us now look at the Federal Reserve's use of its other credit control instruments and at the relationship between them and open-market policy.

DISCOUNT RATES

In several steps the Federal Reserve increased its effective discount rates on loans to banks. In March and April 1946, it withdrew from nonmember banks the privilege of borrowing on the basis of government security collateral at the discount rate applicable to loans to member banks. Thereafter these banks had to pay the rate applicable to loans to nonbank borrowers.[18] Then in April and May the Federal Reserve ended the 0.5 percent preferential rate on loans to member banks secured by governments

[18] Board of Governors, *Annual Report*, 1946, pp. 91-92.

maturing within a year.[19] This left in effect a discount rate of 1 percent on loans to member banks secured by governments. The discount rate was advanced to 1.25 percent in January 1948 and then to 1.5 percent in August of that year.

Though these advances of the discount rate may have exerted some influence toward firmness their effects were probably small, for banks were largely out of debt to the Federal Reserve and were likely to remain so while they held so many short-maturity governments that they could at their option sell to the Reserve banks to

TABLE 81. Maturity Distribution of Commercial Bank Holdings of
U. S. Government Securities on Selected Dates, 1946-1948
(In millions of dollars)[20]

	June 1946	December 1947	September 1948
Treasury bills	$ 1,142	$ 2,052	$ 2,191
Certificates	16,676	6,538	7,474
Bonds and notes due or callable within 1 year	5,655	8,244	4,219
1-5 years	25,285	33,415	31,468
5-10 years	21,933	6,090	6,275
more than 10 years	5,858	5,003	3,672
Total	$76,549	$61,370	$55,318

secure money cheaply and without the onus of having become indebted to the Reserve System. (See Table 81.) When the 0.5 percent preferential rate was eliminated in early 1946, thereby establishing a discount rate of 1 percent, commercial banks were holding more than $1 billion of Treasury bills which they could sell at a 0.38 percent discount, and $22.3 billion of other governments due or callable within a year which they could sell at a loss of yield of not more than 0.88 percent. The increase of the rate to 1.25 percent in January 1948 found the banks holding $2 billion of bills on which the yield was less than 1 percent, and $14.7

[19] *Ibid.,* pp. 92-93.
[20] SOURCE: *Federal Reserve Bulletin,* January, 1949, p. 56.

billion of other governments maturing within a year and yielding 1.13 percent or less. The same type of situation prevailed when the discount rate was raised to 1.5 percent in August 1948; the banks were holding $2.2 billion of bills on which the yield was about 1.1 percent, and $11.7 billion of other governments on which the yield did not exceed 1.25 percent. These facts indicate that an increase of discount rates may prevent a decline of market rates below the official pattern set by the Open Market Committee, but it cannot raise market rates above the official pattern so long as the banks hold large quantities of short-term governments and the Federal Reserve continues to act as a passive buyer. Even the "psychological effects" of rate increases are likely to be unimportant when the banks are out of debt and know that they can remain so.

FEDERAL RESERVE BUYING RATES ON ACCEPTANCES

In several steps the Federal Reserve raised its minimum buying rates on bankers' acceptances from 0.5 percent to 1.5 percent. These actions were unimportant, however, both because of the very small volume of acceptances outstanding and because of the factors mentioned above. The market rate on prime acceptances could not rise much above the pegged rate on Treasury bills.

MEMBER BANK RESERVE REQUIREMENTS

We have seen that from October 1942 through the end of the war the Federal Reserve had kept member bank reserve requirements at the highest level permitted by law, except those against demand deposits in central reserve city banks which were at 20 percent as compared with the legal limit of 26 percent. Thus the amount of additional restrictive power that could be exerted through this instrument under existing legislation was quite small, and Reserve officials repeatedly asked for an amendment of the law to permit still further increases of reserve requirements. In mid-1948 President Truman asked a special session of Congress for legislation giving the Federal Reserve more power to raise reserve requirements, but was granted only a part of his request. Congress provided that until June 30, 1949 the Federal Reserve might increase member bank reserve requirements up to these levels:[21]

Highest Level to Which the Federal Reserve Might Raise Member Bank
Reserve Requirements
(In percent)

	Under the Law in Effect Prior to August 1948	Under the August 1948 Law
Demand Deposits		
at central reserve city banks	26	30
at reserve city banks	20	24
at county banks	14	18
Time deposits, all banks	6	7½

The Federal Reserve actually raised member bank reserve requirements three times, all in 1948. The February action raised the amounts of required member bank reserves by about $500 million; the June action increased requirements by another $500 million, and the September action increased them by still another $1.5 billion. Under the usual prewar conditions these actions might have had a highly restrictive effect on bank credit, for in the

TABLE 82.   Member Bank Reserve Requirements, 1942-1948, Percent of Deposits

Period in Effect	Demand Deposits			Time Deposits
	Central Reserve City Banks	Reserve City Banks	Country Banks	(All Member Banks)
October 8, 1942–Feb. 26, 1948	20	20	14	6
Feb. 27, 1948–June 10, 1948	22	20	14	6
June 11, 1948–Sept. 15, 1948	24	20	14	6
Sept. 16-24, 1948 and after	26	22	16	7½

[21] *Federal Reserve Bulletin*, September, 1948, p. 1103.

absence of open-market purchases on the initiative of the Federal Reserve itself the banks could have replenished their reserves only by becoming heavily indebted to the Reserve banks. But in the postwar situation with the banks holding billions of dollars worth of governments and the Federal Reserve standing ready to buy unlimited amounts of them, the banks could easily replenish their reserves, and the increase of reserve requirements could tighten credit only to the extent that banks were reluctant to sell governments to maintain their lending power. That they were not very reluctant to do this is indicated by the fact that following the $1.5 billion increase of their requirements in September, an additional $2 billion of securities were sold to the Federal Reserve. There was an accompanying slight increase of interest rates, but the effectiveness of the increase of reserve requirements was partly negated by the passive open-market policy.

OPEN-MARKET OPERATIONS BY THE TREASURY

The preceding chapter pointed out that the Treasury could exert a potentially great influence on the available volume of bank reserves, for it was handling large amounts of money received as a current cash surplus, at the beginning of the period it held a large balance which was mainly in the form of deposits at commercial banks, it could sell securities out of its investment account, and it could attempt to sell securities to nonbank buyers. By using at least a part of this money to build up its cash and deposits at the Federal Reserve or to retire securities held by the Federal Reserve, the Treasury could drain off large amounts of bank reserves. And it actually did, as was seen earlier, retire $10.6 billion of securities held by the Reserve banks. This would have had a highly restrictive effect on bank credit and on credit in general if the banks had been unable to replenish their reserves or could have done so only by becoming heavily indebted to the Reserve banks. But here again the passive open-market policy of the Federal Reserve greatly reduced the effectiveness of another credit control instrument, for bank reserves could be quickly replenished by selling governments to the Reserve banks. The Treasury action could tighten credit only to the extent that there was a reluctance to part with governments to restore lending power. Table 83 shows that the Treasury net retirement of securities held by the Federal Reserve was in fact largely offset by sales of governments by others to the passive Federal Reserve. During the period from March 1946 to June 30, 1948 Treasury retirements of Federal Reserve-held securities drained off $10.6 billion of bank reserves,

TABLE 83. Net Amounts of Governments Sold to the Treasury and Purchased in the Market by the Federal Reserve, 1946-1948
(In millions of dollars) [22]

Period	Net Retirements by Treasury of Securities Held by Federal Reserve	Net Purchases in Market by Federal Reserve	Net Changes in Federal Reserve Holdings
March 1–June 30, 1946	$ 1,600	$2,500	$ 900
June 30, 1946–June 30, 1947	4,000	2,100	−1,900
June 30, 1947–June 30, 1948	5,000	4,400	−500
Total, March 1946–June 1948	$10,600	$9,000	$−1,500

but the Federal Reserve was forced to restore about $9 billion by purchasing securities offered by others. The point here is not that these Treasury actions were wholly ineffective; they probably did exercise some net restraint on the growth of credit by forcing banks and others to sell governments in order to maintain and increase their lending power. The point here is only that the passive open-market policy of the Federal Reserve greatly reduced the effectiveness of these Treasury actions in restricting the volume and increasing the cost of credit.

[22] These are Treasury estimates. See *Annual Report of the Secretary of the Treasury*, 1946, p. 56; 1947, p. 44; 1948, p. 38.

MORAL SUASION

Throughout this period Federal Reserve officials were constantly warning banks and the public that an excessive expansion of credit was inflationary and might later lead to collapse. In late 1947 all Federal bank supervisory authorities and the executive committee of the state bank supervisors issued a joint statement pointing out the inflationary effects of the current expansion of bank credit, warning against speculative loans, asking that the terms of consumer credit not be liberalized, and urging banks not to overexpand their risk assets relative to their capital.[23] At about the same time the American Bankers Association was conducting its own voluntary campaign, partly to head off governmental action, to prevent "undue" expansions of credit.[24] This type of "jawbone control" may have inhibited speculative loans to some extent, but for several reasons it is doubtful that its total effects were very large: (1) Banks were largely out of debt to the Federal Reserve and could freely add to their lending power by selling some of their governments. (2) Bankers tended to deny that the expansion of bank credit was a major contributing factor to the inflation, and blamed such things as the foreign aid program, government spending, wage increases, the short work week, veterans' bonuses, and agricultural price subsidies.[25] (3) Bankers, like so many others, were misled by the general idea that loans for "productive purposes" are not inflationary—that only speculative loans have this effect. Each banker could see that most of the loans demanded from him were to be used by the borrower to maintain or expand operations within his own firm, and it seemed reasonable to assume that all expansions of productive loans would be accompanied by corresponding increases of real output. They did not seem to realize

[23] Federal Reserve Bank of New York, *Monthly Review,* December, 1947, p. 127.

[24] For some of the ABA speeches see *Banking,* December, 1947 and January and February, 1948.

[25] See the November 1947 statement of the Federal Advisory Council, Board of Governors, *Annual Report,* 1947, pp. 98-100.

that production was already at capacity levels, that under these conditions total output could grow only slowly, and that further large expansions of even "productive" credit would merely bid up the prices of materials and productive factors. Moreover, banks felt free to extend consumer credit on a "sound" basis. Erroneous as they were, these beliefs that a bank should satisfy all demands for "sound," "productive" loans and meet "legitimate" demands for consumer credit greatly decreased the possibility that bankers would respond to moral suasion beyond the point of abstaining from clearly "speculative" loans.

SELECTIVE CONTROLS

On three occasions during this period the Federal Reserve raised margin requirements on security loans. During most of the war period stock purchasers had been required to put up at least a 40 percent "cash" margin. But as the stock market began to rise more rapidly and persisted in this upward movement, margin requirements were raised to 50 percent in February 1945, to 75 percent in July, and to 100 percent in January 1946. Thus the market was placed on a wholly "cash basis" from early 1946 until February 1947. But on the latter date, after stock prices had declined somewhat, these requirements were lowered to 75 percent, at which level they remained through 1948.[26] It is impossible to evaluate the net effects of these high margin requirements, for we do not know what would have happened in their absence. Stock prices actually rose less than would have been expected in the face of rising commodity prices and high corporate profits, and the amount of credit used for purchasing and carrying securities was kept well under control. How much of this was due to the selective control of loans on securities we do not know. About the only conclusions that seem justified are that the use of this instrument probably lessened somewhat the rise of stock prices

[26] For the Board's statements as to the reasons for these actions see *ibid.*, 1945, p. 82-83, and 86-87; 1946, pp. 90-91; 1947, p. 82.

and the expansion of credit for carrying securities, but that it could not cope with the more serious problem of the expansion of credit for consumption and capital construction purposes.

Of more importance was another selective control—the regulation of consumer credit. We have already noted that in August 1941 the Board of Governors, acting under an Executive Order, issued Regulation W to limit the use of consumer credit. Though its provisions varied somewhat depending on the types of things being purchased, they typically required a down-payment of at least one third and limited the length of instalment contracts to 12 months. Partly because of this limitation but more because of the high level of consumer incomes and savings and the very limited availability of durable goods, the volume of outstanding consumer credit declined from its high point of $10.1 billion in the autumn of 1941 to less than $5 billion in 1944, when it again began to rise. The rise became very rapid as consumer durables again became available in quantity and as their prices rose. Regulation W was continued until November 1, 1947, though it was amended on several occasions, some amendments making it more and some less restrictive. Its typical terms required a one-third down-payment and full repayment within 15 months. By joint resolution Congress forced the Federal Reserve to rescind this regulation as of November 1, 1947, and consumer credit was uncontrolled from that time until August 1948. Though banks and other extenders of this type of credit promised to prevent any liberalization of its terms they were not wholly successful in keeping their promises. As soon as a few sellers or lenders in a market tried to improve their competitive position by liberalizing the terms of credit others would retaliate, and a general reduction of down-payments and a lengthening of the period of repayment occurred.[27] Finally, in August 1948, Congress renewed the power of the Federal Reserve to use this selective control until June 30, 1949. The Board thereupon reissued Regulation W, requiring a 33.3 percent down-payment on automobiles and a 20 percent

[27] *Federal Reserve Bulletin,* August, 1948, pp. 897-903.

down-payment on a number of other durable goods, and limiting the period of repayment to 15 months on credits of $1000 or less and to 18 months on credit exceeding $1000. These terms were more liberal than those in effect before November 1947 but less liberal than those evolved during the period while control was suspended.

Consumer credit expanded at an unprecedented rate during this period. From a total of about $5.5 billion on V-J Day it rose $6.5 billion by November 1947, another $2.4 billion while control was suspended, and still another $1.4 billion during the last five months of 1948. Thus the total rise from V-J Day to the end of 1948 was about $10.3 billion. This undoubtedly contributed to inflationary pressures; it helped to swell the rise of consumer spendings and lowered the net amount of consumer saving. The writer believes that consumer credit controls should have been in force throughout the period and that their terms should have been even more restrictive. Such a policy would not have prevented inflation completely, but it would have had several advantages. (1) It would have reduced somewhat the excessive demand for durable goods. (2) By forcing larger down-payments and larger monthly payments for durables, it would have checked somewhat the demand for other consumer goods. And (3) it might have raised somewhat the amount of net personal saving, for "dissaving" could not have been so large if consumer credit had been less available.

This episode indicates the importance of the question of general credit controls *versus* selective controls. Perhaps there is not such a strong case for selective controls when the Federal Reserve is in a position to place effective restrictions on the total amount of credit available. But when, as in this postwar period, it cannot or at least will not place an effective limit on the total amount of credit and spending power there is a strong case indeed for the use of selective controls to limit the amount of credit that may be borrowed and lent for certain types of purchases. And in this period when total spending power was already excessive and the demand for durable goods was far in excess of the available supply it made little sense to permit such a rapid expansion of consumer credit. In fact, selective controls should have been used more widely, especially in the field of housing credit. Required down payments were at most very small indeed; properties were appraised at high levels for loan purposes; periods of repayment were very long; and interest rates were low. The continued shortage of housing was not traceable to a deficient power to buy; demand was far in excess of supply. An FHA policy of requiring larger down-payments, appraising properties at more conservative levels, and shortening the periods of repayment could have prevented some of the inflation in this field and lessened the total amount of credit expansion without lessening the rate of construction.

What should we conclude about the effectiveness of moral suasion and selective controls in the face of a Federal Reserve open-market policy that placed no limit on total lending power and permitted only a small rise of interest rates? This is a difficult question to answer, for we do not know what would have happened in their absence. The following, however, seems to be a fair appraisal. (1) Moral suasion probably discouraged clearly "speculative" loans but had little effect on total credit and total spending. With banks largely out of debt to the Federal Reserve and able to remain so, and with bankers in general believing that they are justified in making any quantity of "sound loans" for "production purposes" as well as to take care of consumers' "legitimate needs," this instrument is not likely to be a very powerful anti-inflationary force. (2) The limitation of loans on securities probably inhibited somewhat the rise of security prices but had little effect on the availability of credit for consumption and capital spending. (3) Regulation W probably decreased somewhat the expansion of consumer spending, but it did not prevent large inflationary pressures from the side of consumer credit. It should have been kept in force throughout the period and made more restrictive. (4) Selective controls might have been used advantageously in other fields, especially in housing credit. (5) If general credit policy was to be revolutionized by relinquishing control over total lending power the development of much more far-reaching selective controls was justified.

POSTWAR CREDIT POLICY AND THE COST AND AVAILABILITY OF CREDIT FOR PRIVATE PURPOSES

The fact that during the postwar period open-market policy was of over-riding importance and that its principal objective was to keep within narrow limits the rise of yields on government securities has already been noted. But what were the effects of this policy on the cost and availability of credit for private purposes? Was it possible to keep down the yields on governments and simultaneously to increase the cost and decrease the availability of credit for individuals and businesses? It will be contended here that this postwar credit policy made it impossible to reduce significantly the availability of credit for private use and that the cost of private credit could not rise significantly relative to the yields on governments.

This contention is based on two principal facts. (1) The Federal Reserve, in order to prevent yields on governments from rising above its selected pattern, had to purchase all the governments offered to it regardless of the type of seller and regardless of the purpose for which the proceeds would be used. It had to purchase not only from commercial banks but also from insurance companies, savings banks, corporations, individuals, and all other types of investors, and the option remained with these security holders. This represented an almost revolutionary change in the theory and practice of the Federal Reserve. Before the war the System had been expected to affect the supply of money and loanable funds primarily through the commercial banking system. It was a system of "bankers' banks"; it lent primarily to commercial banks, and even its open-market operations were undertaken primarily to affect the volume of bank reserves and lending power.

But with this new policy, every holder of governments received access to Federal Reserve credit; he could secure money by selling governments to the Federal Reserve, which had to issue the money regardless of its use to swell spendings directly, to increase the volume of loan funds, or to enhance idle balances. This might have been a relatively unimportant change if the nonbank groups had held only small quantities of governments, but such was far from being the situation. (2) All types of investors—not only banks

TABLE 84.   Holdings of U. S. Government Securities Direct and Fully
Guaranteed, 1940 and 1945
(In billions of dollars)[28]

	June 30 1940	Dec. 31 1945	Net increase June 1940- Dec. 1945	Holdings in Dec. 1945 as Percentage of Holdings in June 1940
Commercial banks	$16.1	$ 90.8	$ 74.7	564
Mutual savings banks	3.1	10.7	7.6	345
Insurance companies	6.5	24.4	17.9	375
State and local governments	0.4	6.5	6.1	1625
Other corporations and associations	2.5	29.1	26.6	1164
Individuals	9.7	63.5	53.8	655
Total held outside the Federal Reserve and U. S. Government agencies and trust funds	$38.3	$225.0	$186.7	587

but also individuals, businesses, and all types of financial institutions—held tremendous amounts of governments which were either redeemable by the Treasury on demand or salable in the market at any time. As shown in Table 84, holders other than the Federal Reserve and U. S. Government agencies and trust funds held $225 billion of governments at the end of 1945, or nearly 5.9 times as many as in mid-1940. All of these were easily and cheaply convertible into money, for some were redeemable by the Treasury on demand and all others were salable at or above the Federal

[28] SOURCE: *Federal Reserve Bulletin,* August, 1947, p. 1012.

Reserve support prices. In two principal ways these large security holdings assured the easy availability of money for private spending. In the first place, many holders could secure money for their own consumption or investment spendings by the simple process of selling governments. To the extent that private spendings were financed in this way, the spenders did not have to go into debt, did not have to prove to some lender their own credit worthiness, and did not have to pay the interest rates applicable to private loans. The cost of money for consumption or investment was merely the yield sacrificed on the governments sold. It is impossible to estimate the extent to which private spendings were financed in this way, but the evidence indicates that it was on a large scale. That consumers employed it widely is suggested by these facts: Redemptions of Series E bonds totalled $13 billion in the three years following 1945, the percent of all spending units holding governments declined from 63 in 1946 to 48 in 1948, and a decrease of liquid asset holdings was used more frequently than consumer credit to finance personal dissaving in 1946 and 1947.[29] Corporations and other businesses also sold governments to secure funds for spending. It is estimated that nonfinancial corporations alone liquidated $6.5 billion of their governments in 1946 and another $1.5 billion in 1947.[30] A number of state and local governments also sold a part of their accumulated securities to obtain money for spending.

In the second place, possession of huge amounts of governments enabled lenders to offer large amounts of private loans on very favorable terms. If the funds were not available from other sources the lenders could liquidate governments to secure money for lending, and if other buyers would not purchase the governments at prices at least equal to those offered by the Federal Reserve the funds had to be supplied by the Reserve banks, thereby tending to increase both the money supply and bank reserves. And it must be emphasized that the commercial banks were not the only lenders

[29] *Federal Reserve Bulletin,* August 1947, p. 953 and August 1948, p. 916.
[30] *Survey of Current Business,* February, 1948.

who could and did liquidate governments in order to increase their other types of credit. Various others did so, but insurance companies did so on the largest scale. Their net sales of governments amounted to a billion dollars in 1947 and $2.8 billion in 1948, and virtually all the resulting funds were used to swell insurance company purchases of mortgages, corporate bonds, and other obligations. This illustrates a very important fact; any tendency to reduce the lending power of one type of lending institution was likely to be at least partially offset by the ready availability of credit at other types of institutions which could dispose of governments in order to satisfy the demand.

Thus the ability of financial institutions and others to lend huge amounts for private purposes was assured by their large holdings of highly liquid and low-yield governments which could be sold to the Federal Reserve. It did not, of course, assure that lenders would be willing to liquidate these securities in order to lend large amounts to private borrowers at low interest rates. Credit is not perfectly mobile. Several factors could allow yields on private securities to rise relative to those on governments and inhibit the shift from government to private obligations: (1) A rise of the estimated risk and illiquidity of private securities relative to governments. This could be important with the onset of deflation, but it was not likely to occur to any considerable extent while the inflation continued. (2) Inertia. Having already made up their portfolios, some investors may be slow to sell governments in order to purchase private securities whose yields have risen. (3) Specialization of financial institutions and individual investors. Since some investors specialize in holding certain types of securities, their funds do not flow freely into other branches of the money market. (4) Policies of "balanced portfolios" and diversification of types and maturities held. Strongly imbued with these ideas, many investors may be reluctant to upset what they consider to be a balanced portfolio in order to shift to other securities. Commercial banks, with their low ratio of capital accounts to total assets, may in some cases be reluctant to load themselves heavily with higher-risk obligations. All these factors contribute to the immobility of funds among the various branches of the money market and might permit some tightening of credit for private purposes while yields on governments are held constant. The Federal Reserve was apparently relying largely on these "frictions" when it expressed hope that by increasing member bank reserve requirements it could tighten credit somewhat without a significant rise of the yields on governments. But it overestimated the immobility of credit.

Several developments since the prewar period tended to increase the mobility of funds from government securities into other branches of the money market. Among these were: (1) The huge volume of governments held by institutional and other investors. These were greater than all other outstanding debt obligations and equal to many times the annual net increase of private debt. Even if the flow of current savings were very small and the demand for funds very high, investors as a group would have to sell only a small percentage of their governments to be able to absorb all new private issues during any year. The importance of this point is magnified by the fact that every net sale of governments to the Federal Reserve, whether by banks or others, adds an equivalent amount to member bank reserves and permits a multiple expansion of commercial bank loans and investments. (2) The widespread ownership of governments. If most of these securities had been owned by only a few types of financial institutions specializing in a few types of private credit, the mobility of funds out of governments and into other branches of the money market might have been quite restricted. But this was not the case, as is shown in Table 84 above. The mobility of credit seems to have been enhanced by the fact that virtually all types of institutional and individual investors who ordinarily lend in all branches of the money market held large volumes of easily cashable governments. (3) The fact that investors' government holdings were so much larger, as a percentage of total assets as well as in absolute amounts, than they were in the prewar period. For example, government securities as a percentage of their total assets increased between the end of 1939 and the end of 1945 from 40 to 73 percent in commercial banks, from 30 to 66 percent in mutual savings banks, and from 20 to 48 percent in life insurance companies. This great growth in their government holdings—which in many cases had occurred largely because of the scarcity of other debt

TABLE 85.   Yields on Selected Government and Private Obligations,
1944-1948
(Yields in percent)[31]

	9-12 Month Certificates	4-6 Month Prime Commercial Paper	U. S. Govt. Taxable Bonds, 15 Years and Over	Corporate Bonds		
				Aaa	A	Baa
1944	0.79	0.73	2.48	2.72	3.06	3.61
1945	0.81	0.75	2.37	2.62	2.87	3.29
1946	0.82	0.81	2.19	2.53	2.75	3.05
1947	0.88	1.03	2.25	2.61	2.87	3.24
1948	1.14	1.44	2.44	2.82	3.12	3.47

	Yield on Commercial Paper as Percentage of Yield on 9-12 Month Certificates	Yields on Corporate Bonds as Percentage of Yields on Taxable U. S. Bonds, 15 Years and Over		
		Aaa	A	B
1944	92	110	123	145
1945	93	110	121	138
1946	99	116	126	139
1947	117	116	127	144
1948	126	115	128	142

obligations—made for an increased willingness to shift out of governments and into other types of securities, for many investors felt that their position was overly safe, overly liquid, and overly dependent on governments. (4) The prevailing low yields. With yields on all debt obligations at levels below those to which they had been accustomed many investors felt impelled to "reach out"

[31] SOURCE: *Federal Reserve Bulletins.*

for the higher yields on private obligations. (5) The prevailing optimism accompanying postwar prosperity. In this situation lenders appraised the safety and liquidity of private obligations at a higher level than in the prewar period and were therefore more willing to shift to them.

We are therefore led to some important conclusions regarding the relationship between postwar Federal Reserve policy and the availability and cost of private credit. (1) Despite elements of immobility in the credit market investors were highly willing to shift from governments to private obligations. (2) Though Federal Reserve policy was aimed directly at keeping down yields on governments, it effectively kept down the yields on private obligations as well and assured the easy availability of credit for private purposes. Table 85 shows the behavior of yields on certificates and long-term governments relative to those on prime open-market commercial paper and three grades of corporate bonds. The parallelism of movement, though not perfect, indicates a high degree of mobility of credit.

CONCLUSIONS

Postwar monetary policy was profoundly influenced by a number of very important changes in the conditions and attitudes created by the war. Among these were: (1) The huge wartime growth of the federal debt. By the end of the war these securities represented 60 percent of all debt outstanding in this country and constituted a major part of the security holdings of financial institutions, other business firms, and individuals. Much of it was in the form of nonmarketable securities that were redeemable on demand and another large part was of short maturity, so that the Treasury faced large and frequent refunding operations. Annual interest charges alone amounted to about $5 billion. We had no experience with the management of a debt of this magnitude and could not foresee the problems that it would raise. It is therefore little wonder that the objective of holding down interest charges on this debt and of preventing or limiting fluctuations of its prices should have received an unprecedented amount of attention. (2) The increased power of the Treasury over monetary policy. The traditional view in this country has been that monetary policy should be determined by authorities who are largely independent of the executive department of the government. But during the war the Treasury attained a dominant position; it determined the interest rates at which it would borrow, and the Federal Reserve took whatever steps were necessary to assure the success of the Treasury program. The Treasury's power was only slightly less dominant in the postwar period. The Federal Reserve was at times able to influence the Treasury's decisions, but in the last analysis it was the Treasury that fixed the interest rates on its new issues and the Federal Reserve maintained yields on governments in line with these interest rates. This rise of the Treasury's power was bound to affect the type of monetary policy followed, and in general this shift of power tended toward a policy of cheaper money. Though the Treasury also took into consideration the effects of its interest rates on the behavior of the economy as a whole, it almost inevitably attached great importance to the burden of its interest costs, the stability of government security prices, and the ease of carrying out its refunding operations. Its primary responsibility was for debt management, and it was greatly impressed by the difficulties of carrying out this function; it was not officially charged with responsibility for general monetary management. It is more than a half truth that in monetary management the Treasury wielded power without responsibility while the Federal Reserve had responsibility without power. One of the big problems remaining to be solved is that of allocating responsibilities and powers for monetary and debt management in such a way as to secure a proper weighing of the various objectives against each other. (3) The fear of unemployment and the new stress on maintaining "full employment." The Great Depression was vividly remembered and many people in official positions feared that widespread unemployment would again emerge. They appeared to be afraid that strong anti-inflationary policies would lead to a serious loss of production and jobs.

These were some of the principal developments accounting for the long delay in initiating a more restrictive monetary policy and in holding within such narrow limits the permitted rise of interest rates in 1946, 1947, and 1948. The policies followed in these years were not without their restrictive effects on private investment and total spendings; they did increase the cost of borrowed funds after mid-1947, and they did decrease somewhat the availability of credit by creating uncertainty regarding the future course of interest rates. But these effects were quite limited; interest rates were not allowed to rise above depression levels, and the availability of credit could not be markedly reduced by an expectation that interest rates would rise so long as officials proclaimed their determination that for the "foreseeable future" yields on the longest-term governments would not be allowed to rise above 2.5 percent. Such an easy monetary policy would not have been inflationary if the willingness to spend for capital purposes had been at a low level or if the propensity to provide savings out of current income had been high. But with the willingness to spend at very high levels and with the propensity to save at very low levels, the assurance of a large supply of credit at low interest rates could not fail to encourage the inflation.

The following chapter will consider further the economic significance of this policy.

XIV

||||||||||||||||||||||||||||||||||||||||||||||||||||||||||||||||||||||||||||||||||||||||||||||||||||||||||||||||||||||||||||||||||||||||||||||||

The Relation of Postwar Monetary
Policy to the Inflation

THE preceding chapter described the postwar credit policies
of the Federal Reserve, emphasizing their objective of holding within narrow limits the yields on government obligations,
and the derivative effect of assuring the continued easy availability and low cost of credit for private purposes. Though these
policies did contribute to the postwar inflationary process they
should be put in perspective and should not be overemphasized.
They were not the only factors contributing to commercial bank
reserves and to the expansibility of the money supply in the postwar period; the expansion of spendings was not made possible
wholly by a postwar expansion of the money supply; and the war
and postwar expansion of the money supply was not the "sole
cause" of the inflation.

POSTWAR DETERMINANTS OF BANK RESERVES

As emphasized earlier, the expansion of spendings between the
end of 1939 and the end of 1945 was accompanied and made
possible by a very great increase in the money supply. The amount
of coin and currency in circulation increased by about $20.8
billion, and the great expansion of deposits raised by $8 billion

the amount of reserves required of member banks.[1] Funds to supply these needs came from several sources; member banks drew down their excess reserves by $3.5 billion, an increase of the monetary gold stock contributed $2.5 billion, and a rise of outstanding Treasury currency supplied $1.4 billion. But by far the

TABLE 86. Member Bank Reserves and Their Determinants, 1939-1945
(Monthly averages of daily figures, in millions of dollars)[2]

	Dec. 1939	Dec. 1945	Change, Dec. 1939-Dec. 1945
Sources of funds			
F. R. holdings of govt. securities	$ 2,510	$23,708	$21,198
Other F. R. credit	102	1,036	934
Total F. R. credit	2,612	24,744	22,132
Monetary gold stock	17,518	20,047	2,529
Treasury currency outstanding	2,956	4,322	1,365
Total sources	$23,086	$49,113	$26,027
Less: Competing uses of these funds			
Money in circulation	$ 7,609	$28,452	$20,843
Treasury holdings of cash and deposits at the F. R.	3,018	2,894	−124
Other competing uses	987	1,740	753
Total competing uses	11,614	33,086	21,472
Equals: Member bank reserves	11,473	16,027	4,554
Addendum: Excess reserves	$ 5,011	$ 1,498	$−3,513

largest part of these funds was supplied by an expansion of Federal Reserve credit; this amounted to $22.1 billion, and the major part of it, or $21.2 billion, represented increased Federal Reserve holdings of governments. Thus there can be no doubt that during the defense and war period as a whole the increase of Federal Reserve credit was the major contributor of money to

[1] A small part of the increased volume of required reserves resulted from the increase of reserve requirements in percentage terms.
[2] SOURCE: *Federal Reserve Bulletins.*

meet the rising demand for coin and currency and to supply increased bank reserves to enhance bank lending power.

The postwar period presents quite a different picture, as is shown in Table 87. The amount of coin and currency in circulation changed but little from the end of 1945 to the end of 1948, though the volume of required member bank reserves rose by

TABLE 87.   Member Bank Reserves and Their Determinants, 1945-1948
(Monthly averages of daily figures, in millions of dollars)[3]

	Dec. 1945	Dec. 1946	Dec. 1947	Dec. 1948	Change, Dec. 1945- Dec. 1948
Sources of funds					
F. R. holdings of U. S.					
govt. securities	$23,708	$23,767	$21,905	$23,002	$ −706
Other F. R. credit	1,036	979	953	976	−60
Total F. R. credit	24,744	24,746	22,858	23,978	−766
Monetary gold stock	20,047	20,488	22,712	24,218	4,171
Treasury currency outstanding	4,322	4,552	4,556	4,584	262
Total sources	$49,113	$49,786	$50,126	$52,780	$ 3,667
Less: Competing uses of these funds					
Money in circulation	$28,452	$28,997	$28,937	$28,423	$ −29
Treasury holdings of cash and deposits at the F. R.	2,894	2,812	2,297	2,717	−177
Other competing uses	1,740	1,458	1,630	1,651	−89
Total competing uses	33,086	33,267	32,864	32,791	−295
Equals: Member Bank Reserves	$16,027	$16,517	$17,261	$19,990	$ 3,963
Addendum: Excess Reserves	$ 1,498	$ 900	$ 987	$ 797	$ −701

$4.7 billion, partly because of the rise of bank deposits and partly because of the increase of percentage reserve requirements. By far the greatest net contributor to increased bank reserves was the monetary gold stock; this rose by $4.2 billion during the period. Total Federal Reserve credit actually declined $766 million, most of this representing a net decrease of Federal Reserve holdings of governments during the period.

[3] SOURCE: *Federal Reserve Bulletins.*

What are some of the implications of these facts? The first, of course, is that the increase of our monetary gold stock, resulting almost entirely from gold imports, was the great contributor to bank reserves and to bank lending power during the period. As foreigners shipped gold to this country to pay for a part of our exports, this not only enhanced foreign spending for our output but also directly added to the money supply and to bank reserves. And the amount of funds supplied from this source was approximately equal to the total increase of bank reserves during the period. This fact alone should prevent us from attributing to Federal Reserve actions all the increase of the money supply and all the ease of credit during the postwar period.

Does this mean that Federal Reserve policy was "neutral" and contributed to neither the rise of the money supply nor to the continuance of easy credit? Such conclusions do not necessarily follow. In the first place, the Federal Reserve cannot be "neutral." It is officially charged with the responsibility for monetary management, and in the absence of its concern for an "orderly market for governments" it could have sold securities to mop up the added reserves supplied by gold imports and it could even have reduced the volume of bank reserves. Though Federal Reserve policy has been characterized as "passive" it was positive in the sense that Reserve officials at least tacitly approved current economic developments. In the second place, our use of figures for the whole period from the end of 1945 to the end of 1948 hides the fact that at several times within the period Federal Reserve purchases of securities supplied reserve funds which probably prevented a tightening of credit. For example, between early April and December 1946 the Federal Reserve increased its government holdings by about $2 billion, between June and December 1947 it increased them by about a billion, and between June and December 1948 it increased them by considerably more than enough to supply the funds needed to meet enhanced reserve requirements. In the absence of this Federal Reserve policy a significant tightening of credit might have occurred at times—perhaps enough to exert a marked damping effect on the boom. In the third place, the maintenance of this Federal Reserve policy seems to have increased the willingness of lenders to extend credit even when they did not actually sell governments to secure the funds for lending. The knowledge that current Federal Reserve policy made their governments highly liquid and that at any time they could secure money by selling these obligations probably reduced the amount of money that investors held idle and enhanced the amount made available to borrowers. And in the fourth place, the widely-publicized Federal Reserve policy of preventing greater increases of interest rates, especially of long-term rates, on governments undoubtedly reduced the rise of rates on private loans and enhanced the availability of credit at these low rates. The supply of loans at any time is markedly affected by expectations as to the future course of rates. If rates are expected to rise there is a tendency to withhold loans, especially long-term loans, until current market rates have risen to levels comparable with those that are expected to rule in the future. And, ironically, an initial rise of rates may actually reduce the current supply of loans, for it may create an expectation of still further rate increases. It is probable that in the absence of the Federal Reserve policy that has been described, there could have been created an expectation of a marked rise of interest rates, that interest rates would in fact have risen considerably more, and that the upward movement of rates would have created still more uncertainty about the future of rates and would have reduced somewhat more the availability of credit.

It can be concluded, therefore, that though the increase of bank reserves during this period was largely attributable to gold imports and not to an expansion of total Reserve bank credit, the current Federal Reserve policy nevertheless was an important contributor to the continuance of low interest rates and to the easy availability of credit at these rates.

THE MONEY SUPPLY AND SPENDINGS
IN THE POSTWAR PERIOD

This question now arises: "To what extent was the postwar expansion of spendings financed by an increase of the money supply, and to what extent by a more rapid turnover of money?" The facts regarding the money supply are shown in Table 88. During the three years following 1945, the money supply (privately owned demand deposits plus currency outside banks) rose

TABLE 88.   The Money Supply and Its Determinants, 1945-1948
(In billions of dollars)[4]

	Amounts as of End of Each Year				Net Change, 1945-1948
	1945	1946	1947	1948	
Sources					
Monetary gold stock	$ 20.1	$ 20.5	$ 22.7	$ 24.2	$ 4.1
Treasury currency outstanding	4.3	4.6	4.6	4.6	0.3
Total Federal Reserve credit	25.1	24.7	22.9	24.0	−1.1
Commercial bank loans and investments	124.0	114.0	116.3	114.3	−9.7
U. S. Security holdings	90.6	74.8	69.2	62.5	−28.1
other investments	7.3	8.1	9.0	9.1	1.8
loans	26.1	31.1	38.1	42.7	16.6
Total sources=total amounts used	$173.5	$163.8	$166.5	$167.1	$ −6.4
Less: Amounts absorbed by competing uses:					
U. S. Government deposits and cash holdings	$25.9	$ 5.8	$ 3.5	$ 4.4	$−21.5
Time deposits at commercial banks	29.9	33.9	35.4	35.7	5.8
Other competing uses	15.3	14.1	14.0	15.6	0.3
Total competing uses	$71.1	$53.8	$52.9	$55.7	$−15.4
Equals: The money supply					
Privately owned demand deposits	$ 75.9	$ 83.3	$ 87.1	$ 85.7	$ 9.8
Currency outside banks	26.5	26.7	26.5	25.7	−0.8
Total money supply	$102.4	$110.0	$113.6	$111.4	$ 9.0

[4] SOURCE: *Federal Reserve Bulletins.*

by $9 billion. It rose $7.6 billion in 1946 and $3.6 billion in 1947; in 1948, however, there was a decrease of about $2.2 billion. Table 88 also shows the factors accounting for these changes in the money supply. Nearly half of the net increase during the period was accounted for by the rise of Treasury currency outstanding and

TABLE 89.   Effects of Commercial Bank Operations on the Money Supply, 1945-1948

(In billions)[5]

	During 1946	During 1947	During 1948	During the entire 3-yr. period
Factors tending to increase the money supply				
Increase of bank loans	$ 5.0	$ 7.0	$ 4.6	$16.6
Increase of other bank investments	0.8	0.9	0.1	1.8
Decrease of Treasury deposits at commercial banks	20.1	2.3	−0.9	21.5
Total	$25.9	$10.2	$ 3.8	$39.9
Less: Factors tending to decrease the money supply				
Decrease of bank holdings of governments	15.8	5.6	6.7	28.1
Increase of time deposits at commercial banks	4.0	1.5	0.3	5.8
Increase of commercial bank capital accounts	0.6	0.5	0.5	1.6
Total	$20.4	$ 7.6	$ 7.5	$35.5
Equals: net effect on the money supply	$ 5.5	$ 2.6	$ −3.7	$ 4.4
Addendum: Net change of the actual money supply	$ 7.6	$ 3.6	$ −2.2	$ 9.0

the monetary gold stock, mostly the latter. The remainder was due to various other changes shown in the table. The role of commercial bank credit in the expansion requires further clarification. The figures in the table might suggest that the net effect of commercial bank operations was toward reducing the money supply, for these banks reduced their total loans and investments, their holdings of

[5] Computed from data in *Federal Reserve Bulletins* and *Treasury Bulletins*.

governments declining more than their other investments and loans rose. This, however, is misleading, for it fails to show that the reduction of bank holdings of governments was largely offset by the cancelling of Treasury deposits at these banks. While commercial bank holdings of governments fell by $28.1 billion during this period Treasury deposits at these banks fell $21.5 billion, so that the decline of the banks' *net* loans to the Treasury (bank holdings of federal debt minus Treasury deposits at these banks) fell only $6.6 billion. (See Table 89.) At the same time bank loans and other investments rose $18.4 billion so that the net increase of bank loans, *net* loans to the Treasury, and other investments was $11.8 billion. About $7.4 billion of these funds were absorbed by the increase of time deposits and bank capital accounts, but the remaining $4.4 billion went to swell the money supply. Thus, commercial bank operations accounted for nearly half of the increase of the money supply during the three years following 1945, and they accounted for much more than half during 1946 and 1947.

The postwar expansion of the money supply offers some interesting contrasts to that occurring during the war period. (1) It was much smaller each year. (2) The expansion during the war was due almost entirely to the increase of government holdings by the commercial and Federal Reserve banks; the postwar expansion resulted from gold imports and from the expansion of commercial bank loans and other investments and it occurred despite a considerable reduction of government holdings by the banks. In short, the wartime expansion reflected a monetization of government debt, but the postwar expansion reflected a monetization of gold and private debt. (3) The wartime expansion of the money supply was accompanied by a less than proportional increase of spendings for output, but the postwar expansion of spendings was proportionally greater than the postwar expansion of the money supply. The latter is shown in Table 90.

From its postwar low in the first quarter of 1946, the GNP rose 35.8 percent by the last quarter of 1948. During the same period the money supply rose only 8.6 percent and the income velocity of money rose 25.1 percent. This suggests that about 75 percent of the increase of spendings for output during this period was financed by an increase in the income velocity of money and only 25 percent by an increase of the money supply. This conclusion is reached, however, only if we measure changes

TABLE 90. The Gross National Product, the Money Supply, and the Income Velocity of Money, 1945-1948

(Money figures in billions of dollars)[6]

				Index, First Quarter of 1946=100		
Period	GNP (Annual Rate)	Average Money Supply	Income Velocity of Money (Col. 1 ÷ Col. 2)	GNP	Average Money Supply	Income Velocity of Money
1945—1Q	$222.6	$ 93.7	2.38	111.8	91.7	122.1
2Q	225.0	97.7	2.30	113.0	95.6	117.9
3Q	213.0	99.7	2.14	107.0	97.6	109.7
4Q	200.3	104.4	1.92	100.6	102.2	98.5
1946—1Q	199.1	102.2	1.95	100.0	100.0	100.0
2Q	206.3	104.9	1.97	103.6	102.6	101.0
3Q	221.1	107.3	2.06	111.0	105.0	105.6
4Q	224.0	109.4	2.05	112.5	107.0	105.1
1947—1Q	228.2	107.3	2.13	114.6	105.0	109.2
2Q	233.6	107.9	2.16	117.3	105.6	110.8
3Q	232.4	109.8	2.12	116.7	107.4	108.7
4Q	248.6	112.6	2.21	124.9	110.2	113.3
1948—1Q	251.4	109.9	2.29	126.2	107.5	117.4
2Q	261.6	108.2	2.42	131.4	105.9	124.1
3Q	266.5	109.3	2.44	133.9	106.9	125.1
4Q	270.3	111.0	2.44	135.8	108.6	125.1

from late 1945 or early 1946 when income velocity was at the lowest level of which we have any record. If we measure from some earlier level we find that increases of the money supply become of greater relative importance. For example, from the first quarter of 1945 to the last quarter of 1948 spendings for output rose 21 percent, the money supply 18.5 percent, and the income velocity of money only 2.5 percent. And from 1939 to

[6] Computed from data in *Federal Reserve Bulletins* and *Surveys of Current Business.*

the last quarter of 1948 GNP rose 196 percent, while the money supply rose 224 percent and the income velocity of money declined 11 percent.

In short, the movements were as follows: (1) During the defense period the rise of spendings for output was financed by

TABLE 91.   The Gross National Product, the Money Supply, and the Income Velocity of Money, 1929-1948
(Money figures in billions of dollars) [7]

| | | | | Indexes, 1939=100 | | |
Period	GNP	Average Money Supply	Income Velocity of Money	GNP	Average Money Supply	Income Velocity of Money
1929	$103.8	$ 26.4	3.93	113.7	78.1	145.6
1930	90.9	25.4	3.58	99.6	75.1	132.6
1931	75.9	23.3	3.26	83.1	68.9	120.7
1932	58.3	20.8	2.80	63.9	61.5	103.7
1933	55.8	19.8	2.82	61.1	58.6	104.4
1934	64.9	21.4	3.03	71.1	63.3	112.2
1935	72.2	25.1	2.88	79.1	74.3	106.7
1936	82.5	29.0	2.84	90.4	85.8	105.2
1937	90.2	30.4	2.97	98.8	89.9	110.0
1938	84.7	30.4	2.79	92.8	89.9	103.3
1939	91.3	33.8	2.70	100.0	100.0	100.0
1940	101.4	39.1	2.59	111.1	115.7	95.9
1941	126.4	45.5	2.78	138.4	134.6	103.0
1942	161.6	54.8	2.95	177.0	162.1	109.3
1943	194.3	71.5	2.72	212.8	211.5	100.7
1944	213.7	83.6	2.56	234.1	247.3	94.8
1945	215.2	98.9	2.18	235.7	292.6	80.7
1946	212.6	106.0	2.01	232.9	313.6	74.4
1947	235.7	109.4	2.15	258.2	323.7	79.6
1948	262.4	109.6	2.39	287.4	324.2	88.5

increases in both the money supply and a higher turnover of money. (See Table 91.) (2) During the war period itself total spendings for output rose less rapidly than the money supply; the income velocity of money declined as individuals and businesses elected to hold larger money balances in relation to their spendings.

[7] Computed from data in *Federal Reserve Bulletins* and *Surveys of Current Business*.

The decline of velocity was especially large after 1942. We have already noted the principal reasons for this—the scarcity of civilian goods and direct controls to limit private spendings and the decision of private savers to hold a large part of their savings in the form of money rather than other assets. There can be no doubt that by the end of 1945 there were very large private "hoards"

TABLE 92.   Approximate Estimates of Idle Money Balances, 1943-1948
(In billions of dollars)[8]

Period	Col. 1 Actual Money Supply	Col. 2 Amount of Money That Would Have Been Required to Finance GNP with Velocity at 1939 Levels	Col. 3 Amount of Money That Would Have Been Required to Finance GNP with Velocity at 1929 Levels	Col. 4 Col. 1 Minus Col. 2	Col. 5 Col. 1 Minus Col. 3
1943	$ 71.5	$ 72.0	$49.4	$ —0.5	$22.1
1944	83.6	79.1	54.4	4.5	29.2
1945—4Q	104.4	74.2	51.0	30.2	53.4
1946—1Q	102.2	73.7	50.7	28.5	51.5
2Q	104.9	76.4	52.5	28.5	52.4
3Q	107.3	81.9	56.3	25.4	51.0
4Q	109.4	83.0	57.0	26.4	52.4
1947—1Q	107.3	84.5	58.1	22.8	49.2
2Q	107.9	86.5	59.4	21.4	48.5
3Q	109.8	86.1	59.1	23.7	50.7
4Q	112.6	92.1	63.3	20.5	49.3
1948—1Q	109.9	93.1	64.0	16.8	45.9
2Q	108.2	96.9	66.6	11.3	41.6
3Q	109.3	98.7	67.8	10.6	41.5
4Q	111.0	100.1	68.8	10.9	42.4

of money, in the sense of private holdings in excess of the amounts "needed" to finance current private spendings for output. (3) During the postwar period, dishoarding out of idle money balances accumulated by the end of 1945 was one of the principal methods of financing increased spendings for output. This is indicated by the postwar rise of velocity. Unfortunately we have no way of

[8] Computed from data in *Federal Reserve Bulletins* and *Surveys of Current Business.*

measuring accurately the volume of "idle" money balances, for we do not know how much money is "needed" to finance spendings for output and other current transactions. It is possible, however, to compute approximate maximum and minimum amounts by comparing the actual supply of money in existence at a given time with the amounts that would be required to finance current spendings for output if the income velocity were as high as it was in some prewar period. This is done in Table 92. Column 1 shows the average amount of money actually in existence during each period. Column 2 shows the amount that would have been required to finance GNP during each period if the income velocity had remained at 1939 levels. It is computed by dividing GNP during the period by 2.7, the income velocity in 1939. Column 4 shows the excess of the actual amount of money outstanding over the amount that would have been required to finance GNP at 1939 levels of income velocity. This indicates that by the last quarter of 1945 "idle balances" in this sense amounted to about $30 billion. During the postwar period, however, dishoarding occurred, so that by the end of 1948 idle balances in this sense were about $11 billion. But these figures probably underestimate the level of "idle balances" at the end of the war and also during the postwar period, for there seems to have been a considerable amount of "hoarding" in 1939. In that year the income velocity of money was only 2.7 as compared with 3.93 in 1929; it had declined 31 percent during this depression decade. If we deduct from the actual money supply the amounts that would have been required to finance current spending for output with income velocity at 1929 levels we get the results shown in column 5. "Idle balances" in this sense had reached about $53 billion in the last quarter of 1945, but by the end of 1948 they had been drawn down to around $42 billion.

These figures, though only rough approximations, point to several conclusions. (1) At the end of the war the private sectors of the economy were already holding very large balances in excess of the amounts needed to finance their current rate of spendings. (2) A large part of the postwar increase of spendings was financed not by a postwar increase of the money supply but by dishoarding out of money balances accumulated during the war period. (3) Even at the end of 1948, the income velocity of money had not yet risen to even the depression levels of the 1930's. (See Tables 90 and 91.) A phenomenon common to inflations—the flight from money to goods—did not occur on a large scale. (4) These facts do not necessarily indicate that a different postwar monetary policy—one that would have prevented the money supply from increasing at all above the levels that prevailed in mid-1945 —would have been ineffectual in damping somewhat the rise of spendings and prices. Such a policy, which would have necessitated an abandonment of the passive open-market policy and would have required a sterilization of gold imports, would unquestionably have raised interest rates to some extent. But what would have been the reaction to a rise of interest rates and the unavailability of additional bank credit? Would holders of idle balances have dishoarded larger amounts to take advantage of slightly higher yields and thus have assured a continued easy availability of money for private spendings? Would the income velocity of money have risen enough more to compensate for the failure of the money supply to rise further? Or would such a policy have had the opposite effect? Would the rise of interest rates have created expectations of still further rises, so that idle balances would not have been drawn down any more than they actually were? The writer is inclined to the belief that the latter would have happened, and that the postwar increase of the money supply played a larger role in the postwar rise than would be indicated by the figures. There is a strong possibility that the prevention of any increase in the money supply in the postwar period and the publicity accompanying such a policy would have inhibited spendings and the inflation by creating a general belief that prices would not rise so much and might fall soon.

THE ROLE OF MONEY AND MONETARY POLICY
IN THE INFLATION

We come now to some other highly controversial questions. What was the role of postwar monetary policy in the inflation? Was monetary policy "the cause" of the inflation? Or did the money supply "merely adapt itself to the needs of the economy" with "the cause of the inflation" to be sought elsewhere? Too many answers to these questions are overly simple and dogmatic and construe "causal" relationships too narrowly.

In the first place, it should be emphasized that Federal Reserve easy money policies may not, in an unfavorable economic situation, succeed in maintaining spendings at a level sufficiently high to prevent widespread unemployment, let alone produce an inflation. The most they can do is to make money easily available, to depress interest rates and create a general belief that they will remain low, and perhaps tend to improve somewhat the public's expectations as to the future course of business. To illustrate this point let us assume that the Federal Reserve purchases very large amounts of government securities from nonbank holders. The immediate effect is (1) to increase bank reserves, thereby *permitting* a multiple expansion; and (2) to increase the amount of money held by the public. This unquestionably increases total lending power and this, as well as the Federal Reserve purchases themselves, tends to lower interest rates. But it should be noted that this operation increasing bank reserves and the public's money supply is solely on "capital account"; it does not directly raise anyone's income or total savings. The sellers of the securities now hold money rather than securities on capital account, and the banks hold more reserves among their assets to balance their higher deposit liabilities. This increase of liquidity may well increase the supply of loans offered on the market, but an inflation cannot result in the absence of a willingness of the private sectors or the government to borrow in order to spend for consumption or investment purposes. Our experience after 1932 amply demonstrated the fact that an inflation cannot be generated simply by making money available at low interest rates. To get inflation, there must also exist a willingness to borrow and spend.

During the war period, the government supplied the willingness to demand money for spending. Monetary policy made the additional money available; deficit spending created the necessary demand for additional money and injected it into the income stream. And the additional money received by the private sectors of the economy was not on capital account but *on income account*. Received as payments for goods and services, this money could be spent for consumption goods without making the recipients any less rich than they were at the beginning of the period, or it could be saved to enhance the recipients' wealth. This creation of money as a part of the process of creating income certainly makes its recipients more willing to spend it than they would have been if they had secured it merely by selling previously accumulated capital assets.

We come now to the postwar period. The Federal Reserve continued, as we have seen, to assure the easy availability of low-cost credit. But after mid-1946 the Treasury ceased to supply the willingness to borrow and spend money; its deficits were converted to surpluses. The private sectors of the economy supplied this willingness. As indicated earlier, the profitability of private investment was very high indeed, and enterprisers demanded and used very large amounts of money for investment purposes, these amounts rising as the prices of capital goods rose. At the same time the propensity to consume was very high; many consumers were spending beyond their current incomes by drawing on past savings and demanding consumer credit, and others were saving only small parts of their incomes. Spendings, in the form of investment and dissaving, were continuously tending to rise above the amounts being saved out of current incomes, and the excess was financed by dishoardings out of money balances accumulated earlier and by increases of the money supply. There was not lacking any willingness to spend and, if necessary, to borrow money for the purpose.

Thus, when we compare the postwar period with the 1933-1939 period, there can be no doubt that factors other than postwar monetary policy and to some extent other than wartime monetary policy were the "dynamic causes" of the postwar inflation. Federal Reserve policy was little if any more liberal in permitting an expansibility of the money supply than it had been after 1933. The great difference was in the willingness of the private sectors to spend and if necessary to borrow money for the purpose. The huge wartime accumulation of savings that made people and businesses richer was one factor creating both the ability and willingness to spend; but also of key importance were such things as the accumulated depreciation and obsolescence of capital, the backlog of unsatisfied desires for consumer durables, and the general desire to have a good time after the wartime period of real or imagined deprivation.

We can even go farther in emphasizing the passive role of money in the expansion of both spendings and the money supply. Much of this increase was elicited by an accompanying or prior rise of wage rates and of prices of important products. We have already emphasized the fact that demands for output were so insistent and price-inelastic that capacity output could be sold even in the face of marked price increases; as prices rose buyers spent more, and if the purchases were made with borrowed money they borrowed more. Thus a general increase of wage rates did not lead to unemployment, but led employers to spend more for labor and in many cases to borrow more for the purpose. An increase in the price of houses enhanced the amount of money borrowed and spent for this purpose. Increases in the prices of automobiles elicited more rapid increases in consumer credit. And so on.

In short, a realistic description of the postwar inflation must emphasize: (1) The role of factors other than monetary policy that greatly increased the willingness of the private sectors to spend, that made them willing to spend more as prices rose, and that made them willing and even insistent on borrowing more; (2) that the causal sequence was not necessarily from an increased money supply to increased money spendings to increased prices— in some cases it was from the demand for increased prices to a higher rate of spendings to a higher money supply; and (3) that aggressive demands for wage increases and the high-price policies of some sellers contributed heavily to the expansion of spendings, to the rise of the demand for credit, and to the expansion of bank credit and the money supply. These facts correctly indicate that the inflation would have been less extensive, the increase of spendings smaller, and the expansion of the money supply less if by direct controls or otherwise wage rates had been prevented from rising so much and if some industries with administered prices had been less generous with themselves in their estimates of an "adequate profit."

But even though the "dynamic" upward pressures arose in other areas of the economy it does not at all follow that a restrictive monetary policy could not have reduced the extent of the inflation. Though the easy availability of money for spending is not a "sufficient cause" of inflation, it is certainly a "necessary condition." A significant amount of inflation cannot occur without an increase of spendings and this requires a rise of (1) the money supply or (2) the income velocity of money, which is the same as a drawing down of idle balances. In the absence of its concern over the government security market the Federal Reserve could have prevented the postwar rise of the money supply. It had no direct control over the rate of use of existing money, but it seems reasonable to conclude that a prevention of further increases of the money supply would not have increased the amount of dishoarding. Such a restrictive credit policy might actually have decreased dishoarding because of the accompanying greater rise of interest rates and the engendered greater uncertainty concerning their future, and also because a widely publicized tight money policy would have made expectations regarding future spendings and prices less bullish.

For these reasons the writer strongly disagrees with the policy implications of some of the statements made by the Federal Advisory Council in November 1947.

We find nothing in bank loans themselves to suggest that growth of loans has been an active inflationary factor. It rather appears to have been a reflection of the very high level of business activity and high prices. . . .

Commercial banks are influenced by high prices and active movement of agricultural and manufactured products for the foreign aid program. . . .

High wages and high costs of materials have meant that business needed more money to take care of its customers. . . .

There is nothing in the figures or our experience to suggest that there exists any substantial lending for speculation or for unnecessary uses. . . .

The causes of our inflation are not in current banking policies but are found in the great wartime expansion of buying power together with unusual events and public policies since that time.[9]

These statements were made at a time when the money supply had been allowed to rise $10 billion above its level at the end of 1945 and $18 billion above its level in mid-1945. And a considerable part of this increase was traceable to commercial bank operations. To suggest that banks should be permitted to satisfy all demands for "sound" loans that are not to be employed for "speculation" or "unnecessary uses" in the midst of inflation is in effect to suggest that a rise of prices should not be at all inhibited by any shortage of spending power.

The writer also questions the wisdom of those who believed that a significant tightening of credit would have been undesirable because its primary effect would have been to reduce total production and employment. The argument ran somewhat as follows: The fundamental cause of the inflation is the rise of wage rates far in advance of the rise of labor productivity. Workers insist on such increases and will not work for less. If credit is not allowed

---

[9] Board of Governors, *Annual Report*, 1947, p. 98.

to expand at least enough to meet the "increased needs of trade" resulting from these increases of wages and prices the result will inevitably be unemployment and underproduction. The same argument applies if sellers insist on larger profits and will not produce for less. We therefore had only two alternatives: (1) to maintain the existing ease of credit and expansibility of the money supply, which would support more inflation; or (2) tighten credit and experience serious unemployment and loss of production. Both the reasoning and the conclusions are questionable. In the first place, there is no reason to believe that, in order to avoid setting off a deflationary spiral, it was necessary to maintain the prevailing easy availability of credit in the face of the abnormally high profitability of new investment and the high propensity to consume. To argue otherwise is, in effect, to say that the Federal Reserve should never try to stop or even to retard an inflationary boom, for this might start a cumulative deflation.

In the second place, those who used this argument failed to see that the continuance of such easily available credit at such low cost greatly encouraged large and successive wage demands and sellers' demands for larger profits as a condition for producing. Unions and workers do sometimes tend to price themselves out of employment, but they are usually realists. In at least a vague way they try to estimate the magnitude of the demand for their employers' products and gauge their wage demands accordingly. Moreover, most sellers have the capacity to adjust their ideas of "adequate profits" to the magnitude of the demand for their products. A restrictive credit policy could have had a significant restrictive effect on total demand, and it probably would have lessened considerably the amounts of additional wages and profits demanded as a condition for continuing a high level of production.

In the third place, it is not clear what Federal Reserve policy should be when employers and employees *in general* are demanding such great increases of money wage rates and money profits as to exert strong upward pressures on the general level of prices. It is clearly not the function of the Federal Reserve to prevent increases of wages at the expense of profits or vice versa, or even to prevent increases of wage rates, profits, and prices within particular segments of industry so long as these occur within the framework of a relatively stable general price level. But when there is a *general* and rapid upward movement of wage rates, profits, and prices and the Federal Reserve passively supplies, or permits the supplying of, additional spending power to support the upward wage-profit-price spiral, it cannot escape responsibility. In following such a policy the Federal Reserve in effect says to employees and employers, "Your bargaining need not be confined within the framework of a generally stable price level and a national money income that rises only with productivity. You may, if you wish, arrive at much higher wages while maintaining or expanding the volume of your profits and we will supply, or permit to be supplied, all the added spending power needed to support mounting price levels. We remain unconcerned if this means that powerful labor and employer groups gain at the expense of those classes whose money incomes and money wealth cannot rise so fast." The distribution of national income among the various classes of claimants is bound to change with the passage of time, but the shifts will be arbitrary indeed if redistribution is effected through a continuing decline of the purchasing power of the dollar.

Before the war, the Federal Reserve repeatedly stated that its dominant peacetime objective was to secure and maintain a satisfactorily high level of production and employment and relatively stable price levels. It is possible that the two elements of this objective may in the future prove to be incompatible with each other in the face of "big labor" and "big employers" who aggressively try to improve their real income positions by increasing their money wage rates and money profits and refuse to produce if their demands are not met. If such an unfortunate situation arises the monetary authorities will face a difficult decision. To maintain full employment they will have to allow a rising volume of spendings to support rising price levels, with obviously deleterious effects on those with relatively fixed money incomes and money wealth. But if they decide to hold down spending power in order to protect the purchasing power of money, the demand for rising money wages and rising profits in excess of the rise of productivity may lead to underproduction and underemployment. Difficult as such a decision would be, it is at least arguable that the central bank should endeavor to prevent large increases of price levels and force other control agencies in the economy to reconcile the conflict between labor and employers within the framework of generally stable prices.

XV

‖‖

Wage Policies During the Inflation

B Y mid-1948 average hourly wages of American workers had risen to approximately twice their levels in 1939. There can be no doubt that this great increase, unaccompanied by anything like an equivalent increase in output per man-hour worked, was a major contributing factor to the height of the inflation. Wage increases were not, of course, the only "cause" of the inflation, and they could not have occurred to the extent that they did in the absence of other policies and conditions, such as the easy fiscal-monetary policy, the high propensity to consume, the high profitability of private investment, and the high level of government and foreign demand for output. The demand for labor is, after all, derived from the demand for output, and labor is not likely to win a succession of large wage increases in the face of a low demand for output and widespread unemployment. But the fact remains that the large increases in money wages did intensify the inflation. This chapter will therefore present a brief outline of our national wage policy and the following chapter will indicate its relation to the inflation.

First, however, it is necessary to clarify some concepts. Increases in money wage rates can influence the course of prices in three principal ways—through (1) their cost effect, (2) their income effect, and (3) their effect on expectations and the willingness to spend. The cost effect of wage increases is the one usually emphasized. Unless accompanied by an offsetting rise of productivity an increase of wage rates within a particular plant does increase labor cost per unit of output and may lead to an increase in the price of the employer's product. This is especially likely to happen where labor is a large part of total cost and the wage increase is large. But a rise of wage rates does not assure that the price of an employer's output will rise at all, much less that it will rise enough to cover the entire wage increase. Some prices are not cost-determined in the short run; agricultural prices are an outstanding example. Moreover, other factors may prevent price increases even in those industries where employers tend to price their products on the basis of cost. Other elements in cost may decline. For example, general overhead, selling, and administrative cost per unit fell in many industries as the rate of output rose above 1939 levels and as numerous economies of larger-scale operation were realized. Or the employer may find that market conditions will not support higher prices. This is most likely to happen when the wage increase is limited to one firm in an industry; if competitors have not experienced wage increases and do not increase their prices the one unfortunate firm may have to choose between absorbing the wage increase and losing a large part of its sales. The feasibility of passing along a wage rise through higher prices is increased if the wage rise is uniform and covers the entire industry, though even in this case the industry may lose business to the products of other industries where wages have not risen. The feasibility of translating wage increases into price increases is greatest where all industries have to pay higher prices for their labor. We shall see that the probability that wage increases would raise prices through their cost effect was increased by the fact that wage increases were both large and widespread.

The income effect of wage increases—the tendency to raise total personal incomes and spending power—is often given too little attention. It is true that an increase of wage rates limited to one firm or even to one industry is not likely to have a large effect on aggregate personal incomes and spending power. But the case is far different when wage rates in general are increased. With compensation of employees accounting for more than half of our national income a large rise of hourly pay unaccompanied by a decrease of employment or a decline of other incomes can raise very significantly the amount of personal spending power. And in general this was the situation during the period of inflation; employment rose instead of declining, and other types of money income also rose. The wage increases provided rising spending power, were a major factor in raising the prices of things whose prices are not cost-determined, such as farm products, and they contributed greatly to the ability of sellers in general to raise their selling prices at least enough to cover all cost increases.

The effect of wage increases on expectations and the willingness to spend is more intangible but probably important. It is generally believed that wage increases will be very difficult to rescind and that they are likely to lead to price increases. This almost certainly contributed to a feeling that there was little point in waiting for prices to fall and that purchases should be made without delay. Moreover, the rise of wage rates tended to speed up mechanization, thereby encouraging private investment.

We shall use several statistical series to measure the increase in the compensation of labor: average hourly earnings, average weekly earnings, and the aggregate amount of wages and salaries received by labor. Let us look briefly at the characteristics of each of these measures, and at the types of analysis for which each is useful.

Average hourly earnings during any period are computed by dividing the total wage and salary bill by the number of man-hours worked; they include overtime as well as regular pay. These statistics are useful for measuring the income effect of wage increases, but they have several shortcomings for measuring cost effects. Changes in average hourly earnings are a resultant of several factors: (1) Changes in basic wage schedules—by which is meant changes in the rates of pay applicable to particular jobs in particular plants. Increases in basic wage schedules do tend to raise the labor costs of the particular product involved as well as to raise incomes. (2) Upgrading or downgrading of labor—raising or lowering a worker's classification while he continues to do the same type of work. This accounted for a significant part of the rise of average hourly earnings during the war and it, too, tended to raise costs per unit of output. (3) Shifts between lower- and higher-skilled jobs, between lower- and higher-wage plants within an industry, and between lower- and higher-wage industries. Shifts of these types also accounted for a considerable part of the rise of average hourly earnings during the war. Many of the war-created jobs required above-average skill, the rise of employment in the durable

TABLE 93. Average Hourly Earnings in All Manufacturing Industries, 1939-1945[1]

Period	Average Hourly Earnings		Estimated Average Straight-Time Hourly Earnings—Current Weights		Estimated Average Straight-Time Hourly Earnings Weighted by 1939 Employment	
	In Cents	Index, Jan. 1939= 100	In Cents	Index, Jan. 1939= 100	In Cents	Index, Jan. 1939= 100
Jan. 1939	63.2	100	62.3	100	62.3	100
Jan. 1941	68.3	108	66.4	107	64.8	104
Jan. 1942	89.3	141	83.9	135	78.2	126
Jan. 1945	104.6	116	97.0	156	89.4	144
July 1945	103.3	163	96.9	156	90.6	145
Dec. 1948	137.6	218	—	—	—	—

goods industries where wage-rates have traditionally been above the average was larger than elsewhere, and there was a shift away from farms, stores, and service establishments where wages had been low. Increases of average hourly earnings attributable to these shifts of workers need not tend toward higher costs per unit of output, though they do tend to raise money incomes. (4) Changes in the amount of overtime, with higher hourly rates for overtime. This was an important factor in the movement of average hourly earnings. The large amount of overtime worked during the war raised average hourly earnings considerably, but the loss of over-time after the war's end tended in the other direction. In some situations, as when workers drew time-and-a-half for overtime without any increase in the number of hours that a plant operated,

[1] SOURCE: Various issues of the *Monthly Labor Review*.

the rise of overtime work tended to raise costs per unit of output. In some other cases, however, this did not occur.

Table 93 indicates the importance of these factors during the war. Between January 1939 and January 1945 average hourly earnings in manufacturing rose 63 percent, but after eliminating the effects of overtime we find that average straight-time hourly earnings rose only 56 percent. Even the latter figure includes the effects of shifts from lower- to higher-paid jobs. Average straight-time hourly earnings weighted by the 1939 distribution of employment rose only 44 percent. Basic wage schedules rose even less. When we look at postwar developments we shall find that the reduction of overtime work and the shift back toward lower-paid occupations tended to lessen the rise of average hourly earnings.

Average weekly earnings reflect changes in not only average hourly earnings but also in the average number of hours worked per week. The rise of the latter caused the percentage rise of weekly earnings to exceed that of hourly earnings between 1939 and the peak of the war effort, but the tendency was in the opposite direction after the war as overtime work declined and as unions bargained for shorter work-weeks. Higher weekly earnings traceable to longer hours of work are directly relevant to the income effect, but they need not raise costs per unit of output. We shall make little use of statistics relative to average annual earnings per worker, but these obviously reflect not only changes in average hourly earnings and the average number of hours worked per week but also the average number of weeks worked per year.

In discussing the relevance of wage policy to inflation we shall also refer to the aggregate annual amount of wages and salaries; this is of little use in discussing cost behavior but it is directly relevant to the total income and spending power of employees. It varies, of course, with average hourly earnings, the average number of employees at work, and the average number of hours worked by each employee during the year. Table 94 shows, in a highly approximate way, the behavior of each of these. Let us look first at the increase between 1939 and 1944, the peak year of the war effort. Aggregate wages and salaries rose from $45.7 billion to

$116.9 billion, a rise of 156 percent. This reflected increases of 46 percent in the number of full-time and part-time employees at work, 24 percent in the average number of hours worked by each employee during a year, and 41 percent in average hourly earnings. We find, therefore, that during this period the rise in the number of employees at work accounted for about 41 percent of the rise

TABLE 94. Aggregate Wages and Salaries in the United States, 1939-1948
(Index, 1939=100)[2]

Year	Index of Aggregate Wages and Salaries	Index of the Average Number of Full-Time and Part-Time Employees	Index of the Average Number of Hours Worked Each Year by Each Employee	Index of Average Hourly Earnings
1939	100	100	100	100
1940	108	105	101	103
1941	135	116	107	109
1942	179	128	115	121
1943	231	142	122	133
1944	256	146	124	141
1945	257	141	125	146
1946	244	126	122	159
1947	267	126	120	176
1948	296	129	121	190

of aggregate wages and salaries, the increase in the average number of hours worked accounted for about 22 percent, and the rise of hourly earnings accounted for about 37 percent. Without in any way minimizing the importance of the rise of average hourly earnings it should be emphasized that about 63 percent of the increase of total wages and salaries was accounted for by the increased number of people employed and by the longer hours worked by each employee. The further 15 percent rise of aggregate

[2] This table was computed by the writer. The basic data as to aggregate wages and salaries and as to the average number of full-time and part-time employees are from *Surveys of Current Business*. The index of average hourly earnings is the composite index by the Federal Reserve Bank of New York. The index of the average number of hours worked per employee was computed by the writer and is very approximate. It was arrived at by dividing the index of aggregate wages and salaries by the product of the index of average hourly earnings and the index of the average number of employees.

wages and salaries between 1944 and 1948 is quite a different story. It was solely attributable to the further 35 percent rise of average hourly earnings. In fact, the further rise of total wages and salaries during this postwar period was almost solely due to increases of basic wage schedules, which tended not only to raise the aggregate income of employees but also to raise labor costs per unit of output.

Let us now sketch the main outlines of wartime wage policy.

WARTIME WAGE POLICY

Federal limitations on wage increases were of little importance until after Pearl Harbor. There appear to have been three principal reasons for this. The first was the large amount of unemployment. As noted earlier, there were more than 9 million unemployed in early 1940, and at the beginning of 1942 the number was still as high as 4 million. It was felt that the existence of a large labor reserve would prevent "excessive" wage increases, and that some rise of wages would help to restore full production. By January 1942, however, average straight-time hourly earnings in manufacturing were 22 percent above their level of three years earlier. A second factor was the dislike for direct controls in general, and a third factor was the reluctance of both Congress and the executive department to impose unpopular limitations on a very large and politically powerful group.

Though other authorities had some power in the field, the National War Labor Board (WLB) was the principal wartime agency for limiting wage increases and for solving industrial disputes. This body, composed of four representatives each from labor, management, and the public, was established by Executive order on January 12, 1942.[3] Several facts about the WLB at this

[3] This body was the successor to the National Defense Mediation Board, which had been established in March 1941 but which had become inoperative in November 1941 after the resignation of its two CIO members. The principal purpose of the NDMB was to settle labor disputes, and any limitation of wage increases was incidental to its other operations.

stage of its operations should be noted: (1) It was set up primarily to settle labor disputes. At a conference held in Washington in mid-December 1941 both labor and management had agreed with the President that "for the duration of the war there shall be no strikes or lockouts, and that all labor disputes shall be settled by peaceful means, and that a National War Labor Board be established for the peaceful adjustment of such disputes." The Executive order therefore provided that the WLB should not take jurisdiction until other available procedures for settlement had been exhausted, but that, "After it takes jurisdiction, the Board shall finally determine the dispute, and for this purpose may use mediation, voluntary arbitration, or arbitration under the rules established by the Board." Since the Board's primary duty was to settle labor disputes and prevent the loss of production it is easy to understand why it was tempted to purchase peace at the price of wage increases. (2) The Board had jurisdiction over wage rates only in those cases where there was a dispute between labor and management, and where this dispute was not solved without recourse to the Board. It had no authority over wage increases agreed upon by labor and management, and there were many of these. This was the situation until October 1942. (3) The order setting up the WLB contained no statement of national wage policy to guide settlements of wage disagreements. As early as 1941 many had urged that the pending price control bill should cover wages as well as the prices of commodities and other services, but this was not done. The WLB therefore had to work out its own standards, guided only by the general admonition of the Price Control Act to all federal agencies, "to work toward a stabilization of prices, fair and equitable wages, and cost of production." It is therefore little wonder that the Board, bearing a heavy work load and subject to many pressures, was slow to evolve a well-defined and consistent policy.

The first months of 1942 were hectic ones for all federal stabilization agencies. Prices, including those of cost-of-living items, continued to rise, labor disputes multiplied, some wildcat strikes occurred, disputes piled up before the Board, and the latter found itself besieged on the one side by labor to grant wage increases to offset increases in living costs and on the other side by OPA officials demanding that wage increases be prevented in order to prevent further increases of prices. In mid-March the President instructed the Bureau of the Budget to take the lead in developing an integrated anti-inflation program.[4] In its report ten days later the Bureau proposed, among other things, to freeze prices as of April 1 and to freeze all basic wage and salary rates except those below 40 cents an hour. The proposal for a wage freeze met opposition within the administration, especially from the Secretary of the Treasury, and was not adopted. On April 27 the President sent to Congress his famous seven-point program, one of whose points was to "stabilize the remuneration received by individuals for their work." Because of this and other pressures, the WLB worked toward a less liberal policy on wage increases over which it had jurisdiction. This culminated in the "Little Steel Formula," enunciated on July 16, 1942.

This formula, which with modifications was to guide national wage policy during the remainder of the war, stated that wage increases would be permitted for only three purposes: (1) To raise average straight-time hourly earnings 15 percent above their level on January 1, 1941, (2) to "remove inequalities," or (3) to remedy substandard conditions. Chairman William H. Davis has described how the Board arrived at the "15 percent rule."[5] At first it considered a general wage freeze at the levels prevailing in early 1942, but found "that the levels were about as level as the Himalaya Mountains. The changes in different industries had been quite different in amount, so that to freeze them as of the April 1942 date would freeze a great many inequalities. . . . I was insisting, and I still insist that you cannot stabilize anything except with reference to a base or period of stability."[6] The Board

---

[4] U. S. Bureau of the Budget, *The United States at War,* 1946, pp. 250-251.

[5] *Testimony Before the Senate Banking and Currency Committee on Stabilizing the Cost of Living,* September 15, 1942, pp. 86 ff.

[6] *Ibid.,* pp. 88, 90.

found that for three years preceding January 1941 wages and the cost of living had borne a relatively stable relationship to each other. It therefore adopted January 1, 1941 as its base period. It also found that the cost of living had risen 15 percent between January 1941 and May 1942 and that most straight-time wage rates had risen at least this much. It believed, therefore, that the 15 percent formula would have the double advantage of preventing general wage increases and of not penalizing the minority whose wage rates had not risen enough to offset the rise of living costs up to May 1942. It should be noted that though the Board agreed to permit average straight-time hourly earnings to rise enough to offset the rise of living costs that had already occurred up to May 1942 it did not promise to allow further wage increases to offset any increase in the cost of living that might occur after that time. This was to become a burning issue.

Throughout the summer of 1942, inflationary pressures continued to mount and the whole stabilization program appeared to be in danger of collapse. Prices, especially those of foods and other farm products, continued to rise, labor was growing more restive, wage increases continued to occur, and it became increasingly obvious that tighter controls would have to be instituted. The President therefore requested and received from Congress an amendment to the Price Control Act, which tightened somewhat the price control provisions relating to food and farm products and directed the President to establish an Office of Economic Stabilization. This he did by Executive Order 9250 on October 3, 1942. The OES was not to assume administrative functions, but only to formulate and develop appropriate national economic policies and to integrate the policies and operations of the various administrative agencies. The administration of wage control was left in the hands of the WLB. The Executive order increased the power of the WLB and directed it to tighten its controls. (1) It provided that wage rates could be neither increased nor decreased unless notice of the change had been filed with and approved by the WLB. After that date all wage increases, not just those in dispute, were subject to WLB control. (2) It also provided that, "The National War Labor Board shall not approve any increases in the wage rates prevailing on September 15, 1942, unless such increase is necessary to correct maladjustments or inequalities, to eliminate substandards of living, to correct gross inequities, or to aid in the effective prosecution of the war." With a few amendments these were the general criteria governing the WLB's decisions through the end of the war.

We shall not describe in detail the Board's interpretations of these broadly worded directives. The general hope of the order was clear—"Please don't permit too many wage increases!" But the Board faced difficult questions. To what extent should labor shortages in particular plants and areas be solved by granting wage increases rather than by direct manpower controls? How great should a "maladjustment, inequality, or inequity" be before it justified a wage increase? If a wage increase was found to be justified, how large should it be? Many other such questions arose. The Board employed what has been called "an elastic defense of the Little Steel formula."[7] As before, it stood ready to approve such wage increases as were necessary to raise average straight-time hourly earnings 15 percent above their levels on January 1, 1941. It approved further increases only where they were considered necessary "to support a minimum level of decent living," to correct "inequalities" or "inequities" where wage rates in one plant were seriously out of line with rates paid by other plants for similar work or where rates for a job in a plant were out of line with other rates in the same plant, or to help the War Manpower Commission solve labor shortages. The total of wage increases granted for these purposes was substantial, and average straight-time hourly earnings in manufacturing weighted by 1939 employment rose 16 percent between October 1942 and July 1945. This brought the total increase between January 1941 and July 1945 to 40 percent.

Elastic as it was, the WLB's wage policy was considered by most

[7] U. S. Bureau of the Budget, *op. cit.*, p. 198.

labor organizations to be too tight. They wanted to discard the Little Steel formula and to secure considerably higher wage rates. In support of their position they repeatedly pointed to the great increases in farmers' incomes, to swollen business profits, and to the ability of business in general to pay higher wages without increasing prices. They brushed aside the argument that the weekly take-home pay of workers had, because of overtime and other factors as well as increases of straight-time hourly earnings, risen

TABLE 95.   The Cost of Living in the United States, 1941-1945
(May 1942=100) [8]

Date	All Items	Food	Clothing	Rent	Fuel Electricity and Ice	House Furnish- ings	Miscel- laneous
Jan. 1941	87	80	80	96	96	82	92
May 1942	100	100	100	100	100	100	100
Jan. 1943	104	109	100	98	102	101	102
June 1943	108	117	101	98	103	103	104
Jan. 1944	107	113	109	98	104	105	107
June 1944	108	112	109	98	104	113	110
Jan. 1945	110	113	113	99	105	118	111
June 1945	111	116	115	99	105	119	112
Aug. 1945	111	116	116	99	106	119	112
Jan. 1946	112	116	119	99	106	122	113

more than the cost of living, and insisted that straight-time hourly wage rates should rise at least enough to offset all increases in the cost of living. The argument became especially bitter in 1943 as the cost of living began to rise more rapidly above the levels prevailing in May 1942. (See Table 95.) In effect, many labor leaders wanted to convert the Little Steel formula from a "15 percent rule" into an escalator clause which would permit increases in straight-time wage rates to offset all increases in the cost of living since the beginning of 1941. And for this purpose they were not willing to accept the validity of the official cost-of-living index. From early 1943 until the end of the war they insisted that

[8] This is the BLS cost-of-living index converted to a May 1942 base.

the cost of living had risen far more than was indicated by this index, for it failed to give adequate weight to quality deterioration, to the disappearance of low-priced goods, and to changes in modes of living necessitated by wartime conditions.[9] Special emphasis was placed on the increases of food and clothing prices. The WLB did not accept labor's criticism of the cost-of-living index and it did not abandon the Little Steel formula. Labor peace was in general maintained by a three-point program: (1) By the use of delaying tactics. A decision was delayed for a long period awaiting detailed reports on the validity and meaning of the cost-of-living index. (2) By "judicious exceptions" from the Little Steel formula. And (3) by tightening price controls over cost-of-living items, and especially over foods. It seems highly doubtful that larger wage increases could have been avoided without widespread labor unrest if the OPA had not greatly improved its control over food prices and actually rolled some of them back in 1943.

Two principal points in this controversy should be kept in mind. The first is that labor was not content with an increase in its aggregate real purchasing power traceable to longer hours of work, steadier employment, overtime pay rates, and incentive bonuses. It also insisted that the real purchasing power of each hour of standard work should be kept at least as high as in the prewar period. And this was at a time when a large part of total output was not available for consumption purposes, but was being used for war purposes. The second point is the real conflict of interest between employees, urban as well as rural, and farmers. Workers were demanding that each hour of their work purchase as much food and clothing as it did before the war. At the same time farmers were contending that the prices of farm products had been too low relative to other prices in the prewar period, and that they should be allowed to rise more than other prices. If wage rates had been permitted to escalate with food prices and farm

[9] See Office of Economic Stabilization, *Report of the President's Committee on the Cost of Living*, U. S. Government Printing Office, 1945.

prices to escalate with the prices of industrial products (in whose costs labor was the most important single factor), the inflationary spiral could have been greatly encouraged.

POSTWAR WAGE POLICY

On August 18, 1945, very soon after V-J Day, the government took the first of several steps toward a relaxing of its wage controls. Several factors in the situation help to explain federal policy and subsequent developments in the labor market. (1) The "no strike and no lockout" pledge subscribed to by leaders in labor and management in December 1941 expired with the end of the fighting war. Attempts by the President to obtain a similar commitment for the reconversion period met with practically no success. (2) Labor leaders, and probably large numbers of individual workers, entered the postwar period with a deep feeling that they had been treated illiberally during the war—that the Little Steel formula was too restrictive, that their incomes had been kept too low relative to farm incomes and business profits, and that they should have been permitted to take more advantage of tight labor market conditions. (3) Large numbers of workers faced the prospect of sizeable declines in their take-home pay as war production was cut back. The loss of overtime work alone would reduce their income markedly, for a 48-hour work-week had been required in many industries since early 1943, and overtime work was common elsewhere. Moreover, employers were required to pay time and a half for all work in excess of 40 hours a week. Thus, a man whose basic wage rate was a dollar an hour and who worked 48 hours had a weekly income of $52, of which $40 was for regular time and $12 for the 8 hours of overtime. The loss of all overtime work without any change in basic rates would reduce his weekly earnings by $12, or about 23 percent. Seeing no prospect of a comparable decline in living costs, workers were highly reluctant to accept such a decrease of income. In addition, many faced the prospect of being downgraded or of having to shift out of high-wage war jobs to less lucrative employment. That average weekly earnings did decline, especially in the heavy industries, between January 1945 and the early months of the reconversion period is shown by Table 96. (4) There was widespread fear of deflation and unemployment during the transition period. This inclined many government officials to favor wage

TABLE 96. Average Weekly Earnings in Selected Manufacturing Industries, 1945

(In dollars)[10]

Industry	1939	1945 Jan.	1945 Sept.	1946 Jan.	Percentage Increase or Decrease (−) Jan. 1945– Sept. 1945
All manufacturing	$23.86	$47.50	$40.87	$41.15	−14.0
Automobiles	32.91	59.42	44.65	46.19	−24.9
Blast furnaces, steel works, and rolling mills	29.88	55.04	47.51	44.93	−13.7
Machinery (except electrical)	29.27	55.92	48.12	47.84	−13.9
Transp. equipt. (except autos)	30.51	62.61	48.98	49.29	−21.8
Nonferrous metals and their products	26.74	50.92	44.41	46.13	−12.8
Lumber and timber basic products	19.06	33.72	33.41	32.15	−0.9
Rubber products	27.84	54.49	47.20	46.71	−13.4
Cotton mfgrs. (except small wares)	14.26	27.88	28.32	29.01	1.6
Apparel and other finished textile products	18.17	32.42	31.81	33.24	−1.9
Food and kindred products	24.43	39.51	39.36	41.37	−0.4
Paper and allied products	23.72	40.18	40.96	41.17	1.9
Chemicals and allied products	25.59	44.41	43.01	42.61	−3.2
Products of petroleum and coal	32.62	56.20	54.70	52.06	−2.7

increases and provided labor with the argument that wages should be raised to restore spending power. This point was made as early as November 1944 by the Secretary-Treasurer of the American Federation of Labor:

The failure of straight-time hourly wage rates to rise as our national producing power expands and our gross national product increases will be an insurmountable deflationary force paralyzing our efforts for

[10] SOURCE: *Statistical Supplement to the Survey of Current Business*, 1947, pp. 65-67.

full employment. Reconversion will sweep away the various devices by which workers' take-home pay has been maintained, such as continuous overtime, rapid upgrading, the 6-day week and special bonuses in war work. The elimination of overtime, the layoff of extra workers and demobilization of armed forces will reduce consumer buying power by 23 billion dollars when both wars end. Subtracting this from our present level of 128 billion dollars in consumers income available for purchase of goods and services will leave only 105 billion dollars, according to Commerce Department estimates. But studies of the Commerce Department and the Federal Reserve Board show that we shall need 114 to 116 billion dollars of consumer purchases to maintain full employment. There will be a shortage of 9 to 11 billion dollars unless present wage rates are raised.[11]

This argument that higher wages were necessary not only for the workers' welfare but also for the general health of the economy was to be heard over and over again during the following years. (5) Not only workers but practically all other elements in the economy wanted to escape government controls, and the relaxation of wage controls was only a part of the broader program of decontrol.

As noted earlier, the first step toward relaxing wage controls was taken with the issuance of Executive Order 9599 on August 18, 1945. This order stated that the government's policy was, "To move as rapidly as possible without endangering the stability of the economy toward the removal of price, wage, production and other controls and toward the restoration of collective bargaining and the free market."[12] Its principal provisions relative to wages were these: (1) Employers were permitted to grant wage and salary increases *without securing government approval* if such increases "will not be used in whole or in part as the basis for seeking an increase in price ceilings, or for resisting otherwise justifiable reductions in price ceilings, or, in the case of products or services being furnished under contract with a federal procurement agency, will not increase the costs to the United States."

[11] A letter from George Meany to the President. *Report of the President's Committee on the Cost of Living,* pp. 37-38.
[12] *Federal Register,* August 21, 1945, p. 10155.

(2) Any wage increase that an employer intended to use as a basis for requesting price increases continued to require WLB approval, and this was to be given only when the increase was necessary for one of the purposes for which the WLB had approved increases during the war or was necessary "to correct maladjustments or inequities which would interfere with the effective transition to a peacetime economy." Moreover, any proposed wage or salary increase which was expected to require a change in price ceilings was not to become effective until it had been approved by the Director of Economic Stabilization as well as by the WLB. The OPA was admonished to stabilize the cost of living and, "so far as is reasonable, practicable, and necessary for the purpose," to see that price increases granted at one level were not allowed to cause price increases at later levels of production or distribution.

The general intent of this order was clear. Freedom of bargaining between employer and employee was to be restored where wage increases would not endanger existing price ceilings or raise prices paid by the government. Other wage increases were to be held in check, and those considered necessary were, where feasible, to be absorbed by producers and dealers and not passed along to final buyers in the form of higher prices. This program was soon modified. Workers were insistent on much higher wage rates which employers were unwilling to grant if they had to absorb them for the time being and wait an indeterminate period for what they considered "adequate" price increases. It appeared that this policy would prolong labor disputes and interfere with reconversion.

The next step in the liberalization of wage controls came on October 30, 1945 with the issuance of Executive Order 9651. This order relaxed wage controls in several ways. (1) It definitely scrapped the Little Steel formula, ordering the Stabilization administrator to approve wage increases "where the percentage increase in average straight-time hourly earnings in the appropriate unit since January, 1941 has not equalled the percentage increase in the cost of living between January, 1941 and September, 1945." The rise in the cost of living index during this period had been

28 percent. (2) It also ordered approval of increases to correct inequities among plants in the same industry and locality and to aid in the recruitment of manpower in industries designated as essential to reconversion. (3) It assured employers that they could grant unapproved wage increases and that after a "reasonable" test period, which would usually be six months, the OPA would take even these unapproved increases into consideration in determining whether increases in price ceilings were required. Even these provisions proved to be unacceptable, however; labor demanded large increases, and employers were unwilling to wait six months for price adjustments and felt that OPA standards for determining the amounts of price increases were too tight. Labor disputes continued to multiply.

We need not trace out in detail the government's continued retreat from the wage policy enunciated at the end of the war. It is enough to note that in a series of steps it resorted to the use of fact-finding boards which recommended sizeable wage increases, that these recommended increases were approved for price-determining purposes, that the wage-control authorities were ordered to approve all wage increases that were in line with the pattern of increases that had occurred since the end of the war, and that the OPA was directed to liberalize its granting of price increases where wage increases had occurred. By this general process the government gave more than tacit approval during early 1946 to the general pattern of 18½-cent per hour wage increases. Then in November 1946 an Executive Order swept away all remaining wage controls and practically all price controls. The upward spiral was thereafter to be uninhibited.

Let us now outline the behavior of wage rates from the end of the war to the end of 1948. The first round of wage increases occurred early in 1946. The leaders in this fight for wage increases were the big CIO unions, especially those in the automobile and steel industries, and their principal argument was that wage rates had to be increased to offset the loss of overtime, to restore labor's purchasing power, and to prevent general deflation. They there-

fore demanded 52 hours' pay for 40 hours of work—a 30 percent
increase in basic wage rates. In the end, however, they settled for
an increase of 18½ cents an hour, and this became the general,
though not universal, pattern for wage increases in 1946. For a
few months workers enjoyed a real increase in the purchasing power
of their hourly earnings, but by the end of 1946 the increase in
the cost of living, following first the weakening and then the

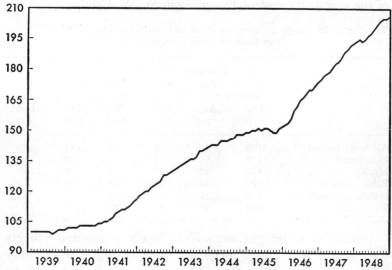

Chart 10.   Index of Average Hourly Earnings of Wage Earners,
Monthly, 1939-1948 (1939 average = 100).

scuttling of price control, had wiped out all this earlier gain and
the purchasing power of hourly earnings was slightly lower than
it had been in late 1945. This set off demands for a second round
of wage increases, which occurred in 1947. The big CIO unions
again demanded a 30 percent increase but finally settled for increases of 15 cents an hour. This again set the pattern for wage
increases, but it was less generally followed than was the 18½
cent pattern in 1946. Subsequent developments were similar to
those in the preceding year; for a time the purchasing power of
each hour of work was increased, but by the end of 1947 the cost

of living had risen so much that real hourly earnings had again fallen to the levels of late 1945. The third round of wage increases in 1948 amounted to about 11 to 13 cents an hour in the heavy industries, but it was considerably less general than were the increases in either of the two preceding years. The continued rise of living costs up to the autumn of 1948 wiped out some of these gains, but real earnings per hour increased during the remainder of the year as the cost of living began to fall slightly.

TABLE 97.   Percentage Increases in Average Hourly Earnings of Wage Earners in Current Dollars, 1939-1948

	Percentage Increase During Period					
	Av. 1939- Dec. 1948	Av. 1939- Aug. 1945	Aug. 1945- Dec. 1948	Aug. 1945- Dec. 1946	Dec. 1946- Dec. 1947	Dec. 1947- Dec. 1948
All wage earners	106	50	37	16	11	7
Manufacturing	117	62	34	12	12	7
Mining	112	43	48	17	16	9
Public utilities	82	32	38	17	11	6
Private construction	105	50	37	11	13	8
Trade and service	104	46	40	21	9	6

In addition to straight increases in hourly wage rates, workers were able to get "fringe increases," such as shorter work-weeks without a reduction of pay, paid vacations, paid lunch periods, retirement benefits, health benefits, and so on. Some of these added significantly to production costs.

THE BEHAVIOR OF WAGES AND SALARIES

Before going on to an analysis of the relationship between wage rates and the inflation, it will be useful to summarize briefly the movement of wages during the period. Let us look first at average hourly earnings for all wage earners except those working for the government and for farmers. These are shown in Chart 10 and a summary of their changes is given in Table 97.[13] Several important

[13] These are the indexes prepared by the Federal Reserve Bank of New York.

facts stand out. The first is that by the end of 1948, hourly earnings for all wage earners had risen 106 percent above their 1939 levels; more than half of this increase occurring after V-J Day. The second is that the increase of hourly earnings was not limited to one area but was spread throughout the economy. The rise was not uniform for all branches of industry, but the disparities were not as great as one might expect in a period of rapid change. This was especially true of the postwar increases.

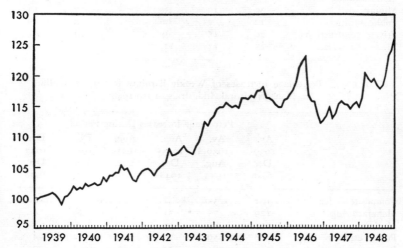

Chart 11.   Index of Average Hourly Earnings of Wage Earners, in 1939 Dollars, Monthly, 1939-1948 (1939 = 100).

Chart 11 and Table 98, which show average hourly earnings in 1939 dollars, indicate that a part of the wartime gains and most of the postwar gains of hourly earnings in terms of money were wiped out by increases in the cost of living. The 50 percent increase in hourly money earnings between 1939 and August 1945 was accompanied by only a 15 percent rise of real purchasing power for each hour's work. Despite the further succession of wage increases, the purchasing power of each hour of work was little if any higher at the end of 1947 than it had been on V-J Day.

TABLE 98.   Percentage Changes of Average Hourly Earnings of Wage Earners in Dollars of 1939 Purchasing Power, 1939-1948[14]

	Percentage Increase or Decrease ($-$) During Period					
	Av. 1939- Dec. 1948	Av. 1939- Aug. 1945	Aug. 1945- Dec. 1948	Aug. 1945- Dec. 1946	Dec. 1946- Dec. 1947	Dec. 1947- Dec. 1948
All wage earners	26	15	10	-2	2	10
Manufacturing	33	25	6	-6	3	11
Mining	30	10	18	-3	9	12
Public utilities	12	2	10	-1	2	9
Private construction	26	15	9	-6	4	12
Trade and service	25	12	11	2	0	9

TABLE 99.   Percentage Increases of Weekly Earnings in Current Dollars in Nonagricultural Industries, 1939-1948[15]

	Percentage Increases During Period					
	Av. 1939- Dec. 1948	Av. 1939- Aug. 1945	Aug. 1945- Dec. 1948	Aug. 1945- Dec. 1946	Dec. 1946- Dec. 1947	Dec. 1947- Dec. 1948
Composite index	101	53	31	14	9	6
Manufacturing	129	75	31	11	13	4
Mining	155	83	39	22	9	4
Public utilities	88	50	25	7	12	4
Private construction	142	81	34	10	12	9
Trade and service	99	42	40	21	9	6
Clerical and professional	73	37	26	12	5	7

Most of the postwar gain came during 1948 when the rise in the cost of living was first slowed down and then reversed. It will be noted, however, that throughout the war and postwar period real earnings per hour were above the 1939 level.

The behavior of average weekly earnings in current dollars is shown in Chart 12 and summarized in Table 99. It will be noted

[14] These figures were computed by dividing the New York Federal Reserve indexes of hourly earnings by the cost of living index converted to a 1939 base.

[15] Chart 12 and this table are based on the indexes by the Federal Reserve Bank of New York.

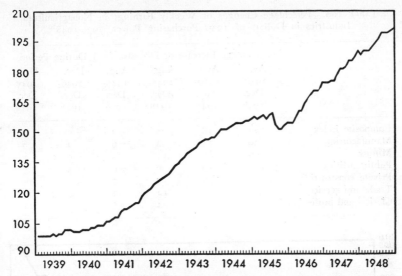

Chart 12. Index of Weekly Earnings in Nonagricultural Industries, in Current Dollars, Monthly, 1939-1948 (1939 = 100).

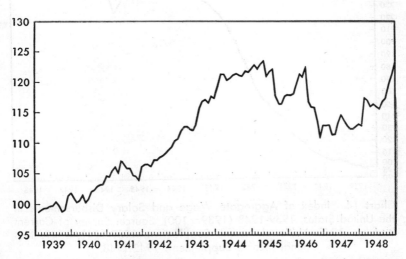

Chart 13. Index of Weekly Earnings in Nonagricultural Industries, in 1939 Dollars, Monthly, 1939-1948 (1939 = 100).

TABLE 100.   Percentage Changes of Weekly Earnings in Nonagricultural Industries in Dollars of 1939 Purchasing Power, 1939-1948[16]

	Percentage Increase or Decrease (−) During Period					
	Av. 1939-Dec. 1948	Av. 1939-Aug. 1945	Aug. 1945-Dec. 1948	Aug. 1945-Dec. 1946	Dec. 1946-Dec. 1947	Dec. 1947-Dec. 1948
Composite index	23	18	5	−4	0	9
Manufacturing	40	35	4	−6	4	7
Mining	56	41	11	3	0	7
Public utilities	15	15	0	−9	3	7
Private construction	48	39	7	−7	2	13
Trade and service	22	9	12	2	0	10
Clerical and professional	6	5	1	−6	−3	11

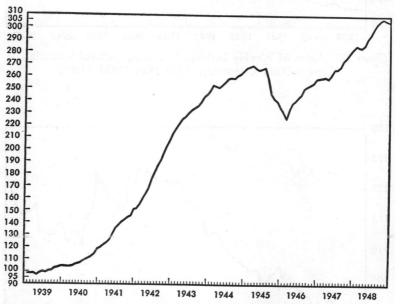

Chart 14.   Index of Aggregate Wage and Salary Disbursements in the United States, 1939-1948 (1939 = 100). **Source:** Survey of Current Business, 1947: National Income Supplement, 1939-1941; 1949: National Income Supplement, 1942-1948.

[16] These figures were computed by dividing the New York Federal Reserve indexes of weekly earnings by the cost of living index converted to a 1939 base.

that during the defense and war period weekly earnings rose more than hourly earnings as a result of the lengthening of the average work-week, but that in the postwar period there was a tendency for the reverse to be true as the average work-week was again shortened. But here again, as shown in Chart 13 and Table 100, much of the gain was dissipated by increases in the cost of living.

Aggregate wage and salary disbursements, reflecting not only increases of hourly earnings and the lengthening of the work-week but also the increased number employed and the larger number of weeks worked per year, rose more between 1939 and 1948 than any of the indexes shown above. This is indicated by Chart 14.

The following chapter will discuss the relationship of these changes in wage rates to the inflationary process.

XVI

‖‖

The Relations of Wage Increases
to the Inflation

WE COME now to the difficult question of the relationship of wages and wage policies to the war and postwar inflation—difficult because of the lack of precise statistics relative to some aspects of the problem but even more because of the intricate causal relationships involved. We shall not succeed in presenting a complete and integrated picture of all these interrelationships, but we can consider some of them.

COST EFFECTS OF INCREASES IN WAGE RATES

As indicated in the preceding chapter, there can be no doubt that increases in wage rates did exert, through their effects on costs of production, a strong upward pressure on many prices. With money wage rates rising to double their 1939 levels and with output per man-hour increasing to a much smaller extent in most industries, the result could only be an increase in the labor cost per unit of output. (See examples in Table 101.) The cost effect of wage increases on the course of the inflation should not be minimized. It was highly important.

On the other hand, it is a gross oversimplification to say that the price inflation was due solely to the cost effects of wage increases. This explanation is clearly inapplicable to the great rise in the prices of farm products. These prices are not, in the short run, cost-determined, much less labor-cost-determined. Farmers do much of their own work, wages of employees make up only a small part of total cost, and the whole history of farm prices is one of wide fluctuations relative to cost levels. It is clear that an explanation of the movement of farm prices is to be found largely

TABLE 101. Output per Man-Hour and Unit Labor Costs in Selected
Industries, 1939-1947
(1939=100)[1]

	1940	1941	1942	1943	1944	1945	1946	1947
Agriculture								
Output per man-day	103.5	107.5	118.9	116.7	123.6	120.7	122.0	116.9
Mining								
Output per man-hour	102.1	103.9	104.0	101.7	105.0	106.7	110.1	114.3
Unit labor cost	97.6	107.6	120.7	137.8	147.1	149.8	160.1	180.4
Electric Light and Power								
Output per man-hour	108.6	123.2	145.8	182.7	191.1	182.5	160.7	166.6
Unit labor cost	93.7	85.9	78.1	65.9	66.1	71.1	88.3	92.3
Footwear, except rubber:								
Output per man-hour	104.1	108.5	107.0	108.3	106.1	111.3	116.5	106.6
Unit labor cost	99.6	107.0	125.4	134.2	146.6	149.9	162.6	193.7
Tobacco products:								
Output per man-hour	101.0	104.8	104.9	103.9	109.1	117.9	116.5	117.2
Unit labor cost	103.2	105.7	117.4	130.4	136.2	136.4	157.4	171.8
Cement:								
Output per man-hour	100.4	108.3	108.4	94.7	93.8	90.1	108.7	110.8
Unit labor cost	101.2	100.3	109.4	133.2	157.1	150.8	137.7	152.4
Clay construction products:								
Output per man-hour	104.5	102.3	94.6	77.9	80.4	84.2	100.0	99.8
Unit labor cost	89.4	98.1	115.0	154.0	156.0	158.4	157.0	173.8
Bread and other bakery products:								
Output per man-hour		105.1	106.9	112.2	111.1	110.2	111.7	106.9
Unit labor cost		102.9	110.6	114.9	123.1	130.9	145.1	174.1

on the side of demand rather than that of cost. The same is true, though perhaps to a lesser extent, of other products.

It is a serious mistake to assume that even big corporations with a degree of control over their prices arrive at the prices to be charged by applying an invariable percentage or dollar makeup to their labor costs or even to their combined labor and material costs. Here, too, the magnitude and elasticity of the demand for

[1] SOURCE: Bureau of Labor Statistics, *Handbook of Labor Statistics*, 1947, pp. 155-159. All figures for productivity are for output per man-hour, except for agriculture where they relate to output per man-day.

their products is highly important in determining their prices. Does a corporation always refuse to raise the price of its product in the face of an increased demand just because its costs per unit have not risen? Does it lower the price of its product with every decrease in its unit costs? Does it always raise its prices enough to offset each increase in its unit costs no matter what the state of demand? Every sales manager and purchasing agent knows that the answer to all these questions is in the negative. The magnitude and elasticity of demand are always important factors in price determination, and it is certain that prices would not have risen so much even in the face of the wage increases that did occur if demand had not risen so greatly and had not become so price-inelastic. Great numbers of employers increased their prices considerably more than was necessary to cover their cost increases and to give them liveable rate of return on existing and new investment. The truth of these statements was borne out by developments in 1949 when many employers, faced with a lessening of demand, lowered their prices somewhat, despite the failure of wage rates to decline.

Moreover, it is a mistake to neglect demand for output as a factor affecting the extent of wage increases. Causation was not solely from higher wages to higher costs to higher prices. To a marked degree it was from a higher total demand for output to a higher demand for labor to higher wages. In the absence of such a high and price-inelastic demand for output labor would not have asked for such large wage increases and employers would not have granted them. On the other hand, if unions and their members had been content to maintain prewar wage rates neither labor costs nor labor's money demand for output would have risen so much, though other demands for output would have risen and some inflation, though a smaller amount, would have occurred.

The above discussion makes it clear that further attention should be given to total demand for output and to the relationship between wage policy and that demand. Let us look first at the war period.

THE INCOME EFFECTS OF WAGES DURING THE WAR

An earlier chapter emphasized that the increase of personal income, and especially of disposable personal income, was one of the important sources of inflationary pressures during the war. Personal income rose 128 percent from 1939 to 1944, and 75 per-

TABLE 102. Indexes of Man-Hours Worked, Physical Output, and Aggregate Wages and Salaries, 1939-1948

(1939=100)[2]

Year	Col. 1 Index of Man-Hours Worked per Year	Col. 2 Index of GNP at 1939 Prices	Col. 3 Percentage of GNP Available for Consumption	Col. 4 Index of Consumption Goods and Services at 1939 Prices	Col. 5 Index of Consumption Goods and Services per Man-Hour Worked (Col. 4 ÷ Col. 1)	Col. 6 Index of Aggregate Wages and Salaries
1939	100	100	74	100	100	100
1940	105	110	71	106	101	108
1941	124	131	65	115	93	135
1942	148	151	56	115	78	179
1943	174	171	53	122	70	231
1944	182	185	52	131	72	256
1945	176	182	57	141	80	257
1946	153	166	69	156	102	244
1947	152	161	71	154	101	267
1948	156	167	68	154	99	296

cent of this total increase was contributed by the rise of wage and salary receipts. The latter rose 154 percent. A part of this increase was drained off by higher tax collections, but the amount of disposable income left in the hands of workers was far larger than before the war. By no means all of this increase in aggregate wage and salary receipts was due to increases in hourly earnings; as

[2] Some of these indexes are so approximate that they should be viewed only as indicators of general magnitude. Column 1 was computed by dividing the index of aggregate wages and salaries (including the military) by the New York Federal Reserve composite index, which includes average hourly earnings of wage earners and average weekly earnings of clerical and professional employees. Columns 2 and 4 were arrived at by deflating the Department of Commerce figures by the cost-of-living index.

estimated earlier, about 37 percent of the rise was due to this factor and 63 percent to the great rise in the aggregate number of man-hours worked, reflecting the increased number employed and the increased number of hours worked annually by each employee. All of the increase in disposable wage and salary receipts, whether due to increased hourly earnings or to increases in employment, enhanced labor's spending power. One might assume, however, that the increase of labor income attributable to the rise of employment would not be inflationary, for it would be balanced by an increased output of goods and services available for purchase by labor. It is true that the rise of employment was accompanied by a roughly corresponding increase of total output, but not by a corresponding increase in consumption goods. This is shown in Table 102. In 1939 GNP amounted to $91.3 billion, and 74 percent of this output was available for consumption purposes. GNP at 1939 prices had risen about 85 percent by 1944 but the volume of consumption goods and services available had risen only about 30 percent. About 47 percent of total output was being used for war purposes, for other governmental uses, for net exports, and for capital maintenance and accumulation. The demands for these purposes were almost completely price-inelastic; these essential demands were to be satisfied regardless of the behavior of price levels. The total volume of consumer goods available was greater than before the war, but the amount available per man-hour worked was about 30 percent less than in 1939 and 1940. As a group, therefore, workers could increase their consumption proportionally with the increase in the number of hours worked only at the expense of other types of consumers, and they found that as they tried to do this by getting higher money incomes and spending more money some other types of consumers, especially farmers and enterprisers, could play the same game. Spirited bidding among these groups for consumer goods tended to bid their prices up, and the rise was limited only by price controls.

The war period emphasizes several important facts relative to real wages and wage policies. (1) The amount of real goods and services that can in fact be consumed by labor in exchange for each hour of work depends not only on total output per man-hour but also on the amount of that output utilized for other purposes. If output per man-hour declines as the amount of employment increases, or even if output per man-hour remains constant and an increased proportion of it is used for war, other government, net export, or capital purposes, the amount of goods and services that can be consumed by labor in exchange for each hour of work must

TABLE 103.   Indexes of Food Utilization, 1940-1948
(1935-1939=100)[3]

Period	Total Food Utilization	Food Utilization by Civilians	Food Utilized by the Military and for Export
1935-1939 av.	100	100	100
1940	110	110	96
1941	114	110	309
1942	126	112	700
1943	131	109	1061
1944	140	114	1239
1945	136	115	1052
1946	137	126	613
1947	138	127	609
1948	133	125	487

decline unless labor can bid output away from other consumers. Increases in hourly wages could not enable labor to bid additional goods away from the government and essential private capital purposes during the war, and they could be used to bid goods away from other consumers only to the extent that they were larger than increases in other consumer incomes and that the rationing and price control system would permit it. (2) A large increase of employment is likely to be accompanied, especially in the short run, by a decrease in the amount of food that can be commanded by each hour of work. This is because total food output is usually

[3] Computed from data in *The National Food Situation*, U. S. Department of Agriculture, NFS-48, April-June, 1949, p. 2. Index numbers represent quantities weighed by average farm prices in the period 1935-1939.

not so easily expansible as are industrial products when the expansion starts from depression levels. It is true that to understand the actual course of farm prices one must remember the government's solicitude for farmers. But the politics of the situation must not be allowed to obscure the fact that the basic reasons for the great rise of farm prices were the limited expansibility of farm output, the rise in the demand for military and export purposes, and the combination of the great increase of consumer money incomes and of the desire of people to use a considerable part of their enhanced incomes to increase the quantity and quality of their food consumption. A major part of the increase of civilian demand must have come from workers enjoying increased employment and increased hourly earnings. The behavior of the total amount of food available for utilization and the amount utilized by civilians is shown in Table 103. (3) Even in the absence of any increase in hourly earnings, aggregate wage and salary receipts would have risen about 80 percent between 1939 and 1944 because of the increase in total man-hours worked. This, together with the prevailing tax policy and the huge government demand for output, would have produced large inflationary pressures. And the increase in average hourly earnings enhanced the rise of the total wage and salary bill and labor's total spending power. (4) This great rise of aggregate wages and salaries, accounting for 75 percent of the total increase of personal income between 1939 and 1944, must also have accounted for a large part of the rise of personal savings during the war.

In view of labor's insistence during the war period that "the purchasing power of each hour of work should be kept at least as high as it was in the prewar period," it is worth noting two different meanings of this term: (1) That labor should in fact continue to buy and consume currently a constant amount of real goods and services for each hour worked, and (2) that the amount of money received for each hour of work and used by labor for current consumption *and for saving* should have a "potential" purchasing power equal to that received before the war. The first was, as we have seen, practically impossible of attainment during the war, with such a large part of output definitely committed to war and related purposes. The second, however, was possible of achievement if labor and other recipients of personal income would save a sufficiently high proportion of their incomes instead of using them currently to demand consumption goods. This did occur; the "potential" real purchasing power of average hourly earnings rose about 11 percent between 1939 and 1944. But it should be emphasized that this maintenance of the "potential" purchasing power of hourly earnings could continue only so long as consumers continued to save such an abnormally large part of their incomes; a general insistence on spending the prewar proportion of incomes for consumption would have decreased considerably the purchasing power of each dollar of income. This is, in general, what happened in the postwar period when the freedom to spend had been restored and not only labor but other consumers as well elected to save only a small part and to spend a large part of their money incomes.

It is also worth noting that wage increases tended in at least two ways to increase the government's deficit during the war period. In the first place, some wage increases enhanced the *net* price paid for goods and services by the government, either by raising the initial price or by reducing the amount recovered from employers through renegotiation. Such increases in the net prices paid by the government were not by any means fully offset by increased tax collections out of workers' increased wage receipts. And in the second place, even those wage increases which were at the expense of employers' profits reduced government revenue, for the marginal tax rate applicable to workers' incomes was in most cases far below that applying to employers' profits, and especially that applying to excess profits. Tax revenues might have been reduced much more if the government had accepted labor's argument that wage rates should be allowed to rise in those cases where employers could afford to pay them without raising prices. By increasing the federal deficit, wage increases raised the net contribution of the government to total demand for output, increased the total amount of private savings accumulated during the war, and tended to increase the amount of new money created by the banking system to meet the government's deficits.

Though the rise of hourly earnings during the defense and war period was an important source of inflationary pressure, it is well to recognize that in this field, as in that of taxes, the government had to consider the relation of its policy not only to inflation but also to other aspects of the economy. In the first place, it had to consider the relation of wage policy to the labor supply and to the productivity of labor. It wanted to increase the labor force as much as possible, to increase the number of hours worked each week, to minimize work stoppages, to secure maximum productivity, to transfer millions of people from less essential to more essential occupations, and so on. It therefore had to decide to what extent it would rely on direct controls over manpower to achieve these ends and to what extent it would use wage increases as incentives.

In the second place, the government faced the problem of justice in the distribution of income. Corporate profits, both before and after taxes, incomes of unincorporated enterprises, farm incomes, and the incomes of self-employed professional people were soaring. Labor felt strongly that it too should be permitted to receive much larger incomes and to save large amounts for the postwar period. The very low wage rates in some areas posed a third problem. To what extent should a war period be used to correct social injustices that had developed in the prewar period, especially when the government's previously announced policy was to eradicate such injustices?

WAGES AND THE POSTWAR INFLATION

The movement of wage rates after the end of the war has already been described. In a series of increases, average hourly earnings of American workers rose about 38 percent between September 1945 and the end of 1948. It goes almost without saying that these large increases exerted a strong upward cost effect on prices. Most of them represented increases in basic wage schedules rather than increased amounts of overtime, upgrading, or net shifts from low-wage to high-wage jobs; employers could not, to the same extent as in the period 1939-1943, offset wage increases by reductions of overhead costs accompanying expanded operations; labor productivity did not increase rapidly; and most employers could not have granted wage increases of 38 percent and still have operated profitably with their prices at the levels of late 1945. None of the following statements is meant to deny that the cost effects of the large postwar wage increases were a potent factor in raising prices. Yet, for the reasons indicated earlier, the cost effects of wage increases cannot fully account for the postwar inflation. They cannot explain the large rise of agricultural prices, such large wage increases could not have been achieved in the absence of a very strong and rising demand for output, and employers could not have raised their prices so much if demand conditions had not been favorable. Again, therefore, we must analyze demand and its relationship to wage rates.

Between the final quarter of 1945 and the last quarter of 1948 aggregate wage and salary receipts rose 26 percent, and this was due solely to the increase of hourly rates. Thus the rise of wage and salary rates accounted for all of the increase of labor's money income during the postwar period and for at least 60 percent of the increase of total personal income. It was therefore a major factor in the postwar increase of consumer spendings for output.

The direct income effects of wage increases do not, however, explain all of the increase in the demand for consumption goods, let alone the entire increase in the total money demand for output. Some of the most important of the other factors were these: (1) The marked rise in the propensity to consume. During 1943 and 1944, for the various reasons indicated earlier, people spent only about 77 percent of their disposable incomes for consumption and saved about 23 percent. But after the war, as they regained freedom of choice, people no longer were willing to save more than about 4 to 8 percent of their disposable incomes; they insisted on consuming between 92 and 96 percent of them. They wanted more consumption goods and were willing to hold only a much smaller part of their incomes as savings for future use. This is reflected in the fact that while disposable personal incomes rose $46 billion between 1944 and 1948 personal consumption spendings rose $57.6 billion. And it must be emphasized that, in general, the demand for consumption goods appears to have been not only very large but also price-inelastic. As prices rose people were willing to spend rising amounts to satisfy their desires for these goods. (2) The large and price-inelastic demand for output for government use, for net exports, and for private capital maintenance and expansion. The various factors that made demands for these purposes so large in the postwar period have already been described. Here again the demand appears to have been highly price-inelastic; the amount of output taken for these purposes seems to have been little affected by price increases. In each of the years 1946 through 1948 about 30 percent of output was used for these purposes and about 70 percent for personal consumption.

The facts brought out in the preceding paragraph are highly important. In the first place, they explain why employers were able to grant such large wage increases, to maintain and even to expand their own profit margins, and to pass along the increases in both wage rates and profit margins in the form of higher prices without suffering a reduction of real sales. This would not have been possible if individuals had not had such an urgent desire to convert their increased incomes into consumption and if the demand for output for government, net export, and private capital purposes had been smaller and more price-elastic.

In the second place, these facts indicate that under the conditions actually prevailing in the postwar period it was impossible for labor as a whole to achieve the increases in *real earnings per hour* that it urgently sought. To make this point we shall not deal with labor's original larger wage demands but only with the 1946 pattern of 18½ cents an hour, and we shall assume that subsequent wage increases were only for the purpose of restoring real hourly wages to the level sought by the 1946 increase. In September 1945 real wages per hour, in the sense of average hourly earnings deflated by the cost of living index, were about 12 percent above their level in 1939.[4] The first round of wage increases was designed to raise average real wages per hour about 15 percent above the September 1945 level, or about 29 percent above 1939. Was it possible for labor to achieve such a large increase in real hourly earnings in such a short period? Or were increases in money wages almost certain to be dissipated by induced increases in the cost of living as soon as price controls were removed? In answering these questions we must recall the two meanings of the term "real wages." It might have been possible for labor to realize large increases in the "potential purchasing power" of each hour's wages if in fact not only labor but other consumers as well had been willing to continue saving a very large proportion of their incomes and to offer only an abnormally small proportion currently for consumption goods. But this did not occur; as rapidly as they were freed from controls, consumers in general elected to use an abnormally large part of their incomes to demand current output for consumption. This brings us to the second meaning of real wages—the amount of goods and services actually consumed in exchange for each hour of work. The upper limit on real wages in this sense depends on several factors. (1) The amount of real output per man-hour worked. Though we have no reliable figures on the changes of labor productivity in industry as a whole it seems highly unlikely that output per man-hour rose much more than 10 percent between 1939 and 1948, and the increase may have been smaller. With real output per man-hour rising at only

[4] This is a minimum figure arrived at by deflating the New York Federal Reserve bank composite index of average hourly earnings of wage earners and of average weekly earnings of clerical and professional employees. The real hourly earnings of wage earners alone had risen about 20 percent. The lower of these figures was deliberately selected so as to understate rather than overstate the case.

this slow rate it is clear that labor could increase by 29 percent the amount of goods and services purchased by each hour of work only by reducing far below prewar levels the proportion of real output used for other purposes. (2) The proportion of real output used for government, net export, and private capital purposes and to supply the needs of consumers other than labor. It was clear that the proportion of national output available for consumption could be markedly increased above the wartime levels as large numbers of men were released from the armed forces and made available for civilian production and as the government decreased greatly its demand for the output of private industry. At the peak of the war period the government took more than 40 percent of output; in the postwar period this percentage fell back to 12 to 15 percent. It was not at all clear, however, that the proportion of output represented by consumption goods could be raised above the prewar levels. However much consumers, including labor, might wish to consume a larger proportion of total output, they had to face the fact that the government wanted to use at least the prewar proportion of output for its purposes, that foreigners as a group wanted more than their prewar proportion of our output as net exports, and that enterprisers wanted more than the prewar proportion of our output with which to maintain and expand our supply of capital goods. After direct controls were removed, consumers could in fact get a larger percentage of output for their uses only if they could bid it away from the other classes of competing buyers, and they found that these other buyers—the government, foreigners, and investors in capital goods—not only could get larger amounts of money but were also willing to spend them for output. In no year during the postwar period covered by this study was more than 71 percent of output taken for consumption; this compares with 75 percent in 1939 and 72 percent in 1940. About 30 percent of output was used for government, net export, and private capital purposes. Because of these general conditions labor as a whole was not able to raise its real hourly earnings—in the sense of money wages corrected for the rise in the cost of living—consistently above their September 1945 level until after the end of 1947, though hourly earnings in terms of money rose about 26 percent.

Do these facts prove that labor as a whole gained nothing from its three rounds of postwar wage increases? Would its real wages per hour have been as high if it had maintained the same money wage rates that prevailed at the end of the war? Not knowing what would have happened in the absence of the large wage increases, we cannot answer these questions with any certainty. It may, however, be possible to cast some light on them by considering a series of less comprehensive questions. (1) Are the effects of general and uniform wage increases different from those of differential wage increases? The answer here is clearly in the affirmative. Those who were able to get wage increases greater than the average clearly increased their real purchasing power. For example, the coal miners increased their purchasing power at the expense of teachers, government employees, and so on. But, in a period of full employment, general and uniform wage increases can lead to an increase of real earnings per hour only at the expense of the nonlabor part of the community. The following discussion will deal only with general and uniform wage increases. (2) What were the effects of general wage increases on the proportion of output taken for government use? It seems probable that this demand for output had some price-elasticity; to the extent that the rise of wages contributed to the rise in prices, it probably reduced somewhat the amount of real output taken by the government. Some school projects were postponed, some other government services were curtailed or prevented from rising as much as they otherwise would, and so on. But the price-elasticity of this demand was probably not very large. A large part of the government's activities was considered essential and was not to be allowed to shrink regardless of the rise of prices. (3) What were the effects of general wage increases on the physical volume of our net exports? Here again there may have been some price-elasticity. As prices rose the purchasing power of accumulated dollar balances, of gold, and of each dollar of grants or loans was reduced. But here, too, the price-elasticity was probably small. The foreign demand was urgent, this country was almost the only source of many goods; our prices, even after their rise, were low relative to those in most other countries; and, in general, our dollar grants and loans to foreigners seem to have been increased to offset a large part of the rise of prices here. (4) What were the effects of general wage increases on the proportion of real output used for private capital maintenance and growth? No one knows the answer to this question, but it seems most likely that the succession of wage increases actually increased the proportion of our output used for this purpose. It is probably true that some capital projects, especially in the field of housing, were either postponed or abandoned because of wage increases. But, on the other side, are the facts that the wage increases were expected to be permanent and created expectations of still further wage increases, that wage increases contributed somewhat to an inflation psychology that tends to swell investment, that the rise of wage rates in the face of continued low interest rates made mechanization more attractive, that labor's expenditure of its increased wages swelled business profits and provided enterprisers with additional money with which to purchase investment goods, and that monetary policy assured business of adequate funds at low cost even though the prices of investment goods rose. (5) What were the effects of general wage increases on the proportion of our output commanded by other types of consumer income and by accumulated savings? There is no question that labor, by raising its money wages, was able to bid a part of output away from some classes of income receivers. This fact will be granted immediately by annuitants, landlords, pensioners, interest receivers, those living on accumulated savings fixed in terms of money, and others in the same general category. Moreover, labor gained at the expense of those who spent wartime savings which had been accumulated in the form of money, bonds, and savings accounts. But it is highly doubtful that the rise of money wages increased the ability of labor as a whole to bid goods away from farmers and other receivers of entrepreneurial income.[5] The very increase of wage rates which enhanced labor's income and spending power, combined with labor's insistence on spending its increased earnings, permitted farmers and other enterprisers to increase their money incomes by at least as great a proportion as that of labor.

It is evident from the tenor of the preceding paragraphs that only limited conclusions regarding the relationship between money and real hourly earnings are justified. (1) In fact, the doubling of average money earnings per hour between 1939 and the end of 1948 was accompanied by only a 20 percent rise in the purchasing power of hourly earnings, and of the latter increase about half occurred in 1948, while only 14 percent of the total rise of money wages occurred in that year. The general rise of wage rates was itself responsible for a considerable part of the rise of living costs during the period. (2) Those classes of labor that achieved the largest wage increases gained real purchasing power at the expense of those whose wages or salaries rose by a smaller percentage. (3) The general rise of money wages almost certainly had the net effect of increasing the real hourly wages of labor in general, for it reduced the purchasing power of consumer incomes that were relatively fixed in terms of money, it decreased the amount of output that could be purchased by each dollar of wartime savings accumulated by nonlabor groups, and it may have enabled labor to bid some, though probably not many, goods and services away from the government and from net exports. It is doubtful, however, that the increases of money wages reduced at all the proportion of output used for capital purposes. The very rise of wage rates, combined with labor's very high propensity to spend, enabled enterprisers to raise their prices enough to protect, if not actually to improve, their money income positions; and the rise of wage rates seems not to have reduced the amount of real output used for investment. (4) If the above analysis is even approximately correct, the net increase in the amount of goods

---

[5] Though it is true that corporate dividends did not rise proportionally with wages, business earnings rose more than in proportion, and all these earnings were spendable for either consumption or investment goods.

and services that labor could consume in exchange for each hour of work as a result of increases in money wage rates was largely at the expense of the relatively fixed types of consumer money income.

CONCLUSIONS

The doubling of money wage rates was an important factor in the inflation. It raised costs of production, contributed greatly to the increase of private disposable incomes and spending power, and enhanced expectations that price levels would rise and remain far above prewar levels. It also contributed to the rise of government spendings and deficits during the defense and war period, augmented the growth of private savings, and helped to increase the growth of bank credit and the money supply by increasing the amount of credit demanded to carry out government and private projects. The inflation would have been smaller if wage rates had not risen so much.

Yet it is misleading to infer that wage increases were the "sole cause" of the inflation or even that they were "purely autonomous causes." To a very considerable extent they, like the increases of many other prices, were induced by other factors. Such large increases in wage rates could not have occurred in the absence of the various other factors that contributed so much to a large and price-inelastic demand for output, and thereby created such a large and price-inelastic demand for labor. Labor would not have demanded and employers would not have granted such large wage increases in the absence of a combination of conditions including the huge government demand for output during the war, the huge accumulation of private savings, the liberal and passive monetary policy, the great rise in the propensity to consume after the war, and the large and price-inelastic demand for output to be used for private capital formation, net export, and government purposes. Thus wage policy was an important contributing factor to the inflation, but it was only one of many.

XVII

||||||||||||||||||||||||||||||||||||||||||||||||||||||||||||||||||||||||||||||||||||||||||||||||||||||||||||||||||||||||||||||

Inflation and the Distribution of
Wealth and Income

T
HE primary purpose of this study has been to describe the
process of inflation between 1939 and 1948 and to analyze
the principal public and private policies that contributed to the
process. It has not been our purpose to trace out the far-reaching
social and economic effects of the inflation, which would itself be
a lengthy and difficult task. Nevertheless, it will be useful to make
a few comments regarding the behavior of the distribution of
wealth and income, for these are among the most important social
consequences of inflation. The purpose of these comments will not
be to provide definitive answers but only to indicate some of the
most important issues.

Most discussions of the effects of inflation on the distribution
of wealth and income assume that the rise of prices starts from a
situation of "full employment" and "full production," so that
neither the total amount of real income (output) nor the total
amount of real wealth is altered by the rise of prices. Under these
conditions it would necessarily follow that any real gain by one
group would have to be balanced by real losses of other groups.
The real gains of those whose money income and money wealth
rose more than price levels could be only at the expense of real
losses by those whose money income and money wealth rose less
than price levels. This is not, of course, a realistic description of

the actual behavior of real incomes between 1939 and 1948, for real output during the postwar period was about 60 percent higher than in 1939, and a major part of the increase was available for private consumption and capital formation.

Table 104 shows that between 1939 and 1948 the cost of living rose 72 percent; the dollar lost 42 percent of its purchasing power over cost-of-living items. This meant, of course, that those whose money incomes rose less than 72 percent suffered a decrease of

TABLE 104.   Price Levels and the Purchasing Power of the Dollar, 1939-1948
(1939=100)[1]

Year	Cost of Living		Wholesale	
	Price Index	Purchasing Power of the Dollar over Cost-of-Living Items	Price Index	Purchasing Power of the Dollar over Wholesale Items
1939	100.0	100.0	100.0	100.0
1940	100.8	99.2	101.9	98.1
1941	105.8	94.5	113.2	88.3
1942	117.2	85.3	128.1	78.1
1943	124.3	80.5	133.7	74.8
1944	126.3	79.2	134.9	74.1
1945	129.2	77.4	137.2	72.9
1946	140.1	71.4	157.1	63.7
1947	160.2	62.4	197.3	50.7
1948	172.2	58.0	214.1	46.7

real income while those whose money incomes rose more than 72 percent enjoyed an increase of real income. Table 105 shows, however, that money incomes in general rose far more than 72 percent. Between 1939 and 1948 total disposable personal income in current dollars rose 174 percent despite the marked increase of tax rates, and average disposable income per capita rose 145 percent. In dollars of 1939 purchasing power the increases were nearly 60 percent for total disposable personal income and more than 40 percent for average disposable income per capita. With such a great rise in the amount of real income to be shared, a

[1] These are the indexes of the Bureau of Labor Statistics, converted to a 1939 base.

marked change in the percentage distribution of national income could occur even if no one suffered an absolute reduction of his real income. Large numbers of people did indeed suffer such reductions as their money incomes rose less than the cost of living. Among these were people whose money incomes consisted solely or largely of interest, annuities, pensions, rentals on property that had been fully occupied before the war, and wages or salaries that rose only belatedly and slowly. Their loss of relative income position was even greater because they did not participate in the general rise of real incomes during the period. Many others who

TABLE 105. Disposable Personal Income, 1939-1948[2]

Year	Disposable Personal Income in Current Dollars		Disposable Personal Income in 1939 Dollars		Index of Disposable Personal Income in 1939 Dollars (1939=100)	
	Total (In billions)	Per Capita	Total (In billions)	Per Capita	Total	Per Capita
1939	$ 70.2	$ 536	$ 70.2	$536	100.0	100.0
1940	75.7	574	75.1	569	107.0	106.1
1941	92.0	691	87.0	653	123.9	121.8
1942	116.2	863	99.2	736	141.3	137.3
1943	131.6	964	105.9	776	150.9	144.8
1944	145.6	1,054	115.3	835	164.2	155.8
1945	149.4	1,070	115.6	828	164.7	154.5
1946	159.2	1,127	113.6	804	161.8	150.0
1947	173.6	1,205	108.4	752	154.4	140.3
1948	192.6	1,314	111.8	763	159.3	142.4

escaped an absolute reduction of their real incomes nevertheless slipped down the scale of relative incomes as their money incomes rose less than the average. On the other hand, the more fortunate experienced both an absolute and a relative improvement of their income positions as their money incomes rose more than the cost of living and also more than the average increase of incomes.

Because of the marked rise of output, it is necessary to distinguish conceptually, even though it may be difficult to do so statistically, between the change in the distribution of income that ac-

[2] Computed from data in *Midyear Economic Report of the President*, July, 1949, p. 91. The data on disposable personal income in 1939 dollars were arrived at by deflating the figures in current dollars by the cost-of-living index converted to a 1939 base.

tually occurred during the inflation period and the changes that resulted from the inflation of price levels and the accompanying dispersion of individual prices. Only a part of the actual change in income distribution was a consequence of the rise of price levels; a very significant part of the change was due to the rise of employment and output, and such a change in income distribution could have occurred even if price levels, including the prices of labor and other services, had not risen at all. For example, in 1939 more than 9 million were unemployed, many others were working less than full time, and many firms were operating far below full capacity. A major part of the low-income groups must have been composed of the families of those who were wholly or partially unemployed or who were proprietors of small enterprises suffering from the low level of demand. The rise of employment, without any increase of money wage rates, would have increased the percentage share of national income going to those who were formerly at least partially unemployed. The incomes of these people would have risen more than the incomes of those who were already fully employed and also more than other relatively fixed types of money income. Moreover, the rise of employment opportunities in the higher-wage industries helped those in low-wage occupations to secure wage increases that were greater than the average increase for all industries. Similarly, the rise of output and sales by the firms that had formerly been most depressed would have tended to increase the percentage shares of national income received by the owners of these firms even if the prices of their products had remained stable, for with higher volume their overhead costs per unit of output would have fallen and their profit per unit would have been multiplied by a larger physical volume of sales.

This fact is highly important for public policy if one believes that it would have been possible to achieve and maintain relatively full employment and production with far less inflation of price levels than that which actually occurred. It probably would have been impossible to attain high levels of employment and output without some rise of prices above their 1939 levels; the price levels of that year included too many individual prices that were too low relative to cost schedules to make full employment profitable. But this situation seems to have been largely remedied by the price increases that had occurred by early 1942. On the whole, this early rise of prices and the rise of employment and output accompanying it probably tended toward a more equal distribution of income. (1) The rise of employment tended to increase the share of national income going to those who had previously been in the lowest income groups because of unemployment. (2) The increase of employment opportunities helped those with the most depressed wage rates to secure wage increases beyond the average. (3) The firms and industries that had been hardest hit by the depression tended to show the largest percentage increase in output and sales. (4) Farmers, whose incomes had been among the lowest in the economy, enjoyed a marked improvement in their position as the prices of farm products rose more than other prices; by 1942 the parity ratio had risen to 106 as compared with 77 in 1939 and 55 in 1932. (5) The rise of prices by 1942 had not yet reduced the purchasing power of the people with fixed money incomes below the levels prevailing during the late 1920's. In 1942 the cost of living was about 17 percent above the 1939 level but it was still 5 percent below its level in 1929. The major part, if not all, of the tendency toward a more equal distribution of income after 1939 was most probably due to the rise of employment and output and to the early price increases which made possible these increases of output. It seems doubtful that the rise of prices after full employment had been reached, and especially the price increases after the war, contributed much if anything to the greater equality of incomes. It is even less likely that the postwar price increases, with their arbitrary effects on individuals and families, promoted equity in the distribution of wealth and income. In short, widespread unemployment probably tends toward a more unequal distribution of income, and for this situation a rise of employment and output is a corrective. It does not necessarily follow, however, that further price increases after relatively full employment has been attained tend toward "equity," however that term may be defined.

In interpreting the following statistics relative to income distribution the following facts should be borne in mind. (1) The behavior of the percentage shares of income was a resultant not only of price changes but also of changes in the level of employment and output. (2) Many of the statistics do not reflect changes in

TABLE 106. Percentage Shares of the Total National Income Originating in Business, by Legal Form of Organization, 1939-1948[3]

	1939	1940	1941	1942	1943	1944	1945	1946	1947	1948
All Legal Forms of Business	100.0	100.0	100.0	100.0	100.0	100.0	100.0	100.0	100.0	100.0
Compensation of employees	61.7	59.5	57.8	56.7	57.4	57.9	58.6	60.0	59.5	58.4
Income of unincorporated enterprises[a]	18.3	18.1	18.2	19.5	19.1	19.8	22.0	22.9	21.6	21.3
Corporate profits[a]	9.0	12.8	15.9	16.7	17.2	16.2	13.3	11.7	14.0	15.8
Rental income of persons	5.6	5.2	4.8	4.6	4.4	4.4	4.4	4.1	3.7	3.3
Net interest	5.3	4.4	3.3	2.5	1.9	1.7	1.6	1.4	1.3	1.2
Corporate Business	100.0	100.0	100.0	100.0	100.0	100.0	100.0	100.0	100.0	100.0
Compensation of employees	80.7	75.9	72.6	71.4	71.7	72.9	76.2	78.9	76.2	73.8
Corporate profits[a]	15.5	21.2	25.5	27.0	27.3	26.2	22.9	20.6	23.4	26.0
Net interest	3.8	2.9	1.9	1.6	1.1	0.9	0.9	0.5	0.4	0.2
Sole Proprietorships and Partnerships	100.0	100.0	100.0	100.0	100.0	100.0	100.0	100.0	100.0	100.0
Compensation of employees	38.3	37.3	36.1	35.5	35.4	35.9	36.0	36.5	35.8	35.0
Income of unincorporated enterprises[a]	59.0	60.3	62.0	63.3	63.7	63.4	63.4	63.0	63.8	64.6
Net interest	2.7	2.4	1.9	1.2	0.9	0.7	0.6	0.5	0.4	0.4

[a] These are profits before taxes but after inventory valuation adjustment.

private purchasing power due to increased tax burdens. And (3) the broad aggregates hide wide differences in the behavior of their components.

FUNCTIONAL SHARES OF INCOME

It will be useful to look briefly at the percentage shares of income going to the various types of productive factors. Table 106 shows how that part of national income originating in business

[3] Computed from data in Tables 7 and 12 of the *National Income Supplements to the Survey of Current Business*, July 1947, 1948, and 1949.

was shared. In broad outline, the table shows that (1) the percentage share represented by net interest payments declined markedly, (2) the percentage share represented by personal rental incomes also declined, but to a lesser extent, (3) the share represented by corporate profits and income of unincorporated business enterprises rose considerably, and (4) the employee's percentage share was remarkably constant, though slightly below 1939 levels.

Table 107 shows the behavior of the functional shares of total personal income. The first part of the table indicates the percentage of total personal income represented by each functional share during the period, and the second part presents indexes showing the size of percentage shares in the various years relative to the percentage share in 1939.[4] These were the principal developments: (1) The greatest losers of relative position were personal interest and rental incomes. (2) The greatest gainers were farm incomes and the incomes of unincorporated business and professional enterprises. (3) Corporate dividends declined as a percentage of personal income, but this was solely the result of highly conservative dividend policies, for corporate profits after taxes rose markedly relative to total personal income. (4) The percentage of personal income represented by the compensation of employees rose somewhat during the war and then declined to the 1939 level after the end of the war.

Though statistics relative to the functional shares of income are useful for some purposes they are quite inadequate for describing the behavior of individual family incomes. There are two principal reasons for this. (1) The various functional types of income are of varying importance to different families. The incomes of some families consist solely of wages and salaries; others receive only rentals; still others receive two or more types of income. Thus different families are affected in quite different ways by changes in the functional shares of national income. (2) Each functional share is a very broad category and conceals wide differences in the

[4] That is, the index for year $X = \dfrac{\text{the percentage share in year } X}{\text{the percentage share in 1939}} \times 100$.

behavior of its components. For example, some farmers enjoyed very great income increases while others improved their income position very little. The profit experiences of corporations varied widely. Some landlords whose properties were fully rented before

TABLE 107.   Functional Shares of Personal Income, 1939-1948[5]

A. Functional Shares as a Percentage of Total Personal Income

	1939	1940	1941	1942	1943	1944	1945	1946	1947	1948
Total personal income	100.0	100.0	100.0	100.0	100.0	100.0	100.0	100.0	100.0	100.0
Wages and salary receipts and other labor income	62.9	63.2	64.5	66.3	69.6	70.0	67.9	62.8	63.0	63.8
Income of unincorporated business and professional enterprises	9.3	9.9	10.0	10.3	9.9	10.3	10.9	11.8	11.9	11.6
Dividend receipts	5.2	5.2	4.7	3.5	3.0	2.8	2.7	3.3	3.6	3.7
Farm income	6.2	6.3	7.3	8.6	7.8	7.1	7.3	8.1	8.0	8.7
Rental income of persons	4.8	4.6	4.5	4.4	4.1	3.9	3.6	3.5	3.4	3.1
Personal interest income	7.5	6.9	5.7	4.4	3.7	3.6	3.9	4.2	4.0	3.9
Transfer payments	4.1	4.0	3.3	2.6	2.0	2.2	3.6	6.4	6.0	5.2
Addendum:										
Total corporate profits after taxes	6.9	8.2	9.8	7.7	7.1	6.5	4.9	7.9	9.9	10.0
Total compensation of labor	65.9	66.1	67.4	69.2	72.7	73.0	71.6	66.1	65.9	66.2

B. Index of Shares of Total Personal Income (Percent of personal income in 1939=100)

	1939	1940	1941	1942	1943	1944	1945	1946	1947	1948
Wages, salaries, and other labor income	100	101	103	105	111	111	108	99	100	101
Income of unincorporated business and professional enterprises	100	107	108	111	106	111	117	127	128	125
Dividend receipts	100	100	90	67	58	54	52	63	69	71
Farm income	100	102	118	139	126	115	118	131	129	140
Rental income of persons	100	96	94	92	85	81	75	73	71	65
Personal interest income	100	92	76	59	49	48	52	56	53	52
Transfer payments	100	98	81	63	49	54	88	156	146	127
Addendum:										
Total corporate profits after taxes	100	119	142	112	103	94	71	114	143	145
Total compensation of labor	100	100	102	105	110	112	111	100	100	100

the war and who enjoyed no rise in rental rates actually suffered a decline of their net incomes while some other landlords received very large increases because of higher occupancy, or higher rental rates, or both. Some workers who were already fully employed and who received only small wage and salary increases enjoyed

[5] Computed from data in the *Survey of Current Business.*

little or no increase of their money incomes while others who enjoyed increased employment or large increases in their wage or salary rates received very large increases in their money incomes. This widely varying behavior of incomes within each broad category is illustrated, though in an incomplete way, by the following statistics relating to annual earnings of full-time employees in various industries.

TABLE 108. Average Annual Earnings per Full-Time Employee, 1939-1948[6]

Industry	Rank in 1939	1939 Earnings as Percentage of 1939 av.	Rank in 1944	Rank in 1948	Percentage Increase 1939-1948	Rank in Percentage Increase 1939-1948
Security and comm. brokers, dealers, exchanges	1	226.5	1	1	85.6	52
Radio broadcasting	2	145.9	3	5	63.9	64
Air transport (comm. carr.)	3	187.9	13	15	49.0	68
Finance, n.e.c.	4	164.7	11	12	67.4	61
Engineering and other professional services	5	159.2	4	6	91.3	49
Insurance carriers	6	159.1	28	35	55.2	65
Motion pictures	7	159.1	34	40	50.4	67
Banking	8	158.9	39	38	54.0	66
Pipeline transportation	9	155.8	8	2	110.7	29
Insurance agents and combined offices	10	151.9	27	23	78.6	57
Railroads	11	151.5	17	9	91.0	50
Mfg.: petroleum and coal products	12	149.5	7	3	119.4	20
Fed. govt. civilian except work relief	13	148.7	19	31	72.0	59
Business services, n.e.c.	14	147.5	14	8	97.7	43
Fed. govt.: govt. enterprises	15	146.9	36	37	66.6	62
Wholesale trade	16	143.1	20	7	104.3	37
Electric and gas utilities	17	142.6	30	27	80.8	54
Mfg.: autos and auto equipment	18	142.6	6	14	98.5	41
Mfg.: printing & publishing	19	138.7	35	13	86.4	36
Local railways and buslines	20	137.3	29	32	86.2	51
Crude petroleum and natural gas	21	135.9	23	10	112.2	28
Mfg: machinery (except electrical)	22	135.7	9	19	102.7	39
Mfg.: transportation equipment (except autos)	23	134.5	5	17	106.0	34
Nonprofit organizations n.e.c.	24	131.9	32	11	115.5	23
Mfg.: chemicals, etc.	25	130.0	21	22	109.9	30
Misc. repair services and hand trades	26	129.4	10	28	98.9	40
Mfg.: electrical machinery	27	129.2	24	33	96.1	46
Telephone and telegraph	28	129.1	46	46	76.2	58
State and local govt.: govt. enterprises	29	127.4	40	36	93.0	47

[6] SOURCE: *National Income Supplement to the Survey of Current Business*, 1947, 1948, and 1949, Table 26.

TABLE 108.   Average Annual Earnings per Full-Time Employee, 1939-1948

Industry	Rank in 1939	1939 Earnings as Percentage of 1939 av.	Rank in 1944	Rank in 1948	Percentage Increase 1939-1948	Rank in Percentage Increase 1939-1948
Water transportation	30	125.3	2	4	151.6	8
Mfg.: iron and steel and their products	31	125.0	12	20	119.0	21
Mfg.: rubber products	32	124.9	18	29	105.7	35
State and local govt.: non-school except work relief	33	123.5	50	52	65.6	63
Commercial and trade schools, and employment agencies	34	123.4	16	30	108.1	33
Mfg.: nonferrous metals and their products	35	122.8	15	25	115.2	25
Metal mining	36	122.5	31	24	120.5	19
Mfg.: paper	37	114.1	41	26	126.8	16
Religious organizations	38	113.8	62	66	34.0	69
Anthracite mining	39	113.5	26	18	143.7	10
State and local govt.: public educ.	40	113.2	55	48	91.8	48
Mfg.: food and kindred prods.	41	110.7	45	43	108.4	32
Mfg.: stone, glass and clay prods.	42	109.7	42	41	114.8	26
Mfg.: misc. manufacturing	43	107.9	39	42	115.4	24
Highway pass. transportation	44	105.2	33	44	118.9	22
Agriculture and similar service establ.	45	103.1	47	61	68.3	60
Amusement and recreation except motion pictures	46	103.1	57	56	83.5	53
Services allied to transportation	47	102.4	37	45	122.3	18
Contract construction	48	102.3	22	34	146.9	9
Local public services n.e.c.	49	100.1	49	53	96.4	45
Educational services	50	99.9	59	59	79.3	56
Retail trade and auto services	51	98.8	54	49	113.5	27
Legal services	52	97.3	63	60	80.7	55
Bituminous & other soft coal	53	96.6	25	21	183.0	4
Nonmetallic mining	54	94.5	44	39	154.4	7
Fed. govt.: military	55	93.9	52	47	132.5	13
Real estate	56	92.3	61	58	97.6	44
Mfg.: furniture	57	91.8	48	51	127.0	15
Mfg.: leather and leather prod.	58	83.8	51	55	132.1	14
Mfg.: apparel	59	82.7	53	54	137.1	11
Personal services	60	81.4	64	63	103.7	38
Fisheries	61	80.9	43	16	245.7	2
Mfg.: textiles	62	77.5	56	50	170.4	6
Hotels and lodging places	63	77.3	65	67	98.0	42
Mfg.: lumber	64	77.2	60	57	137.7	10
Mfg.: tobacco	65	73.9	58	64	122.7	17
Medical and health services	66	73.2	67	65	109.8	31
Private households	67	42.0	68	68	171.5	5
Forestry	68	33.9	66	62	396.0	1
Farms	69	30.5	69	69	245.2	3

Addendum:
Average annual earnings in 1939=$1239
Average percentage increase, 1939-1948=121.4

TABLE 109. Average Annual Earnings of Paid Employees in School
Systems, 1938-1948[7]

	Earnings in Current Dollars			Earnings in 1938-39 Dollars		Index of Earnings in 1938-39 Dollars 1938-39=100	
	1938-39	1946-47	1948-49	1946-47	1948-49	1946-47	1948-49
All Regular Classroom Teachers							
Cities 2,500-5,000 pop.	$ 1240	$ 2044	$ 2655	$1350	$1598	109	129
Cities 30,000-100,000 pop.	1748	2458	3150	1624	1896	93	109
Cities over 500,000	2787	3580	4242	2365	2554	85	92
Supervising Principals, Elementary Schools							
Cities 2,500-5,000 pop.	1928	2900	3692	1915	2223	99	115
Cities 30,000-100,000 pop.	2467	3328	4195	2198	2526	89	102
Cities over 500,000	3994	5077	5907	3353	3556	84	89
Principals of Junior High Schools							
Cities 2,500-5,000 pop.	——	3083	3483	2036	2097	——	——
Cities 30,000-100,000 pop.	3215	4016	4788	2653	2883	83	90
Cities over 500,000	5306	5909	6906	3903	4158	74	78
Principals of Senior High Schools							
Cities 2,500-5000 pop.	——	3283	4032	2168	2427	——	——
Cities 30,000-100,000 pop.	4055	4700	5468	3104	3292	77	81
Cities over 500,000	5550	6396	7321	4225	4408	76	79
Superintendents of Schools							
Cities 2,500-5,000 pop.	3244	4225	5106	2791	3074	86	95
Cities 30,000-100,000 pop.	6125	7307	8772	4826	5281	79	86
Cities over 500,000	11667	14333	16000	9467	9633	81	83
Superintendents of Buildings							
Cities 2,500-5,000 pop.	1800	2925	3340	1932	2011	107	112
Cities 30,000-100,000 pop.	2581	3361	4280	2220	2577	86	100
Cities over 500,000	4700	6431	7500	4248	4515	90	96
Head Janitors							
Cities 2,500-5,000 pop.	1131	1875	2228	1238	1341	110	119
Cities 30,000-100,000 pop.	1968	2794	3210	1845	1933	94	98
Cities over 500,000	3920	4554	5179	3008	3118	77	80

[7] From data in the *National Education Association Research Bulletin*, 1949,
Vol. 27, pp. 47, 49, 51.

Table 108 shows that average annual earnings per full-time employee in industry as a whole rose 121.4 percent between 1939 and 1948. But there was a wide dispersion from this average. At the upper extreme, average annual earnings per full-time employee in forestry rose 396 percent. At the lower extreme was the 34 percent rise for employees of religious organizations. In ten industries the increase was not sufficient to offset the 72 percent increase in the cost of living; in ten others the increase was more than twice as great as the rise of living costs. In general, the industries with the lowest annual earnings per full-time employee in 1939 showed the greatest percentage increases, but there were many exceptions to this rule. The numerous shifts in rank between 1939 and 1944 and 1948 are shown in the table.

If the categories were broken down still further the dispersion would become even more apparent. Even within a given industry there would be widely differing percentage changes in pay for different kinds of jobs, for younger and older workers, for high-wage and low-wage workers, and so on. For example, the table above shows that average annual earnings of full-time educational employees of state and local governments rose 92 percent between 1939 and 1948. This represented a 12 percent rise of real income, which was far below the 29 percent average rise for full-time employees in industry as a whole. But there were wide differences within this group, as is shown in Table 109. (1) In general, those with the lowest pay in 1938-1939 received the largest percentage increases. Some of them were even able to improve their real incomes, though only a few enjoyed real increases as large as those for employees in general. (2) Most of those who were among the more highly paid educational employees in 1938-1939 not only failed to share in the general rise of real income but actually suffered a loss. (3) Most of the educational employees in larger cities suffered an actual loss of real income. These statistics go far toward explaining the restiveness among educators in the postwar period and the serious shortage of teachers and educational administrators.

SOME CONCLUSIONS

Though the preceding sections of this chapter have not attempted to present a comprehensive survey of the behavior of income and wealth distribution between 1939 and 1948, they do point to certain conclusions and to certain implications that merit more detailed study. (1) The usual descriptions of the effects of inflation on the distribution of wealth and income do not fit this period as a whole, for they assume that the total amount of real wealth and income to be shared remains unaffected by the rise of spendings. In this case, however, the amount of real income to be shared rose about 60 percent. (2) The actual changes in income distribution during this period were due not only to the rise of price levels and the dispersion of individual prices but also to the rise of employment and output. (3) The available statistics indicate some tendency toward a more equal distribution of income, with the lowest income groups receiving an increased share. (4) A large part, if not all, of the tendency toward a more nearly equal income distribution was probably due to the rise of employment and output and to the rise of prices in the early part of the period rather than to the further inflation of prices during the latter part of the war and the postwar period. (5) Further price increases after full employment has been attained do not necessarily tend toward either equality or equity in the distribution of income and wealth. They cannot produce further increases of total output and they favor those whose money income and wealth are highly volatile, at the expense of those whose wealth and income are either fixed in terms of money or cannot be increased so rapidly or to such a great extent. (6) Though one can hardly object to the changes in income distribution resulting from a diminution of unemployment and from the minimum rise of prices required to produce relatively full employment, it does not follow that further large increases of price levels after relatively full employment has been attained are equally defensible.

The following sections deal with some other implications of

the rise of prices that occurred after relatively full production had been attained.

INFLATION AS A CAPITAL LEVY

Some people are disposed to defend a postwar inflation as a method of reducing the real burden of the national debt and of extracting purchasing power from those who profited unduly during the war period. They believe this is a satisfactory type of capital levy with which to reduce the buying power of those who profiteered during a war period and paid insufficient taxes. It would be difficult to devise a more capricious method of redistributing real wealth and income. In the first place, a postwar inflation does not reduce the purchasing power of all the "excess" income received during a war. It affects only that part of wartime income that is saved and held in the form of claims whose money values do not rise as much as the cost of living—such forms as money, savings accounts, life insurance, annuities, bonds, and preferred stocks. The receiver of "excess" income during a war can escape the "tax" imposed by postwar inflation either by consuming all the income before the postwar inflation occurs or by investing his wartime savings in claims whose prices rise at least as much as the cost of living. In fact, some wartime "profiteers" may actually increase their wealth still more by investing their wartime savings in claims whose prices rise more than the cost of living; and the greater the postwar inflation, the greater their potential gain. In short, a postwar inflation is not a "tax" on wartime income or on wartime savings; it is a "tax" on holding savings in the form of money, government securities, or other claims whose prices do not rise at all or do not rise as much as the cost of living.

In the second place, a wartime and postwar inflation "taxes" relatively fixed-price forms of savings accumulated before the war just as surely as wartime savings, and the "tax" on prewar savings, which reflects the full effect of the price increase, is the greater. For example, those who laboriously saved during the 1930's and accumulated money, savings accounts, bonds, mortgages, and other fixed-price assets lost about 42 percent of their purchasing power between 1939 and 1948. On the other hand, those who saved in the prewar period and bought real estate, other durable goods, or common stocks escaped with a smaller loss of purchasing power or actually gained as the value of their equities rose more than the cost of living. The latter was especially true of those who used their savings to make down-payments on volatile-priced assets and borrowed to cover much of the purchase price.

In the third place, such an inflation produces many other shifts of wealth and income by causing some prices to rise so much more than others.

It may well be true that action should be taken in a postwar period to alter the distribution of wealth and income that has developed during a war. For this purpose various types of taxes or capital levies might be employed. But inflation is one of the least satisfactory ways of trying to accomplish such a purpose. It injures some and rewards others without any necessary relation to ability to pay or benefit received. It affects prewar as well as wartime savings; it cannot take into account the total wealth or income, the age, the state of health, or the number of dependents of those whom it injures or rewards; and it is just as capable of rewarding the rich and injuring the poor as it is of accomplishing the opposite result.

INFLATION AND THE AGED

The inflation seriously injured the economic position of many of the older people in the population. This is especially true when one considers the longer-run effects and accepts the fact that the cost of living is highly unlikely to fall back to anywhere near the prewar level. Consider, for example, the case of those who had already retired before the war or who retired before enjoying much of the wartime inflation of money incomes and then had to rely for a livelihood on wealth or income which had been fixed in terms of money before the rise of prices. They had no chance to earn further amounts of income or to accumulate more wealth, and the purchasing power of their bonds, savings accounts, life insurance, annuities, private pensions, or public assistance was reduced by more than 40 percent between 1939 and 1948. This was serious for many of those who thought they had provided liberally for their old age, but it was tragic for those who had barely enough to meet their needs even at prewar price levels.

For several reasons the inflation also injured many of the older members of the population who had not yet retired by the end of 1948 but who would have to retire within a few years while the cost of living was still far above prewar levels. (1) During most of their working lives they had received only the lower money incomes prevailing before the war, and their ability to save was based largely on these lower income levels. (2) Many of the older people who were already in the top ranks of their occupations did not receive wage and salary increases commensurate with those granted to younger workers. Their basic wage or salary rates were not increased so much, and they did not receive the accelerated promotions and up-grading enjoyed by younger people. (3) The inflation seriously reduced the purchasing power of their fixed-price savings accumulated during the years when price levels and money incomes were much lower. (4) The amount of benefits provided by many public and private retirement plans was based on lifetime earnings or average earnings over many years, and for these older workers the prewar years would be weighted heavily. Only those whose retirement benefits were based on earnings during their last years of employment were more fortunate, and some of them had not received wage or salary increases commensurate with the rise in the cost of living.

There were, of course, members of the older group who benefited from the inflation because their money income and money wealth increased more than the cost of living. Nevertheless, so many were injured that the inflation has undoubtedly been an important factor in creating the demand for greatly liberalized public and private old-age benefit programs. Whether or not such programs will repair the damage done by the inflation remains to be seen.

OTHER EFFECTS OF INFLATION

A more comprehensive study of the incidence of inflation would have to deal with many other effects—the plight of churches and private schools, colleges, hospitals, and charitable institutions that rely heavily on interest receipts to meet their operating expenses; the decline of real income suffered by many state and local employees; the loss of purchasing power by annuitants and pensioners; and so on. It would also have to describe the great gains by debtors and many others. But enough has been said to indicate that the inflation period claimed many victims. It may be true that there is less suffering during a period of full employment and inflation than there is during a period of widespread unemployment and deflation, but this is hardly an adequate defense of further large price increases after relatively full employment has been reached.

XVIII

||||||||||||||||||||||||||||||||||||||||||||||||||||||||||||||||||||||||||||||||||||||||||||||||||||||||||||||||||||||||||||||||||||||

Conclusions

A SUMMARY OF THE INFLATIONARY PROCESS

IN ITS broad outlines, the American inflation of 1940-1948 is easy to explain. It was an almost inevitable product of the types of government policies followed during the war and of certain other conditions created by the war, though it was aggravated by postwar policies. The original inflationary impetus came from the government's fiscal policy. Reflecting its decision to take constantly increasing amounts of national output for war purposes, the federal government spent huge amounts for goods, labor and other services, its spendings rising to a peak of about $100 billion a year and amounting to more than $383 billion during the six years following June 1940. This willingness of the government to commandeer output and to pay great amounts into private incomes was not by any means matched by an equal willingness to commandeer money incomes through increased taxes. It is true that effective tax rates were increased markedly and that federal tax collections aggregated nearly $197 billion during the six years following June 1940. But this was far too little to prevent private money incomes after taxes from rising to unprecedented levels. Federal tax collections were far too small to extract from private incomes as much as federal spendings were contributing to them, so that the federal deficit amounted to nearly $187 billion during the six years following June 1940. The total federal deficit during these

384

six years was greater than total federal spendings during the preceding century and a half.

This huge deficit-spending program had a triple effect on the private sectors of the economy. (1) It directly contributed a great increase to the total money demand for output, thereby helping at first to restore full employment and then to create inflationary pressures as obstacles to increased production began to appear. (2) It fed huge amounts into the disposable money incomes of individuals and business firms. Enjoying rising amounts of disposable income and expecting still further increases of income and prices, the private sectors were both willing and able to spend rising amounts. During 1940, 1941, and early 1942, private spendings did in fact rise markedly, thereby contributing to the rise of total spendings for output and to inflationary pressures. Throughout the war period itself private consumers and enterprisers continued to be both willing and able to spend much larger amounts and added their inflationary pressures to those emanating from the huge government spendings, but the actual rise of private spendings was held in check by several factors. The general feeling of patriotism and the Treasury's dramatic pleas to save and to lend to the government provided some check on private spending, but they appear to have been largely ineffective for this purpose as compared with direct controls. Most of the credit for holding private spendings in check during the war must go to the system of direct controls over prices, wages, and the purchase, production, and use of goods and services. The rise of actual consumption spendings was held down by price ceilings, the limited availability of consumer goods and services, and consumer rationing. And private investment spendings were held at low levels by price ceilings, wage ceilings, and direct government limitations on the amount of goods and services made available for private capital maintenance and accumulation. Throughout the war period itself there was a large amount of "suppressed inflation"; the abnormally high rate of private saving was achieved only under compulsion, and a major part of it represented "forced saving." (3) It created a huge amount of private savings. Private gross savings during the six years 1940-1945 appear to have totalled nearly $234 billion. Individuals and business firms entered the postwar period far richer in terms of money than they had been at the beginning of the war, and for this federal deficits were largely responsible. To the extent that government spendings were covered by tax collections, the private sectors were left with only their receipted tax bills to evidence their contribution to war finance. But to the extent that government spendings were covered by borrowings, the private sectors received claims against the government which were valuable assets. In the first instance, however, the savings of the private sectors were made in the form of money.

While the aggregate amount of private saving was largely determined by the size of the federal deficit, it was federal borrowing policy that largely determined the form and liquidity of the assets that would represent these private savings at the end of the war. It would have been possible to institute a plan for compulsory lending so that private savings would have had to be exchanged for claims against the government and these claims could have been made cashable only under conditions consistent with the maintenance of economic stability. In this way the liquidity of private savings could have been controlled. Compulsory lending was employed to only a very minor extent, however, and the Treasury relied almost solely upon a voluntary lending program. Individuals and business firms were left free to decide for themselves whether they would hold their savings in the form of money or whether they would exchange the money for government securities or other claims. The inevitable result of this reliance on voluntary lending was that the private sectors entered the postwar period with the major part of their savings in highly liquid forms. To entice lenders to part with their money and buy governments on a voluntary basis the Treasury had to make all of its securities almost completely liquid and cashable on demand; the buyers of these securities still retained the freedom to determine when, for what purpose, and at what rate they would convert them into money.

Even so, however, individuals and nonfinancial corporations elected to exchange less than half of their money savings directly for government obligations; they elected to hold more than half in the form of currency, checking deposits, time and savings deposits, and other claims. As a result, the Treasury had to borrow very large sums from various types of financial institutions, and nearly half of its borrowings were from the Federal Reserve and commercial banks which created new money in exchange for the securities. Thus, as a result of the reliance upon voluntary lending, individuals and nonfinancial business firms entered the postwar period not only much richer in terms of money than they had been in 1939 but also with the major part of their huge wartime savings in highly liquid forms. The various types of financial institutions also entered the postwar period with huge accumulations of liquid governments which they could either continue to hold or could convert into money at their option.

This huge wartime accumulation of savings served in several ways to increase both the ability and the willingness of the private sectors to spend rising amounts in the postwar period. Some people actually used some of these savings to consume more than their current incomes after the war, and many others did not consume beyond their current incomes but felt free, because of their backlog of savings, to consume an abnormally large proportion and to save an abnormally small proportion of their incomes. The large accumulations of savings by business firms made many of them both more willing and more able to spend for capital replacement and net accumulation. The great accumulation of liquid government securities by financial institutions was a major factor in enabling them to provide the private sectors of the economy with a very large supply of low-cost credit during the postwar period.

The great financial accumulations were not, however, the only legacies of the war that contributed to the willingness to spend large and rising amounts in the postwar period. Among the other important conditions created by the war were the following: (1) The large accumulated backlog of domestic demand traceable to the limited availability of many types of civilian goods during the war and to the low rate of capital construction during the depressed decade of the 1930's. At the end of the war business inventories of some goods were virtually nonexistent and in many others they were inconveniently low relative to the high rate of production and sales; consumers' durable goods had been produced in only very small quantities since early 1942; the production of some types of consumer nondurables had been small relative to swollen private incomes; the shortage of housing was acute; public works programs had been held to minimum levels for several years; and private capital construction had been limited to essentials during the war. In the meantime population had continued to rise and capital obsolescence to accumulate. (2) The accumulation of huge foreign needs for economic relief, reconstruction, development, and prevention of the spread of communism and other social unrest. These factors accounted for the large foreign demand for our output, for the willingness of our government to grant large amounts of foreign aid, and for our continued large military expenditures. (3) The accumulated dissatisfaction with the wartime distribution of income. Practically all elements in the economy—farmers, workers, manufacturers, merchants, and others—felt that they should have been allowed to profit to a greater extent from the great demands for their goods and services and entered the postwar period with a determination to improve their income positions by getting increased prices for their goods or services.

There can be little doubt that the huge wartime accumulation of liquid savings and the other conditions generated by the war accounted for the major part of the postwar inflation. But various postwar policies also contributed to the extent of the inflation. (1) The rapid removal of direct controls. Consumer rationing and most other direct controls over the production and use of goods and services were removed before reconversion was complete. Wage controls were weakened soon after V-J Day and completely abolished about a year later. Price controls were seriously weakened by July 1946 and swept away in November of that year. The destruction of these controls, which had been the principal bulwark against inflation during the war, unleashed private demands on the market and enabled the various private sectors of the economy to try to bid goods and services away from each other by spending more money, and to try to improve their real incomes by demanding higher money incomes for their productive services. (2) The postwar fiscal policy that enabled the private sectors to retain a larger part of their mounting money incomes. The Treasury's collection of tax surpluses between mid-1946 and mid-1948 did tend to limit inflation but it did little to prevent inflation, for a major part of the surplus was itself generated by the inflationary rise of money incomes. (3) The highly liberal monetary and credit policy. For nearly two years after V-J Day interest rates in general were rigidly held at their low wartime levels, and the rise after mid-1947 was narrowly limited and controlled. The immediate objective was to hold down the yields and to support the prices of federal securities, but the broad effect was to assure an almost unlimited availability of cheap credit for private purposes. The supply of money and credit was allowed to respond to the demand for it.

Though other elements would have to be introduced to explain exactly the timing and the extent of the inflation, the factors mentioned above appear to have been the principal contributors to the inflationary process. It will now be useful to look at some of the principal lessons to be found in the inflation.

SOME LESSONS OF THE INFLATION

With the benefit of hindsight and of an analysis of the principal causes of the inflation it is possible to offer a number of suggestions as to how the extent of the inflation might have been reduced without an undue sacrifice of other objectives.

Tax Policy. Given the volume of government spendings, the greatest single inprovement in the anti-inflation policy would have been to increase tax collections to a far greater extent. The inadequate wartime tax policy, and the huge deficit that resulted from it, allowed a great increase in private disposable incomes and was largely responsible for the upward pressure of private spendings and for the creation of the huge volume of savings that the private sectors had accumulated by the end of the war. For the purpose of holding down private spending power and of preventing an accumulation of private savings there appears to be no substitute for heavier taxation.

It certainly would not have been feasible to tax heavily enough to cover all the government's wartime spendings. The extremely high average and marginal tax rates that would have been necessary for this purpose would probably have imposed extreme hardships on some persons and they would have interfered seriously with total production and with the shift of productive resources in accordance with wartime needs. However repugnant it may be to our moral sense, it is probably true that even in wartime there is no complete substitute for the pecuniary incentive toward efficiency, hard work, long hours of work, and the necessary shifts of productive factors. For this reason alone it was probably infeasible to tax heavily enough to meet all government expenditures. On the other hand, the writer contends that it would have been feasible to collect a much larger volume of taxes from persons and some more from business, and that for this purpose exemptions should have been lowered at an earlier date, tax rates on taxable income graduated more rapidly, and improvements in tax administration introduced earlier in the war. This would have lessened inflationary pressures during the war and would also have reduced the accumulation of private savings. Tax collections should also have been larger in the postwar period. This would have held down private disposable incomes, drained off private holdings of liquid assets, and provided the Treasury with larger receipts to be used for restricting the supply of money and credit.

Borrowing Policy.   Though the size of the federal deficit largely determined the volume of private savings, federal borrowing policy relative to the sources of its loans and to the characteristics of the securities issued was the major determinant of the liquidity of private savings at the end of the war. The almost exclusive reliance on voluntary lending was another major shortcoming of the war finance program. It meant that private individuals and business firms retained full control over the forms in which they would hold their savings, and in practice it forced the Treasury to make all its securities almost completely liquid and to borrow large amounts from the Federal Reserve and commercial banks. The government should have employed a compulsory lending program to cover the major part of its deficit. This would have had several advantages for the purpose of inflation control. (1) It could have been used to hold down the private propensity to spend during the war period. (2) It could have distributed more equitably any sacrifice involved in lending to the Treasury. And (3) it would have enabled the government to retain control over the cashing of claims against itself. It could have made the claims cashable only under conditions consistent with inflation control. This would have been a very valuable addition to the government's monetary powers, though it obviously presented a number of difficulties. The alternative of issuing almost completely liquid claims that are spendable at the option of their holders is an invitation to inflation.

Monetary Policy. During the war general monetary policy obviously had to be the slave of fiscal policy. It was unthinkable that the monetary authorities would fail to provide the Treasury with all the money it needed beyond its tax collections and its borrowings from nonbank sources. The greatest improvement in wartime monetary policy would have been a more nearly adequate tax policy to reduce the size of the deficit and a compulsory lending program to cover most of the deficit and reduce the amounts to be borrowed from the banks. But given the type of taxing-borrowing policy actually used by the Treasury there was little chance to improve on general monetary policy during the war period. Even the low-interest policy seems not to have enhanced wartime inflationary pressures very much, for it probably had little effect in decreasing the private propensity to save or in increasing private investment spendings. These were largely determined by fiscal policy and direct controls over the prices and supplies of goods and services.

There were, however, at least two measures that should have been seriously considered during the war to regulate the monetization and demonetization of the public debt by the banking system. (1) To forbid the banks to acquire any regular federal issues in excess of their holdings on some base date, any further acquisitions to be limited to special issues eligible for holding only by the banks. This would have permitted a more accurate control over the amount of debt monetization by the banking system. And (2) to require the banks to hold a 100 percent reserve against the increase of their deposits above some base-date level, the reserve to be in the form of special issues of federal securities or interest-bearing or noninterest-bearing deposits at the Federal Reserve banks. This would have prevented a multiple expansion of bank credit on the basis of Federal Reserve purchases of securities and would have immobilized a great volume of government securities and prevented their sale in the postwar period for the purpose of making private loans. Of course such a policy would have been anathema to bankers and might therefore have decreased their coöperation in the bond-selling program. Moreover, it would have been a poor substitute for heavier taxes and compulsory lending.

Though the very easy monetary policy did not itself contribute much to inflationary pressures while private demands were held in check by a harness of direct controls it became an important contributory factor as direct controls were relaxed and abandoned, as the private sectors regained their freedom to raise prices and spend as they wished, as the propensity to save declined, and as private investment spendings soared. The maintenance of low yields on federal obligations, which constituted more than half of all outstanding debt, had the effect of assuring that great amounts of credit would be easily available at low cost for all private purposes.

For nearly two years after V-J Day, no rise of interest rates was permitted, and the rise after mid-1947 was closely controlled. Such an easy-money policy in the face of great unleashed private demands for credit could not fail to feed the inflation.

A rise of interest rates and the accompanying uncertainty as to the future course of rates should have occurred sooner and should have been allowed to progress further. This is not to say that the monetary authorities should not concern themselves with the prices and yields of federal obligations. With these securities representing more than half of all debt and with their prices and yields exerting a marked influence on the prices and yields of all other debt obligations, it is unthinkable that the monetary authorities, who are charged with general credit regulation, should abandon the market to random, panicky, and disorderly movements. Stabilization activities of a type that will prevent disorderly movements that serve no useful purpose in the economy are clearly in order. What is objectionable is a policy of maintaining an almost inflexible level of interest rates, and doing so by surrendering control over the money supply despite wide fluctuations in the demand for credit to be spent for consumption and investment purposes. Such a passive monetary policy can only accentuate deflation and inflation if, in fact, the demand schedules for investable funds fall greatly at one time and rise greatly at another. A monetary policy of this type will inevitably accentuate economic instability instead of tending toward stability. This is not, of course, to argue for a restrictive policy so severe that it would produce deflation and unemployment. Nor is it to argue that prices of federal obligations should have been allowed to decline as much as they did in 1920 and 1921. Such a great decline would not have been necessary to exert a significant damping effect on the inflation.[1]

The effect of rising interest rates on the size of the carrying

[1] For an elaboration of this point of view, see Lester V. Chandler, "Federal Reserve Policy and the Federal Debt," *American Economic Review*, March, 1949, pp. 405-429.

charges on the federal debt and on the capital value of long-term federal obligations is, of course, of some concern. They do not appear, however, to be of sufficient importance to justify the discarding of monetary policy as a stabilizing device and the conversion of it into a device for aggravating instability. In a period of inflation, it is better to see interest charges on the federal debt rise than to condone a continuously easy monetary policy. And if it is decided that holders of the long-term securities should be protected against capital depreciation this should be accomplished by shifting the risk to the Treasury through raising coupon rates or through some other comparable device. It should not be achieved during inflation by a passive policy of monetizing this debt at almost inflexible low-yield rates.

Direct Controls.   Only a few conclusions regarding direct controls over prices, wages, and the production and use of goods and services can be noted here. The principal conclusion is that while they were in effect they constituted the principal bulwark against inflation and were far more effective than had been expected at the time of their introduction. Some of their principal achievements were these: (1) They uneasily held in check competitive attempts by the various interest groups to increase their absolute and relative income positions by raising the prices of their goods and services. (2) Consumer rationing and other controls over the purchase, production, and use of goods and services held down private demands for output and contributed greatly to the success of price and wage controls. (3) Direct controls over prices, wages, and the purchase, production, and use of goods and services held down private consumption spendings and forced very large amounts of private savings. Thus they were a major contributor to the Treasury program for selling securities to nonbank buyers. These controls also held private investment spendings in check. (4) By holding down prices and wages they held down federal spendings and the size of the federal deficit. (5) By increasing private saving out of each level of income, by holding down private investment spendings, and by limiting the size of the federal deficit they held in check the wartime rise of the money supply. With the supply of money made almost completely responsive to the demand for it at low interest rates, the harness of direct controls limited the expansion of money by holding in check the demand for it.

Thus the numerous direct controls constituted the principal bulwark against inflation while they were in effect, and it is frightening to contemplate how much more inflation would have occurred before V-J Day if they had been absent and if fiscal monetary policy had not been altered. Because of their success during the war period itself there is some danger that in a future comparable period they will be considered a complete substitute for an adequate tax and borrowing policy. They will be a necessary and valuable part of the general control program in such a situation, but for several reasons it would be dangerous to attempt to use them as a substitute for rather than as only a supplement to a restrictive fiscal policy. (1) They might break down even during the war period itself. Great increases in private disposable incomes place a serious strain on price and wage ceilings, rationing, and other controls over goods and services; too much money income left in the hands of the private sectors is a temptation to black-market operations. No one knows how much more private disposable incomes could have risen during World War II without breaking down the direct controls or how well the direct controls would have worked if the war had continued for several more years. (2) With an inadequate fiscal policy direct controls cannot prevent the private sectors from accumulating large amounts of savings. And (3) reliance on direct controls during a war means that there will be a large amount of "suppressed inflation" at the end of the war. An early removal of the direct controls unleashes the danger of a cumulative postwar inflation. This danger became an actuality at the end of World War II.

There are, of course, wide differences of opinion as to whether direct controls should have been retained longer after the end of the war. Their retention for a longer period would have involved many difficulties in administration and in the allocation of productive factors and output. But under the circumstances, their relaxation was almost certain to unloose inflationary price and wage increases. The hope that price increases could be quickly choked off by a rise of real output was purely illusory, and it was unrealistic to expect that wage rates could be held down while the cost of living and other prices were free to rise. In another such period direct controls should either be kept for a longer period, or monetary and fiscal policy should be such as to choke off a wage-price spiral, or some less formal method of securing a moratorium on price and wage increases should be developed, or a combination of these methods should be employed.

Selected Bibliography

U.S. GOVERNMENT PUBLICATIONS

Board of Governors of the Federal Reserve System:
Annual Reports
Federal Reserve Bulletins
Bureau of the Budget
The United States at War, Washington, 1946
Bureau of Labor Statistics
Monthly Labor Review
Commerce Department
Survey of Current Business, especially National Income Supplement, July 1947, July 1948, and July 1949.
Congress
Banking and Currency Committees of the House and Senate, various hearings on price control and economic stabilization, 1941-1948
Joint Committee on the Economic Report
Hearings Before the Subcommittee on Monetary, Credit, and Fiscal Policies, 1949
Statements to the Subcommittee on Monetary, Credit, and Fiscal Policies, 1949
Report of the Subcommittee on Monetary, Credit, and Fiscal Policies, 1950
Ways and Means Committee of the House and the Finance Committee of the Senate, hearings on various revenue acts, 1940-1948
Office of Economic Stabilization
Report of the President's Committee on the Cost of Living, 1945
President's economic reports to congress, 1947-

Treasury Department
Annual Reports of the Secretary
Treasury Bulletin

BOOKS

Bach, G. L., *Federal Reserve Policy Making,* Knopf, New York, 1950.

Goldenweiser, E. A., *Monetary Management,* McGraw-Hill, New York, 1949.

Harris, S. E., *Inflation and the American Economy,* McGraw-Hill, New York, 1945.

Hart, A. G., Allen, E. D., and others, *Paying for Defense,* Blakiston, Philadelphia, 1941.

Murphy, H. C., *The National Debt in War and Transition,* McGraw-Hill, New York, 1950.

Paul, R. E., *Taxation for Prosperity,* Bobbs-Merrill, New York, 1947.

ARTICLES

Abbott, C. S., "The Commercial Banks and the Public Debt," *American Economic Review,* May, 1947, Supplement.

Allen, E. D., "Treasury Tax Policies in 1943," *American Economic Review,* December, 1944.

Carr, H. C., "The Problem of the Bank-Held Government Debt," *American Economic Review,* December, 1946.

Chandler. L. V., "Federal Reserve Policy and the Federal Debt," *American Economic Review,* March, 1949.

Fellner, W., "War Finance and Inflation," *American Economic Review,* June, 1942.

Fellner, W., "Postscript on War Inflation," *American Economic Review,* March, 1947.

Friedman, M., "The Tax [on spending] as a Wartime Measure," *American Economic Review,* March, 1943.

Goldenweiser, E. A., "Federal Reserve Objectives and Policies," *American Economic Review,* June, 1947.

Gordon, R. A., "Government Spending and Income Velocity," *American Economic Review,* June, 1950.

Hagen, E. E., and Kirkpatrick, Nora, "Forecasting Gross National Product and Employment During the Transition Period," *Studies in Income and Wealth,* National Bureau of Economic Research, New York, 1947, vol. 10.

Harris, S. E., "Subsidies and Inflation," *American Economic Review,* September, 1943.

Hart, A. G., "Flexible Taxes to Combat Inflation," *American Economic Review,* March, 1942.

Holben, R. E., "General Expenditure Rationing with Reference to the Kalecki Plan," *American Economic Review,* September, 1942.

Mints, L. W., (Ed.), "A Symposium on Fiscal and Monetary Policy," *Review of Economic Statistics,* May, 1946.

Mosak, J. S., and Salant, W. A., "Income, Money and Prices in Wartime," *American Economic Review,* December, 1944.

Musgrave, R. A., "The Wartime Tax Effort in the United States, the United Kingdom, and Canada," *Proceedings of the National Tax Association,* 1943.

Newcomer, M., "Congressional Tax Policies in 1943," *American Economic Review,* December, 1944.

Poole, K. E., "Problems of Administration and Equity" [of the tax on spendings], *American Economic Review,* March, 1943.

Robinson, R. I., "Money Supply and Liquid Asset Formation," *American Economic Review,* March, 1946.

Seltzer, L. H., "Is A Rise of Interest Rates Desirable or Inevitable?" *American Economic Review,* December, 1945.

Seltzer, L. H., "The Changed Environment of Monetary-Banking Policy," *American Economic Review,* May, 1946, Supplement.

Shere, L., "Taxation and Inflation Control," *American Economic Review,* December, 1948.

Shoup, C., "Problems in War Finance," *American Economic Review,* March, 1943.

Simmons, E. C., "Federal Reserve Policy and the National Debt During the War Years," *Journal of Business of the University of Chicago,* April, 1947.

Slichter, S., Harris, S. E., and Dunlop, J. T., "Wage Policy—A Symposium," *Review of Economic Statistics,* August, 1947.

Sproul, A., "Monetary Management and Credit Control," *American Economic Review,* June, 1947.

Thomas, W., "The Heritage of War Finance," *American Economic Review,* May, 1947, Supplement.

Villard, H. H., "The Problem of Bank-Held Government Debt," *American Economic Review,* September, 1947.

Wallich, H. C., "Debt Management and Economic Policy," *American Economic Review,* June, 1946.

Wallich, H. C., "The Changing Significance of the Interest Rate," *American Economic Review,* December, 1946.

Whittlesey, C. R., "Federal Reserve Policy in Transition," *Quarterly Journal of Economics,* May, 1946.

Willis, J. B., "The Case Against the Maintenance of the Wartime Pattern of Yields on Government Securities," *American Economic Review,* May, 1947, Supplement.

Index

$4.50

Inflation in the United States 1940-1948

BY LESTER V. CHANDLER

This is the only work of its kind—a careful, detailed study, by a financial authority, of the process of inflation during a period covering the pre-war, war, and post-war years—a cycle that today appears to be in the making once more. As such it should be of immediate importance to everyone concerned with the economic welfare of the country. Emphasis is placed upon fiscal and monetary policies, but much attention is given to other principal factors affecting timing and extent of the inflation, such as the behavior of real output, controls over prices, wages, and the production of goods and services, private controversies over income distribution, wartime accumulation of a backlog of demand for output, and foreign conditions that affected the demand for our exports.

This study was made possible by a grant from the Merrill Foundation for the Advancement of Economic Knowledge.

See the note on the author on the inside back flap.

No. 8600